AN ASCENDANCY ARMY

ALLAN BLACKSTOCK

An Ascendancy Army
The Irish Yeomanry, 1796–1834

FOUR COURTS PRESS

Set in 10.5 on 12.5 point Ehrhardt for
FOUR COURTS PRESS
Fumbally Court, Fumbally Lane, Dublin 8, Ireland
e-mail: info@four-courts-press.ie
and in North America by
FOUR COURTS PRESS
c/o ISBS, 5804 N.E. Hassalo Street, Portland, OR 97213.

A catalogue record for this title
is available from the British Library.

ISBN 1-85182-329-8

Printed in Great Britain
by the Martins Printing Group, Bodmin, Cornwall

070199-4500X8

To Mary, Peter and Alice

Contents

List of Illustrations

LIST OF MAPS

List of Abbreviations

BL add. mss	British Library, Additional Manuscripts
BNL	*Belfast News Letter*
CO	Colonial Office
FJ	*Freeman's Journal*
HC	House of Commons
HMC	Historical Manuscripts Commission
HO	Home Office
HRO	Hampshire Record Office
IESH	*Irish Economic and Social History*
IHS	*Irish Historical Studies*
IS	*Irish Sword*
KAO	Kent Archives Office
LHL	Linenhall Library Belfast
NAM	National Army Museum
NHI	New History of Ireland
NLI	National Library of Ireland
NS	*Northern Star*
NA	National Archives (Ireland)
OP	Official Papers
PRO	Public Record Office, London
PRONI	Public Record Office of Northern Ireland
QUB	The Queen's University of Belfast
RP	Rebellion Papers
SUL	Southampton University Library
TCD	Trinity College, Dublin
WO	War Office

Preface

I would like to thank the following individuals and institutions for permission to quote from collections in their keeping: the Earl of Gosford; the Deputy Keeper of the Records, P.R.O.N.I.; the Director of the National Archives of Ireland; the Council of Trustees, National Library of Ireland; the Board of Trinity College Dublin; the Public Record Office, London; the British Library; the National Army Museum; the Centre for Kentish Studies (formerly the Kent Archives Office); the Hampshire Record Office; the Linenhall Library, Belfast; Armagh County Museum; Nottinghamshire Record Office. Crown Copyright is acknowledged for the Home Office, War Office, Colonial Office and Wellington Papers. I would also like to thank the Belfast Harbour Commissioners for permission to use the Thomas Robinson painting on the cover, the Trustees of the Ulster Museum for permission to use photographs of various yeomanry artefacts to illustrate the text and Dr Peter Stoddart for permission to quote from his unpublished thesis 'Counter-Insurgency and Defence in Ireland, 1790–1805'. My thanks and gratitude is also due to the many members of staff at the various archival institutions and libraries for their help and patience.

The writing of this book was made possible by a fellowship from the Institute of Irish Studies at the Queen's University of Belfast. I would like to express my gratitude to the Director, Professor Brian Walker, and to all the other members of staff and fellows who helped with their support and encouragement. I would also like to thank the Esme Mitchell Trust for subvention towards the cost of publication.

It would be exhaustive to list all the historians who have stimulated my interest in the period and helped with their subsequent advice and encouragement, but a particular debt of gratitude is due to Professor Peter Jupp, Dr A.T.Q. Stewart, Professor Thomas Bartlett, Professor David Hempton, Dr Alvin Jackson, Dr A.P.W. Malcomson and Professor Louis Cullen. I am also most grateful to Dr David Hayton for reading the chapters in draft and, on a very practical level, to Tony Sheehan of Queen's Arts Computing Unit for his patience with a newcomer to word-processing and to Maura Pringle and Gill Alexander of Queen's School of Geosciences for their help with maps.

Finally, I would like to thank George Meharg for his design and artwork on the cover, everyone at Four Courts Press for their patience and last, but certainly not least, my wife and family for their support.

Introduction

Some years ago a county Down farmer was ploughing one of his fields not normally given over to tillage. His children followed the plough looking for the buried treasure of their fairy tales. They found no glittering bracelets or golden coins, only a dull, oval-shaped metal disc of no obvious significance. Disappointed, they handed the object to their father who cleaned off the soil to reveal the following engraving: 'Armed Associations of 1798'. Curiosity aroused, he sent the disc to the Ulster Museum, where it was identified as a military cross-belt plate. The term armed associations was used at the time to refer to civilians enlisted as auxiliaries to yeomanry corps as the authorities prepared for the United Irish insurrection. Groups like these were raised in county Down, particularly in the Downpatrick area, and the belt plate probably originated from there. However, its historical significance is much wider. The year of its manufacture, 1798, also witnessed French invasion attempts in Ireland and the spread of the conflict with Britain and her allies from Europe and the colonies to the mouth of the Nile, a conflict which revolutionised warfare by the rise of the citizen soldier. Despite this, the Irish Yeomanry has been almost totally neglected by historians, indeed the mode of the object's discovery is curiously symbolic of the past's refusal to be ignored. However, the story of the yeomanry does not begin in 1798.

Those who like their history to contain clear turning points look to 1789, the year of the French Revolution, as a point in time after which things 'changed utterly'. However, as a watershed in military affairs, the year 1793 was of infinitely greater significance. This was the year of national conscription in France, the nation-in-arms or *levee en masse* which revolutionized theories of war and defence throughout Europe, Britain and Ireland included, by vastly increasing the size of armies and replacing the formal formations and manoeuvres of the eighteenth century with the dash and *élan* of the citizen soldier. Previously there had been 'limited warfare' fought with relatively small armies. In 1790 the French regular army stood at between 130,000 and 150,000. However, Carnot's compulsory levy in 1793 raised 500,000 men.[1]

1 J. Gooch, *Armies in Europe*, p. 27; Major General J.F.C. Fuller, *The Conduct of War, 1798–1961*, p. 31.

This frightening development necessitated a great increase in the manpower needed by all European armies. In Britain and Ireland this demand was met by reforms in the regular army and a number of traditional defence measures implemented on a larger scale. The shock waves from Paris brought the danger of invasion and domestic tumult to the British Isles and stimulated a semi-conscript militia, fencible regiments[2] and heavy citizen volunteering for part-time military service. The Irish Yeomanry was of the latter type. However, though it can and should be seen in the context of European mass militarisation, its real origins and characteristics were rooted in Irish soil.

To some contemporaries and many subsequent historians Irish yeomen have an unsavoury reputation. 'The Yeomanry', wrote Lord Cornwallis, as he grimly surveyed the smouldering embers of rebellion in July 1798, 'are in the style of the loyalists of America, only much more numerous and powerful, and a thousand times more ferocious; these men have saved the country but they now take the lead in rapine and plunder'.[3] These were the words of a newly arrived English soldier-administrator who despised colonials with the imperialist's hauteur and attacked amateur warriors with professional contempt. However, this reputation has been frequently renewed ever since. Few accounts of Ireland in the period of the French wars, and especially the 1798 period, fail to mention yeomanry. Yet, as so often in Ireland, the relationship between reputation and reality has never been properly investigated.

Irish historians have largely been content with reputation and received opinion. Reams have been written on political and social radicals but conservatism has been largely neglected. The yeomanry have long languished in the historiographical shadow of the United Irishmen and the Irish Volunteers, yet at its height over 80,000 Irishmen joined the ranks, representing almost every propertied family in the country and many of their tenants and retainers. The problem is that, although almost every text mentions the yeomanry, there is little dispassionate analysis of their origin, organisation and political and social impact. Moreover, contemporary writers tended to use the yeomanry as polemical ammunition for politically motivated rebellion histories. Sir Richard Musgrave highlighted the dismissal of Catholic yeomen from corps in Wicklow and Wexford in 1797 and 1798 in order to sustain his specious argument that because Catholicism and loyalty were demonstrably so incompatible the rebellion was a popish plot. He judiciously omitted to mention that Presbyterian yeomen were also purged from corps in Armagh and Tyrone at the same time

---

2 Fencibles were troops raised by landowners for wartime home service. A small number of Irish fencibles were raised but it was mainly a British measure. English, Scots and Welsh fencibles served in Ireland. They were rather unfairly denigrated as a poor relation to the regular army as the following doggerel shows: Oh, did you see the Fencibles,/ Commanded by insensibles, / Devoid of all good principles / Detestable are they: quoted in W.J. Fitzpatrick, *The Life and Times of Lord Cloncurry*, p. 139.   3 N.A.M. 6602–45 f. 5, Cornwallis Papers, Cornwallis to Ross, 24 July 1798.

lest it disturb his rationale. The Catholic Committeeman and United Irishman Edward Hay similarly yoked the yeomen into a causal theory. Hay was embittered at the failure of emancipation and believed England wanted to rule Ireland by exploiting its religious divisions. He argued that the Irish Volunteers of 1782 had resisted this invidious policy but, following their suppression in 1793, Protestant bigotry was revived by 'upstart' *nouveaux riches* magistrates who, together with their brutal and bigoted yeomen, goaded the 'people' into rebellion.[4] Like Musgrave, Hay omits any ingredients which would spoil the broth, not mentioning liberal Protestant magistrates who also raised yeomen, like Captain Edwards of Bray,[5] or the United Irish policy of trying to infiltrate corps.

By locating the Irish Yeomanry firmly in the horrific carnage and bitter polarisation of 1798, these polemical works have helped create the reputation, of a brutal and partisan force, which has darkly shadowed them ever since. Objectivity became difficult, particularly as attitudes to yeomanry were inextricably linked to the Catholic Question after 1795 when Fitzwilliam suggested that a largely Catholic yeomanry could follow emancipation. Support for the yeomanry became more a shibboleth for Protestant Ascendancy than an assessment of their strategic value, while opposition was a rejection of ascendancy and the refusal of 'the disaffected' to accept the contribution their own actions had in scaring Protestants away from radicalism. After the initial crop of rebellion histories, later historians have tended to gloss over the yeomanry. Lecky was a notable exception but his tendency to present Irish history as the history of the Anglo–Irish elite loses much of the essential context.[6] By portraying the yeomen as adjuncts to the gentry, Lecky misses altogether the populist element. This historiographical neglect has largely continued into the twentieth century. The destruction of the entire Yeomanry Office records in the 1922 Four Courts fire is a partial explanation. However, a perusal of the extant source material, which ranges from the papers of viceroys and their chief secretaries to the papers of landed families, quickly reveals ample material for a reconstruction. In the mid-twentieth century some light broke into the dark cellars of neglect, albeit often a reflected light. Two monographs on related subjects brought in their train some consideration of the formation, functions and composition of the yeomanry. Sir Henry McAnally's study of the Irish Militia compared the military role of each force. He saw the yeomanry as largely taking over the militia's anti-disturbance duties, because of the fear of United Irish infiltration of the largely Catholic rank and file. Hereward Senior's pioneering work on early Orangeism necessarily devoted much discussion to populist movements among lower-class northern Protestants.[7]

4 Musgrave, *Memoirs of the Different Rebellions in Ireland*, pp 160, 200; Hay, *History of the Rebellion in the County of Wexford*, passim. 5 I am indebted to Professor L. Cullen for drawing my attention to Captain Edwards. 6 W.E.H. Lecky, *Ireland in the Eighteenth Century* (hereafter: Lecky, *Ireland*). 7 McAnally, *The Irish Militia, 1793–1816*; Senior, *Orangeism in Ireland and Britain, 1795–1836* (hereafter: Senior, *Orangeism*).

He investigated the role of the proto-yeomanry Dungannon Association, in the delicate and shifting relationship between the mid-Ulster gentry and their tenants. However, Senior underplayed the significance of yeomanry by over-emphasising the importance of the Orangemen, without whom, he claimed, yeomanry could not have functioned. More recently, yeomanry have come under the scrutiny of Thomas Bartlett who uses both this civil-military hybrid and the militia to examine developments in the political consciousness of the levels of society represented in the ranks of both forces. Bartlett claims the co-existence of these two 'native' forces at a time of great polarization allied with the potential of both for politicizing their members meant 'The Yeomanry and the Militia can best be regarded as the military expressions of two rival "nations" that had emerged in Ireland in the years after 1800'.[8] At last the Irish yeoman begins to break free of the polemical strait-jacket and present himself as a fit object for serious historical study.

When one looks behind the tired polemical rigmaroles the hazy outline of a very different force begins to emerge, whose longevity, numbers and geographical extent makes it highly significant in its impact on social and political life. A thorough re-examination is essential, but when this is contemplated a basic problem arises. Huge gaps are revealed in historical knowledge about the raising, administration, duties and membership of the yeomanry. This study first aims to fill these gaps, and then to analyse the wider impact of this 'Ascendancy army', and its contribution to longer-term trends and traditions. It is based on a comprehensive and detailed coverage of the relevant primary sources, both printed and manuscript, including official and parliamentary records, the private papers of politicians, papers of landed families newspapers, pamphlets and a wide variety of local sources such as yeomanry detail books. Before this can be done it is necessary to look back into the eighteenth century and establish the social, economic, political and demographic background to the yeomanry, and then to examine its generic roots, from the earliest feudal ideas of military service to its immediate military and paramilitary origins in the turbulent closing decades of the century.

8 T. Bartlett, 'Militarisation and Politicization in Ireland', p. 135.

I

The eighteenth-century background

The eighteenth century is sometimes portrayed as a rare period of stability in the turbulent course of Irish history, apart from the troubled 1790s. In this view, the political calm following the religious, ethnic and dynastic upheavals of the previous century made steady improvements possible in the economic and social fabric of the country, as reflected by the confident classical building style and in institutions and societies designed to promote agriculture and manufacturing, such as the Linen Board and the Dublin Society. There was also a growing interest in the study of Irish culture, language and history, reflected in the formation of the Royal Irish Academy in 1785. This view of eighteenth-century Ireland tends to make the events of the 1790s, including the raising of the yeomanry, look like a spontaneous convulsion and over-emphasises the role of imported ideology in lighting the fuse. However, notwithstanding the significance of the French connection, the expectations, fears and assumptions of the society which spawned the yeomanry in 1796 were grounded in a contextual framework which stretched back into the eighteenth century and beyond. It is necessary to establish this context by looking back at the economic, social and political developments in the eighteenth century.

THE ECONOMIC BACKGROUND

The Irish economy grew markedly, though unevenly, during the eighteenth century. It was grounded mainly in agriculture but, as the century progressed, commerce and industry, in particular domestic linen production became increasingly important. The rearing of livestock, particularly cattle, dominated agricultural production until the 1780s when tillage increased rapidly. Annual exports and imports increased from £814,746 and £792,473 in 1700, to £4,855,319 and £3,829,914 respectively in 1790. Most exports were for the British market, although foreign trade grew in the latter part of the century from growing ports like Galway, Limerick and Belfast. The production of linen cloth increased dramatically, with the 1730s seeing the most rapid expansion. In 1700 about one million yards were exported. By 1770 this had increased to twenty million, with as much again produced for the domestic market as linen became the most valuable element of the economy. Ulster became the main centre for linen production through a combination of capitalisation, availability of skills and the natural suitability of the environment for flax cultivation (though the industry had also spread significantly into other parts of Ireland by the 1790s).[1] In the 1780s, one out of every five male workers in the nine counties of Ulster was employed in linen weaving.[2] Linen was not evenly produced throughout Ulster, so the true proportion would have been much higher in areas like county Armagh, the Lagan valley and counties Antrim and Londonderry. Linen brought prosperity, and, because it enabled a weaver to support himself with only a minimum of land, meant that the weaving districts were heavily populated. In 1759 the linen district between Monaghan town and Carrickfergus was described as being well cultivated, with neat cottages, gardens and orchards interspersed with gentlemen's residences. Arthur Young, travelling in Ulster in 1776 was also struck by the affluent appearance of the linen districts, which compared unfavourably with other parts of the country.[3]

The appearance of the countryside altered in response to these economic changes. At the beginning of the century many parts remained largely as the Elizabethan adventurers had found them: inaccessible and dangerous. The Irish parliament and the Dublin Society encouraged landowners to improve their estates by planting hedges and draining bogs. Change came unevenly. Forest and wilderness areas remained in the remoter western parts and in Ulster in the flat wastes surrounding Lough Neagh.[4] The road network expanded rapidly from the 1730s to accommodate the growth in inland trade stimulated by the textile industry (wool was also significant, though its importance declined towards the end of the century). Often these were built by turnpike trusts, comprised of interested traders, but, with new legislation in 1765, the county grand juries were given authority to raise the capital by levying the 'cess' on areas served by the road.[5] By 1800 a expanded network of market towns had grown up, and ports like Cork, Galway, Waterford, Belfast and Newry flourished. Dublin's century-long economic and administrative growth was elegantly reflected in public buildings of international significance, such as the Parliament Building, completed in 1739, and later the Customs House and Four Courts. Coach roads now linked major towns with inns and post towns at suitable intervals. The signal for the 1798 rising – the burning of the mail coaches radiating out from Dublin on old May Day – was, in twentieth century terms, as strategically sophisticated as hijacking a national television station in a political coup d'etat. A canal system developed to facilitate the passage of goods, agricultural produce and raw

1 L. Cullen, *An Economic History of Ireland since 1660*, pp. 54, 61. 2 D. Dickson, *New Foundations: Ireland, 1660–1800*, pp. 96, 100. 3 J.L. McCracken, 'Social Structure and Social Life, 1714–60', *NHI*, v, p. 44; A. Young, *A Tour in Ireland*, pp. 124–5. 4 McCracken, ibid., pp. 43–5. 5 L. Cullen, ibid., p. 88.

materials from the interior. The Newry Canal, completed in 1742, which linked the port to the huge Lough Neagh catchment via the Upper Bann, was the first purpose-built canal in the British Isles. So profound was the modernisation in the physical environment, that one historian has claimed 'the Irish man-made landscape' to be 'essentially one of the eighteenth century'.[6]

Yet, despite these overall economic advances, progress was erratic. Notwithstanding the growth of markets, and perhaps because of the concentration on pasturage for the export market, many small cottiers, especially in the west, were dependent on subsistence agriculture. Frequent crop failures led to local famines. Even the linen industry was not immune to slumps such as that in the 1770s which underlay the Steelboy protests in Ulster. Land was a good investment. Leases set at low wartime rents in the 1690s expired in the 1720s and 30s and were re-let at higher rents in more stable conditions. Rents doubled between 1745 and 1770, a period of sustained economic growth, and doubled again between 1776 and 1813. Landlords prospered enough by the 1750s to diversify into mining and textiles. Rents are reckoned to have increased sixfold during the century.[7] However, owing to the practice of long leases being granted when rents were low, sub-letting middlemen soaked up much of the benefit before it reached the head-landlord. The distribution of wealth changed somewhat during the century. In 1791–2, though approximately 59 per cent of the population had annual incomes of £5 or less and a smaller group of around 11 per cent had £20 or over, a significant middle sector was emerging with incomes of between £5 and £20.[8] Ireland's real wealth and political power, was largely in the hands of the 5,000 or so owners of landed estates: the Anglo-Irish Ascendancy. In 1770 the rents paid to this small group rents accounted for 20 per cent of the country's total income. But henceforth the accelerating growth of towns and the rise of manufacturing entrepreneurs began to challenge the landed monopoly of wealth.[9]

The tensions and jealousies created were later reflected in frequent references to the United Irish leaders as 'overblown tradesmen'. Although the disturbances of the 1790s which gave rise to the Irish Yeomanry were fundamentally political and sectarian rather than economic there was some substance in these fears, particularly in Ulster. The growth of the linen industry had seen linen bleachers, merchants and manufacturers increase in wealth and sometimes diversify into trade. These people were usually Presbyterians but could also include some Catholics, like the Teelings of Lisburn. Denied the political influence to which their wealth should have entitled them, many of these rising men identified with the American colonists' resent-

6 L. Cullen, 'Man, Landscape and Roads: the changing eighteenth century', in W. Nolan (ed.), *The Shaping of Ireland* (Cork, 1986), p. 124. 7 L. Cullen, *The Emergence of Modern Ireland, 1600–1900*, pp. 41, 43–4, 169; K. Whelan, 'Settlement and Society in eighteenth-century Ireland' in G. Dawe and J.W. Foster (eds), *The Poet's Place: Essays in Ulster Literature and Society*, pp. 45–62. 8 Dickson, op. cit., pp. 98, 106–7. 9 Cullen, *The Emergence of Modern Ireland*, p. 241.

ment at 'taxation without representation'. Some went no further than supporting parliamentary reform, but others followed a revolutionary course and became the driving force behind the northern United Irishmen.

POPULATION

The political explosion at the end of the eighteenth century was prefaced by a population explosion. The most recent research on population in this period reduces Professor Connell's estimates made in the 1950s (see table).[10] Despite revisions the trend still shows a population growing rapidly towards the end of the century.

Year	Estimated population (millions)
1706	1.75 - 2.06
1712	1.98 - 2.32
1725	2.18 - 2.56
1732	2.16 - 2.53
1744	1.91 - 2.23
1749	1.95 - 2.28
1753	2.20 - 2.57
1791	4.42

Population distribution was also changing. Although the greater part still lived in the country, the proportion of town dwellers was increasing. Dublin's population almost tripled during the century, from 62,000 in 1700 to 180,000 in 1800. Belfast, though still relatively small, had increased fivefold during the same period to 20,000. Other towns and cities showed hefty increases. Cork grew from 17,000 to 60,000, Limerick from 10,000 to 42,000, Waterford from 7,000 to 22,000 and Kilkenny from 4,000 to 14,000.[11] Belfast's expansion was made possible by a mid-century linen boom and was continued by the resultant growth in the volume of imports and exports.[12] Newry and Derry also benefited from linen to become substantial urban centres. By the late 1790s, Cork's trade and population flourished so much that contemporaries felt it would soon rival Liverpool as a commercial centre.[13] Smaller towns also followed the trends set by larger centres. Armagh shows rapid population growth in the latter half of the century. Its population stood at around 1,000 in 1714,

10 D. Dickson, C. O'Grada and S. Daultrey, 'Hearth Tax, Household Size and Irish Population Change, 1672–1821', *Royal Irish Academy Proceedings* C 82/6 (1982), pp. 125–81.   11 Whelan, op. cit., p. 58.
12 W.H. Crawford, 'Change in Ulster in the late eighteenth century', in T. Bartlett and D. Hayton (eds), *Penal Era and Golden Age*, p. 186.   13 M. Murphy, 'The Economy and Social Structure of Nine-teenth-Century Cork', in D. Harkness and M. O'Dowd (eds), *The Town in Ireland*, p. 125.

had doubled by 1770, but really took off thereafter, reaching 8,500 by 1821.[14] Armagh's growth was triggered by its prominence as a centre of linen weaving and bleaching. Rural areas also experienced sustained growth during this period. In Ulster, rural population density correlates with linen production, as a weaver could survive on a smaller patch of land than the smallest farmer. The linen manufacturing counties of Antrim, Armagh and Monaghan were reckoned to be the most populous in Ireland.[15]

In an age before official censuses, the exact denominational breakdown of this population cannot be computed with certainty. The first official census of religious affiliation was not carried out until 1861. However, two earlier surveys give an impression of the relative proportions. In 1732–3, hearth tax collectors were asked to record the religion of each household in their survey. Professor Connolly reckons that, allowing for the usual deficiencies, the proportion of Catholics was between 73 and 79 per cent. In 1834 a survey by the Commissioners of Public Instruction included religious affiliation. This was done reasonably accurately, and the findings correspond with the 1861 census in relative proportions. The main point is that the proportion of Catholics does not change radically over the entire period, and can be confidently estimated at around three-quarters of Ireland's population by 1790s.[16] The national denominational summary in the 1834 returns tallies with these estimates. It found that from a total of 7,954,100 inhabitants, 6,436,060 were Roman Catholic, 853,160 Anglican, 643,058 Presbyterian and 21,882 Protestants belonging to other sects.[17] If 4.5 million is taken as a reasonable estimate of the total population in the 1790s, and the proportional breakdown of 1834 taken as a rough guide, this would approximate to 3,600,000 Roman Catholics, 500,000 Anglicans and 362,000 Presbyterians with the remainder smaller denominations such as Methodists, Baptists and Quakers.

The distribution of denominational populations did not change much. The 1732–3 hearth tax returns show the highest concentrations of Catholics in Munster and Connaught with significant numbers also in rural Leinster, though they underestimate the proportion in Ulster. Outside Ulster, the main Protestant strength was in the towns. At the end of the seventeenth century, Dublin had one-third of Leinster's Protestant population, Protestants were a majority in Drogheda and a large majority in Dundalk. However the expansion of towns during the eighteenth century brought more Catholics in from rural hinterlands and in many cases urban Protestant strength was eroded. Drogheda's majority had disappeared by the 1730s.[18] Dublin's hearth tax returns show Protestants as a two-thirds majority in 1732, though

14 L.A. Clarkson and E.M. Crawford, *Ways to Wealth: the Cust Family of Eighteenth-Century Armagh*, p. 13.   15 J.H. Andrews, 'Land and People, *c*.1780', *NHI*, iv, p. 249.   16 J.C. Beckett, intro; *N.H.I.*, p. xiv; S. J. Connolly, *Religion, Law and Power*, pp. 144 –5; *Priests and People in Pre-Famine Ireland*, pp. 281–2.   17 *Parl. Papers*, HC 1835 [45] [46] *First report of the Commissioners of Public Instruction, Ireland, with appendix*, xxxiii, pp. 70–4.   18 S.J. Connolly, *Religion, Law and Power*, p. 147.

recent research more realistically puts the proportion about equal as the first computation ignored servants. During the century significant numbers of Catholics from
Kildare, Wexford and Wicklow settled in the city. The political ramifications of this
were felt in the 1790s.[19]

A glance at the diocesan figures from the 1834 census illustrates the regional
differences in religious populations. The diocese of Down in the episcopal province
of Armagh contained 28,025 Anglicans, 58,484 Roman Catholics, 99,652 Presbyterians and 3,544 miscellaneous Protestants. In parts of the south and west, Protestants were heavily outnumbered. The diocese of Ross, in the province of Cashel,
had 6,061 Anglicans to 108,225 Roman Catholics. Neither group would have felt
threatened by the two miscellaneous dissenters.[20] Most Presbyterians were settled
in Ulster, where, despite emigration, they enjoyed numerical dominance over Anglicans, whose numbers were also high. It is reckoned that up to 125,000 Presbyterians left the north of Ireland during the period 1718–74, mainly destined for the
American colonies.[21] The most heavily Presbyterian counties were Antrim and Down.
Belfast was also a Presbyterian stronghold. In 1752 Bishop Pococke estimated that
of 400 households in the town, only 60 were Anglican.[22] Despite growing Presbyterian numbers and wealth in the second half of the century, its corporation was dominated by Anglican nominees of the Donegall family, the town's landlords. By the
1790s this oligarchic government had pushed Belfast to the forefront of radical politics.

THE POLITICAL BACKGROUND

Eighteenth-century politics, like their twentieth-century equivalent, were about
people and power. However, similarities should not be assumed, even in such
reductionist terms. The people who participated in and benefited from the political
process were vastly different then than now. Power was conceived of and exercised
in a different manner. Voting rights in county and borough elections were confined
to a narrow social and religious constituency. The right to sit in parliament was
limited to an even smaller social band. As the section on the penal laws shows, the
Irish parliament had made it illegal for Catholics to vote and *de facto* illegal for
Catholics to sit in parliament. Presbyterians could sit in parliament, but their opportunities of election were restricted by the Test Act until 1780. Even so, the percentage of Protestants who could vote was as low as 5.5 per cent (about 60,000 in
counties and boroughs) on the eve of the 1793 reform, which restored the vote to
Catholic freeholders. This percentage was approximately the same as in England,
but higher than in Scotland.[23]

19 Whelan, op. cit., p. 60.   20 Commissioners of Public Instruction, ibid.   21 J.L. McCracken, *NHI*,
p. 32.   22 S.J. Connolly, *Religion, Law and Power*, pp. 161–2.   23 S.J. Connolly, ibid., p. 98.

The franchise for the two-seat county constituencies was restricted to those holding freehold or leased land with a minimum value of forty shillings, while that for the 117 borough seats varied rather idiosyncratically according to the type of borough. In corporation boroughs such as Belfast, which were the main type, the vote was restricted to a narrow oligarchy of members of the corporation, aldermen, common councilmen or burgesses. In other types, it was given to freemen, in still others, to 'potwallopers' (substantial householders).[24] Despite these differences, the general rule applied that voting rights depended on possessing some recognised unit of property. In addition, the forty shilling criteria was so narrowly prescriptive as to exclude owners of considerable property who fell outside the terms of reference, yet sufficiently ill-defined to facilitate the deliberate creation of freeholds for votes by unscrupulous landlords.[25]

MPs were typically country gentlemen or the scions of aristocratic families, plus a few lawyers, soldiers and merchants.[26] Many were under the sponsorship of an aristocratic patron. Men like the marquises of Abercorn and Downshire traded in the control of seats to build up a strong political 'interest' which could be offered to or courted by the government. In 1793 Downshire controlled nine seats while Abercorn had six.[27] Such control came from influence and popularity in the county, alliances with other families or the purchase of seats for 'close' boroughs controlled by an individual or a clique and immune from 'open' competition. The price for such support was patronage: the right to dispose of government jobs and offices. This system appears now to be hopelessly oligarchic, venal, unrepresentative and corrupt. However, it should be remembered that, although politics was operated by an elite, this elite was not totally closed, nor was it completely unresponsive to public opinion. There were sufficient people from non-aristocratic backgrounds, like Castlereagh's family the Stewarts of Newtownards, to keep a humbler foot in the door. The Irish parliament and its supporting political system should not be compared with a modern democracy: it represented the property of the country. For the most part, reformers wanted to improve the existing system, not overturn it. The trade in borough seats, one of the most apparently 'corrupt' political practices, was part of a political culture which saw seats as a species of property. An omnipresent and fastidious sense of honour acted as a brake on blatant corruption and unaccountability. 'Close' borough seats were not regarded as carrying the same weight as 'open' county and borough seats, though in simple numerical terms they were equally important. Moreover, the same prickly honour which could lead an MP to fight a duel with another whose rhetoric had exceeded the bounds of propriety would also

24 J.L. McCracken, *The Irish Parliament in the Eighteenth Century*, passim. **25** P.J. Jupp, *British and Irish Elections, 1784–1831*, p. 153. **26** McCracken, ibid., p. 13. **27** A.P.W. Malcomson, 'A lost natural leader: John James Hamilton, first Marquess of Abercorn' in *Proceedings of the Royal Irish Academy* 88C, iv, pp. 61–86.

make him stand against the government and all its patronage if a 'popular' measure demanded it.[28]

The most important issue of concern to the eighteenth-century Irish MPs was the constitutional relationship of their parliament with Westminster and with Dublin Castle. The Irish executive, the lord lieutenant, chief secretary and the various Castle officials, were appointed by and answerable to the ruling administration in London rather than to the Irish parliament. Although the Castle officials were semi-permanent, the lord lieutenant was automatically changed with each new British administration, a factor which mitigated against continuity of experience and the acquisition of any deep knowledge of Irish affairs. Moreover, for most of the century, the Irish parliament's legislation was subject to veto by the British privy council. This subsidiary position infuriated Irish parliamentarians, most of whom were of direct English ancestry, and who preferred to view Ireland as an equal, sister kingdom.

Although the Anglo-Irish relationship should have been one of mutual dependence, there were tensions at varying levels of intensity throughout most of the century. Contemporaries put a word on this tension: 'Patriotism'; historians have tended to call it 'Protestant Nationalism'. Certain issues, usually involving the raising of finance by the Irish parliament, were likely to upset 'patriotic' feelings. During the century, 'patriotic' sentiment peaked in a series of crises. It manifested itself within parliament as a rejection of government measures, and outside as unruly demonstrations by the Dublin mob. The famous Money Bill dispute of 1753 was the most damaging of these crises, with many government supporters patriotically biting the hand that fed them. The eventual freeing of the Irish parliament from London's legislative veto in 1782 was achieved by parliamentary patriots acting in conjunction with the Irish Volunteers functioning as an armed expression of public opinion.

Legislative independence – the so-called 'constitution' of 1782 – was one of the great political changes of the century; the other was the introduction and growth of the Catholic Question, which eventually became an issue of massive importance at both the political and sub-political levels of society. The conditions engendered by both issues provide the backdrop to the troubled 1790s. Grattan's parliament was never a satisfactory arrangement from a British viewpoint, leaving dangerous ambiguities in vital areas such as foreign affairs, control of the navy in Irish waters and, as was demonstrated in the Regency crisis of 1788–9, the relationship between parliament and the monarch. Moreover, the post-1782 arrangements did not please everyone in Ireland. Some of the more radical Volunteers wanted further constitutional reform. Many were Presbyterians who wanted the parliamentary representation altered, to accommodate a wider range of interests. An even smaller number of reformers also wanted the franchise to include Catholics. One important by-prod-

28 A.P.W. Malcomson 'The Parliamentary Traffic of this country', in *Penal Era and Golden Age*, p. 138.

uct of 1782 was that the British government began to seriously consider the Irish Catholics as an important third player in the game of governing. It is necessary to look at the Catholic Question in some detail as it was to become intimately embroiled in the raising of yeomanry.

THE CATHOLIC QUESTION

The immediate context of the penal laws was the Williamite wars of 1688–90. However to understand fully the underlying attitudes it is necessary to briefly look back into the seventeenth century. The great Irish rebellion of 1641 looms large but it is wrong to assume this was the first challenge to the plantations. Individual attacks were made by 'woodkerne' on plantation castles and bawns between 1609 and 1641. Both planters and government blamed the influence of Catholic priests. The 1641 rising itself started as a plot among disenchanted native Irish landowners like Sir Phelim O'Neill to capitalise on divisions in England between Charles I and parliament by claiming royal authority for a strike against planters of English origin, however, a deeper vein of popular resentment was touched and the attacks soon threatened both English and Scottish planters. Although the extent of the slaughter of Protestants has been exaggerated, massacres did occur leaving a deep and lasting scar on the Protestant psyche. A.T.Q. Stewart claims the Protestant 'siege mentality' originated in 1641.[29] When Catholics of old English ancestry and the native Irish came together in the Confederation of Kilkenny in 1642 and declared for Charles, it made Protestants begin to see their relationship with England in a more ambivalent light. Obviously their minority position ultimately depended on English support, as Cromwell was soon to prove, yet the fact that Ireland could be made subservient to English interests was a potential source of insecurity. The Cromwellian land settlement of the 1650s further reduced native Irish landholding and imported a hard new type of Protestant settler often with a military background. The rebellion and wars of 1641–52 had another important legacy. The Presbyterian system of church government came over with the parliamentarian General Munro's Scottish army.

In 1660 Irish Protestants, particularly Presbyterians, entered into an uneasy acceptance of the restored Stuart monarchy, but with the birth of a Catholic heir to James II in 1688, England once more proved a source of both threat and deliverance. James's lord deputy in Ireland, Tyrconnell, had been following a catholicizing policy since 1687, particularly in the army and the legal profession. James naturally looked to Ireland after his expulsion from England and the invitation to William and Mary to take the throne. Ireland became the cockpit of James's struggle to reclaim his

---

29 A.T.Q. Stewart, *The Narrow Ground*, pp. 46, 52.

throne, and the war between Williamites and Jacobites one of international significance. However, the sight of Tyrconnell's raw Catholic levies renewed Protestant
memories of 1641 and caused a panic-stricken scramble for the relative safety of
defensible towns like Derry and Enniskillen. During the struggle, James called a
parliament in Dublin, the so-called 'Patriot Parliament', almost totally composed of
Catholic nobles and gentlemen. It repealed the Restoration land settlement and
passed an Act of Attainder appropriating the property of around 2,000 'traitors'.
The military struggle ended in Jacobite defeats at the Boyne, Aughrim and Limerick. Deliverance from Tyrconnell's hordes became part of Protestant mythology
along with siege traditions of resistance and self-reliance. Many members of the
subsequent 'Williamite parliament' had featured in the proposed Jacobite land ap-
propriations. In consequence they burned for immediate revenge and craved long-
term security following two attempts at Catholic resurgence within fifty years.

Eighteenth-century Ireland is sometimes represented as the century of the Anglo-
Irish Ascendancy on the one hand and the victims of the penal laws on the other: a
land of 'haves' and 'have nots', divided along lines of religious affiliation. In this
analysis, the earthquake of 1798 which levelled the houses of rich and poor alike,
was a disaster waiting to happen. In a sense this was true, given the climate of change
and increased expectations from about 1780 onwards. However, recent research has
shown not only that the penal laws were far different in their implementation than
the letter, but also that the economic fortunes of important sections of the Catholic
community actually revived in the first half of the eighteenth century.[30] If fully implemented, there is little doubt the main corpus of legislation enacted between 1697
and 1709 would have extinguished Catholicism in Ireland. This legislation targeted
the essentials of Catholicism in both its structure and practice, as well as Catholic
property and political power. The Bishops' Banishment Act of 1697 declared that
'all popish archbishops, bishops, vicars general, deans, Jesuits, monks, friars and all
other regular popish clergy and all Papists exercising ecclesiastical jurisdiction, shall
depart out of this kingdom before 1 May 1698'.[31] The law was doubly significant
since by excluding bishops and preventing Catholics from attending educational
institutions abroad, no new priests could be ordained. Other Acts forbade Catholics
bequeathing land to the eldest son in the traditional manner, unless he 'turned' to
become Protestant. Failing this, the estate was 'gavelled', divided equally amongst
all the sons, thus breaking it up as an economic and political unit. Catholics were
still able to lease land, but, by the Popery Act of 1704, the period was limited to
thirty-one years. They were excluded from the legislative, judicial and executive
functions of the state, both centrally and locally. They could not sit in parliament,
nor, after 1728, vote for those who did, and they were debarred from borough cor-
porations and county grand juries. They could neither practise law as barristers or

30 T. Bartlett, *The Fall and Rise of the Irish Nation* (henceforth: Bartlett, *Fall and Rise*), p. 46.   31 9
Will. III, cap. 1.

solicitors, nor could they execute it as magistrates or even humble constables. Catholics could not serve in the king's army, nor could they freely hold arms, whether to fire at the king's enemies or at rooks in the cornfield.[32] Their exclusion from public office was largely shared by Presbyterians, who were seen as a threat to the establishment because of their system of church government, their numbers, and their 'Commonwealth' traditions. They were effectively disqualified from crown and municipal office by the sacramental test clause in the 1704 Popery Act.[33] Though Protestant dissenters were spared the other religious, political and economic strictures of the penal code, it rankled none the less with those who had supported William to share the 'punishment' of the Catholics they had helped defeat, and to have helped maintain the parliament which now legislated against them.

For a variety of reasons, the penal laws did not destroy Irish Catholicism or complete the work of the Reformation in Ireland. Not least was the hard reality that wholesale conversions would have meant diluting the Protestant landowning elite's monopoly minority status. There were some genuine conversion attempts by zealous Anglicans like Archbishop Edward Synge of Tuam. However, the resistance of local communities to centralised ideological initiatives, allied to the notorious weaknesses in law enforcement, ensured the uneven implementation and eventual failure of the penal laws. Indeed, recent research shows that the period 1690–1760, 'far from being a "penal era" in which Catholics were uniformly downtrodden and oppressed, in fact witnessed a considerable Catholic resurgence'.[34]

The dynamism of the eighteenth-century Catholic community was derived from two associated factors: the survival of a semi-gentry, and the rise of 'strong' farming families who intermarried and branched out into trade in both country and town. Kevin Whelan has shown that Catholic economic resurgence centred on a 'core area' of South Leinster and East Munster and radiated outwards along kin and trade links. The crucible of recovery contained 'a leadership class based on surviving Catholic landed families and increasingly assertive mercantile and big farm groupings'.[35] The importance of continental trade-links was a major feature, not least by providing safe investment locations for Catholic capital. Consequently, ports like Galway, Cork and Limerick held strong and coherent groups of Catholic trading families. Despite a fall in the outright ownership of land held by Catholics in fee simple, they still maintained a considerable 'interest' in land. Often this was obscured. It has been estimated that up to ninety per cent of all 'discoveries' of Catholic land by Protestants under the penal laws were actually collusive: gentlemen's agreements, worked out according to the dynamics of local family connections, whereby the real ownership remained in Catholic hands with the authorities merely notified of the nominal new Protestant owner. Additionally, although their leases

32 J.C. Beckett, *The Making of Modern Ireland*, chap. 8, passim; Lecky, *Ireland*, i, p. 146.   33 2 Anne, c. 6.   34 Bartlett, *Fall and Rise*, pp. 25, 36, 46.   35 Whelan, 'Catholic mobilisation, 1750–1850' in *Culture et Pratique Politiques*, p. 236.

were legally limited to thirty-one years, Catholics could increase their interest in land by lease speculation or twist the law to wring out *de facto* possession in the form of perpetually renewable thirty-one year leases.[36]

This constricted vibrancy in key sections of the Catholic community had great significance for events later in the century. Like Presbyterians in Ulster, the wealth, influence and entrepreneurial intellects of these 'strong' farmers and traders became ever more incompatible with exclusion from the polity in the 'enlightened' spirit of the times. The American and French revolutions proved that ingrained orthodoxies could be overturned by the collective efforts of the people. However, unlike the Presbyterians, reinstatement of Catholic power would radically alter the *status quo* in Ireland because of their numerical majority in the population. This caused increasing anxiety to Anglicans, whose position was necessarily supported by continuing Catholic impotence and by the guarantee that their interests and those of Hanoverian Britain coincided in protecting Ireland from the Jacobite threat within or without. While the Jacobite danger and Catholic espousal of the Stuart cause was real, this British support was not in doubt, but the belligerence of the 'independent' Irish parliament after 1782 and, particularly, the outbreak of war with France in 1793, caused British ministers to re-evaluate their position.

The most recent scholarship traces the beginnings of agitation for Catholic relief back to the political upheaval surrounding the Money Bill dispute of 1753, which fractured the Anglo-Irish governing consensus sufficiently to encourage some influential Catholics to plead their case.[37] It opened the door, which had been slammed shut in the reigns of William and Anne, sufficiently to allow the first foot of Catholic grievance across the threshold. These pleadings were accompanied by frequent and genuine loyal declarations. Although there was clearly emotional support for the exiled Stuarts in the first decades of the century, it was inactive due to a lack of cohesive leadership and the switch of Jacobite invasion plans from Ireland to Britain. By the time of the Young Pretender's rising in 1745, even this notional support had become equivocal, with many Catholics reluctant to jeopardise the non-implementation of the penal laws.[38] The first Catholic Association was founded in 1756 with the limited objectives of trying to influence opinion by issuing pamphlets revising some of the myths surrounding 1641 and seeking parliamentary support against legislation hostile to their interests.[39] Strategic considerations were always close to British government thinking on the Catholic issue. The penal laws locked up a potentially great recruiting resource in the Catholic population, one of which continental powers were quick to take advantage. Britain's imperial wars created an unprecedented demand for soldiers, particularly the Seven Years' War of 1756–63. To demonstrate Catholics' loyalty and thus their suitability for relief Lord Trimleston

36 Bartlett, *Fall and Rise*, pp. 47–8.   37 Bartlett, ibid, p. 44.   38 S.J. Connolly, *Religion, Law and Power*, pp. 233–6, 247.   39 Bartlett, ibid., chap. 4, passim.

offered to raise seven regiments to serve the crown. He was refused, but the important fact for the future was that the proposal received serious consideration by the British government. Irish Catholic loyalty was now seen as vital in wartime. This set a pattern for the future, as did the manner in which the approach was made, directly to London. The Catholic Committee was now well aware that Irish parliamentarians, remembering Tyrconnell, feared an armed and trained Catholic population and were confident that the Protestant militia of 1739–40 and 1745 was sufficient to protect Ireland from internal disorder.[40]

The major relief Acts of the period all originated in London and had strategic and political undertones. Luke Gardiner's relief bills of 1778 and 1782 were government-sponsored measures, intended to secure Catholic loyalty during the American war and to trade off Irish 'patriot' demands. Indeed, in 1782 the intention was to prevent the 'patriots' disingenuously embracing the Catholic cause themselves to make their campaign for legislative independence appear to come from the entire country.[41] Never again could Irish Protestants automatically assume uncritical British support. These two Acts were modest enough in their terms, removing restrictions on the leasing, ownership and bequeathing of land, rescinding the restrictions on priests and legalising Catholic schools. However, they were symbolically significant to Protestants, whose anxiety grew apace as agitation continued for further relief.

In 1792 and 1793 major relief Acts were passed against an ominous background darkened by the threat of war with revolutionary France, and domestic disorder from the Catholic Defender movement spreading from Ulster into Louth.[42] Moreover, the Catholic Committee was mobilising popular Catholic opinion under a more assertive middle-class leadership who had ousted its aristocratic founders. The 1792 Act was a prelude to that of 1793. It removed the remaining restrictions on education, intermarriage and entry to the legal profession but, as a compromise to the Irish parliament, did not include, as the British government wanted, the right to vote in county elections, sit on juries or bear arms. The arms issue was to be a particularly sore point with poorer Protestants and was to feature in sectarian troubles in county Armagh and influence attitudes towards Catholic participation in the yeomanry. The right to bear arms had profound significance. It was taken to symbolise citizenship and gave poorer Protestants a status they would have been otherwise denied by their lowly position in the social hierarchy. The progressive removal of the penal code put such people on the defensive. A major feature of the Armagh troubles was arms raids on Catholic houses by Peep O'Day Boys, gangs of lower-class Protestants. The 1793 Act opened the municipal and parliamentary franchise to Catholic forty-shilling freeholders and all but the most important civil and military posts. The only major concession denied was the right to sit in parliament.

40 S.J. Connolly, ibid., p. 201.   41 Bartlett, ibid., chap. 6, passim.   42 For a discussion on the Defenders see chapter 2.

LAW AND ORDER: THE FRAMEWORK

The Irish landowning gentry, like their British counterparts, served as local representatives of government in a voluntary and unpaid capacity in the main local agencies which executed government business and enforced the laws. County governors and sheriffs were responsible for maintaining law and order, with sheriffs also acting as returning officers in elections, appointing juries and parish officers. The real spade-work of local law enforcement was done by the magistrates, appointed by the lord lieutenant but nominated locally, and usually men owning property in the county they served. The typical working magistrate was a man of local influence with a sizeable tenantry, the same type of gentleman who would later raise yeomanry. Major landowners headed the county bench of magistrates, but their role was honorary and symbolic rather than practical. The county benches were large. The 1796 list for Down contained 121 names, though not all were resident nor was every resident 'active'. This was a major problem with the Irish magistracy. Because of uneven Protestant settlement, particularly in the south and west, it was difficult to get enough fit people on the bench.[43]

Magistrates were the main point of contact between most members of the public and the law. By the eighteenth century there was such a vast and complex amount of legislation to be administered that it became necessary, as in England, to issue voluminous law guides, like Edward Bullingbroke's massive tome.[44] Magistrates had a dual role, part judicial and part executive. In addition to hearing cases and passing judgement, they directed the various law enforcement officers in the days before a police force: the parish constables and the watchmen in towns and cities. In both roles magistrates could act either as individuals or in consort on the county bench.[45] Much of the local everyday work, such as checking the weight of loaves or chasing up the fathers of bastards, was handled in the magistrate's individual capacity, as was the execution of the law against petty criminals. More serious cases were dealt with by a specially convened gathering of magistrates or deferred to the quarter sessions for judgement by the assembled county bench assisted by a jury appointed by the sheriff.

Still graver cases, such as murder, manslaughter and treason, were 'presented' to the county grand jury at the twice yearly assize courts. The grand jury's function was to deliberate on the admissibility of these presentments for judgement, along with others for raising money for the construction or upkeep of roads and bridges. Such criminal or financial presentations as they approved were called 'true bills' and submitted to the assize judge for decision.[46] The judges were centrally appointed

---

43 R.B. McDowell, *The Irish Administration*, p. 112.   44 E. Bullingbroke, *The duty and authority of Justices of the Peace and Parish Officers for Ireland* (Dublin, 1764).   45 D.W. Hayton, 'Ireland and the English Ministers, 1707–16'; McDowell, ibid., p. 69.   46 Hayton, ibid. p. 69; McDowell, ibid., p. 164.

and travelled in circuit throughout the provinces for the lent and summer assizes. The powers of these courts were extensive, ranging from gaol through transportation to capital conviction. The grand jury was also an important opportunity for the county gentlemen to meet. There was a social dimension: gargantuan conviviality was the norm and the assizes probably contributed to more cases of gout than the hunt ball. Moreover, such meetings were ideal for the transmission of government policy via the circuit judges, and conversely for the relaying of local concerns back to government in the form of resolutions. As the century wore on, increasing use was made of newspapers to publicise resolutions. Carrying the agreement of the most 'respectable' men, they carried weight, and represented what the eighteenth-century political world recognised as public opinion. This method of collective action could also take the form of an 'association' of gentlemen pledged to suppress organised disorder. Such associations could cover several counties and were one of the traditions which fed into the yeomanry. Throughout the eighteenth and into the nineteenth century the main concern of local government was law and order. In addition to associations, the magistrates had access to a range of options depending on the scale of the problem. They could use the parish officers, organise citizen volunteers or request military aid from central government.

LAW AND ORDER: THE CHALLENGES

It is perhaps a misnomer to speak of law and order being challenged in the early eighteenth century. This statement would presuppose a functional, uniformly operated law and order system, which was being systematically opposed. It is more accurate to see the onus resting on the system to challenge groups and regional areas which, for various reasons, resisted the rule of law. S.J. Connolly has argued that in the first half of the century, 'there were segments of Irish society in which the normal processes of law and order were largely ignored and others in which they operated at best imperfectly'. He sees three basic types of lawlessness, all of which declined after about 1750. Although 'toryism', which originated in land confiscation, had died out with the spread of military barracks in the early eighteenth century, it had been replaced by banditry in remote areas like south Ulster and west Galway. Secondly, in some areas the landed gentry ignored the law when it ran contrary to their own interests, rather in the way that English gentry in coastal districts toasted the king in smuggled brandy. The third problem area was in the larger towns and cities, where unruly mobs often proved beyond the power of the municipal magistrates and their watchmen.[47]

These types of opportunistic, unpredictable and unco-ordinated lawlessness de-

47 S.J. Connolly, *Religion, Law and Power*, pp. 215, 217.

clined and were replaced from around 1760 by large-scale popular protest movements with specific agrarian or economic objectives in Munster, Leinster and parts
of Ulster. Magistrates in the south and west were faced with Whiteboys and
Rightboys, while their Ulster counterparts had to deal with Oakboys and Steelboys.
Though agrarian protest was a feature of the second half of the century, these groups
were pre-figured to an extent by the 'Houghers' of 1711–12 in Connacht and the
midlands, who were protesting against the spread of stock-rearing, which created
less employment than tillage. Like later agrarian groups, the Houghers' objectives
were defensive; they wanted to preserve the *status quo* of traditional agricultural
practice. They did so by houghing (slashing) the tendons of the graziers' livestock,[48]
a gruesome practice which survived in attacks on soldiers later in the century.

The agrarian protesters of the 1760–90 period shared similarities, but equally
each had its own composition and orientation, and the various groups should be
seen as local or regional phenomena. This is not to say that disturbances were localised. At least twenty-two counties were affected in this period, but the degree of
disturbance varied and only Waterford, Tipperary and Kilkenny were constantly
seriously troubled.[49] These were the counties affected by the Whiteboys, who protested against a range of grievances including tithes, priests' dues, grain prices and
the enclosure of common land.[50] Unlike the Houghers, who were partly gentry-led,
the Whiteboys were a genuinely popular movement and an oath-bound, secret society. The significance of the Whiteboy oath, which swore allegiance to Queen Sive, a
Celtic goddess, was that it enabled them to spread easily. The very name Whiteboy,
derived from the wearing of white apparel over ordinary clothes on midnight raids,
bespoke cohesiveness and anonymity. Like the Houghers, the Whiteboys framed
their own rules based on natural justice and tried to enforce them by violence. However this was now directed at the persons as well as the property of those who
resisted them. Although the Whiteboy disturbances were self-evidently economic,
many nervous Protestants saw in them the bogey of Catholic resurgence particularly as outbreaks of 'Whiteboyism' coincided with Britain being at war with France.
Some even saw the spectre of Jacobitism returning to haunt them in white cockades
and shirts. There were similar reactions to the outbreak of Rightboy disturbances in
Cork and Kerry between 1785 and 1788. The Rightboys were mostly small cottiers,
but included some Protestants and larger farmers. They protested against the auc-
tioning of leases, the increase in taxation at a time of falling returns, and, more
particularly, the exactions of Anglican and Catholic clergy. Despite this, as has been
conclusively argued, it suited the more conservative element within Protestantism

---

48 S.J. Connolly, ibid., p. 219; 'Law, Order and Popular Protest ... the case of the Houghers', in P.J.
Corish (ed.), *Radicals, Rebels and Establishments.*   49 S.J. Connolly, 'Violence and Order in the Eighteenth Century', in P. O'Flanagan, R. Ferguson and K. Whelan (eds), *Rural Ireland, 1600–1900: modernisation and change*, p. 53.   50 J.S. Donnelly Jnr, 'The Whiteboy Movement of 1761–65', *IHS*, xxi, 81
(1978), pp. 20–55.

to utilise the opportunity the Rightboys presented to raise the Catholic bogey against more liberal elements who favoured reform and Catholic relief, and consequently initiated the concept of a Protestant 'Ascendancy' under attack.[51]

Around the time of the first Whiteboy outbreak in the 1760s a movement known as the Hearts of Oak or Oakboys emerged in the linen-producing Tandragee district of Armagh. The Oakboys' grievances centred on the county cess. They quickly spread into Monaghan, Cavan, Tyrone and Derry and were composed of the lower classes of all denominations. Their leadership came from the same social group, though recent research suggests some gentry involvement.[52] Their tactics were to frighten the gentlemen of the grand juries into reducing the cess by large daylight demonstrations carrying the implicit threat of force. Unlike the Whiteboys, they threatened rather than actually used violence. A typical experience was that of an Anglican clergyman, Theophilus Martin, who encountered the Tyrone Oakboys near Cookstown in July 1763. Led by a 'captain', they surrounded his chaise in large numbers, jostled him and threatened a lynching unless he swore an oath against raising cess 'for building useless bridges'. Although on enquiry he was told that nobody had yet been hanged, the prudent cleric took the oath and was given a sprig of oak for his hat as a safe pass.[53] The Oakboys faded in the later 1760s, but were soon replaced by a more dangerous society known as the Hearts of Steel or Steelboys. Starting around 1769 on the Upton and Donegall estates in South Antrim, the Steelboys protested against steep increases in the price of leases then falling in for renewal. On the Donegall estate the grievance has been shown to have arisen not just from insecurity but from the frustrated ambition of under-tenants who had hoped to become direct tenants but had been outbid by wealthy middlemen (including some Belfast merchants) able to afford the new leases. Once successful, the middlemen would hike up the under-tenants' rent without compunction.[54] Unlike the Oakboys, there were ominous sectarian undertones to these economic grievances, as some renewals went to Catholics who could bid higher. One Steelboy declaration explicitly proclaimed:

> we are all Protestants and Protestant Dissenters ... groaning under oppression ... are forced to join ourselves together to resist. Some of us refusing to pay the extravagant rent are turned out and our lands given to Papists, who will promise to pay the rent.[55]

51 J. Kelly, 'The genesis of Protestant Ascendancy: the Rightboy disturbances of the 1780s and their impact on Protestant opinion' in G. O'Brien (ed.), *Parliament, Politics and People*, pp. 93–127.   52 I am grateful to Dr Eoin McGuinness of QUB for this informaion.   53 J.S. Donnelly Jnr, 'Hearts of Oak, Hearts of Steel', *Studia Hibernica* 21 (1981), pp. 7–75; 8 July 1763, P.R.O.N.I. G.M. Stewart Papers, T1442/6.   54 W.A. Maguire, 'Lord Donegall and the Hearts of Steel', *IHS*, xxi, 84 (Sept. 1979), pp. 351–76.   55 Quoted in J.A. Froude, *The English in Ireland*, ii, pp. 121–2.

Given the prevailing economic problems of the time, a slump in domestic weaving coupled with growing competition for land, the Steelboys soon spread into counties Down, Londonderry and Tyrone. The Steelboys were an oath-bound, secret society, more like the Whiteboys than the Oakboys. They also used similar methods to the Whiteboys of enforcing compliance to their rules, including destruction of crops and cattle, forced contributions and assassination.[56] Moreover, there seemed to be an underlying system. The earl of Abercorn's agent, James Hamilton noted, 'What makes these rioters more formidable [than the Oakboys] is that they form and execute their acts of mischief in nightly meetings'.[57] At one stage the Steelboys became confident enough to march in force into Belfast and rescue a prisoner. Needless to say, the gentry were worried by what was, by Ulster standards, a serious challenge to law and order. Around Portstewart, for example, the gentlemen's houses were barricaded with 'bags of sand nailed up in most of our windows'.[58] However, the Hearts of Steel melted away around 1773 when the magistrates called in troops and were granted special powers.

In the mid-1780s a sinister development occurred in county Armagh: disturbances started between the lower classes of Protestants and Presbyterians on the one side and Catholics on the other. These troubles rolled on with changes of manifestation and location into the mid-1790s and proved to have a resonance far beyond their place and time. At first they took the form of fair-day feuds between gangs, known on the Protestant side as 'fleets' because of the recent currency of the term in naval warfare. Ominously, they soon began raiding Catholic homes for arms. These raiders styled themselves 'Peep O'Day Boys' from their habit of attacking in the early hours of the morning. The Catholics banded together as 'Defenders' to resist. In 1788 the emphasis shifted from fair-day riots and arms raids to more violent struggles for local territorial dominance, often resulting in fatalities. The sectarian violence had died down in north Armagh by early 1790 (though Defenderism persisted in Catholic districts in the south of the county), only to flare up again in 1791 following the brutal mutilation and murder of a Protestant woman in Forkhill. The early 1790s saw the fire spread into Monaghan, Tyrone and west Down, while burning even more intensely at its heart in central and southern Armagh.[59] These territorial confrontations climaxed near Loughgall in September 1795, when the 'Battle of the Diamond' was fought between a large force of Defenders and Protestants from Armagh and west Down. The Protestants, though numerically smaller, were better armed having access to Volunteer guns. They were also forewarned and took the best ground, routing the Defenders who left around thirty dead on the field and more 'found afterwards by the reapers along the line of their flight'.[60] The

56 Maguire, op. cit. pp. 351–2; Donnelly, 'Hearts of Oak', ibid., p. 67.   57 Hamilton to Abercorn, 13 Mar. 1772, P.R.O.N.I. Abercorn Papers, T2541/1A1/10.   58 Mrs O'Neill to Mrs Tobin, 27 Mar. 1772, P.R.O.N.I. Knox Papers, D115/2.   59 D.W. Miller, 'The Armagh Troubles, 1785–95', in S. Clarke and J.S. Donnelly Jnr, (eds), *Irish Peasants: Violence and Political Unrest*, pp. 165, 173.   60 Colonel Blacker, quoted in: C. Kilpatrick (ed.), *The Formation of the Orange Order*, p. 16.

consequences of this affair were far-reaching. The first Orange Lodge was formed in its immediate aftermath, from the various Protestant groups involved. There then followed the 'Armagh Expulsions', a pogrom against Catholics conducted by the victors, who engaged in assassination and 'racking', economic intimidation involving the wrecking of houses and particularly looms. By the end of 1796, several thousand Catholics had fled, mostly to Connacht.[61] The refugees took their resentment with them, which helped to spread the Defender movement outside Ulster and inspired a general Catholic fear of Orangemen well in advance of the actual establishment of lodges in the south. There is little doubt the early Orangemen were involved, though their gentry leaders later claimed that their organisation checked such lawlessness. Richard Jephson recounted one instance where Orangemen had shot a man in a potato field and defied the magistrates to bury or remove the victim.[62]

Historians have offered various interpretations of the Armagh troubles. Until recently, the favoured approach was an economic-demographic analysis predicated on the inter-related growth of population and linen weaving. Hereward Senior detected continuities between the Steelboys and Peep O'Day Boys, insofar as both feared Catholics outbidding them for leases. For Senior, the reaction against Catholics having arms was secondary to this economic motive.[63] Peter Gibbon also saw economic change as a causal factor, but in a different way. In his view, the trouble originated in the plight of those whose independence and status were being undermined by modernisation in the linen industry, which led to weavers being employed by manufacturers rather than acting as free agents.[64] David Miller, looking at contemporary interpretations of the troubles, found that 'breakdown' theories were the most common. Concentrating on the first phase of troubles from 1784–90, Miller considered that the main cause of breakdown was the impact of weaving, in freeing young men from familial restraint and making them less amenable to paternalistic gentry control. He agreed with Senior in seeing the Volunteers as a further cause of instability. Their admission and arming of Catholics annoyed poorer Protestant weavers, too socially and economically disadvantaged to be considered themselves as Volunteers, thus provoking attacks on Catholics.[65] All these interpretations are grounded in a belief that the undoubted demographic and economic idiosyncrasy of county Armagh spawned the instability which led to disorder.

However, recent research has shown that only a political explanation can explain both the events in Armagh and the spill-over into areas with a different economic structure, such as Louth.[66] In this analysis, electoral politics destabilised Armagh starting with the 1783 general election in which the Cope family of Loughgall em-

61 Bartlett, *Fall and Rise*, p. 216. 62 Jephson to Charlemont, 9 Oct. 1795, H.M.C. *Charlemont*, pp. 265–6. 63 Senior, *Orangeism*, p. 8. 64 Gibbon, *The Origins of Ulster Unionism*. 65 Miller, 'Armagh Troubles', passim. 66 L. Cullen, 'The Political Structures of the Defenders' in H. Gough and D. Dickson (eds), *Ireland and the French Revolution*, pp. 117–38.

braced radicalism as the best vehicle for their ambitions. This radical interest, which supported Catholic relief and encouraged Catholics to join the Volunteers, continued into the 1790s. The by-election of 1795, when the Copes narrowly failed to capture one of the county seats, saw a bitter electioneering campaign in which 'Church and King' mobs were pitted against the radical interest. Raising up such sentiments was playing with fire and could be counter-productive if the 'boys' got unruly enough to make government think the gentry had lost control. By 1788 some Volunteer companies around Benburb were admitting Peep O'Day Boys to their ranks in order to counteract this.[67] Presbyterians were the key players in this ongoing, shifting conflict of alliances. Many Armagh Presbyterians were politically radical and some favoured an alliance with the Catholics. Others were not, or were at least susceptible to instinctive anti-Catholicism in an area which saw atrocities in 1641. Lord Gosford, the leader of the conservative interest in the county, noted in 1788 that most arms raids in central and north Armagh were by 'Protestant Dissenters who attack and rob Roman Catholic houses under the pretence of arms searches'.[68] Gosford was deluding himself if he thought that robbery was the motive. The Peep O'Day Boys wanted to rob Catholics of what they saw as symbolising political rights: Volunteer guns. This political explanation is convincing, though the intensity of the violence was undoubtedly influenced by its demographic complexity. Presbyterians, Anglicans and Catholics lived cheek-by-jowl in county Armagh, and memories of 1641 massacres lingered long.

The Armagh troubles were a much more serious challenge to law and order than the agrarian protests of the 1760–80 period. The danger was not confined to Armagh alone. Defenderism developed an intrinsically political, sectarian and revolutionary character and spread widely. This diffusion should be seen in the wider context of the French Revolution and renewed agitation by the Catholic Committee, particularly the 1792 campaign to elect a Catholic Convention, which spread politicisation to every parish and in the widespread riots against the enlisting of militia in 1793. In 1791 the Defenders were confined to an area of sectarian feuding in Ulster. By 1793 they were raiding for arms in Louth and Meath. By 1795 the movement had spread to twelve counties and had already reached Dublin, where tacit liaisons developed with urban radicals then controlling the Catholic Committee.[69] The extent and intensity of militant Defenderism was perturbing. In January 1795 the new lord lieutenant, Fitzwilliam, complained, 'not a day has passed since my arrival, without intelligence of outrage committed in Westmeath, Meath, Longford or Cavan'.[70]

Defenderism was a hybrid growth comprising many strands of the Irish past and

67 Cullen, ibid., p. 119; Miller, ibid., p. 172.   68 Gosford to Acheson, 8 Feb. 1788, P.R.O.N.I. Gosford Papers, D1606/I/125C.   69 J. Smyth, 'Defenderism and the Catholic Question', in Gough and Dickson, ibid., pp. 111–13; Lecky, *Ireland*, iii, p. 445.   70 Fitzwilliam to Portland, 10 Jan. 1795 P.R.O. H.O.100/ 56/ff. 57–60.

present which flourished in the heated conditions of the time. It combined elements of millenarianism with a militant anti-Protestantism, which, by defining Protestants as 'heretics' harked back to the Reformation.[71] Camden, Fitzwilliam's successor, called the Defenders 'successors of a class of people who have never been made good subjects'.[72] Traditional grievances about dispossession were updated by the Catholic Committee's politicising activities. Moreover the old Jacobite idea of looking for deliverance from overseas was resurrected as the Defenders looked to revolutionary France for inspiration and material support. A paper found on a Cavan Defender bore the ominous missive: 'The French Defenders will uphold the cause and Irish Defenders will pull down British laws.'[73] Revolutionary atheism seemed less important than than the fact that France was waging war against Protestant Britain and Ireland. By now a spectre which haunted the Irish government, a Presbyterian-Catholic alliance, became tangible in the alliance between Catholic Defenders and radical Presbyterians in the Society of United Irishmen.

The first United Irish society was formed in Belfast in October 1791 as a club for advanced radicals who wanted a thorough reform of parliament. These men were mainly Presbyterians and many were involved with the radical section of the old Volunteer movement, which had increasingly begun to draw inspiration from the French Revolution. Many retained an atavistic fear of Catholicism but, principally through the efforts of Wolfe Tone, began to link the Catholic cause to their own. The Catholic Committee astutely kept its distance, though Tone was their secretary and his influential pamphlet *An argument on behalf of the Catholics of Ireland* was an official production. William Drennan, who may originally have coined the idea of a united Irish 'Brotherhood', complained the Catholics had 'two strings to their bow'. They hoped the unofficial alliance with Presbyterians and reformers would itself forward their case for full emancipation; or, alternatively, that the fear of such a combination would induce the British government to offer emancipation to detach Protestants from the alliance. Though the Catholic Committee remained aloof, individual Catholics and some Anglicans joined as the United Irish society spread to Dublin in November 1791. Behind their immediate aims of reform and emancipation, the long-term objective of founder members like Drennan, Neilson, Russell, Tone and Tandy was meaningful independence for Ireland under a republican form of government. Between 1791 and 1794 the societies disseminated propaganda and tried to mobilise public opinion behind their demands. They established new Volunteer corps, modelled on France's national guard, until Volunteering was banned when war broke out in 1793. Propaganda was also spread by the written word, in particular by Samuel Neilson's newspaper, the *Northern Star*. A reform petition was presented to parliament in 1794 but rejected out of hand as reform was off the agenda in wartime. Although the United Irishmen were an open society

71 Quoted in Bartlett, *Fall and Rise*, p. 212.   72 Camden to Portland, 25 Sept. 1795, P.R.O. H.O.100/58/f. 344.   73 21 June 1795, P.R.O. H.O.100/58/ff. 201–5.

operating within the law, the Irish government were extremely wary of them and waited the chance to strike. This came in 1794 with the arrest of a French agent, the Reverend William Jackson, whose brief confirmed what had long been suspected; that the French wanted to use Irish discontent strategically. The United Irishmen were immediatley banned, and as a result, nearly destroyed as an organisation. However, after the initial shock, they began to re-organise from 1795 as an underground secret society, based on a cellular system and closely allied with the Defenders. Irish discontent thus acquired the mass-based appearance the French needed to seriously consider an invasion.[74] The Defenders were willing partners and had already begun to infiltrate militia regiments, largely Catholic in their rank and file. The Defenders capitalised on the discontent over the raising of the militia in 1793 and Catholic disappointment at the recall of the radical viceroy, Fitzwilliam. He had followed a pro-Catholic policy, which included a purge of 'Ascendancy' Protestant office-holders. The hopes of full emancipation thus raised were soon dashed when it became known that Fitzwilliam acted on his own initiative, without British government authority. His hurried recall in March 1795 hightened Catholic anger without allaying Protestant insecurity. In these circumstances, the United Irish-Defender alliance was a high-risk strategy, given the latter's sectarianism. By 1795 the local magistrates were being swamped by the increasing scale and violence of the disturbances.

LAW AND ORDER: THE RESPONSES

Traditionally the responses available to magistrates varied according to the extent of the problem. For routine law enforcement they used medieval survivals known as high and petty constables. The urban equivalent were the watchmen who were also organised on parish lines. These officials could be supported by civilians who volunteered their services.[75] They were of limited value against organised protest and the system was moribund. Some improvements were attempted during the century. In 1734, in the apparently frequent cases where the sheriffs and seneschals were not doing their duty properly, the powers of appointment transferred to grand juries and magistrates. Between 1787 and 1792 chief constables were centrally approved for each barony or half-barony, to superintend up to eight sub-constables appointed by the grand jury. These baronial police, contemptuously nicknamed 'barnies', were a charge on the county and this, added to resentment at central interference caused thirteen counties, including all nine in Ulster, to opt out in 1792. Another manifestation of an embryonic centralising and reforming tendency was the appointment in 1786 of police commissioners to superintend the Dublin Watch, an initiative so

74 N. Curtin, *The United Irishmen*, chapter 2, passim.   75 S.J. Connolly, *Religion, Law and Power*, p. 203.

bitterly resented by the corporation that it was revoked in 1795.[76] Further moderni-
sations of the police system would have to await the arrival of Sir Robert Peel in the
nineteenth century. The government's half-hearted attempts to renovate Ireland's
law and order system extended to the magistracy. There were weaknesses in the
Irish magistracy, such as the dearth of sufficiently active people in some areas, and
the questionable neutrality of others in places like Armagh. The 1787 Preservation
of the Peace Act, which charged the cost of suppressing disturbances to the county
authorities, was originally intended to abolish the property qualification for magistrates and replace them with a mixture of paid professionals and government nominees.[77] Like other tentative reforms, this was shelved in the face of opposition from
the landed interests dominating local government who were in practice mostly left
to control the localities as they pleased. When faced with situations where the number
of rioters exceeded his capacity to cope, the magistrate could, in combination with
the sheriff or under-sheriff and at least one other magistrate, call on 'the power of
the county', raised from 'the king's liege people ... except women, clergymen, persons decrepit and infants' to suppress the disturbance and arrest the ringleaders.[78]
This body was called the *posse comitatus* and could be armed 'against such riots as
savour of rebellion'.[79] This meant *de facto* exclusion of Catholics, who were debarred
by the penal laws from bearing arms and serving as sheriff, magistrate or constable.

When dealing with widespread agrarian combinations beyond the power of the
local law enforcement officers and their civilian helpers, magistrates could apply for
military assistance either in the form of detachments of militia or regular soldiers.
Regulars were more often used in practice, because up to 1756, the militia, though
Protestant in composition, was only embodied intermittently and not considered
well armed or trained.[80] There was a break in militia provision throughout the worst
years of agrarian disturbance, until war in 1793 necessitated a new militia which,
though mostly Protestant in command, was largely Catholic in rank and file. The
regular army was more readily available and a more useful tool. The British parliament's suspicion of standing armies since the Glorious Revolution meant that the
permanently embodied part of the British army, in peacetime around 12,000 men,
was kept in Ireland as a garrison and strategic reserve. A programme of barrack
building had spread this force over the country, making it more accessible to the
magistrates.

Using soldiers to enforce the civil law was a touchy subject throughout the cen-

76 McDowell, *The Irish Administration*, pp. 135–7.   **77** K. Boyle, 'Police in Ireland before the Union',
in *Irish Jurist*, viii (1973), pp. 90–116.   **78** E. Bullingbroke, op. cit., p. 627.   **79** T.W. Williams, *The
whole law relative to the duty and office of a Justice of the Peace*, iv, p. 34. Author's note: though published
in England these provisions seem to have applied equally in Ireland. The set of Williams in P.R.O.N.I.'s
library is signed by George Stephenson, probably the same man who captained the Hillsborough Yeoman Cavalry.   **80** S.J. Connolly, *Religion, Law and Power*, pp. 201–2.

tury. There were political, military and practical objections to its indiscriminate use. Irish Whigs were always likely to be affronted at anything which seemed to breach the 'constitution' or savoured of arbitrary power. Moreover, the soldiers themselves disliked civil duty which their commanders found tangled the lines of authority as they always had to be accompanied by the magistrate who called them out, otherwise it was technically martial law. The government were also wary lest lazy or electioneering magistrates used troops as an easy option or disingenuous device. Calling for troops was seen as a fail-safe, an ultimate option if other expedients had proved ineffective.[81] This was not an exclusively Irish practice. Magistrates throughout the British Isles were equally ready to call in the army to deal with riots or organised protest. It took around 15,000 horse and foot to quell London's Gordon Riots in 1780.[82]

A further additional manpower resource available to the magistrates, which conveniently bridged the civil-military ambiguity, were corps of locally raised volunteers. The Irish Volunteers of 1778–84 were the largest and historically best known manifestation of this phenomenon. However, there were other localised volunteer corps raised when no militia was available, as in Ulster in 1760 against a small French invasion. Theoretically these volunteers were raised under the old Militia Act of 1715, but in practice they were spontaneous, locally organised and orientated.[83] In addition to bridging gaps in the military defences, the magistrates used volunteer corps as a back-up for law enforcement. Some of the first volunteer corps of the 1770s were raised specifically to tackle southern Whiteboyism. The day-to-day functions of the Irish Volunteers raised during the American war involved 'police' duties. Though military in appearance, the Volunteers were a civil force never subject to the Mutiny Act, as militia and regulars were. Sometimes it is difficult to distinguish on paper between local volunteers and the associations already described but the practical distinction would have been clear enough as the Irish Volunteers were more a paramilitary force than a collection of armed gentlemen. Volunteers and associations were the main alternatives to requesting troops to suppress major disturbances. However, magistrates sometimes pragmatically combined civilian and military assistance. This sort of *ad hoc* response was typical of the time. It was not ideal and lacked any long-term planning, yet had the advantage of being flexible and adaptable. These pragmatic manpower additions were matched by empirical boosts of emergency legislative power like the 1764 Whiteboy Act which indemnified magistrates against exceeding the law.[84] Similar provisions were available to northern magistrates facing the Steelboys, including the trying of suspects outside their home counties to counteract intimidated or sympathetic juries.[85] The 1787 Whiteboy Act

81 S.J. Connolly, ibid., p. 201.   82 K. O. Fox, *Making Life Possible: a study of military aid to the Civil Power in Regency England*, passim; A. Babington, *Military intervention in Britain*, p. 26.   83 A.T.Q. Stewart, *A Deeper Silence*, p. 19.   84 Boyle, 'Police in Ireland', *Irish Jurist*, vii (1972), passim.   85 F.J. Biggar, *The Ulster Land War*, p. 82; Donnelly, 'Hearts of Steel' p. 63.

made activities like arms raids and forced contributions capital offences while administering and taking illegal oaths brought transportation for life and seven years respectively.[86]

Ireland can appear a severely disturbed country for most of the eighteenth century, given the longevity and regional range of agrarian problems, the range of optional additional forces and severe statutory sanctions available. However, recent historical scholarship points to the low number of actual convictions despite the potential severity of the criminal code. S.J. Connolly detects a more sparing use than in England of the death penalty and transportation and considers that 'social order in eighteenth-century Ireland cannot be seen as having been upheld by a ruthless application of legal terror'.[87] In a seminal article Thomas Bartlett concluded that a mutual, tacit understanding between ruler and ruled of the 'limits' of protest and reaction, the 'moral economy', existed up to the early 1790s. This bond was weakened by the 1793 Catholic Relief Act and shattered by the anti-militia riots of 1793, in which about 230 lives were lost, around five times the number killed in agrarian disturbances.[88] In these riots lower-class Catholics protested against getting nothing from the Relief Act which enfranchised forty shilling freeholders, while at the same time, as the group most affected by the militia ballot, they were being *de facto* conscripted, since wealthier people could buy substitutes.

In many respects the Irish Yeomanry of 1796 was a combination of old and new. It provided a meeting place where traditional assumptions which drew on this eighteenth-century background were rudely confronted with the escalating and potentially revolutionary problems of the 1790s. The origins of the force itself were also a mix of ancient and modern. It is to these origins that we now turn.

2

Antecedents and origins

THE TERM 'YEOMAN'

Though the Irish Yeomanry of 1796 was influenced by contemporary military thinking, its ancestry stretched into the distant past. The term 'yeoman' has an interesting lineage which combines the concepts of economic and military service. A seventeenth-century treatise spoke of the 'yeomanry or common people, for they be called
of the Saxon word "Ge man" which doth signify common, which have some lands
of their own [*sic*]'. The O.E.D. traces the word's etymology to the Middle English
period [*c*.1150–*c*.1350] when it was rendered as 'yeman': a servant to a royal or noble
household. The range of meaning also included armed service, such as the Squire's
'yeman' in Chaucer's *Canterbury Tales*: 'clad in cote and hood of grene' with 'a sheef
of pecock arwes, bright and kene'.[1] The concept of the yeoman was an enduring one
in war and peace which became embedded in literary and oral culture. G.M.
Trevelyan noted: 'The motif of the English yeoman – his independence, his hearty
good nature, his skill in archery – fills the ballads from the Hundred Years' War to
the Stuart era'. As well as a place in literature the yeoman had a place in society.
William Harrison, an Elizabethan cleric, ranked the yeoman third in the social hierarchy, beneath landowners and merchants but above ordinary wage-earners. Some
were forty-shilling freeholders but most were 'farmers to gentlemen'.[2] The status
implicit in this connection is embodied in the seventeenth-century proverb: 'Better
be the head of the yeomanry than the tail of the gentry.'[3] In a pre-democratic age,
the yeoman was an icon of good order, providing sufficient independence to ensure
hierarchy did not become autocracy while, at the same time, defending the establishment with loyal military service. This long tradition of 'feudal' military service
based on economic standing fed directly into the civilian levies of the French wars.
Ian Beckett claims, 'the origins of auxiliary military forces are undoubtedly rooted
in the military obligations of the Anglo-Saxons'.[4] The dual economic and military
concept of the yeoman was carried over to Ireland with the plantations.

1 HMC 6th Report appx., *Mss of Rt Hon Lord Leconfield*, f. 15. 2 Trevelyan, *English Social History*, pp.
10, 167. 3 *Dictionary of Proverbs and Quotations* (Everyman, London, 1982), p. 361. 4 I.F.W. Beckett,
The Amateur Military Tradition, p. 2.

THE PROTESTANT DEFENCE TRADITION

Following the Elizabethan conquest, and subsequent plantations from England and Scotland, the plough and the sword became almost synonymous: cultivation mirrored conquest. The incomplete, partial nature of conquest and plantation and the ever-present danger of attack by the dispossessed meant a tradition of self-defence became established amongst the settlers. Given the failure of the Reformation, the dichotomy this represented was Protestant against Catholic as well as settler against native. The Irish Yeomanry drew on, refined and perpetuated this formidable tradition, which sometimes merged with wider military strategies to make Protestant self-defence and the defence of Ireland seem synonymous. Ian Beckett distinguishes between two types of amateur military service: centrally-organised and armed militias and local, self-sufficient volunteer-type forces.[5] The Protestant defence tradition embraced both but also included a wider spectrum of organisations ranging from a paid militia to transitory local defence groups. Indeed, such groups were an integral part of the plantation scheme. The Ulster undertakers were required to build houses for their Protestant tenants near the defensive bawn and provide arms.[6] This propensity for protective banding together was underpinned, on the Presbyterian side, by the 1638 National Covenant to oppose prelacy in Ireland and Scotland. When Catholic revanchism under James and Tyrconnell forced Protestants to abandon their holdings and flee to defensible towns like Enniskillen and Derry, this was replaced by a more generalised banding of Anglicans and Presbyterians in 'county associations'.[7]

In part this panic was occasioned by fears of another 1641. That rebellion shook the plantation to its roots and left psychological scars and fears which haunted the Irish Protestant psyche for centuries. The fears were more than mere folk memories. The planters' descendants could not forget that their lands once belonged to the indigenous Irish. Each year on 23 October, the anniversary of the start of the 1641 rising, a thanksgiving sermon was delivered to Irish parliamentarians. This reinforced memories by depicting subsequent crises, though less severe, as a continuing pattern of native Irish rebellion. Even in the 1760s, these sermons reminded Protestants they dwelt in an 'enemy's country'.[8] Sir John Temple's *The Irish Rebellion*, a strongly anti-Catholic account of 1641, was re-printed at least ten times between 1646 and 1812.[9] Atavistic fears were easily triggered. When the United Irishmen and Defenders made common cause in the mid-1790s, Lord Clare, ironically of Catholic ancestry, spoke for many Protestants who feared 'the scenes of 1641 repeated again'.[10]

---

5 Beckett, ibid., pp. 2–3.   6 P. Robinson, *The Plantation of Ulster*, p. 64.   7 D. W. Miller, *Queen's Rebels*, pp. 13, 25.   8 T. C. Barnard, 'The uses of 23 October 1641 and Irish Protestant Celebrations', *English Historical Review*, cvi (1991), pp. 889–920.   9 Bartlett, *Fall and Rise*, p. 7.   10 Clare to Camden, 28 Aug. 1796, K. A.O. Pratt Papers, U840/0183/6.

Following the Jacobite defeat and the Catholic interest's emasculation by the penal laws, the Protestant local defence network was perpetuated in a series of 'Boyne Societies', initially of Williamite veterans, but later open to all classes of Protestant. Their organisation is shadowy. It is known they existed in at least twelve counties, being well represented in areas of substantial Protestant settlement. They adopted names like the Royal Boyne Society, the Apprentice Boys, the Boyne Men, the Orange Boyne Society and, in Dublin, the facetiously named Aldermen of Skinner's Alley.[11] For much of the eighteenth century these clubs functioned at a mainly social and informal political level, enjoying great dinners and thundering toasts. However they were also a sleeping defence network which could be roused if the ghosts of rebellion disturbed the Georgian calm.

Concurrent with these unofficial 'skeleton' groups, a government-organised militia existed periodically for most of the eighteenth century. Under the penal laws, Catholics were debarred from militia service. The first Irish Militia Act was passed in 1715 to co-ordinate pre-existing local militias under a regular system.[12] Until the Jacobite invasion threat of 1715 forced rationalisation, militia in Ireland was a fluid term, comprehending organisations such as the Boyne Societies and temporary *posse comitatus* groupings.[13] The militia was raised on a county basis by the governors and influential gentlemen with a basic role of domestic peacekeeping. They were granted commissions to array all Protestants aged between sixteen and sixty and chose the best for enlistment into companies. When this was done the men were grouped into a combination of county regiments and separate small companies, known as 'independent troops'. The mix of regimentation and separate corps varied according to county. Some, like Armagh, had no regimentation at all in the 1756 array. Given the financial constraints, it was never reckoned to be a very effective force and was supplemented by loosely organised groups of armed local Protestant volunteers during the Jacobite scares of 1711, 1715 and 1745. The term 'volunteer' was one of flexible usage. In 1760, during a small French landing at Carrickfergus companies of volunteers marched to defend Belfast. These 'volunteers' were actually militiamen from various independent companies (the term denoted offered service as opposed to the ballot of the array). Similar groupings were also used against agrarian rioters like Whiteboys and Steelboys in the 1760s and 1770s when no militia was arrayed. The Militia Act was renewed twelve times between 1715 and 1776 when it lapsed.[14] Although many of these renewals were academic exercises, the statute's continued existence and the latent underlying organisational framework perpetuated the Protestant self-defence tradition.

11 Senior, *Orangeism*, p. 2; Kilpatrick, Murdie and Cargo (eds), *The History of the Royal Arch Purple Order*, pp. 10–11.   12 2 Geo. 1 c. 9   13 For further discussion see: D.W. Miller, 'Non-Professional Soldiery' in T. Bartlett and K Jeffrey (eds), *A Military History of Ireland*, pp. 315–34.   14 P.D.H. Smyth, 'The Volunteer Movement in Ulster', unpublished Ph.D. (QUB, 1974), pp. 25–34; Miller, 'Non-Professional Soldiery', op. cit., p. 326; J. O'Donovan, 'The Militia in Munster' in G. O'Brien (ed.), *Parliament, Politics and People*, pp. 31–3.

THE IRISH VOLUNTEERS

The Irish Volunteers of 1778–82 are the best known expression of this Protestant defence tradition. They require detailed description being, in some respects, an earlier manifestation of the same national tendency which helped form the yeomanry and bear a fruitful comparison with them. The raising of the Volunteers was sparked by the same circumstances which normally activated militia service. The outbreak of the American war meant that regular soldiers were drained from Ireland. This was coupled with the possibility of invasion when France and Spain joined the colonists in 1778. The militia legislation had lapsed and attempts at resurrecting it by Henry Flood and George Ogle failed because insufficient money could be found. The normal garrison of 12,000 regulars fell to around 4,000.[15] Fear of domestic order rose, as troop levels fell and landowners and businessmen began raising Volunteer companies. Had new militia legislation been available, many of the leaders of the first Volunteer corps, which included surviving *ad hoc* independent corps raised against agrarian rioters, might well have accepted commissions and the nominal changes they brought, since separate voluntary corps like theirs had co-existed with militia since at least 1715. However an invasion scare in June 1779 saw volunteering rapidly expand and become a recognisable national 'movement' in terms of coherence and numbers.[16] These Volunteers had no legislative basis, other than that, as Protestants, they were allowed to bear arms and they had been given no commissions by government. From mid-1779, the movement's rapid expansion and subsequent transformation into a powerful political pressure group marked it as different from earlier 'volunteers'.

Henry Joy Jnr, owner of the *Belfast Newsletter*, was involved in the political side of the Volunteers, and attempted to write the movement's history in the 1820s. He described the philosophy as follows:

> The declared principle of the Association was the defence of the town and country, the expense of array to be bourne [*sic*] by themselves; and no manner of pay to be accepted from Government, nor any military oath whatever taken. So far they differed from all former irregular corps, raised against invasion or rebellion; as the preclusion of an oath of military duty prevented their officers from having the offer, or having it in their power to accept, either of Commissions or pay under the Crown.[17]

To the government's alarm, the corps functioned in a proto-democratic way, as officers were elected from the ranks. Although there had been Volunteers in Munster

15 *c.*1786, R.I.A., Charlemont Mss., MS12 R7.   16 D.W. Miller, 'Non-Professional Soldiery', ibid., p. 327.   17 L.H.L. Joy Mss., v, pp. 58–9.

to combat the Whiteboys, Belfast claimed the honour of the first of the new generation with its first company, formed on St Patrick's Day 1778.[18] Similar corps soon
organised in different parts of the country, either of the Belfast type, composed of
merchants, businessmen and professionals, or rural corps raised by the gentry from
their tenants. These corps were predominantly infantry, with some cavalry and a
small number of artillery companies. Rank and file membership averaged around 70
but could range from 30 to over 180.[19] It is difficult to obtain accurate national
returns for the Volunteers. Being a highly politicised organisation, it is not surprising that estimates of its total size ranged widely. According to the most recent research, it seems the initial tide of enthusiasm seems to have enabled about 12,000 to
be raised by early 1779, enough for the missing regulars' law and order role. Real
fears of invasion throughout 1779 kept up the momentum and estimates of the national total for the middle of that year vary between 40,000 and 45,000.[20] The movement peaked in mid-1782 when it reached almost 89,000. This was comprised as
follows:

Ulster	34,152
Connacht	14,336
Munster	18,056
Leinster	22,283[21]

The heavy bias towards Ulster reflected both its originating initiative and large Protestant population. There were very few Catholic Volunteers initially, though in some
areas middle-class Catholics provided financial support for local corps. From 1784,
some corps admitted Catholics, despite the penal laws regarding arms. Presbyterians were heavily represented in the ranks and command of the northern Volunteers.
A number of Presbyterian ministers were captains. The Reverend William Bruce
preached at Lisburn in the blue coat with red facings of the Lisburn True Blues.[22]
Anglicans were also involved, but the role of the established clergy was not as great
as that of dissenting ministers, with the notable, and eccentric exception of Frederick
Hervey, the earl-bishop of Derry. Initially volunteering appealed particularly to those
of a whiggish disposition, who saw it as a contemporary manifestation of the classi-
cally-based 'true whig' principles of the Glorious Revolution: the citizens asserting
their right to arm for self-defence and resisting arbitrary government. The leaders
of the two main volunteering areas belonged to this whig tradition. The Leinster
and Dublin city Volunteers acted under the duke of Leinster while the earl of
Charlemont became the Ulster commander-in-chief.

18 A.T.Q. Stewart, *A Deeper Silence*, p. 4.   19 Belfast Monthly Returns, May 1781, L.H.L. ibid., p.
82.   20 J. Kelly, 'A secret return of the Volunteers of Ireland in 1784', *IHS*, xxvi, 103, (May 1989), pp.
269–92; P.D.H. Smyth, 'The Volunteers, 1778–84', (P.R.O.N.I. facsimile pack).   21 Kelly, op. cit., p.
270.   22 P. Rogers, *The Irish Volunteers and Catholic Emancipation*, pp. 45–6.

When volunteering expanded rapidly in 1781, a diverse membership was revealed both in terms of social standing and ideology. Although typically middle-class in the ranks, the landed gentry had also become involved, some through principle, others, like Abercorn's agent James Hamilton, who wanted to retain an influence on the direction it was taking. Hamilton was concerned that 'the first cause of their associating [to oppose invasion, is] not even spoken of now, but openly declared [to be] to have the laws reformed to what they think their right'.[23] Ordinary Volunteers were people able to afford the leisure and equipment to drill and parade as citizen soldiers. Yet such independence was unsettling, as it upset traditional social norms. If leisure was not a gentry monopoly, certainly those beneath them were expected to engage in more traditional pursuits than those of the Rathfriland Volunteers described as 'all men in business who lose at least half their time in learning the use of arms'.[24]

Rank and file Volunteers, broadly speaking, fell within two potentially incompatible stand-points in Protestant ideology. Volunteering encompassed both libertarian 'true whigs' and the Boyne society men of rural Armagh and elsewhere: put simply, those who looked to 1688 for liberty and those who remembered 1690 and victory. The resolution of such tensions by the parliamentary patriots and the subsequent use made of the Volunteers as a political pressure group gave the 'Volunteers of 1782' their place in Irish history. However, before examining these aspects it is necessary to understand their practical function and organisation.

Though comprised of civilians under officers without commissions, in terms of their structure, appearance and role the Volunteers were primarily a military force. However, like the militia, their day-to-day duties involved the domestic peacekeeping aspect of military service, so common in Ireland and Britain, with their anti-invasion role always latent. Henry Joy described this law-and-order role in glowing terms:

> The country at large made greater advances in the first years of the Volunteer institutions than ... in a century. The villain could find no screen, nor the laws be trampled on with impunity as the particular [ie local] knowledge of such numerous bands ... enabled them to detect every species of criminal.

Joy then quotes Henry Flood's pronouncement that: 'The King's writ was taught to run in tracts of country where his Majesty's name and his Courts of Law had seldom been heard of.'[25] Hard fact underlay this bombast: the extensive territorial coverage and local knowledge of permanently organised, armed residents was a more

23 Hamilton to Abercorn, 28 May 1780, P.R.O.N.I. Abercorn Papers, T2541/IAI/13/34.   24 Morgan to Lord Hillsborough, 1 June 1779, P.R.O.N.I. Downshire Papers, D607/203.   25 L.H.L. Joy Mss., v, p. 47.

effective tool for magistrates than temporary troop detachments. Even an unsympathetic observer like Hamilton conceded their efficiency as a police force: 'the Volunteer associations in Ireland have been ... the chief means by which a most dangerous and numerous set of robbers ... have been suppressed'.[26] Local magistrates used the force for serving warrants, making arrests, assisting with evictions as well as in the prevention or suppression of riots.[27] However, doubts existed about their anti-invasion role as it was felt they were unable to move from home for any extended time.

This territorial fixity was seen as a military weakness, dissipating the movement's overall strength. It was overcome by gathering together individual corps into battalions and regiments. Like most Volunteer innovations, this more militarised structure started in Ulster. In January 1780 all local commanders in county Armagh met at Tandragee and elected Lord Charlemont as colonel of the first Ulster regiment of 1,000 men in two battalions, mainly infantry but including a small number of cavalry and artillery corps.[28] The process soon spread throughout Ulster then to the rest of Ireland. This stage in volunteering was characterised by large reviews: gatherings of local battalions and guest corps for joint drills and training. There was much ceremonial and ostentation by the proud amateur soldiers. In July 1780 the Belfast Battalion fired three volleys in a *feu de joi* to celebrate the Battle of the Boyne.[29] Every 4 November their Dublin counterparts marked William III's birthday by parading around his statue in College Green. Until the troubled 1790s this was not incompatible with the 'true whig' version of the Williamite tradition and was supported by liberals and even radicals, who associated William's memory with civil liberty and religious toleration.[30] In 1781 the reviews grew larger and more dramatic. The Belfast review of July 1781 was typical, comprising 5,072 Volunteers from Belfast, Down, Antrim and Tyrone who, as well as the usual drilling and speechifying, fought an elaborate mock battle.[31] These gatherings were more than military occasions. With large camps on short summer nights, they were a heady mixture of boy-scoutism, social mixing and rivalry outside the normal constraints of the workaday world. Volunteering became fashionable and the gaudy uniforms were a status symbol. Newry vied with Belfast for the ultimate in patriotic chic. However, behind the glittering facade and social gambolling a wider and more profound *esprit de corps* was being cultivated. The small local corps soon began to feel part of a great society as they listened to the speeches and drank the toasts. Those controlling the Volunteers, in conjunction with the parliamentary patriots, understood the movement's potential and had political objectives in mind. Large gatherings enabled the Volun-

26 Hamilton to Abercorn, 28 May 1780, P.R.O.N.I. Abercorn Papers, T2541/IAI/13/34.   27 D.W. Miller, 'The Armagh Troubles, 1784–95', S. Clarke and J.S. Donnelly Jnr, (eds), *Irish Peasants and Political Unrest, 1780–1914*, pp. 123–4.   28 Rogers, op. cit., p. 51.   29 L.H.L. Joy Mss., v, p. 68.   30 J. R. Hill, 'National festivals, the State and "Protestant Ascendancy" in Ireland, 1790–1829', *IHS*, xxiv, 93 (May 1984), pp. 30–51.   31 L.H.L. ibid., pp. 82–3; Rogers, op. cit., p. 51.

teers to be represented as speaking with one voice. Differing ideological viewpoints could be easier handled this way, glossed over in the general excitement as toasts were roared into the warm night air to descend in the cold reality of the printed word in the following day's newspapers as pointedly political resolutions.

The Volunteers had drifted into a 'unique' relationship with patriot politicians. By 1782 at least 23 Volunteer officers sat in the Commons and around 12 in the Lords.[32] The first political manifestation of this relationship was non-importation associations, started by co-ordinated grand jury resolutions in 1779. These complemented the patriot agenda of opposition to restrictions on Irish trade. The most visible effect was seen in the vivid scarlet, green, blue and orange Volunteer uniforms which were home-made from Irish wool.[33] The campaign to free Irish trade from restrictions imposed at Westminster marked the Volunteers' entry into the political arena, as a pressure group touting a very explicit threat of force. On the anniversary of King William's birthday, the duke of Leinster's Volunteers were reviewed opposite the parliament building. They fired repeated musketry volleys and ominously draped slogans like 'Free Trade or this' from cannon barrels.

Although it was felt that trade restrictions were responsible for the current economic depression, the issue reactivated long-nurtured grievances about Irish subordination. Inevitably the campaign switched to the status of the Irish parliament. This raised problems. Not everyone in parliament, or every Volunteer, wanted radical change. Some Volunteers aimed their sights at parliamentary reform, together with full political rights for Catholics, whereas the parliamentary patriots merely wanted to put an end to the Irish parliament's subordinate position. The danger for the patriots was that the moment would pass and the momentum dissipate itself in division. Accordingly a grand delegate convention was held at Dungannon in February 1782. Resolutions were passed calling for legislative independence and further Catholic relief, adroitly conveying to British ministers the impression that all Ireland backed the demand while, at the same time, preventing the government from enticing Irish Catholics themselves.[34] Although the Catholics were 'used' at Dungannon, they learnt a lesson, as it provided a model for the Catholic Convention of 1792, to which Catholic delegates were elected from all parts of the country. The Dungannon Convention also cemented the entire Volunteer movement together as grand juries all over Ireland adopted its resolutions. This co-ordination achieved results. With intense domestic pressure over Lord North's handling of the American War, Grattan's demands for 'legislative independence' were irresistible. The game of political bluff succeeded because Britain was not in a position to call it. The logical outcome of armed resistance would have been unthinkable for Protestant 'nationalists' in the Irish parliament and their Volunteer allies. Put to the test, the Volunteers and patriots would have preferred to accept the devil they knew rather

32 P.D.H. Smyth, 'The Volunteers and Parliament', in T. Bartlett and D. Hayton (eds), *Penal Era and Golden Age*, p. 113. 33 Lecky, *Ireland*, ii, p. 237. 34 Bartlett, *Fall and Rise*, pp. 99–102.

than to hazard their already privileged position in an attempt to improve it. Nevertheless, their brinkmanship set political precedents for the future. The gun was introduced into Irish politics and England's weakness became Ireland's opportunity.

The year 1782 marked a watershed in Volunteer politics. The more moderate leaders were satisfied that they had made their patriotic point to England and enhanced parliament's status without weakening their position in it by countenancing reform. Not all Volunteers thought this way and the movement began to split. The first cracks were caused by not reform but by interpretations of the legal validity of the Irish parliament's independence. Die-hard patriots wanted to press Westminster further to renounce formally its right to legislate for Ireland, as opposed to the simple repeal of the legislation achieved by Grattan. This was a red herring floated by Henry Flood, who had been eclipsed by Grattan in the patriot movement and wanted to regain his position. 'Renunciation' was achieved, but made no difference. The much lauded 'constitution of 1782' was unsatisfactory and Anglo-Irish relations remained dangerously ill-defined.

In mid-1782 the government attempted to hasten the disintegration of the Volunteer movement by offering commissions to enlist fencible regiments, as a locally-raised military alternative. Though some were accepted, the political tide still ran strongly against central interference and the fencible scheme failed. The more radical Volunteers pressed on for more political concessions. They were split between those who wanted reform and emancipation and looked to the earl-bishop of Derry for leadership, while Flood led those wanting reform alone. Still confident in their ability to influence parliament with large displays, these radicals organised a national convention at Dublin's Rotunda in November 1783. The old showiness remained. Bishop Hervey paraded to the convention in full regalia, flanked by his Volunteers and looking more like a ridiculous clan chief than an Anglican bishop. Flood arrogantly took the reform proposals to parliament in full Volunteer uniform but he had gravely miscalculated. While unresolved internal divisions split the Volunteer movement over the Catholic issue, parliament basked in the light of 1782 and was in no mood to listen to a red-coated opportunist or, in the attorney-general's words, countenance the 'edicts of another assembly or receive propositions at the point of a bayonet'.[35]

There was another attempt to gather support for reform in 1784 but the moment had passed. Most original Volunteer leaders and many ordinary members had left, satisfied with their achievements. Attempts were made to maintain numbers by recruiting Catholics. Little is known of those corps which lingered on during the later 1780s. However, a transformation came in 1789 when the French Revolution revitalised radicalism, reviving calls for reform and emancipation. New corps began to form and others were re-formed. The initiative again came from Ulster par-

35 Quoted in A. T. Q. Stewart, *A Deeper Silence*, p. 50

ticularly in Belfast where the Volunteers began calling themselves 'National Volunteers' in ominous imitation of France's National Guards. Dublin radicals, led by Napper Tandy, formed a similar movement. As numbers increased there was a return to large public demonstrations. In 1792 the Belfast Volunteers celebrated the falling of the Bastille and sent supportive addresses to the French National Assembly. These francophile Volunteers included most members of the United Irish societies recently founded in Belfast and Dublin.[36] Wolfe Tone attended the Belfast celebrations in 1792 as delegate of the Catholic Committee with a brief to cement the alliance with the reformers and get a resolution in favour of emancipation.[37] Another sort of volunteering revival was occurring contemporaneously in southern Ulster, where growing Catholic assertiveness and the emergence of Defenderism led to the establishment of more conservatively-minded corps in the tradition of the Boyne Societies. Some admitted ex-Peep O'Day Boys in order to keep them under some control. David Miller has convincingly argued that these new Volunteer companies significantly altered the character of the ongoing sectarian disturbances in Armagh. From around 1788, the nature of these disturbances changed from arms raids on Catholic homes and fair-day fights to battles for local dominance. This had a marked impact in the number of fatalities in clashes, with nine lives lost between 1788 and 1791, as opposed to two between 1784 and 1788.[38] Although gentry leadership eventually controlled the turbulent new recruits, Catholic opinion inevitably had difficulty in making distinctions. From a Castle perspective, any sort of volunteering was a de-stabilising influence, and the movement was suppressed on the outbreak of war in 1793.

THE IMMEDIATE ORIGINS OF THE IRISH YEOMANRY

The Irish Volunteers proved to Dublin Castle the danger of not having full control of Ireland's military resources. The volunteering precedent set up a classic dilemma. Government feared putting armed power back to the localities in case it was translated into political opposition, yet knew they could not defend Ireland in an emergency without recourse to its Protestant inhabitants. Because a large standing force had been associated in England with arbitrary government ever since the Glorious Revolution, Ireland provided a convenient peacetime base for the army. However, during wartime, much of this force was withdrawn from Ireland, leaving successive viceroys with a double defence problem: insufficient troops for domestic peacekeeping and the need to secure the country against invasion. The Volunteers ostensibly met both expedients, yet there was arguably no real danger of either. For the Castle the volunteering experience re-defined the problem as one of securing Ire-

36 Stewart, ibid., pp. 180–6.   37 M. Elliott, *Wolfe Tone*, p. 172.   38 Miller, 'Armagh Troubles', pp. 173–4.

land by securing her defenders. The Revolutionary wars intensified this problem. By 1796 there was a very real threat of invasion, coupled with the prospect of a concurrent insurrection. The immediate origins of the Irish Yeomanry are to be found in the various proposals put forward to meet this problem at central and local levels. However, there was to be no clear path to the eventual formation of the yeomanry. Rather, the idea evolved by a process of elimination. Often proposals defined what was not possible rather than what was.

Though thinking on the defence of Ireland remained static in the 1790s, the new political and military context of the times ensured that traditional measures assumed new forms. Various forms of fencible regiments were tried, and a new militia raised in 1793. The fencible concept occupied one strand of thinking in the evolution of a plan for a yeomanry. Fencibles were a British concept, first tried during the Seven Years' War. The Irish fencibles proposed to replace Volunteers in 1782 were described by the commander-in-chief as 'a means of restoring the power of the sword to the crown'.[39] However, the plan fell foul of most Volunteers, who regarded alternative defence proposals as insulting their own efforts. The ending of war in November 1782 removed the immediate need for fencibles, and Portland's successor, Temple, gladly let the matter drop. In November 1784 a motion for a new militia bill was debated. This time an amendment by William Brownlow was included, to satisfy the Volunteers' pride by reiterating parliament's gratitude for their wartime service. It should have allowed the 'original' Volunteers to re-emerge as a national militia, but Westmorland was totally opposed to the proposal, fearing it might resurrect the dread spirit of political volunteering. The issue was shelved as proactivity was sacrificed to political expediency, until war in 1793 necessitated hasty and reactive militia legislation. The inclusion of Catholics in the ranks for the first time since the penal laws caused problems. The militia ballot sparked widespread rioting among those too poor to purchase substitutes, who saw the compulsory levy as an insult cancelling the benefits of the recent Catholic Relief Act.[40] Again, the defence of Ireland was proving a sticky issue.

By 1796 troop levels stood at 35,000, of which only 5,500 were regulars, the rest being mistrusted militia or untried British fencibles, sent over in default of regular reinforcements. The government wondered how to stretch its resources to meet the militarily antithetical demands of invasion and insurgency.[41] The former needed flexibility and the ability to concentrate large numbers quickly, whereas the latter required a static presence spread widely. The logical answer was a locally recruited defence force, but this risked restarting volunteering in a dangerously unstable climate. In addition to agrarian problems in Munster, the sectarian conflicts in Armagh spread bitter Defenderism into Leinster and Connacht. The United Irish-

---

39 M.R. O'Connell, *Irish Politics and Social Conflict in the Age of the American Revolution*, pp. 337–8.   40 T. Bartlett, 'An End to Moral Economy', pp. 41–64.   41 K. Ferguson, 'The Irish Army and the Rebellion of 1798', p. 93; P.C. Stoddart, 'Counter-insurgency and Defence in Ireland, 1790–1805'.

men were forging links with this burgeoning Defender movement. The reliability of the militia was questioned. By 1796 Wolfe Tone estimated that the Irish militia establishment of 19,000 included no less than 15,000 Catholics.[42] Although the northern county regiments contained many Protestant private soldiers and the officer corps was mainly Protestant, the militia do not fully fit into the Protestant defence tradition. The policy of service outside the home county meant that the mainly Catholic southern regiments were on peacekeeping detachments in the crucible of central Ulster and it was suspected, with good reason, that sectarian conflict was being utilised to promote Defender and ultimately United Irish infiltration. Members of the Westmeath regiment planted a liberty tree in Blaris camp near Lisburn, while 70 Monaghan militiamen confessed United Irish involvement and four ringleaders were shot in May 1797 as an example.[43] With volunteering banned and the 'new' militia unreliable there was now a defence vacuum which left worried magistrates in a quandary. Using the recent British precedents, they made were several attempts to free themselves from this strait-jacket. The attempts were still-born but the ideas behind them re-emerged later as important contributory factors in the formation of yeomanry.

From the end of 1794 some Irish magnates had begun to follow their Scottish counterparts and resurrect the fencible option. Briefly it seemed to provide an answer, but the momentum soon slackened as the scheme slewed into the bog of Irish politics. The Castle was immediately inundated by offers from Irish gentlemen.[44] Westmorland allowed Lords Jocelyn and Glenworth to raise about 300 fencible cavalry, but his successor, Fitzwilliam, stopped the enlistment in favour of six regular Irish brigades. Fitzwilliam wanted Irish Catholics to enlist in these brigades and so demonstrate their loyalty, thus facilitating his own plans for Catholic emancipation. In a somewhat similar vein, Fitzwilliam tried to use the precedent of the English Yeomanry to create the political space for emancipation. This was the first time an Irish yeomanry force had been mooted. Fitzwilliam optimistically claimed, 'we must endeavour to form a strength upon the principle of the English Yeomanry which will have the double effect of a defence against an invasion and an additional power in support of the magistracy'. He envisaged this force comprising 'the better sorts of the people ... between the landlord and the peasant' who would be largely Catholic, except in Ulster. This, he contended, could only be retrospective to full emancipation, otherwise it would mean arming discontented people. If framed in an English context, Fitzwilliam's proposal was not especially radical. It merely meant widening the *status quo* to preserve it from revolutionary upheaval. However, in Irish political terms, it was seen as virtually revolutionary in its implications. Portland saw this clearly. 'I cannot help fearing', he wrote in February 1795, 'if these corps ...

---

42 Curtin, *The United Irishmen*, p. 148; F. McDermott, *Theobald Wolfe Tone*, p. 229.   43 Bartlett, *Fall and Rise*, p. 215. Curtin, ibid., p. 172.   44 Westmorland to Portland, 23 Dec. 1794, P.R.O. H.O.100/53/ f. 52; Westmorland to Portland, 30 Dec. 1794, H.O.100/53/f. 117.

are established and made up out of the materials of which, I believe they can only be composed, that the real power and influence of the country will be placed in the hands of the Catholics.'[45] Fitzwilliam's plan ended with his hasty recall for exceeding instructions on the Catholic issue. His yeomanry scheme was not thought out properly: its implementation would have meant government intervention on an impossible scale over the heads of an alienated gentry. However, Fitzwilliam left an important signpost unintentionally pointing from one sort of Irish yeomanry to another. The association with the Catholic question in 1795, coupled with the ongoing Protestant self-defence tradition, largely predetermined the complexion of the Irish Yeomanry in 1796.

Fitzwilliam's abortive scheme temporarily removed the yeomanry option from the local magistrates and gentry, as it had the effect of increasing the already considerable political risks associated with raising any form of local defence force. Yet, at the same time, the promise, then denial, of emancipation poisoned an already deteriorating situation. The strategic need for a yeomanry grew in proportion to the political difficulties involved in raising one. In the most disturbed counties embattled and embittered landowners, first denied Volunteers, then fencibles and now yeomanry, made desperate attempts to get a self-defence force sanctioned by the new viceroy, Camden. At first they tried to re-open the door to fencibles which Fitzwilliam had slammed shut. More offers to raise fencibles started around April 1795, now with the important proviso that they would only serve within Ireland. Camden was not keen and would only consider Irish fencibles if they could be interchanged with British.[46] It soon became clear the Irish gentry and their viceroy had a completely different conception of what fencibles meant in practice. Camden clearly saw them as part of the overall war effort while the gentry thought solely in terms of self-defence. Camden wriggled from the horns of this dilemma in June 1795, telling Portland he was dropping the measure as too expensive and because regular soldiers would be better.[47]

Extra measures were also necessary. In the autumn of 1795, the future commander-in-chief, Lord Carhampton was sent to Connacht to suppress Defenderism. He was authorised to exceed the normal restraints of the law if necessary.[48] A member of the Ascendancy himself, Carhampton had no scruples about doing so and transported large numbers of suspects to the fleet without trial. Using the English association movement as a precedent, Carhampton, Lord Mountjoy and others planned county associations, armed anti-Defender forces, for Meath, Kildare and Dublin. Knowing the likely reception from a viceroy haunted by the spectre of volunteering, the organisers tried to get their plans near completion before presenting them as a virtual *fait accompli*. It failed. The attempt stung Camden into a shocked

45 Fitzwilliam to Portland, 10 Jan. 1795, P.R.O. H.O.100/56/ff. 57–60; 15–26 Jan. 1795, H.O.100/56/ff. 81, 161; Portland to Fitzwilliam, 16 Feb. 1795, H.O.100/56/f. 251.   46 Camden to Portland, 17 Apr. 1795, P.R.O. H.O.100/54/f. 33.   47 17 June 1795, P.R.O. H.O.100/58/f. 57.   48 Bartlett, *Fall and*

response. He told his chief secretary Thomas Pelham that he was alarmed at not being consulted and feared 'a new system of Volunteers' spinning out of his control. Carhampton was told that the associations could not arm themselves and must confine their activities to those of normal peacekeeping associations organised by grand juries. However, the defence needs of government and gentry simply would not disappear. Once one new proposal from either quarter was dismissed, for whatever reason, another emerged, hydra-like, in its place. The time was fast approaching when strategic necessity would steal the march on Camden's instinctive political caution. What these various attempts to address Ireland's defence conundrum had done was to define the thinking both of the gentry and the Castle and to create the political space to be occupied by the Irish Yeomanry.

Roughly contemporary with Carhampton's Connacht expedition, renewed sectarian violence erupted in Armagh between the Defenders and an amalgam of local Protestant interests known as the Orange Boys. These disturbances culminated in the rout of the Defenders at the Battle of the Diamond in September 1795 and the formation by the victors of a regular system of Orange lodges. A less well known, but perhaps no less important, by-product was the reaction of some members of the local landed gentry, who saw the need to intervene to retain some influence with the turbulent combinations now springing up amongst their Protestant tenants. It is known that William Brownlow of Lurgan, the Blackers of Carrickblacker and the Verners of Churchill became involved early on with the new Orange Order.[49] What is less clear, however, is the timing, the extent and the means of this gentry support.

In 1899, Colonel Robert Wallace started a history of the Orange Order which was never completed. Wallace was an Orangeman who became a County Grand Master, so his manuscript history is scarcely impartial. Nevertheless it did draw on the reminiscences of some very old men who had heard first hand accounts of the 1795–8 period in their youth. Wallace gives details of a new version of the association movement which started at a meeting of the Armagh magistrates in October 1795. Apparently there was an attempt to establish 'Mixed Associations' of Protestants and Catholics, which failed due to the mutual antagonism of each group. This was hardly surprising, considering that the proposal came scarcely a month after the Battle of the Diamond. Then, in early 1796, came another proposal which was to have significance for the formation of yeomanry later in the year. Starting in February, on the Blacker estate, Protestant Associations or District Defence Associations were organised amongst the tenants, and gentry-directed resolutions were passed, pledging assistance to the magistrates. These associations spread to other northern counties as grand juries produced similar resolutions.[50] Although a local initiative, the significance was that landlords were again attempting to organise their tenants and the tenants themselves were now aware of an alternative 'side' to belong

Rise, p. 213.   **49** D.W. Miller, 'The Armagh Troubles', op. cit., pp. 180–1; Senior, *Orangeism*, p. 31.   **50** Kilpatrick, (ed.), *The Formation of the Orange Order, 1795–98*, pp. 8, 31–3, 45–6.

to, given the uncontrollable expansion of the Defenders and United Irishmen. It reawakened memories of the Volunteers and paved the way for yeomanry recruitment.

Government slowly began to realise that Ireland's defence and Protestant self-defence were not antithetical in the dangerous world of the mid-1790s. Yet both partners in defence, government and gentry, stood with a clutch of failed initiatives in their hands. To be properly effective, the associations needed to be armed and organised. As Carhampton had recently discovered, Camden would not allow anything resembling locally-controlled Volunteers. The next step was to offer control to government.

3

'A task of infinite delicacy': the formation of the Irish Yeomanry

These were John Foster's words in early September 1796, describing plans for the Irish Yeomanry, which had been a matter of intense debate for over two months. Surprisingly, no complete contemporary account exists of this gestation period. The nearest we have is the Reverend William Richardson's 1801 pamphlet on the origins of the yeomanry. He claims the Dungannon Association's plan, first submitted to government in late June, was the prototype for the national yeomanry system.[1] This was a gentry-sponsored law and order association, which compiled loyal resolutions to be signed by reliable inhabitants and submitted offers of service under government control. As Richardson was one of the instigators, his account must be treated with caution. However, the fact that such a polemic was considered necessary just five years after the foundation, and at a time when the yeomanry was a prominent and highly visible feature of Irish life, bespeaks contemporary confusion about its origins. With the exception of Hereward Senior, later historians have been even more taciturn on the yeomanry's formation than on its subsequent history. Senior, like Richardson, sees the Dungannon Association as forerunner to the yeomanry. His thesis is that these loyal associations had two aims. In areas where the gentry were Orange, they would provide a legal basis for arming the lodges. In other districts they could be used to suppress Orange 'wrecking'. In Senior's analysis, government initially hesitated but, around early August 1796, accepted the risk and utilised them on the model of the English Yeomanry.[2] Senior's work has a pioneering value in identifying different interest groups, whose needs sometimes concurred, sometimes conflicted. However his analysis needs re-examination, for two reasons. First, the subsequent importance of Orangeism has introduced a distracting sense of inevitability into his narrative. Second, his neglect of the Home Office and Camden papers, key official sources, leads to an underestimation of government's active role. This interpretation, that the yeomanry was a northern gentry initiative forced on a

---

1 Foster to Camden, 2 Sept. 1796, K.A.O. Pratt Papers, U840/0184/3,4; 37 Geo. III, c. 2; Richardson, *Yeomanry*. 2 Senior, *Orangeism*, pp. 42–5.

reluctant government, has recently been taken up by David Miller.[3] However, the yeomanry's subsequent history cannot be properly understood without a reliable account of the groups and issues involved in its origins. The period of planning and formation must be reconstructed as thoroughly as possible.

On 25 June 1796, Cooke received a letter from Thomas Knox of Dungannon, MP for Tyrone and eldest son of Lord Northland, who owned the town. Knox enclosed for Camden's consideration a copy of a 'plan of association' and draft resolutions. He believed these would 'show the numbers and strength of the well-affected ... and depress and terrify the conspirators' and hoped such associations could become general in Ulster. Knox sent another copy on 6 July, amended after consultation with 'the most intelligent persons' locally. Camden showed interest, and returned the resolutions to be re-drafted 'to make the expression more general', thus preventing other resolutions being grafted on 'of a questionable tendency'. A comparison of the draft with the resolutions as eventually published shows what Camden meant. Deleted from the initial paragraph was the clause 'to oppose the French should they attempt to invade'. Camden obviously saw the danger of United Irishmen exploiting the old Volunteers' traditional anti-invasion response to obtain a concealed presence in any new force. Camden consulted the law officers, one of whom, Arthur Wolfe, the attorney-general, had already been sounded out by Richardson. Satisfied that there was no sinister purpose, Camden told Portland that it might be 'the foundation of a useful plan to strengthen government'.[4] However, he stopped well short of sanction.

The official response to the plan is difficult to disentangle. As we have seen, Camden had aborted embryonic armed associations in 1795, fearing they could precipitate uncontrollable volunteering. Moreover, another local defence option was already on the agenda. Pelham was in England, where Cooke sent him 'some resolutions Knox has published and the purport of which his excellency approved', but noted also that the cabinet were considering a yeomanry cavalry and that Wolfe, Beresford, Clare, Foster and Parnell supported it.[5] These options were therefore seen as different means to the same military end. However, the social and political context of each contained such potential implementation problems that they continued to be considered separately. Yeomanry were already established in England as a property-based force, organised, financed and manned by the county elites. In the vast majority of cases they were cavalry, though occasionally they also contained dismounted troopers.[6] Armed loyal associations, in this context, were local in their application and control and had no parliamentary legislative basis.[7] Such associations existed in England in 1792–3, where they undertook semi-military duties, as,

---

3 D.W. Miller, 'Non-Professional Soldiery', op cit., p. 333.   4 Knox to Cooke, 25 June 1796, 6 July 1796, N.A R.P.620/23/202, 620/24/16; *BNL*, 11–15 July 1796.   5 Cooke to Pelham, 14 July 1796, B.L. Pelham Papers add. mss., 33102, f. 69.   6 A. Gee, 'The British Volunteer Movement, 1793–1807', p. 46.   7 I.F.W. Beckett, *The Amateur Military Tradition*, pp. 73–4.

ASSOCIATION of the INHABITANTS of the Town of DUNGANNON, to Support and Defend the KING and CONSTITUTION, to preserve the Peace of their Town and its Neighbourhood, and to discourage and resist all Endeavours to excite Sedition and Rebellion.

WHEREAS, we have observed with much concern that great pains have been taken of late in many parts of this Country, to excite discontents among his Majesty's faithful subjects, thereby to alienate their affections from his Person and Government, and to induce them to be willing to exchange our excellent free Constitution, for that System of Anarchy and Confusion, which is now spreading desolation over other parts of the world.

AND WHEREAS, we have reason to believe, that some miscreants have carried their wickedness so far as to hold treasonable correspondence with the French, with whom his Majesty is now at open War, to invite them to invade this Kingdom; and, as an encouragement, have held out the following audacious falsehood, viz. that his Majesty's subjects in this Kingdom are ready to rebel against him, and to adopt their principles, and that a few, seduced by the emissaries of the French, through the management of a desperate and traiterous Society, have bound themselves by oaths to be ready, (in furtherance of these purposes) in case of Invasion, either to join them, or to rise and take possession of the Country, and the property of its peaceable Inhabitants.

NOW we whose names are hereunto subscribed, Inhabitants of the Town of Dungannon, sincerely attached to our most excellent Constitution, sensible of the benefits we enjoy under the mild Government of our most Gracious Sovereign, and of the present prosperous state of our Country, prosperous in a degree heretofore unexampled, where Wealth and Comfort are sure to follow honest Industry, unwilling to put at hazard these solid advantages, and abhorrent of the machinations of a set of desperate adventurers, who without Property themselves aim at that of others, and hope to rise to wealth and consequence in a general Confusion.

RESOLVE, that we will at the hazard of our Lives and Fortunes support and defend our Gracious KING GEORGE the Third, against all Foreign and Domestic Enemies.

THAT we will discourage and oppose all treasonable and seditious practices, and resist all attempts to disturb the peace of the Country.

AND further in case of actual Invasion, or Insurrection, should his Majesty in his wisdom require such Exertion, THAT WE WILL EMBODY OURSELVES FOR HIS DEFENCE, AND FOR THE PROTECTION OF OUR TOWN, and all of us, or as many of us as he shall think fit to call upon, will enroll ourselves under such Officers as he shall Commission, and with their assistance, and under their Command will train and discipline ourselves, so as to be able to render him the more effectual service, and frustrate the hopes of the Traitors and Banditti, who vainly rely upon finding the Country naked and defenceless, should the regular Troops be drawn off to oppose an invading Enemy.

HERE follow the names of the associators, too numerous to be inserted.

Session House, Dungannon, July 12, 1796.

WE, the JUSTICES of the PEACE for the County of Tyrone, assembled at the Quarter-Sessions, unanimously approved of the above resolutions, and warmly recommend the adoption of them to the different Towns and Parishes of this County.

NORTHLAND	JOHN STAPLES	T. CAULFIELD	JAMES RICHARDSON
CASTLESTEWART	ROBERT LOWRY	EDWARD EVANS	T. K. HANNINGTON
JAMES STEWART	R. LINDSAY	A. STEWART	W. I. ARMSTRONG
T. KNOX	JAMES VERNER	T. FORESYTHE	SAMUEL STREAN

The Dungannon Resolutions

for example, coastal patrols, but, in 1794, when new defence legislation permitted the embodiment of Volunteer Infantry corps, they were subsumed into the larger organisation. As such they were typically urban and more lower-class than yeomanry. In Ireland the problem with such associations was two fold. First, there was the danger of further de-stabilising the situation by resurrecting volunteering. For this very reason, Camden had stamped on proposals by Carhampton and others in 1795 to start armed anti-Defender associations in Leinster. Richardson knew this and ensured that the offers of service would be acceptable to the lord lieutenant, 'by whom a self-governed army might be deemed dangerous'.[8] Second, the consequences of getting wrong the decision about loyalty were potentially disastrous. Yet Knox had put pressure on Camden's weak spot, hinting that associations and resolutions would be generally adopted in any case if government did not become involved.[9] There were also difficulties with the yeoman cavalry concept, given Fitzwilliam's plans for a largely Catholic yeomanry in 1795. Fitzwilliam was a Portland whig; consequently, any resurrection of the idea was unlikely to meet an enthusiastic reception from the Home Secretary. At this stage, the potential difficulties outweighed the advantages and it is not surprising the matter was left untouched during July. Although the existence of another option on the agenda alters the motivational balance as expressed by Richardson, Senior and Miller, it does not go to the other extreme by showing yeomanry as solely a government measure. Rather, the evidence indicates parallel central and local initiatives. Sometimes these lines of development converge in apparent coherence, on other occasions they move far enough apart to appear separate. Both eventually fused to become the Irish Yeomanry, but to start an analysis at the point of fusion would lead to oversimplification and miss much of the 'infinite delicacy' which helps explain the form yeomanry took and the developing attitudes to it. This reconstruction will trace the formative process along both lines of development.

The next official comment came on 30 July when Camden told Pelham, still in England, that most of his advisors were pressing for something like the English yeomanry. These included Clare, Wolfe, Dillon and Carhampton. Speaker Foster was less enthusiastic, being unwilling to resort to yeomanry till invasion was probable. Camden, uneasy without his trusted, able and understandably unwell secretary, was 'not prepared to say [yeomanry] is necessary at present' and refused to commit himself till Pelham returned.[10] Meanwhile the parallel local initiative made some progress during July but also hit snags. The Dungannon Resolutions were a form of orchestrated public opinion, composed and imposed from above, designed to interest government without alienating loyalists. Richardson, who drafted them, admitted that he had deliberately manipulated loyal opinion to make it appear they originated among the loyalists themselves. The public assembly of the Tyrone mag-

8 Richardson, *Yeomanry*, p. 15.   9 Camden to Portland, 12 July 1796, P.R.O. H.O.100/60/f. 261.   10 Camden to Pelham, 30 July 1796, B.L. Pelham Papers add. mss. 33102 ff. 81–6.

istracy at Dungannon for the July quarter-sessions was chosen to try them out, Richardson having earlier canvassed opinion in other counties. Dungannon's was selected as the best offer and published in the newspapers of Dublin, Belfast, Strabane and Derry, as a template for other places, signed first by the magistrates then by the associators 'too numerous to be inserted'.[11] Public failure risked strengthening the United Irishmen immeasurably, so Richardson had had other places in reserve should Dungannon have failed. In the event the response was uneven. The Down grand jury confined itself to standard resolutions to preserve the peace. The scheme failed outright in Coleraine and had a mixed reception in county Armagh.[12] The Dungannon Association's uneven progress reflects its essential characteristics: it was new and dangerous, disingenuously obscure and underlaid with the personal and political ambitions of Thomas Knox.

The idea of a law and order association was not new either at county or parish level. It was a well recognised procedure for magistrates and gentlemen to band together to deal with disorder by publishing resolutions, organising as a *posse comitatus* to make arrests, and raising rewards by subscription to encourage informers. Indeed, as recently as May 1796 an association was established in the south Derry barony of Loughinsholin where about 60 magistrates and gentlemen resolved to aid the military in suppressing the United Irishmen. Contemporary newspapers reveal a range of somewhat similar parish resolutions offering the magistrates assistance in the form of the *posse comitatus*, such as those from Moira, county Down, pledging information against Orange and Defender rioters.[13] Knox's plan not only offered this usual law and order support to the magistrates; it also offered central government emergency armed service under crown commissions. It was therefore more permanent than the *posse comitatus* and, crucially from the government's perspective, more controllable than the old Volunteers. It therefore contained two levels of response, one familiar and eminently respectable, the other hidden, 'too numerous to be inserted', held in reserve, contingent on governmental acceptance of the associators' advance promises of service. This duality had radical social implications, as the *Northern Star* unwittingly pointed out, in mocking 'the invincible mass of peers, magistrates, butchers, lackeys, informers etc.'.[14] The plan therefore implied a degree of liaison between the gentry and more proletarian elements in society not seen since the Volunteers. However, since the French Revolution such linkages were considered too risky for some. Most Antrim gentlemen feared that associations would produce republican counter-associations.[15] Moreover, in areas where Orangeism was established, in parts of Armagh, Tyrone and west Down, any law and order plan would inevitably encounter the problem of sectarian disorder. If

11 *B.N.L.*, 11–15 July 1796.   12 Richardson, *Yeomanry*, pp. 15, 23; *B.N.L.* 18–22 July 1796; Corry to Cooke, 23 July 1796; N.A. R.P. 620/24/48, Dalrymple to Cooke, 24 July 1796, 620/24/53.   13 *N.S.*, 2–5 May 1796; 27–30 May 1796; *B.N.L.*, 4–7 July 1796.   14 *N.S.*, 1–5 Aug. 1796.   15 O'Neill to Camden, 29 Aug. 1796, K.A.O. Pratt Papers, U840/0130A.

Knox's associations were to function, they had to address this as well as opposing the United Irishmen. The evidence points, not surprisingly, to confusion, some of it deliberate, rather than an open commitment to arm the Orangemen as Senior suggests.

The governor of Armagh, Lord Gosford, recommended adoption of the Dungannon plan at the summer assizes to prevent 'a renewal of the horrid scenes as experienced last winter', meaning the expulsions of Catholics.[16] The sheriff, John Ogle, was also confused about the plan, telling Cooke, 'I can have no doubt Sir but that my Lord Lieutenant is fully apprized of the late associations entered into by the Orangemen ... as also of the avowed opposition of a well meant association at Dungannon'. Ogle feared this would create more problems, and advocated the gentry should, as with the old Volunteers, 'mix with them and point out what was reasonable or otherwise rather than [organise as] another corps associated as themselves pretending to suppress them'.[17] Yet this is what Senior claims Knox and Richardson were quite openly doing. If the Dungannon Association was about legally arming the lodges, then the sheriff and governor in the county where Orangeism started knew nothing of it. In the event the most influential grand jurors were absent at the Armagh assizes. A surprised General Dalrymple, heard it commonly reported that they were avoiding entering into resolutions, and mistakenly inferred indifference or lack of unanimity. However, the real reason was that some Orange 'wreckers' were up for trial. Wrecking was a capital offence under the provisions of the Whiteboy Act, yet these men were acquitted by the rag-tag jury which eventually assembled. Ogle suspected intrigues.[18] Obviously something was happening. The judge noted that neither Knox or Richardson had attended the assizes, which seems strange as Knox had written to Gosford some days before regarding adoption of the Dungannon plan.[19] The probable scenario was that the assizes threatened to bring the subterranean aspect to light prematurely. If the resolutions against lawbreakers passed, as Gosford wished, it would have been impossible to acquit wreckers. Obviously the law and order aspect of the plan was then rapidly withdrawn when it threatened to alienate Orangemen to whom Knox had promised government arms in return for acting within the law. If some of the Dungannon plan's deliberately less well-informed patrons implemented its policy too rigorously before the Orangemen had received the promised government sanction, it would dangerously compromise Knox's position with a volatile section of his father's tenantry. This brinkmanship certainly sits square in the context of attempts, well-described by Senior, by certain mid-Ulster families, the Verners, Blackers, Warings and Knoxes,

---

16 Gosford to Corry, n.d. [July 1796], enclosure in Corry to Cooke, 23 July 1796, N.A. R.P.620/24/48.
17 Ogle to Cooke, 15 July 1796, N.A. R.P.620/24/37.   18 Dalrymple to Cooke, 24 July 1796, N.A. R.P.620/24/53, Kemmis to Cooke 24 July 1796, 620/24/55, Ogle to Cooke, 14 Aug. 1796, 620/24/113.
19 Kemmis to Wolfe, 27 July 1796, N.A. R.P.620/24/188; Corry to Cooke, 23 July 1796, 620/24/48.

to control riotous Orange tenants by enrolling them in loyal associations from 1795, and, as this fell foul of government's fear of restarting volunteering, more recent moves such as allowing them to parade on 1 July, and encouraging rules and resolutions to assist the magistrates.[20] However, as the Armagh example shows, the Dungannon plan was not as clear-cut or overtly Orange as Senior implies. Even in the Orange districts it meant different things to different people. It is hard to imagine someone like James Stewart of Killymoon, a liberal ex-Volunteer and later supporter of Catholic relief, who was personally visited by Richardson and signed the resolutions at the Tyrone quarter-sessions, knowingly associating himself with political pariahs like the Orangemen. Knox's plan also meant something different to government. Camden's fear of volunteering and the prevailing opinion in his 'cabinet' against arming any sections of the population below the level of the gentry, not to mention the political capital the opposition obtained from the Armagh expulsions, make it impossible to believe they would knowingly enter into, as Senior claims the formation of yeomanry implied, a '*de facto* alliance' with the Orangemen.[21] Even Cooke, Knox's channel of communication to the Castle, who may have been privy to the moves to draw the sting from Orangeism, did not support arming them. He had recently reprobated their 'irritating conduct' in continuing to persecute Catholics, and gave Pelham his personal opinion that Ireland's defence needs were best met by cavalry re-inforcements, arming the gentry, reforming the militia, and getting effective generals.[22]

Having had no response to the Dungannon offers, on 13 August Knox wrote Cooke an ambiguously structured letter, complaining that the United Irishmen would be easily suppressed 'if Government would show a decided approbation of the measure or even, privately, intimate to their friends that they wished it well'. Then, undoubtedly with Cooke's censure of the Orangemen's conduct in mind, with desperation behind his delicate phraseology, he tried to maintain the distinction between them and the loyal associations:

> As to the Orange Men we have rather a difficult card to play, they must not be entirely discountenanced, on the contrary, we must, in a certain degree, uphold them, for, with all their licentiousness, on them must we rely for the preservation of our lives and properties, should critical times occur. We do not suffer them to parade, but at the same time, applaud them for their loyal professions. I hope I shall be able to manage it with our Tyrone people that they shall not be lost to the cause of their King and Country and at the same time, be kept within due bounds.[23]

20 Waring to Cooke, 4 July 1796, N.A. R.P.620/24/11; Gosford to Camden, 13 July 1796, P.R.O.N.I. Gosford Papers, D1606/1/1/186; See for example, Waringstown Resolutions, *B.N.L.*, 24–27 June 1796. 21 Senior, *Orangeism*, pp. 45, 49. 22 27 July 1796, B.L. Pelham Papers add. mss. 33102 ff. 74–5. 23 Knox to Cooke, 13 Aug. 1796, N.A. R.P.620/24/106.

What then was the role of Orangeism in the Dungannon Association? When looked at from the local end of the telescope, what the government saw as offers of service from the Dungannon associators 'too numerous to insert', were obviously promises of arms and official approval to the Orangemen. The Orangemen could remain in the background until government sanction arrived in the form of commissions, arms and uniforms, to allow them to emerge having swapped the ominous orange for respectable red. Having kept their side of the bargain by ensuring the gentry-backed resolutions succeeded in Knox's home town it was now up to Knox to keep his, hence the worried letter to Cooke. When the offers of other loyal associations are examined a similar pattern is revealed. Resolutions similar to the original Dungannon ones appeared in the *Belfast Newsletter* from Drumcree and Seagoe parishes in county Armagh.[24] Together they have 30 signatures of gentlemen and magistrates claiming 'connections' with 1,317 other inhabitants. These could be based on a rent-roll, but it looks suspiciously similar to the transaction described by Blacker in raising the Seagoe Infantry. He admitted raising it entirely from local Orangemen in consulta-tion with their leaders as, in October, he had to choose 100 yeomen from his original offer in August of around 1,000. James Verner of Churchill, who supported the Dungannon Association and whose family had had strong Orange connections since the Battle of the Diamond, persuaded 2,383 'loyal inhabitants' to sign a similar resolution in August.[25] Verner's son later described this, saying that as the United Irishmen comprised people of all religious persuasions, and government not know-ing whom to trust, 'my father issued notices calling upon the Protestants to assem-ble at his place', who signed their names, took the oath of allegiance and offered service. Verner then took his list to Camden and 'assured his excellency he would be responsible for every one of them'. In October they were embodied into the Churchill Yeoman Infantry.[26] The idea in these cases seems to have been similar to skeleton regiments in the regular army: a commitment to join when the infrastructure was ready.

Thus far from clarifying and regulating the relationship between gentry and Orangemen as Senior claims, the Dungannon Association's dual structure deliber-ately muddied the waters. Knox's family did have a relationship with the Orange-men, and he exploited this to ensure the scheme's success in his home town. Al-though Knox's example was followed by others like Blacker, who also had Orange links, Knox had ambitions for the plan far wider than the Orange area of central Ulster. He initially intended it would become general throughout Ulster, but, as Richardson's pamphlet mentions consultations with southern gentlemen, Knox's ambitions obviously were not confined even to his own province.[27] These larger ambitions tie up with Knox's political career. He had been Abercorn's political man-

---

24 *B.N.L.*, 5–9 Sept. 1796.   25 Senior, *Orangeism*, p. 58; Richardson, *Yeomanry*, pp. 21, 26.   26 Sir W. Verner, *A Short History of the Battle of the Diamond* (London, 1863), p. 17.   27 Richardson, *Yeomanry*, p. 27.

ager until 1794 when they quarrelled irreconcilably over Knox's resignation from the Tyrone Militia. Knox remained MP for Tyrone but was on borrowed time, as Abercorn would inevitably withdraw his patronage in the 1796 general election.[28] He was now forced to plough his own furrow, as his father, Lord Northland, had stayed with Abercorn. An ambitious man, Knox was obliged to look elsewhere and, given his reputation with government as an active magistrate, the deteriorating 'state of the country' made Camden's difficulty his opportunity. With volunteering suppressed and Camden terrified of re-starting it, with unsuccessful attempts at peacekeeping associations in 1795 and early 1796, the Dungannon resolutions resonate with the need to fill the vacuum in which Ireland's voluntary military potential was dissipating. Since 1782 Dungannon had occupied a special place in Volunteers' minds throughout Ireland. Knox's wider scope for the plan was therefore designed to attract this constituency, Ireland's traditional Protestant garrison. Safely delivering the Volunteers' defence potential would shore up his crumbling parliamentary career, whereas merely linking government with Orangeism would finish him. This explains the initial caution, flexibility and inevitable confusion, since, to keep the plan alive long enough for the transfusion of official approval, he had to meet a variety of magistrates' needs, yet at the same time maintain internal unity. However, the longer government delayed, the more difficult it became to hold both the elite and proletarian components and the less likely became the wider adoption Knox wanted. All this modifies rather than revises Senior's view, of a close yeomanry-Orange connection; but it is an important modification which clarifies some of the dynamics involved in the foundation and subsequent history of the yeomanry.

While Knox sweated in Tyrone, Camden and his advisers deliberated on an official yeomanry scheme in the cool sanctity of the Castle. On 5 August Camden again consulted the law officers on measures to meet the deteriorating domestic situation, now compounded by intelligence of a French invasion attempt. He met Clare, Foster, Parnell and John Beresford to consider recalling parliament early to suspend Habeas Corpus and legalise a yeomanry in case the troops, dispersed on peacekeeping, were suddenly withdrawn to the coast to meet an invasion. Opinion was divided on the viability of a yeomanry. The consensus was that reinforcements of regular cavalry were the best option, but that authority should be given Camden to call parliament early in case he needed to embody a yeomanry. Camden confided to Pelham that he hoped reinforcements would make it unnecessary 'to recur to the measure either of enrolling yeomanry cavalry or adopting associations'.[29] The objections to locally-raised defence options, which appear to have emanated from Foster in particular, centred on the trustworthiness of the proposed force. As reinforce-

---

28 A.P.W. Malcomson, 'A lost natural leader: John James Hamilton, first marquess of Abercorn', in Proceedings of the Royal Irish Academy, 88, No. 4, 1988, pp. 271–303; R.G. Thorne (ed.), *The History of Parliament: the Commons, 1790–1820*, iv, p. 349.   29 Camden to Portland, 6 Aug. 1796, P.R.O.H.O.100/62/ff. 153-63; Camden to Pelham, 6 Aug. 1796, B.L Pelham Papers, add. mss. 33012 f. 96.

ments were unlikely, and while Portland's consent was awaited, the next logical step
was to canvass the localities to check which, if any, of the home-defence options
were feasible.

Camden sent influential men into the localities to canvass the views of the country gentlemen. At this stage their brief was simply to gather opinions rather than try
out or encourage any particular proposal, as the government feared the high levels
of danger, anticipation and excitement would mean spontaneous uncontrolled and
uncontrollable 'volunteering' if there was a whiff of the official plans. However,
some hot-headed canvassers tried to push their favoured mode of local defence.
Carhampton panicked the Roscommon grand jury by using invasion fears to resurrect his armed association idea of 1795. It should be noted at this juncture that, even
in crisis, personal ambition underpinned some of the schemes. Knox's ambitions
were mirrored by Carhampton's, who was canvassing for the post of commander-
in-chief. Although his scare tactics sent the price of cattle plummeting, this did not
prevent his appointment in September.[30] Downshire's men pushed for yeomanry
cavalry on the English model, which so confused some west Down gentry who had
been supporting association schemes, that they considered them separate plans.[31]
The Dungannon Association's supporters used the opportunity to try to spread
their system. Lord O'Neill, governor of Antrim, obtained leave of absence from the
militia to go north and test opinion on yeomanry and associations. He no sooner set
foot on Antrim soil, in the absentee Lord Hertford's town of Lisburn, than he was
accosted by three agitated magistrates who thrust a paper into his hand, proposing
associations on the Dungannon model to try on the county gentlemen, unsuccessfully as it turned out.[32] Hertford's estate was an island of Anglicanism between heavily
Presbyterian districts of Down and Antrim and had been penetrated by Orangeism.
Hertford's agent, Reverend Philip Johnston, in his capacity as a magistrate, had
tried to establish small armed associations on a parish basis, and submitted a plan to
government which, like Knox's, was received without either support or discourage-
ment.[33] The feedback coming into the Castle showed that the Dungannon scheme
was spreading into Hertford's estate. The Reverend Higginson, curate of Ballinderry
and Johnston's confidant and acolyte, submitted resolutions from Orangemen who
had changed their title to 'loyalists' and adopted 'the resolutions lately entered into
at Dungannon as their own' while Johnston's own parishes submitted an even stronger
version. Although rejected by the county elite, parish-based resolutions similar to
Johnston's continued to come in from loyal associations in Derriaghy and Derry-

30 Pelham to the duke of York, 22 Sept. 1796, B.L. Pelham Papers, add. mss. 33113, ff. 47–52; Dillon to
Camden, 22 Aug. 1796, K.A.O. Pratt Papers, U840/0181/5.   31 Dillon to Camden, 13 Aug. 1796,
K.A.O. Pratt Papers, U840/0181/3; French to Cooke, 22 Aug. 1796, N.A. R.P.620/24/141; Waddell to
Ross, 22 Aug. 1796, 620/24/144.   32 Camden to O'Neill, 13 Aug. 1796, O'Neill to Camden, 18, 29
Aug. 1796, K.A.O. Pratt Papers, U840/0130A; O'Neill to Cooke, 17 Aug. 1796, N.A. R.P.620/24/
124.   33 Johnston to Hardwicke, n.d. July 1804, M. MacDonagh (ed.), *The Viceroy's Postbag*, pp. 24–8.

volgie, contiguous parishes along the Lagan valley. Others came from Fort Edward near Dungannon itself.[34] As their parochial origin and clerical input would suggest, these were all composed of Anglicans. In Armagh the situation was somewhat different. General Dalrymple stressed the danger of a selective armament: those excluded would consider themselves 'given up' and become United Irishmen, while to arm in proportion [to local religious demography] would, anticipating Foster's phrase, be a matter of delicacy. Gosford felt that each parish should organise its own defence individually, as 'the plan for one may not do for the other'.[35] The feedback from elsewhere in Ireland indicated less complexity. John Toler, the solicitor general, visited gentry and farmers in the south and west, gathering information rather than giving out encouragement. Toler thought they were reliable, but cautioned against 'the renovation of volunteering' while Lord Dillon simply saw arming all the property as best for Roscommon.[36]

With no official direction, the situation in August was confused. However a number of features stand out. First, armed associations on the Dungannon model were still being considered separately from a yeomanry. Camden assured Dillon that the government was not proposing associations when, as a Roscommon landowner, Dillon complained of Carhampton's heavy-handed tactics. Secondly, Camden still had reservations about arming the gentry as a yeomanry force, telling Dillon that, even under the guard of commissions, 'I confess I think it is a delicate measure to resolve upon', though he saw none better.[37] Moreover, another problem had arisen. Completely unaware of the tacit arrangement with Orangemen in parts of Tyrone, Armagh and Antrim, Camden requested information on reports that the United Irishmen were prejudicing public opinion against Knox's Dungannon Association, construing it as a 'Protestant combination, supported by government against the Catholics'.[38]

The general consensus from the canvass was that some form of locally-raised home defence was necessary. However, amongst the avalanche of letters, a vital one was missing. Camden had not yet received Portland's response. On 17 August he wrote again, requesting authority to proceed. Now Whitehall prevaricated. Portland replied ambiguously on 20 August, putting the responsibility back to Camden. Synonyms for yeomanry were tossed back and forward across the Irish sea. Picking up on Camden's evasive phrase of 6 August Portland authorised 'provincial levies', but thought it unnecessary to call parliament to execute what was a normal wartime expedient. This was certainly not what Camden had in mind. Backed up by the

---

34 Higginson to Cooke, 22 August 1796, N.A. R.P.620/24/156; Various resolutions, n.d. Aug. 1796, 620/24/87,124,130.   35 Dalrymple to [Cooke], 29 Aug. 1796, N.A. R.P.620/24/174.   36 Toler to Cooke, 10 Aug. 1796, N.A. R.P.620/24/102; Dillon to Camden, 4 Aug. 1796, 620/24/81.   37 Camden to Dillon, 15 Aug. 1796, K.A.O. Pratt Papers, U840/0181/3.   38 Camden to Pelham, 13 August 1796, B.L. Pelham Papers, add. mss. 33102 ff. 101–2; Camden to O'Neill, 13 Aug. 1796, K.A.O. Pratt Papers U840/0130A.

opinion of a mass of Irish gentlemen, he replied, with uncharacteristic candour, on 24 August claiming that 'great numbers wish to associate for the preservation of property and to form corps of yeomanry cavalry and infantry' and threatening unilateral action, saying that he could not 'delay my encouragement many days longer', having previously made his government 'thought one of slow decision and want of energy'.[39] Knox, would doubtless have agreed.

Portland's consent came at the end of August, vaguely discernible behind another semantic haze. On 28 August he told Pelham, still in London, that Camden should consider himself authorised to take whatever measures he thought expedient. He distanced himself behind contradictory statements, saying, 'it is true that I do not specifically empower him [Camden] to raise yeomanry corps *eo nomine* [roughly 'in name'] but as I say that I do not conceive it necessary to make the parliament meet earlier than usual for the purpose of raising levies'. Then, in a concluding master-stroke of ambiguity, given the current financial crisis, he said he saw no problem with Camden raising a force in wartime not voted for by parliament. He wrote again the following day to assure Camden that although he did not use the words 'yeomanry' or 'association' he wanted it understood he meant either or both.[40] Fitzwilliam's Catholic yeomanry/Catholic emancipation proposal had soured relations in the coalition so much that Portland must have shuddered at any mention of the word, not to mention the opportunities it would afford the Foxite opposition to embarrass Pitt and Portland. The point was not lost, even on government supporters. Lord Auckland told Beresford, 'Lord Fitzwilliam will have a melancholy topic of triumph over us all eventually'.[41]

With no reinforcements in sight, following further consultations on 30 August with Clare, Beresford, Foster, Parnell, Wolfe and Castlereagh, the question of an internally-raised home-defence force answered itself. The issue now was what form such a force should take. Both options, yeomanry cavalry or armed associations, had been scouted and the feedback revealed both increasing need and implementation problems. Camden admitted 'the difficulty of the measure is extreme'.[42] Both options had awkward connotations. Arming property-owners as cavalry meant *de facto* arming the Protestants, while armed associations, which would be mainly infantry, and, as Johnston's plans had shown, could also be exclusively Protestant, carried the additional danger of reviving the Volunteers. Both risked alienating the Catholics. Castlereagh shared Foster's objections about trustworthiness, but as the summer waned, the tentative policy began resolve into an official plan. Forgetting his Volunteer boyhood, Castlereagh advised, 'strong as the objections are to irregular corps in

---

39 Camden to Portland, 17 Aug. 1796, P.R.O. H.O.100/62/f. 166; Portland to Camden, 20 Aug. 1796, H.O.100/64/f. 173; Camden to Portland, 24 Aug. 1796, H.O.100/62/ff. 190–4.   40 Portland to Camden, 28 Aug. 1796, B.L. Pelham Papers, add. mss. 33102 ff. 113–14; Portland to Camden, 29 Aug. 1796, P.R.O. H.O.100/62/ff. 200–3.   41 28 Aug. 1796, W. Beresford (ed.), *Beresford Correspondence* (hereafter: *Beresford Corrs.*), ii, pp. 125–7.   42 Camden to Pelham, 30 August 1796, B.L. Pelham Papers, add. mss. 33102 ff. 119–20.

a country so recently extricated from their danger, yet I do not think it would be possible ... to resist the eagerness of the gentlemen ... to be permitted to arm for their own defence under commissions from the crown'.[43] Clare felt noblemen and squires would be best stimulated by 'general associations on the plan of that of Dungannon', obviously unaware of the proletarian aspect.[44] Portland put spin on the problem. Claiming to be an admirer of the English Yeomanry, he reminded Camden that its Irish equivalent would necessarily be composed of very different materials. Drawing on his own Irish viceregal experience, he anticipated difficulties from the gentry whichever method was chosen, and recommended circumspection. He warned that choosing cavalry risked starting a body of people 'employed in promoting and aggrandising the power and influence of the person to whose troop they belong' while associations would be made subservient to election purposes.[45] Beset with difficulties and conflicting advice, Camden must have yearned for the tranquillity of his Kentish estate.

These transactions marked an important watershed in the evolution of the yeomanry. As fortified as he could be with such conditional consent, Camden decided to 'feel the pulse of the country', this time with a specific proposal which he called the Fencible County Cavalry Plan. In usual military terms, fencibles were a full-time regular internal defence force raised by bounty for service anywhere in the British Isles during wartime. Camden's plan was very different, in that he envisaged part-time baronial cavalry troops undertaking to train and provide emergency service either in their home county or the next adjoining. Unlike English yeoman cavalry they were to be paid and equipped by government.[46] In reality this measure was a hurried compromise which attempted to square the circle by satisfying Irish needs and English objections, and at the same time secure property-based local defence without risking either delegating too much power to the Irish gentry or risking revived Volunteers. The incongruities of the plan were clear from the beginning. Shortly after it was circulated, Camden admitted that he used the word 'fencible' imprecisely because there were insufficient Irishmen rich enough to be considered yeomen.[47] As events were to show the fencible scheme was destined to set the country gentlemen's blood pressure soaring rather than draw blood from the United Irishmen.

With Portland's warnings ringing in his ear, Camden circularised the plan to 'such noblemen and gentlemen as I shall find expedient for His Majesty's service to entrust with the power of levying an armed force' in areas where troops might be withdrawn. Copies were then distributed to gentlemen within each magnate's sphere

---

43 Castlereagh to Camden n.d. [c.30 Aug. 1796], cited in Sir J.A.R. Marriott, *Castlereagh* (London, 1936), p. 49.   44 Clare to Camden, 28 Aug. 1796, K.A.O. Pratt Papers, U840/0163/6.   45 Portland to Camden, 29 Aug. 1796, P.R.O. H.O.100/62/ff. 200–3.   46 Sketch of a plan for ... a fencible county cavalry, n.d. [c.30 Aug. 1796], P.R.O. H.O.100/61/f. 262.   47 Camden to Portland, 3 Sept. 1796, P.R.O. H.O.100/62/ff. 208-14.

of influence, with letters asking them to attend meetings to discuss the measure. The sources do not specify the criteria by which the magnates were chosen. In some instances county governors were used, but this could not be general practice, as some counties had multiple governors. The evidence indicates that suitability was determined by a combination of criteria: property, influence and the ability to raise men, rather than on political allegiance. Leading conservatives and whigs were used equally. The marquis of Downshire, a strong conservative, was summoned from England to take the plan to Down, while the wealthy whig landowner Thomas Connolly, was used for county Londonderry. Charlemont, another whig, was used for Armagh and Tyrone, the duke of Leinster for Kildare, and Clanricarde for Galway. The archbishop of Cashel was also asked to exert his influence.[48] The choice of Leinster is particularly interesting. His connections were not obviously propitious, as he was related to Charles James Fox, and his brother, Lord Edward Fitzgerald, was becoming notorious as a republican. Although like Charlemont, Leinster was an ex-Volunteer commander, he was himself much more radical in his politics and an implacable opponent of Camden's coercion policy. Although Leinster later resigned from the yeomanry, Camden, at this juncture, took the larger view by putting the respectability and manpower-raising potential of the nobility and gentry above any political idiosyncrasies. At this stage, government's objectives were twofold: to test opinion, and get firm commitments. Downshire's was one of the first county meetings held. Camden viewed it as a precedent and wanted to ensure that no alternative plans were proposed which could have diminished the power inherent in controlling the conditions and terms of the new force. He drafted out the sort of resolutions he wanted, confined to general statements of loyalty, and expected Downshire to get them passed.[49] By late August, therefore the impetus for a new home defence force came as strongly from the centre as in July it had come from the localities. Government newspapers supported and publicised the measure. On the back of a report of impending invasion, the *Freeman's Journal* recommended that 'every man ... who loves his Religion, his country, his family and his King, stand prepared to defend them'.[50]

The canvass revealed that the pulses of the country gentlemen were racing. Given the earlier lack of direction, dangerous confusion was inevitable. James Buchanan of Omagh, unversed in the semantic niceties in vogue at the Castle, bluntly said that he could easily raise 'volunteer cavalry' but they would be Presbyterians who would leave if any Catholic was admitted. Worse still, he gave the impression that they would enlist as independent volunteers without mentioning government's role.[51] Moreover the switch to the fencible plan meant that government owed explanations

---

48 Knox to Cooke, 25 June 1796, N.A. R.P.620/23/202; Camden to Portland, 31 Aug., 3 Sept. 1796, P.R.O. H.O.100/61/f. 63, H.O.100/62/f. 201; Camden's Letter Book, 1 Sept. 1796, K.A.O. Pratt Papers, U840/0130A.   49 Camden to Downshire, 7, 11 Sept. 1796, P.R.O.N.I. Downshire Papers, D607/D/155,160.   50 *F.J.*, 6 Sept. 1796.   51 Buchanan to Cooke, 19 Sept. 1796, N.A. R.P.620/25/133.

to those offering infantry. On 7 September W.C. Lindsay wrote to Cooke about his armed association offer of August, claiming that without encouragement they were being threatened by 'Liberty Men'. Cooke could only say he would have answered the original resolutions if he could, 'but upon the subject of arming associations government has not yet decided'.[52] Expense was used as an excuse. Sir George Hill, who was trying to get resolutions passed in Derry city, complained that 'to hesitate at expense is nonsense'.[53] Doubtless cost was a factor, but a more fundamental reason was the strong opinion in the 'cabinet' against infantry. Speaker Foster now favoured cavalry, fearing that lowering the social level requisite for membership would open the levy to a wider social band, thus making it harder to exclude untrustworthy persons.[54] Opinion fluctuated daily. As news of the cavalry plan broke, Charlemont called personally on Camden, proposing an alternative infantry scheme for Ulster. As though to confirm Charlemont's fears, feedback from meetings in Ulster soon poured in, showing the cautious cavalry plan was a monumental blunder as it excluded the social constituency containing most loyalists. Lord Cole said the Fermanagh gentlemen would be hard pressed to get one cavalry troop from its eight baronies, but could raise 'a well-affected infantry'.[55] In Drumcree, county Armagh, a local gentleman found the potential cavalrymen so far scattered as to render the objectives of property defence unattainable. Yet the Drumcree and Seagoe parish resolutions claimed 'connection' with 1,317 inhabitants.[56] Clearly the plan had to be changed to include infantry. This raised more problems. The *de facto* lower-class membership of infantry corps meant the thorny question of religious composition could not be ignored.

Contrary to received opinion, there was no policy to exclude either Catholics or Dissenters from the cavalry plan. In the age of the French Revolution, property could be confidently equated with loyalty. Camden's attitude to non-Anglican membership was certainly favourable. He asked Lord Waterford to scout local Catholic opinion, telling him he thought it 'inexpedient to refuse Catholics', and that he had encouraged Kenmare, a Catholic aristocrat, to form a corps. He had earlier told Downshire, 'I confess I should think it would be wise to admit those Catholics and Dissenters upon whom you can rely, into these corps'.[57] However the critical words, 'upon whom you can rely', put a veto into the gentry's hands particularly when it came to infantry corps. Indeed, given the delicate balance of obligation and need, offer and acceptance, upon which voluntary service was contingent, sometimes the

52 Lindsay to Cooke, 7 Sept. 1796, Cooke to Lindsay 9 Sept. 1796, N.A. R.P.620/25/29.   53 Hill to Cooke, 9 Sept. 1796, N.A. R.P.620/25/38.   54 Foster to Camden, 2 Sept. 1796, K.A.O. Pratt Papers, U840/0184/3.   55 Camden to Foster, 1 Sept. 1796, K.A.O. Pratt Papers, U840/0184/2; Camden to Portland, 3 Sept. 1796, P.R.O. H.O.100/62/ff. 208–14; Cole to Cooke, n.d. Sept. 1796, N.A. R.P.620/25/133.   56 Smyth to [?Pelham], [early] Sept. 1796, N.A. R.P.620/25/12; *B.N.L.*, 5–9 Sept. 1796.   57 Camden to Waterford, 14 Sept. 1796, K.A.O. Pratt Papers, U840/0174/15; Camden to Downshire, n.d. [*c*.30 August 1796], P.R.O.N.I. Downshire Papers, D607/D/142.

landowner had no choice. Infantry offers were made to Downshire, and later accepted, from the Newry hinterland, which specified that those making the offer would serve with no 'papist'.[58] Here is an example of one of the tragedies of Irish history: potentially constructive new measures are drawn into the gravitational pull of old prejudice.

Government's culpability over Catholic membership was in keeping the policy lines vague rather than in deliberately discriminating. Camden's doctrinaire approach seems to have been overruled by the pragmatism of his advisers who, once decided on a new force, were more concerned that it should succeed in all areas and were prepared to allow the lines of demarcation to evolve according to local conditions. Even Foster was brought round to the necessity for infantry, though not without a parthian shot: 'Lord Charlemont must know the north better than I'. Infantry, in Foster's view, would involve filtering, which to do 'without creating offence or jealously will be a task of infinite delicacy'. Clare, within days of Charlemont's infantry proposal, though agreeing with Camden that umbrage should not be given to Catholics, said he would not dampen loyalists' zeal by making them feel dependent on anyone's approval but Camden's; yet he later maintained, 'it is peculiarly desirable that Catholic gentlemen of property and good principles should come forward in defence of the king and constitution'.[59] Unworthy of the name policy, this at least fulfilled the purpose of local flexibility without alienating Catholic magnates. Characteristically, Camden postponed the decision on Charlemont's infantry proposal until Pelham's return from England, when all feedback could be assimilated into a modified plan.[60]

On 17 September an official plan, certain to lower the blood pressure of the gentry was published and distributed. This contained the critical amendment:

> Troops of cavalry will be preferred ... but as it has been represented in certain parts of the kingdom where it might be difficult to raise cavalry alone that many respectable persons would readily serve on foot, the proportion of mounted and dismounted men in each troop must depend on local circumstances.[61]

Although *prime facie* this was the same as the English Yeomanry, it was tacitly understood by both government and gentry to include acceptance of the armed associations' offers of service. Following Pelham's return it was officially announced on 19 September that a yeomanry force was to be raised. This was the sign Knox had waited for. Richardson claimed it was the day government formally approved the Dungannon Association. Charlemont was given the go-ahead to call meetings to

58 Downshire to Cooke, 25 Nov. 1796, N.A. R.P.620/26/77. 59 Foster to Camden, 2 Sept. 1796, K.A.O. Pratt Papers, U840/0184/3; Clare to Camden, 7 Sept. 1796, U840/0183/8; Clare to Trench, 22 Oct. 1796, P.R.O.N.I. Clare papers, T3244/5/2. 60 Camden to Portland, 17 Sept. 1796, P.R.O. H.O.100/62/f. 226. 61 *F.J.*, 17 Sept. 1796; 17 Sept. 1796, P.R.O.N.I. Atkinson of Crowhill Papers, T2701.

levy mounted and dismounted yeomanry.[62] It was in these in these rapidly altering circumstances and *ad hoc* planning that the Dungannon Association and its northern offshoots were swept into the yeomanry, rather than the other way about. Moreover, from the time infantry were deemed acceptable, resolutions and offers of service began to come in from parish associations in Dublin and surrounding counties. The Armed Association of the Parish of Donard published resolutions in the *Freeman* and recommended other parishes to do the same. Finally, on 7 October, a meeting was held at the Mansion House, offering armed service to government and convening parish meetings for the churchwardens to enlist people into corps so that regiments of infantry and cavalry troops could be raised in Dublin's four ward divisions.[63] Given Richardson's extravagant claims and Knox's known ambitions, these might appear an extension of the northern associations. However there is no evidence that this was so. They partly resulted from the canvass in early September. Simon Purdon, a prime mover in the Finglas Union association, had earlier responded by saying that few mounted men could be got there or in Santry.[64] Now that government had decided a purely property-based, English-style yeomanry was impossible, and that home-defence meant different social classes could inhabit the same space, they were free to offer as infantry. There was another motivation. The government were going through the motions of considering whether Pitt's 'New Levies', a parochially-raised force, could be exchanged with similar levies from Ireland. Given that the Irish government was raising yeomanry, not to mention the natural reluctance of Irish civilians to submit themselves to a ballot and possible overseas service, this proposal was gladly and emphatically dropped.[65]

The period between early September and the issuing of commissions in October was one of intense activity. Feedback still indicated practical problems. Lord Shannon was experiencing difficulties of over-subscription and was uneasy about the government's lack of direction about Catholic membership. He had tried to limit the cavalry troops to 50 per barony as requested, but already had 70 including some wealthy Catholics. He believed this answered local purposes by representing Catholic property, but understanding the issue to be sensitive, decided against having too many without specific guidelines. In areas under no direct United Irish threat there were the predictable queries. In Galway, Clanricarde's gentlemen wanted to know in whose gift the nomination of officers would be. John Pollock, in Meath, could raise men from his own estate, but found 'great jealousies amongst the neighbouring gentry, great diversity of opinion as to the admissibility of Catholics, the utmost difficulty in the recommendation of officers, and a certainty of making every little squire of £200 or £300 per annum indisposed ... if each of them should not be appointed an officer'.[66]

62 Richardson, *Yeomanry*, p. 29; Camden to Charlemont, 20 Sept. 1796, H.M.C. *Charlemont*, ii, p. 284. 63 *F.J.*, 29 Sept., 6–13 Oct. 1796.   64 Purdon to Cooke, n.d. Sept. 1796, N.A. R.P.620/25/133.   65 Pelham to Portland, 26 Oct. 1796, P.R.O. H.O.100/62/f. 298; Camden to Portland, 28 Oct. 1796, H.O.100/65/f. 89.   66 Clanricarde to Pelham, 12 Sept. 1796, N.A. R.P.620/25/133; Pollock to

Following the official announcement, the offers of service flooding in to the Castle could be considered and given verbal acceptance in advance of the legislation. By 27 September John Beresford noted that enrolling was proceeding rapidly.[67] As we have seen, the usual procedure was for the governor or magnate to call a meeting of magistrates and gentlemen to see who would or could raise yeomen. Assuming all went to plan, supporters of the scheme then assembled potential recruits in their own districts, administered the oath, passed loyal resolutions and submitted an offer of service from the best candidates.[68] Some cavalry corps organised subscribers, who contributed money and balloted for those who would actually serve.[69] In accordance with the policy of keeping the yeomanry clear of county political interests, such offers were submitted directly to government. In practice, they were often mediated informally through the local magnate or his member of parliament. The onus was then on government to choose from the various offers. Refusals could cause offence, so care was taken to limit the offers before they reached the Castle. Pelham reckoned that two thirds of the original militia levy would suffice for county Down, and told Downshire to limit himself accordingly, to avoid snubbing anyone in this key county.[70] As the local gentry had responsibility to convene the meetings, much reliance was placed on their ability to judge the validity of the resultant offers. It did not mean all meetings went smoothly. The Catholic Committee sent emissaries to the south and west to stop Catholics from enrolling in cavalry corps.[71] In some parts of Ulster the enrolment meetings gave the United Irishmen a chance to embarrass the local gentry and flex their muscles. At Letterkenny in county Donegal the Oath of Allegiance was refused 'accompanied by expressions of impudent disloyalty'.[72] In practice most offers which got as far as being transmitted to the Castle were accepted. By January 1797 Camden had received 656 offers, 440 of which had been accepted, 125 declined and 91 held under consideration.[73]

The conclusion to be drawn from this formative phase is that where the central and local developments came together in early September, the resulting compromise became the Irish Yeomanry. The force which emerged from this complex process of adjustment became an organisation with inherent paradoxes. It was a uniform national structure which simultaneously contained territorially discrete, regionally diverse and sectionally complex elements. Some of the 'infinite delicacy' involved was to colour the yeomanry later. The lack of official membership directives contributed to denominational exclusiveness in some areas. This in itself could repre-

Pelham, 18 Oct. 1796, 620/25/176; Alexander to Cooke, 26 Sept. 1796, 620/25/122; Shannon to Camden, 1 Oct. 1796, K.A.O. Pratt Papers, U840/0175/8; Camden to Waterford, 14,15,19 Sept. 1796, U840/0130A.   **67** Beresford to Auckland, 27 Sept. 1796, *Beresford Corrs.*, ii, pp. 141–4.   **68** J. Boyd to R Boyd, 5 Oct. 1796, N.A. R.P.620/25/148.   **69** John [?Wroge] to Boyle, 19 Oct. [1796], P.R.O.N.I. Shannon Papers, D2707/A3/4/2.   **70** Pelham to Downshire, 20 Oct. 1796, P.R.O.N.I. Downshire Papers, D/607/D/213.   **71** 'J.W.' to Cooke, 28 Sept. 1796, N.A. R.P.620/36/227.   **72** J. Boyd to R. Boyd, 5 Oct. 1796, N.A. R.P.620/25/148.   **73** 10 Jan. 1797, N.A. R.P.620/28/81a.

sent the local balance of power for the yeomen and their enemies. The government's role in the process was of equal weight with that of the localities. Their apparently ponderous, blunderingly hesitant approach must be seen in context. It was the first time a levy outside the framework of the militia legislation had been attempted. The achievement looks better when we remember that the levy required intimate knowledge of local social, political and religious conditions, which were changing rapidly. That yeomanry were raised at all is an achievement in a pre-census age, when even the population of Ireland was not accurately known.

Given the rushed, *ad hoc* nature of the planning it is not surprising the Yeomanry Bill was to 'regulate' the county corps. It came in with a Bill to suspend Habeas Corpus in order to allow more peremptory strikes at the United Irishmen. Camden wanted both measures passed without delay and the session kept 'as short as possible' so that members could return to their counties and concentrate on raising yeomanry. Pelham and Arthur Wolfe introduced the Yeomanry Bill on 14 October. It was discussed in committee on 17 October and alterations ordered. The following day several amendments were debated and the finalised Bill was given its third reading before going to the Lords.[74] Parliament was then adjourned for six days. The main change at the committee stage reflected the duality of input in the measure. The objective, as stated in the preamble, was 'encreasing [*sic*] the military force of this Kingdom' whereas the Act omitted this arbitrary sounding statement, which gave the impression of primarily addressing government interests, and added a reference to property protection.[75] During the short adjournment, Pelham called the members to a meeting on 20 October to iron out remaining difficulties over the cavalry aspect. Over 70 attended what Shannon described as one of the most tumultuous meetings he had ever experienced. The results of *ad hoc* planning were surfacing. In some areas more men offered than government could afford to equip. Shannon felt it was using gentlemen badly to expect them to reject men whose offers they had just encouraged. To complicate matters, some gentlemen preferred to finance corps by local subscription. The old Volunteer James Stewart of Killymoon berated absentee landlords and proposed they be coerced into subscription schemes to replace government allowances. Fermanagh MP Viscount Cole made 'a great figure ... by the strength of his lungs ... and the frequency of his orations' while Shannon himself sneered at those offended by the proposed cheap uniform: 'some *fine officers* who had planed ornaments of various sorts, and had studied fashions to adorn their bodies'.[76] There is no record of firm decisions being reached; the details were probably left to evolve in practice as the growing expectation of invasion and insurrection necessitated getting the yeomen into action rapidly. Parliament re-assembled on 25 October and the Yeomanry Bill received the Royal Assent two days later.[77]

74 Camden to Portland, 1 Oct. 1796, P.R.O. H.O.100/62/f. 250; Vote of the Irish House of Commons. 75 37 Geo. III, c. 2.   76 Shannon to Boyle, 20 Oct. 1796, P.R.O.N.I. Shannon Papers, D2707/A3/3/22.

The Act provided for yeomen to receive government arms, uniforms and equipment, or allowances in lieu, and pay for two days' exercise per week. To assist with drill, each corps would have a permanent sergeant plus a drummer for infantry and a trumpeter for cavalry. Yeomen would only be under the Mutiny Act if they voluntarily offered to serve as a military corps in the event of invasion or insurrection. They could only be brought before a court martial comprised of yeomanry officers and were exempted from militia service. Each yeoman swore the 'Yeomanry Oath' before a magistrate.[78] The first commissions were issued on 31 October 1796 and after months of 'infinite delicacy' the yeomanry became a blunt and highly visible reality throughout Ireland.

77 Pelham to the Irish Office, 27 Oct. 1796, P.R.O. C.O.906/1.   78 37 Geo. III, c. 2.

4

Volunteer and Orange linkages

There are many superficial similarities between the Volunteers and the Irish Yeomanry. Both were locally raised, gentry-officered and territorially-based and were intended for local and national defence. Both came from a long tradition of voluntary armed service stretching back, through the eighteenth-century Jacobite scares, to defence associations raised in 1641 and 1689.[1] Both were predominantly Protestant with heavy concentrations in Dublin and Ulster. Paradoxically, historians have tended to concentrate on the *differences* between the Volunteers and other manifestations of the Protestant defence tradition rather than investigate their linkages to it. There are two reasons for this. As has already been pointed out, the innovatory nature of 'political' volunteering is inherently interesting and therefore attractive. Secondly, because of their political role in alliance with the parliamentary patriots, the Volunteers have occupied a hallowed place in nationalist hagiography, as representing 'Protestant nationalism'. When nationalism was developing as a political ideology in the nineteenth century, O'Connell's Repeal Association seized on the example of the Volunteers and 'legislative independence' to create a family tree of patriotism which accorded Grattan a place in the canon alongside Owen Roe O'Neill and Patrick Sarsfield. Indeed, they went as far as to start their own 'Repeal Volunteers'.[2] Have historians been misled by the Volunteers' reputation as an armed political pressure group, or as Protestant nationalists, to the extent they either omit or misunderstand the yeomanry linkage? Even the unionist historian, Lecky, sees little connection, noting that 'all who were in known sympathy with the United Irishmen were of course excluded [from the yeomanry] and this shut out the great body of those who composed the Volunteers of 1782'. Senior modifies this statement, perceptively seeing the northern Volunteers as 'in a sense, the progenitor of both the United Irishmen and the Orange movement'.[3] Both historians have drawn their conclusions from assumptions rather than from an analysis of the evidence. But were those assumptions correct? Recent work has indeed underlined strong links between the Volunteers and United Irishmen, both in terms of ideology and per-

---

1 A.T.Q. Stewart, *A Deeper Silence*, p. 6. 2 D.G. Boyce, *Nationalism in Ireland*, p. 161 and cover illustration. 3 Senior, *Orangeism*, p. 6.

sonnel. The first Belfast society of 1791 originated in a secret inner circle of Volunteers, including its progenitor William Drennan, Samuel McTier, Samuel Neilson, Thomas McCabe and William Tennant.[4] Although it is true that Volunteer muskets were used at the Battle of the Diamond, McCracken's men used Volunteer cannon at the Battle of Antrim. This begs the question: how far were yeomanry the old Volunteers new-formed? Circumstantial documentary evidence can be selected to prove almost anything, yet the question is so vital to an understanding of the history of Protestant Ireland that it refuses to go away. By using a different approach, utilising the methodology of the military historian, it can perhaps be asked differently: what levels of continuity between the Volunteers and the yeomanry are indicated by a comparison of the locational structure and membership of the two groups, and do these levels vary over time and place?

Some valuable county studies by Padráig O'Snodaigh in the 1970s examined the linkages from a military historian's perspective. Using yeomanry lists, and statistics gleaned from the few surviving Volunteer lists, plus newspapers, to plot locational and membership continuities, O'Snodaigh found considerable correlation on both counts. For example, in Monaghan, Donegal, and Roscommon, he found around 50 per cent of Volunteer surnames recurring in yeomanry lists. In Meath, from 88 yeomanry surnames, he found 20 in Volunteer lists and a further 23 in the 1756 militia musters. In Limerick and Roscommon, the locational continuity rate is also around 50 per cent, while in Monaghan it is 43 per cent and Donegal 38 per cent. O'Snodaigh's general conclusion is that, far from being the progenitors of the United Irishmen or Orangemen, the Volunteers were 'heirs to the old militia and ancestors of the yeomanry' into whose structure they were absorbed.[5] The strength of this interpretation is that the Volunteers are seen in a military rather than a political context as part of the tradition of Protestant self-defence. However, its weakness is in not examining those parts of Ulster where Presbyterian radicalism made such conclusions less predictable. It must be remembered that the Volunteers in Ulster were a heavily Presbyterian body. Therefore, an investigation of Antrim and Down is necessary then comparisons made with Armagh and Tyrone, more mixed in terms of the Protestant denominations and Fermanagh, the Irish county with the heaviest concentration of Anglicans. A further and unavoidable weakness, as O'Snodaigh admits, is the incompleteness of the sources on membership. Indeed, he leaves names out altogether in his recent and valuable compilation listing the locations of Volunteer units from scattered lists, newspaper references and artefacts.[6]

Similar problems occur when examining the aforementioned Ulster counties. Ideally Volunteer and yeomanry muster lists could be laid side by side and com-

4 N. Curtin, *The United Irishmen*, p. 30; A.T.Q. Stewart, op. cit., pp. 149–54.   5 P. O'Snodaigh, 'Notes on the Volunteers, militia, yeomanry and Orangemen of county Donegal', *Donegal Annual*, vii (1969), pp. 49–73: *Riocht na Midhe*, iv (1978–9) pp. 3–32; *Clogher Record*, ix (1977) pp. 142-66; *Irish Sword*, x (1971), pp. 125–40, xii (1975–6), pp. 15–35.   6 O'Snodaigh, *The Irish Volunteers, 1715–93: A List of the Units*, passim.

pared for membership. However, this is not as easy as it seems. Lists of yeomanry corps by county are available, but these only name the corps, the captains and commissioned officers. The survival of muster lists, naming rank and file members of individual yeomanry corps, is very erratic, given the destruction of official records in 1922. Scattered muster lists do turn up in private papers, but are relatively rare, being dependent on a captain preserving his corps' administrative records. I have been unable to find matching Volunteer and yeomanry muster lists to make a rank-and-file comparison. Even comparisons at officer level are problematic. Since the Volunteers were an unofficial body, complete national lists are rare and the surviving ones incomplete. The most detailed list, which names individual captains was a secret compilation for Castle consumption dating from 1784 when the Volunteers were declining, and is poor for Ulster.[7] Better, from a membership perspective, are lists for the Ulster counties compiled by the antiquarian T.G.F. Paterson. These were also compiled from incidental evidence, mainly newspapers, and are consequently incomplete: for some units no names are known. Antrim is exceptional, as a complete county list of captains survives for 1780–84.[8] In the following membership analysis, Paterson's lists have been used for comparison with the official yeomanry lists for January 1797 and December 1803. However, even in this case, like cannot be compared with like. The 1797 list names captains and lieutenants, whereas the 1803 list only gives captains. Paterson's eclectic methodology meant that surgeons, chaplains, secretaries and ordinary ranks occasionally slip in. The effect can be counteracted to an extent, by only including those above the rank of sergeant for the purposes of comparison. Moreover Paterson's lists for Armagh in the *Ulster Journal of Archaeology* are incomplete. What has been done with these lists is to abstract individual surnames of officers from Paterson's lists, only acknowledging repeats of the surname where it is clear that different families are involved. The obvious weaknesses, apart from the thirteen years separating the last Volunteer and first yeomanry list, is that surnames alone cannot indicate wider family interests through marriage. Thus the membership comparison must necessarily be impressionistic rather than definitive. However, in examining new ground, impressions are better than assumptions.

As the following table shows, Fermanagh tends to follow O'Snodaigh's findings. From 23 distinct Volunteer surnames, 12 recur in either the 1797 or 1803 yeomanry lists. Continuity of service is seen in major magnates such as Lord Enniskillen and the Brooke and Archdall families, through to smaller gentry figures like Watkins of Lisbellaw and Balfour of Lisnaskea. In Tyrone the recurrence rate is less, but still substantial, at 17 from 43, while in Antrim, from 55 identifiably separate Volunteer surnames, 20 are in the yeomanry. In Down the recurrence rate is lower at 35 from

---

7 J. Kelly, 'A secret return of the volunteers in Ireland in 1784', *I.H.S.*, xxiv, 103, pp. 268–92.   8 T.G.F. Paterson, 'The County Armagh Volunteers of 1778–93', *U.J.A.*, series 3, iv (1941), pp. 101–27; v, (1942), pp. 31–61; vi (1943), pp. 69–105; vii (1944), pp. 76–59; 'The Volunteer Companies of Ulster, 1778–1793', *Irish Sword*, vii (1965–6), pp. 90–116, 204–30; viii (1967–8), pp. 92–7, 210–17.

121, but lowest of all is Armagh, where only nine names from 50 reappear. This is not surprising given the incompleteness of the Armagh statistics.

Command Recurrence Rates

County	%
Antrim	26
Armagh	18
Down	29
Fermanagh	52
Tyrone	40

In each county one can see absolute continuity of individuals commanding Volunteer corps in the same location as they later commanded yeomanry. To take some examples, in Down, Matthew Forde commanded at Kilmore and Cumberbridge, Patrick Savage at Portaferry, Blackwood at Killinchy, Ker at Portavo and Kennedy at Holywood while in county Antrim, the Skeffington family commanded at Antrim, Adair at Donegore, Dobbs at Carrickfergus and McManus at Ahoghill. There were notable exceptions to this. Lord Moira supported the Volunteers but would have nothing to do with yeomanry, while, in Tyrone Thomas Knox's family, from the volunteering Vatican of Dungannon, do not figure in Volunteer lists, which no doubt was one of the reasons why government responded to Charlemont rather than Knox when the yeomanry measure was being determined. Although the statistics for these counties, apart from Fermanagh, reveal continuity levels rather less than O'Snodaigh's, allowing for the passage of time, and for incomplete and incongruous lists, they still reveal definite connections at command level. Locational continuity is perhaps a stronger factor for comparison, if for no other reason than the fact that better statistics are available.

Despite the government's initial plans, the location of yeomanry corps was not just determined by baronies or towns, but was contingent on there being a gentleman willing and able to command a corps and sufficient loyalists to man it. Given that some Volunteer corps remaining in existence to the early 1790s functioned as radical clubs and proto-United Irish societies, a locational comparison should reveal any evidence of discontinuity in areas of known United Irish activity. O'Snodaigh's compilation list has been used to establish areas where Volunteer units had existed, and the 1797 and 1803 yeomanry lists used to plot locational continuity, allowing the totality of each organisation to be compared. O'Snodaigh's list charts the locational occurrence of each unit during the entire volunteering period from 1776 or earlier, up to suppression in 1793. Though numerically the yeomanry establishment later exceeded the 1803 total, the 1803 list denotes the locational high water mark following large augmentations and the acceptance of many new corps earlier that year. However, caution is still necessary. The location of all Volunteer or yeomanry corps cannot be precisely plotted. Although both forces mostly comprised small, locally raised, territorially defined companies of infantry and, to a lesser extent in the Volunteers, cavalry troops, from 1780 Volunteers tended to combine into battalions and regiments superimposed on the territorial pattern of individual corps to facilitate co-operative action. These groupings appear in O'Snodaigh's list with locationally imprecise nomenclature such as the Carlow County Legion, the County Limerick Horse, the Central Division of Connacht Volunteers and the Third Ulster Regiments. Moreover, some Volunteer units adopted titles reflecting their politics rather than location. Thus we have the Protestant Association of Meath, the Roman Brigade of Westmeath, the Irish Corps of Cork, the Bill of Rights Battalion of Antrim, the Old Orange Volunteers of Donegal and the even more historical True Milesian Volunteers of county Dublin. Precise location of yeomanry corps can also be difficult. The original conception of the force as baronial meant that many cavalry corps took the name of the barony they were raised in and the exact place of assembly, near which the yeomen were to live, remains unclear. Occasionally it can be deduced indirectly, from primary source evidence. For example, in Down the first and second troops of the Lower Iveagh Cavalry were based at Waringstown and Hillsborough respectively.[9]

Taking the identifiable locations from O'Snodaigh's list as a template reflecting the totality of volunteering, identifiable yeomanry locations will be plotted in two stages, 1797 and 1803, and rendered both in tabular and map form to enable similarities and discontinuities to be assessed. Where lists are imprecise regarding location, or the location they give cannot be found in the 1861 townland index, no note is made on the map. Also, for the purposes of clarity, where a succession of corps or new corps were spawned from the original, no record is made on the map. The resultant maps are therefore not intended to provide definitive coverage records but rather to give a general impression of locational continuity. Where Volunteers and yeomanry units each took the same baronial names but the precise location is not clear enough to plot on the maps, locational continuity is assumed and included in the table. The figures in brackets give the total number of corps listed in the county, including supplementaries.

County	1778–93 Volunteers	1797 Yeomanry	Common	1803 Yeomanry	Common
Antrim	65	9 (10)	3 (5%)	42 (55)	24 (37%)
Armagh	34	13 (14)	8 (24%)	17 (20)	10 (29%)
Down	75	11 (14)	9 (12%)	38 (63)	25 (33%)
Fermanagh	14	8 (10)	5 (35%)	22 (25)	8 (57%)
Tyrone	41	21 (24)	14 (34%)	46 (72)	25 (61%)

9 Resolutions of the Lower Iveagh Cavalry, 16 Apr. 1797, P.R.O.N.I. T714.

Comparing the location of Volunteer and yeomanry corps, the immediate impression is of considerable structural differences between each force. This can be partially explained by the differing nature of each. As unpaid, independent units, the Volunteers tended to proliferate, being unlimited by finance or military strategy. Moreover, as the early 1780s were characterised by domestic calm and political excitement, Volunteer corps often tended to be more ephemeral than yeomanry corps, springing up or amalgamating in response to their role as a political pressure group. Also, from what evidence we can glean, the average size of Volunteer corps was smaller than yeomanry corps. MacNevin's figure of 225 Ulster corps totalling 32,217 supporting the 1782 Dungannon resolutions, gives an average of 143 per corps. However, as his national total was around 100,000, such inflated figures obviously originate in Volunteer propaganda. A more realistic assessment is revealed by Paterson's Antrim list. Compared with yeomanry figures for 1803, this shows both the overall numbers and average size of Volunteer corps significantly smaller than yeomanry corps. Paterson's list shows 54 Volunteer corps totalling 3,359 (average 62) as opposed to 4,674 yeomen in 55 corps (average 85).[10]

The immediately striking feature revealed by both maps and table is the distinct difference between Down and Antrim on the one hand, and central and western Ulster on the other. The further west one goes from the hub of the northern United Irishmen in Belfast, east Down and Antrim, the higher the Volunteer-yeomanry correlation becomes. Moreover, though from both locational and leadership aspects there is evidence of Volunteer-yeomanry linkages in each county surveyed, the degree of continuity was *initially* less in Antrim and Down and never reached the same levels as elsewhere, despite the establishment of many new corps in 1798 and in 1803, which provided a degree of belated continuity. The Down map (fig. 3) shows these new corps in the eastern part of the county, in places like Bangor, Holywood, Donaghadee and Greyabbey, Killinchy and Killyleagh. What factors influenced this tardy and incomplete linkage. Was it the presence of the United Irishmen? Volunteer-yeomanry continuity was strong in Tyrone but, as recent work has shown, the United Irishmen had spread into that county *before* the formation of the yeomanry. It seems then the existence of United Irishmen was not the critical factor. The answer seems to depend upon a coincidence of factors and pre-existing conditions being present within a specific time frame. Individually Down and Antrim each had more Volunteer locations than Fermanagh and Tyrone combined, yet the latter had far higher Volunteer-yeomanry continuity rates. The conditions for poor Volunteer-yeomanry continuity must therefore lie in the factors which made these counties distinctive from the others. These factors are the coincidence of large numbers of Presbyterians, many of whom were liberal in outlook, with heavy

10 T.G.F. Paterson, 'The Volunteer companies of Ulster, 1778–93, *I.S.*, vii (1965–66), pp. 90–116; T. MacNevin, *The History of the Volunteers of 1782* (Dublin, 1846). Parl. Papers, HC [10] 1803–4, A return presented ... of all volunteer and yeomanry corps, xi, pp. 65–100

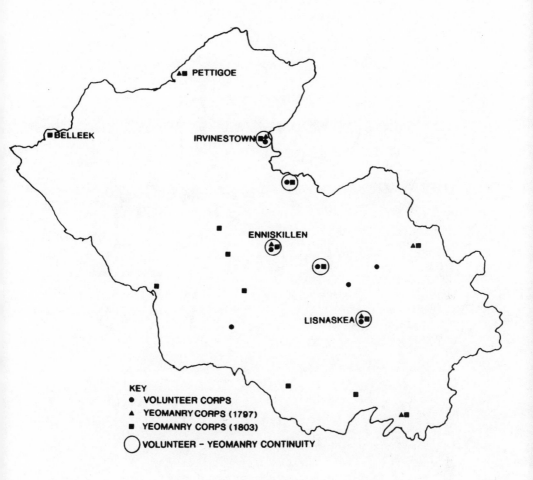

Volunteer and Yeomanry corps in county Fermanagh

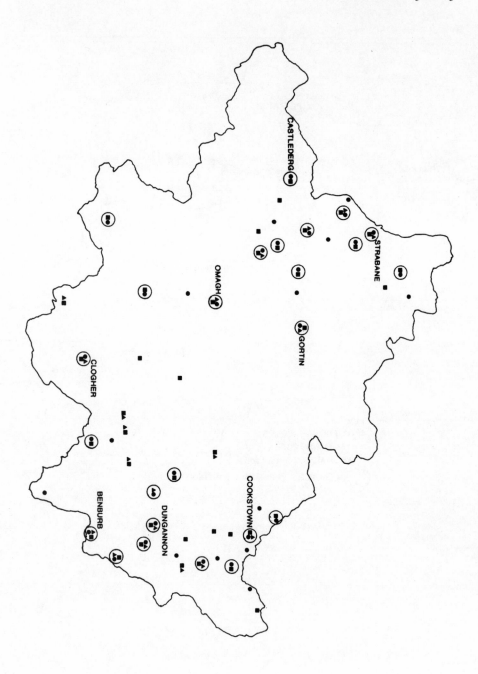

Volunteer and Yeomanry corps in county Tyrone

Volunteer and Yeomanry corps in county Armagh

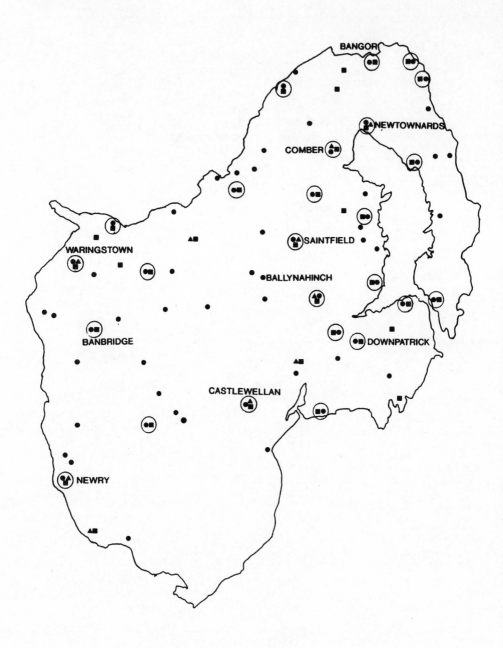

Volunteer and Yeomanry corps in county Down

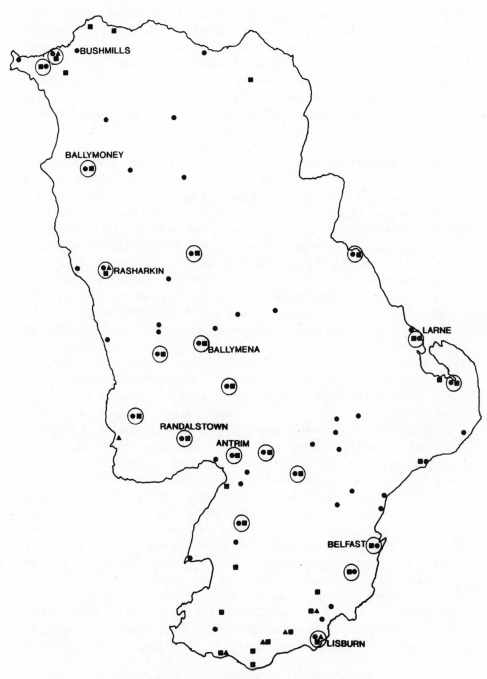

Volunteer and Yeomanry corps in county Antrim

participation in the Volunteer movement in the 1780s and the continuance or resurrection of volunteering up to 1793 and the absence of formalised sectarian tensions. Assuming the pre-existence of these factors, the critical ingredient was the *early* establishment of United Irish clubs, before the Volunteers were suppressed and while the United Irish movement's political aims would have been readily assimilated with the liberal views of the Presbyterians, previously catered for by the Volunteers. In other words, where conditions were favourable, the United Irishmen had first call on the old Volunteers before there was any need to organise a loyal alternative or to formulate alternative propaganda.

Statistics gleaned from military lists therefore provide a useful function in sketching in the outlines of the problem. By establishing patterns, they enable the right questions to be asked. Thus armed, it is time to turn back to the documentary sources, in particular those detailing the United Irish response to the raising of yeomanry in late 1796 and early 1797. This response, which was largely focused on ex-Volunteers, reveals different approaches, distinguished by timing and local conditions, which can be compared with the locational continuity analysis. Initially, in September and October when the yeomanry was being canvassed and organised, the United Irishmen made general appeals to persuade old Volunteers not to enlist. A propaganda onslaught was launched, which alternated between trying to embarrass the old Volunteers by evoking their proud past and misrepresenting the yeomanry as unconstitutional. The *Northern Star* recalled the time 'No standing army was necessary to defend Ireland ... but alas! Volunteers! ... you were PUT DOWN ... because you were attached to the freedom of your country' and pointed out that Downshire, who was enlisting yeomanry, had been involved with raising militia in 1793. In October, the *Star* accused Nicholas Price of Saintfield, a delegate to the Volunteers' Dungannon convention in 1782, of hypocrisy by raising yeomen 'to support the measures of an obnoxious administration'.[11] However by late 1796, when the yeomanry had become a reality, tactics varied: direct physical intimidation was used in particular areas while in other districts the 'hearts and minds' approach continued. The leader of prospective yeomen in the north Antrim barony of Dunluce, an area of significant Anglican settlement which had also produced a Volunteer unit, considered that the corps could not be embodied unless troops were sent, 'otherwise those poor fellows will be murdered'. This was no idle threat. One of Lord Londonderry's Newtownards yeomen was indeed murdered early in 1797.[12] There is no evidence of intimidation in Fermanagh, where United Irish penetration only began in 1797. However in Tyrone, as though fulfilling his own dire prophesies, Thomas Knox reported the yeomen complained that they were '*marked* men'. At Killymoon, near Cookstown, some of James Stewart's old Volunteers, who were attempting to form as a yeomanry corps, had their cottages burnt and their animals maimed. At

11 *N.S.*, 2–5 Sept., 24–8 Oct. 1796.   12 McNaughton to [?] Cooke, 26 Oct. 1796, N.A. R.P.620/25/191; Londonderry to Camden, 28 Feb. 1797, 620/29/3; Curtin, *The United Irishmen*, pp. 68–9.

nearby Stewartstown, those who had refused to join the United Irishmen and chosen to enlist as yeomen were themselves 'cut and maimed'.[13]

However, in parallel with this intimidation campaign, in certain areas the United Irishmen still tried to persuade ex-Volunteers not to become yeomen. In the counties under consideration, this seems confined to Armagh, particularly the city and its hinterland, and Belfast. While Charlemont and his son attended parliament in late October 1796, handbills were distributed to those he had earlier canvassed as prospective yeomen. These amalgamated Volunteer and Presbyterian grievances, predicting that the embodiment of yeomanry would frustrate parliamentary reform and the abolition of tithe. As though in testimony to Charlemont's significance in the Ulster yeomanry, when the earl came north to raise yeomen early in November, he met a concerted and more sophisticated propaganda campaign. Handbills addressed 'To the earl of Charlemont' and 'To the Yeomanry' were scattered on the streets, evoking memories of 1782 by representing the new force as unconstitutional, and claiming that the yeomanry oath simultaneously bound people to support arbitrary measures such as the Insurrection Act and the suspension of Habeas Corpus which, they claimed was the basis of the constitution. All this was taken seriously enough to provoke a counter-campaign by government supporters, who poured scorn on these claims and for their own part also appealed to volunteering sentiment: 'let the people reflect, that it is the *arming of themselves*, that is endeavoured to be prevented by this wicked publication'. At a meeting to raise yeomanry in Belfast in January 1797, the same constitutional argument appeared. Again, the objections focused on the yeomanry oath, as a shibboleth of support for the existing laws. However the meeting resolved not to form as yeomen at all but as Volunteers 'whose memory we revere and whose example we wish to imitate'.[14] There was good reason for the United Irishmen to hope ex-Volunteers in these areas could be won over. When Belfast Presbyterians refused to sign a petition of loyalty, Charlemont lamented lyrically, 'there was a time when my opinion might have some little weight at Belfast, but, alas, those halcyon days are fled'. Meanwhile in Armagh, there was a 'considerable degree of cold thrown on the yeomanry corps' and Charlemont 'deserted by the old people he thought he could depend on'.[15] In the political ferment of the mid-1790s, a crucial feature was the scramble for new allegiances. Bartlett describes the competition between government and radicals for Catholic support as the race for the Catholic, whereas Kevin Whelan points to the competition between conservatives and radicals for Presbyterian support in Armagh in 1795-6.[16] The raising of yeomanry in Armagh is clearly a development in that contest.

13 Knox to Camden, 27 Nov. 1796, N.A. R.P.620/26/83; Newton to O'Connor, 7 Nov. 1796, 620/26/26; Printed Proclamation, 6 Nov. 1796, P.R.O. H.O.100/65/f. 109.   14 Close to Toler, 26 Oct. 1796, N.A. R.P.620/25/190; Handbills, 8-9 Nov. 1796, 620/26/32; Skeffington to Cooke, n.d. Jan. 1797, 620/28/141.   15 Charlemont to Haliday, 12 Sept. 1796, H.M.C. *Charlemont*, ii, pp. 283–4; N. Alexander to H. Alexander, 8 Nov. 1796, N.A. R.P.620/26/32.   16 Bartlett, *Fall and Rise*, passim; Whelan, *The Tree of Liberty*, p. 117.

TO THE
YEOMANRY

As Yeomen have become the Topic of general Converfation, and Doubts having arifen that no Man who is a Friend to his Country, can take the Oath—I think it my Duty fo far to explain it as relates to the fupporting the Laws, many of which, at prefent, form no Part of the Conftitution.—As a Specimen, the following are a Part of what you are called upon to fupport and maintain, viz. a Convention Bill, a Gun-Powder Bill, an Infurrection Bill, and laft of all, the Sufpenfion of the Habeas Corpus Act, which was the Bafis of our Conftituti-on; but now, being repealed, leaves every Perfon at the Mercy of ANY MAN IN POWER to imprifon them during Pleafure, without being in any Way refponfible for fuch ARBITRARY Conduct :—Thefe are the Laws you are called upon to fwear to fupport and maintain ; and to prevent which being carried into Execution, OUR Anceftors fhed their beft Blood, and did not efteem it too dear a Sacrifice for that INESTIMABLE BLESSING—

LIBERTY.

United Irish handbill found in Armagh

When Charlemont came to Armagh in November to enlist his yeomen, the Reverend Richardson noted how 'schisms and feuds' had broken out between 'the old Royalists and the Republican Reformists now disposed to loyalty' among whom were Charlemont's old Volunteers. The 'Royalists', obviously Anglicans, had already associated under the city sovereign, Macan, who was also the Primate's agent and, much to Charlemont's chagrin, refused to serve with 'the very men who three years ago erected the Tree of Liberty in Armagh street, and who since Lord Charlemont came to Armagh, debated an hour whether they should take the Oath of Allegiance or not.'[17] Meanwhile in Belfast, many old Volunteers felt themselves in an intolerable position as the worsening political and security climate threatened to make loyalty and liberalism incompatible. Liberal Presbyterians felt themselves in a cleft stick and tried to keep their options open. Martha McTier told Drennan: 'These, indeed are trying times, and the right path becomes complex' and 'it is all half work here, just enough to damn either side; about a hundred have agreed to arm, many of them old Vol[unteers]'.[18]

In both instances, the yeomanry won the race for the Volunteer. Whelan notes that competing appeals to Armagh Presbyterians were made either by playing upon their radicalism or mediated through the newly-formed Orange Order. However, in the key case of the Armagh city yeomanry, this was not the situation. Richardson suggested splitting the parties into separate corps and the January 1797 yeomanry shows two corps, one under Macan and the other under Johnston, Charlemont's

17 Richardson to Wolfe, 26 Sept. 1796, N.A. R.P.620/25/118.   18 McTeir to Drennan, 13, 30 Jan. 1797, D.A. Chart (ed.), *The Drennan Letters*, pp. 247-9.

old volunteering lieutenant. The point here is not that Charlemont's Volunteers changed from being patriots to persecutors. In this symbolically significant instance, the race for the Volunteer, and perhaps for the Presbyterians as a whole, was won because traditional Presbyterian libertarianism was accommodated by flexibility in the yeomanry structure. This was underlined in 1798 when the government allowed Charlemont to make an exception for them and uphold the voluntary principle, enabling them to do permanent duty without putting themselves under the Mutiny Act.[19] In Belfast yeomanry corps were eventually, if belatedly formed. Compromise was in the air. William Drennan's friend, the liberal Presbyterian minister and ex-Volunteer, Dr Bruce, signed in support of yeomanry with the proviso he would only act when it became necessary. In Belfast and Armagh, yeomanry proved the better option, by being flexible enough in its implementation to absorb wavering radicals. Its very existence provided the comfort of an alternative 'side' to join if it came to choosing the lesser evil. Bruce, who had once preached with his Volunteer musket alongside the pulpit, was to be found guarding the Long Bridge with his yeomanry musket during the Down insurrection.[20]

The examples of Armagh and Belfast seem to mark boundaries between the two general tendencies in the locational continuity analysis. However they do not explain *why* ex-Volunteers were courted for there at the same time as they were being intimidated elsewhere. Obviously the existence of radicalism or at least liberalism among the old Volunteers in both places was a prerequisite, but the answer must lie beyond. In Down and Antrim, the Volunteer–United Irish connection, facilitated by the depth of Presbyterian radicalism, was already sufficiently in place by late 1796 to allow coercion *against* rather than competition *for* those who threatened to break the 'union' by becoming yeomen. In Fermanagh, United Irish organisation was ineffectual but in Tyrone, the United men had a 'significant presence' by October 1796.[21] As is shown by reports of intimidation of yeomen, this presence came from the Defender link. An Anglican clergyman, the Reverend Andrew Newton, noted with perverse satisfaction, that the attacks on James Stewart's Killymoon yeomen would open Stewart's eyes about emancipation. The Presbyterian ex-Volunteers who had earlier offered as yeoman to James Buchanan in Omagh evinced resistance to 'French and Belfast principles' and Catholic membership as a 'spirit of Defenderism and revenge exists in that body'.[22]

So, allowing for the contests in Armagh and Belfast, which in any case resolved in favour of government, the pattern of higher Volunteer-yeomanry continuity the further west we look from Antrim and Down appears to correlate with the findings from documentary evidence. Although much more detailed local work is needed,

19 Camden to Charlemont, 3 April 1798, Charlemont to Camden, 4 April 1798, Charlemont to Johnston n.d. April 1798, H.M.C. *Charlemont*, ii, pp. 318–19.   20 A.T.Q. Stewart, *The Summer Soldiers*, p. 212. 21 Curtin, *The United Irishmen*, pp. 69–70.   22 Newton to O'Connor, 7 Nov. 1796, N.A. R.P.620/26/ 26; Buchanan to Cooke, 19 Sept. 1796, 620/25/133.

the general pattern emerging seems to be that where the United Irish movement was strong, in Antrim and Down, because sufficient old Volunteers were enlisted prior to the formation of yeomanry they could coerce any who considered becoming yeomen. This was compounded, from the perspective of government, by the balance of trust being against having yeomen with volunteering connections in these areas. The heavy concentration of yeomanry on the Hertford estate had, with the exception of Lisburn, no volunteering precedent. Secondly, where the Defender alliance was substantive enough to produce depth of numbers, as in Tyrone, the Volunteers themselves were unlikely to become United Irishmen. Arguably then, outside eastern Antrim and Down, as the United Irishmen gained Defenders they lost Volunteers.

Can we say then that this confirms the findings of O'Snodaigh and Bartlett, that, with the exceptions noted and allowing for accidental structural dissimilarities and time-lapse, the yeomanry was largely built on the pre-existing template of the Volunteers and came from the same tradition and constituency? The circumstantial evidence shows strong continuity. In a number of instances the cross-over between the two forces was so close the old Volunteers insisted on keeping their title. The Dublin Independent Volunteer Association of 1780 offered their services as yeomen. They were not permitted to use their old title but were allowed to join extant yeomanry corps.[23] In urban corps there was strong continuity amongst professional groupings. In Dublin the same professional groupings of lawyers, barristers, revenue officials and merchants run through both Volunteers and yeomanry. In Belfast and Newry there were merchants' corps in both forces. There was considerable membership continuity in the Newry merchants.[24] Clearly in such instances professional *esprit de corps* and associating to defend vested interests was a greater motivational factor to join either force than the 'official' reasons for its existence. Professional groupings formed yeomanry corps in their own image, as they had done in the Volunteers, rather than conforming to any governmental template. De Latocnaye, the French émigré traveller, was in Dublin when yeomanry were forming and commented on this professional exclusiveness, noting that the yeomen were 'all commanded by principle men of their own calling'. He compared Dublin with Edinburgh, where all professional and occupational groups joined one large corps.[25] He also noted another form of continuity, in a common witticism, that the Lawyer's Cavalry needed no training as they already knew very well how to charge!

A 'democratic' ethos, strongly reminiscent of the Volunteers is also seen in many yeomanry corps, particularly with respect to the selection of officers. So insistent were the Dublin corps on this point, that the government gave way on its preferred option, that recommendations should come from the captains. This phenomenon was not confined to urban or professional corps. In Tyrone James Stewart's

23 Smyth to Cooke, 2 Jan. 1797, N.A. R.P.620/28/9.   24 D. Crossle, 'The Volunteers and Yeomanry of Newry', *Newry Telegraph*, 3–5 Apr. 1904.   25 Cited in *Irish Sword*, vii (1965–6), pp. 340–1.

Cookstown yeomen insisted on the right both to elect their officers and serve without pay, as they had in the Volunteers. Obviously such *ad hoc* departures from the norm were made to accommodate a recognisable volunteering 'sentiment' which could be classified as politically independent of government, liberal in outlook and ideologically libertarian in the Lockeian sense of the armed citizen's right to be free to defend his country. Leonard McNally, the informer, reported that when the Catholic Committee canvassed opinion in the Dublin yeomanry a great majority appeared in favour of parliamentary reform. Even Henry Joy McCracken, when in Kilmainham gaol, thought Dublin yeomen far more liberal than their Belfast counterparts.[26] Government's willingness to accommodate liberals in the yeomanry can also be seen in those who led it. The examples of Charlemont and Leinster have already been mentioned. Other men with a strongly independent volunteering background were permitted to raise corps. Thomas Douglas of Gracehall, county Down, had pointedly refused a deputy governorship in 1793 as the position was created to raise militia.[27] An independent and doctrinaire ex-Volunteer, he saw the creation of militia as an arbitrary, coercive move out of keeping with the independent, voluntary spirit of 1782. Yet Douglas was to raise and command yeomanry. John Edwards of Bray is another excellent example of how Volunteer ideology continued into the yeomanry. Edwards was a liberal Protestant who had served in the Volunteers. As a magistrate and yeomanry captain he abhorred the martial law policy of 1798 and threatened to use his corps to arrest any regulars who burned houses.[28] Grattan's stance on the yeomanry was equivocal, because the measure had been associated with Fitzwilliam's emancipation plans. However, so strong was the input of 'Grattan's Volunteers' that he was forced to distinguish between those yeomen who 'adopted the true original principles of the Volunteer association', who paid for themselves and elected their officers and 'An Ascendancy army ... a Revenue army or Church Militants'.[29]

The final words on the linkage must rest with the United Irish writer Charles Teeling. Even in 1828, Teeling's anger is still tangible as he dubs lapsed radical ex-Volunteers who joined the yeomanry as 'double traitors', to their 1782 tradition and to the United Irishmen.[30] However, in reality the Volunteer movement did not fit Teeling's deliberately reductionist analysis. Volunteer cannon may have been used against the troops and yeomanry at the Battle of Antrim but Volunteer muskets were also used against the Defenders at the Battle of the Diamond by those shortly to become yeomen. Moreover, as we have seen, it was not simply a case of there being polarities in volunteering between Francophile radicalism and Williamite conservatism; between these extremes there was a fluidity of opinion responsive to circumstances which was beginning to find an anchor in the yeomanry. This raises various

26 H.J. McCracken to M.A. McCracken, 15 Mar. 1797, T.C.D. McCracken Papers, MS 873; 'J.W.' to Cooke, 25 Feb. 1797, N.A. R.P.620/36/227. 27 Douglas to Downshire, 23 Apr. 1793, P.R.O.N.I. Downshire Papers, D607/B/411. 28 Edwards to Cooke, 16 Apr. 1798, N.A. R.P.620/36/176. 29 *B.N.L.*, 17–21 Oct. 1796. 30 C.H. Teeling, *Personal Narrative of the Irish Rebellion of 1798*, pp. 207–8.

questions. Does this acceptance of volunteering as a broad church and the critical influence in the early yeomanry undermine the traditional view of the primacy of Orangeism in the force, and what precisely was the Orange connection?

ORANGEISM AND THE YEOMANRY

Despite the subsequent reputation of the 'Orange yeomanry', the initial Orange role in the yeomanry was a very limited one. In mid-1796, Orangeism was geographically limited to parts of mid-Ulster and its adherents numbered only several thousand.[31] By February 1797, Richardson described the Orange country as radiating eastwards from Dungannon, through Armagh and well into Down and recalled:

> When the yeomanry business was agitating ... [Orangemen] held meetings quietly and signified their readiness to join ... when it was so far advanced that it was certain government would adopt it, they held pretty general meetings, whence they signified ... they would meet no more as a party ... the best of them are in the yeomen.[32]

However, compared with the first yeomanry levy, the limited Orange role becomes clear. In early 1797, when Richardson wrote, the yeomanry stood at 30,000 men, drawn from every Irish county.[33] Even in the 'Orange' districts there was uneven cross-over between the two organisations. As we have seen, Orangemen comprised the bulk of the proletarian membership of the loyal associations in places like Dungannon and Lisburn, and on the estates of Verner, Blacker and others. However, the existence of a proto-yeomanry loyal association did not necessarily imply Orange yeomen. In west Down, Captain Waddell disbanded Maralin Orange Lodge, released the members from their oath, and replaced it with a Dungannon-type association which he subsequently offered to local Catholics.[34] The extent of the initial linkage was no more than the fact that when some of the loyal associations had their offers of service accepted, the gentlemen or clerical magistrates who organised them as yeomanry made their selections from the local lodge. However this was a localised connection rather than official acceptance. These loyal associations were swept into the yeomanry by dint of a policy decision which had nothing to do with Orangeism and involved deliberately targeting the entire traditional Protestant 'garrison' as ex-Volunteers, rather than the relatively small section who had joined the new Orange societies in mid-Ulster. There simply was no policy to connect with the Orangemen at this stage. When, Verner, for example assured Camden that his

---

31 Senior, *Orangeism*, p. 51.   32 Richardson to Abercorn, 22 Feb. 1797, P.R.O.N.I. Abercorn Papers, D623/A/156/5.   33 Memo on the defence of Ireland, n.d. [Feb. 1797], P.R.O. W.O.30/66/ f. 28.   34 Waddell to [Cooke], 29 July 1796, N.A. R.P.620/24/173.

yeomen were trustworthy, it was all the government needed or wanted to know. The immediate contemporary significance was more in the propaganda it gave the United Irishmen. 'Hibernicus' in the *Northern Star* satirised the Dungannon Association's resolutions: 'Who now are they who have endeavoured to excite discontents among his majesty's faithful subjects? Are they not *Orange-men*? Those "traitors and banditti" ... associated for the diabolical purpose of exterminating their Catholic countrymen'.[35]

Meaningful Orange linkages only developed when the yeomanry was well established in mid-1797 and became progressively closer and more overt as time went on. This process happened in distinct stages related to military policy. General John Knox decided to support the Orangemen in central Ulster as a fail-safe against the United Irishmen. He told Abercorn, 'the only people to take our parts are the Orangemen. They are inclined to be licentious, and it requires much difficulty to keep them within bounds. I have found it necessary to encourage that party'.[36] This was a similar line to that taken by his brother Thomas with the Dungannon Association. However, the crucial difference was that yeomanry were now established, and Knox had government's discretion to augment as he thought strategically expedient. From around March 1797, General Knox began a interrelated series of local measures which were to result in a strengthening of the Orange-yeomanry connection. Knox's intention appears to have been to keep up the distinction between Orange 'wreckers' and Orangemen who would assist the magistrates, which had been promoted in 1796 by his brother and others like Verner, Blacker and the Warings of Waringsford, while at the same time playing a risky game of utilising the Orange 'spirit'. The first indications came in March, when he overtly used yeoman in disarming operations with instructions to ignore unregistered Orange guns, to keep up the animosity between them and the United Irishmen, a strategically desirable situation which was under threat due to the growing power and local dominance of the latter. He also took it upon himself to encourage local landowners to form fencible regiments, which would be composed of Orangemen in areas where they predominated. The overall intention was to find an alternative to the southern militia regiments who served in the north and which were mainly Catholic in their rank and file and strongly suspected of harbouring United Irish and Defender sympathies.[37] In May, having engineered acceptable Orange resolutions about assisting the magistrates and secured Pelham's approval he began, again with Pelham's blessing, to administer a 'test' oath to purge yeomanry corps of those who had infiltrated as United Irishmen or been forced to neutralise themselves as yeomen by taking the United 'oath of secrecy' as protection from the local dominance of their erstwhile adversaries.[38] At the same time as the acceptance of the Orange resolutions, Knox secured official

35 *N.S.*, 1–5 Aug. 1796.   36 11 May 1797, P.R.O.N.I. Abercorn Papers, D623/A/156/4.   37 Knox to Abercorn, 12 Mar. 1797, P.R.O.N.I. Abercorn Papers, D623/A/156/9.   38 Senior, *Orangeism*, p. 69; Knox to Pelham, 22 May 1797, B.L. Pelham Papers, add. mss., 33104 ff. 101–2.

approval to augment yeomanry corps with Orangemen. The entire process had a strategic purpose. The Orange districts of mid-Ulster along with the natural east-west divide of Lough Neagh and the Lower Bann formed a natural barrier between the United Irish heartland and the west of the province. Although the United Irish-men had been spreading west, by encouraging Orangeism as a physical and geo-graphical block, Knox could prevent co-ordinated action and make province-wide co-operation difficult. James Verner's Churchill Infantry, already tacitly Orange, were allowed to attach Orange supplementaries while Joseph Atkinson of Crowhill, county Armagh, was allowed a new corps entirely composed of local Orangemen. This connection had been 'advertised' in April at a yeomanry review in Lord Northland's park near Dungannon, at which General Lake predicted 'we will have plenty of orange ribbons'.[39] Government were not so well prepared and, realising the political dangers, Knox overcame Pelham's reluctance with assurances that the Castle's hands would be clean: 'I do not by any means wish the government should give them [the Orangemen] an avowed protection, as it might do mischief in the south, but that protection may be given silently by permission to enrol themselves in the district corps [yeomanry].[40] From Knox's point of view, encouragement of Orangeism in the yeomanry served not only as a boost to a previously faltering loyalism but also as a means of control. Less than a week after getting permission for the Crowhill corps, Knox was in correspondence with Atkinson regarding an indi-vidual whom he had information against as having drilled United Irishmen. 'If he does not clear up his conduct to his [Orange] lodge', Knox intended to have him arrested.[41] This encouragement of Orangeism, of which enrolment in the yeomanry was a main plank, was a risky expedient and was shot through with contradictions. On the one hand, Knox wanted to use and indeed fire up the Orange 'spirit', yet, at the same time, he tried to make a distinction between those Orangemen who would assist in keeping the law in the yeomanry and those who could potentially break it. Richardson successfully sold the policy to Abercorn on precisely that basis.[42] After the fencible proposals were scuppered by the duke of York, Knox commented on a belated and overt proposal for 'Orange Fencibles' by Alexander Bissett, an Armagh clergyman, that it would be of use by drawing 'that class of men' away from Armagh for service elsewhere.[43] The actions of Orange yeomen in the arms searches that summer was to prove the difficulty of the balance Knox was trying to keep. Indeed, the fact that he was trying to get Orangemen into the yeomanry shows that the structural incompatibly of the two organisations was a barrier to a more extended cross-over at this time. Even with augmentations, yeomanry by their nature were

39 Lake to Gen. Knox, 19 April 1797, N.L.I. Lake Papers, MS56/f. 53.   40 Pelham to Knox, 26 May 1797, Knox to Pelham, 28 May 1797, N.L.I. Lake Papers, MS56/ff. 123–4, 139–40.   41 Knox to Atkinson, P.R.O.N.I. Atkinson of Crowhill Papers, T2701/2/3.   42 Abercorn to Richardson, 17 Mar. 1797, P.R.O.N.I. Abercorn Papers, D623/A/80/41.   43 Knox to Pelham, 16 Mar. 1797, N.A. R.P.620/29/79; Knox to Pelham, 16 June 1797, B.L. Pelham Papers add. mss. 33104 ff. 236

small scattered units not well placed to absorb an organisation with local depth of numbers. Viewed strategically, this was a problem, and, as we shall see, it remained the situation until 1798. The 1797 July celebrations saw Generals Lake and Knox review 15,000 Orangemen, including some yeomen, at Lisburn and Lurgan.[44] Aside from the psychological and propaganda value of Knox's Orange augmentations, their real importance in the linkage process was the precedent they set.

The first really major Orange linkage came in the spring of 1798. Again it was a child of necessity. Between late 1797 and early 1798 Orangeism expanded rapidly in Ulster. By March 1798, Camden reckoned the Ulster Orangemen at 40,000.[45] As the Ulster yeomanry remained below 20,000 until 1799,[46] it neither fully tapped the available Orange manpower nor offered loyalists maximum protection. With insurrection now a question of 'when' rather than 'if', contingency plans were made, in association with the Grand Lodge, lately moved to Dublin, to utilise thousands of Orangemen as an armed civilian back-up to the yeomanry. Official nervousness remained about the Orange offer. Abercromby, the new commander-in-chief, advocated only arming them 'in case of emergency'.[47] Yet internal defence had to be improved. This task fell to Castlereagh, as acting chief secretary. His objectives were to improve the yeomanry's military capacity and gain access to more emergency manpower. The yeomanry were put on permanent duty under the district generals. Castlereagh then expanded on General Knox's local precedent of 1797. A circular to yeomanry captains on 16 April 1798 asked them to organise up to 50 men, 'neither clothed, paid, armed or disciplined', for emergency duty.[48] This apparently innocuous circular concealed the crucial Orange-yeomanry linkage in Ulster and Dublin.

William Elliot, the military under-secretary at the Castle, privately told John Knox:

> Though it is intended (for the purpose of precluding any jealousy or appearance of invidious distribution) to make the measure of enrolment general, yet Lord Castlereagh considers the part of the country falling under your command *particularly* within the object of the plan.[49]

Given Knox's correspondence with Pelham the previous year, this could mean only one thing: sanction at the highest level. Camden later reminded Castlereagh: 'How long is it, my dear Lord C., since we ordered an exclusive armament of supplementary yeomen in the North, and of Mr. Beresford's corps in Dublin?' (Beresford's connection controlled the Dublin Lodge.)[50] This 'understanding' raised 5,000 Or-

44 Senior, *Orangeism*, p. 77. **45** Camden to Portland, 29 Mar. 1798, P.R.O. H.O.100/75/f. 331. **46** Castlereagh to Wickham, 13 May 1799, P.R.O. H.O.100/86/f. 367. **47** Notes on the Defence of Ireland, 25 Apr. 1798, P.R.O. W.O.30/66/f. 211. **48** Lurgan Yeomanry Detail Book, P.R.O.N.I. D3696/A/4/1. **49** 16 Apr. 1798, N.L.I. Lake Papers, MS56/f. 154. **50** 4 Nov. 1798, C. Vane (ed.),

ange supplementary yeomen in Ulster. Yet it should not be taken as wholehearted official endorsement, and acceptance of the Orangemen as the allies of government against the people. By using the yeomanry system as a filter and control, government tried to compromise between the danger of arming the entire Orange body and a strategically suicidal policy of drift. Camden was never happy with this situation. During the rebellion, he agonised to Portland about the dilemma it placed him in: 'how impolitic and unwise ... to refuse the offers of Protestants to enter with the Yeomanry ... yet how dangerous [is] even any encouragement to the Orange spirit, whilst our army is composed of Catholics, as the militia generally is'.[51]

Yet even the supplementary plan failed fully to utilise Orange manpower and the offers of voluntary service continued. In May 1798, the yeomanry were grouped in brigades to overcome their military limitations as self-contained corps. They were to fall back from rural areas to garrison the towns and join the military on the outbreak of hostilities.[52] With the country under martial law, local generals had discretion to utilise all civilian support they could get. When the northern rising started, Orangemen unconnected with the yeomanry and other non-aligned loyalists crammed into the defensible towns. The Downpatrick garrison consisted of 100 York Fencibles, 30 regular dragoons, five outlying yeomanry corps 'with all the Orangemen that can be collected in the area'.[53] In Belfast, 'no people except military and Orangemen *now employed*' were to be seen.[54] Orangeism spread like wildfire in the tense atmosphere of crowded barracks. Edward Hudson told Charlemont of this process at Jonesborough where Orange yeomen from Armagh were quartered with 'Your old Ballymascanlon Volunteers, who six months ago were almost all United Irishmen, are now complete Orangemen'.[55]

This process was quickened as divisional generals used their discretion to arm some lodges openly. The initial shipment north of 5,000 muskets for the 'well affected' only covered the supplementaries.[56] General Nugent distributed confiscated United Irish guns to Downpatrick Orangemen until further supplies arrived. Yet a residual reluctance remained: Nugent opposed a general armament of the Orangemen generally until 'the last extremity' as, once started, it must be total.[57] The Battles of Antrim and Ballynahinch pre-empted Armageddon and the arming fell short of what the Orange leadership wanted. It was reported 'the Orangemen call aloud for arms and to be let loose'.[58] This problem of safely utilising northern Orangemen was never fully resolved. Castlereagh suggested a scheme to Nugent, akin to Knox's

Castlereagh: Correspondence, i, pp. 424–6.   51 11 June 1798, P.R.O. H.O.100/77/f. 132.   52 N.A.M. 6807–174/ff. 433–4, Nugent Papers, Plans for yeomanry division, 22 May 1798; Cavan to Lake, 9 June 1798, P.R.O. H.O.100/77/f. 139; Nugent to Lake, 10 June 1798, N.A. R.P.620/38/121.   53 Nugent to Lake, 10 June 1798, N.A. R.P.620/38/121.   54 Goldie to Lake, 13 June 1798, N.A. R.P.620/38/185.   55 19 May 1798, H.M.C. *Charlemont*, ii, pp. 322–3.   56 Lake to General Knox, 30 May 1798, N.L.I. Lake Papers, MS56/f. 168; N.A.M. 6807–174/ff. 457–8, Nugent Papers, Castlereagh to Nugent, 6 June 1798.   57 Nugent to Hewitt, 4 Sept. 1798, *Castlereagh Correspondence*, i, pp. 332–4.   58 Shannon to Boyle, 9 June 1798, P.R.O.N.I. Shannon Papers, D2707/A3/3/80.

fencible proposal, whereby they could be arranged in bodies of six to seven hundred under gentry commanders for service during the rebellion. A shipment of 7,500 muskets belatedly reached Belfast but the plan was aborted by the new viceroy and commander-in-chief, Cornwallis, who despised irregulars.[59] However, the links were forged. In the hour of danger, the yeomanry and Orange Order were brought into physical, emotional and ideological juxtaposition. The previous limited overlapping became a flood of cross-fertilisation. The term 'Orange Yeomanry', once a United Irish propaganda cliché and something of which the government 'feared to speak', now permeated official correspondence. Reassuring Wickham about the north in June 1798, Edward Cooke confidently claimed: 'the force of Orange Yeomanry is really formidable'.[60]

The Volunteer linkage, outside Antrim and Down, tells us much about where the yeomanry was coming from, but it was the Orange connection which largely dictated the direction in which the force was going. This said, traces of Volunteer independence, and proto-democratic tendencies survived within the yeomanry. These tend to be obscured. Election of officers, or office-bearers was as much a feature of the Orange lodge as it was of the Volunteer corps. The opponents of Union made the argument that, as the Volunteers had secured the 'independence' of the Irish parliament would their direct descendants, the yeomanry, support its dissolution. Perhaps the best way of looking at these influences on the yeomanry is to see it as the place where the two strands of the Williamite tradition met. The independent, anti-autocracy of 1688 and the anti-Catholicism of 1690 combined at a time when Protestants perceived their position as being under physical and political threat. The mixture in the old bottle of the Volunteers soon became the new wine of Orangeism. The effects of this potent brew will be assessed in the chapter on Protestantism. Having established the yeomanry's various connections and its place in the Protestant defence tradition we must now look at the yeomanry force itself.

59 N.A.M. 6807–174/ff. 459–62, 473–5, Nugent Papers, 10, 21 June 1798. **60** 2 June 1798, P.R.O. H.O.100/77/f.21.

5

Profile of the Irish Yeomanry

The appearance of soldiers was not an uncommon sight to anyone living in Ireland, or Britain for that matter, during the last decades of the eighteenth century. The first yeomanry corps in 1796 would not therefore have presented an unfamiliar spectacle. Mainly cavalry and infantry, there were also a very small number of artillery corps in towns or at strategic points. The Dublin Lawyers' corps had an artillery section and, in 1805, the Loyal Loughlinstown Yeomanry Gunners manned the new defensive works at Loughlinstown army camp twelve miles south-east of Dublin.[1] Such corps were never encouraged by the government. Although never overtly stated, the authorities, remembering Volunteer theatricals in College Green, clearly had no wish for an encore. There were a few oddities, such as the Glancree Yeomanry Pioneer corps, who helped build Wicklow's military road and Richard Lowell Edgeworth's yeomanry 'Telegraphic' corps, who guarded his inland communication system between Galway and Kilmainham.[2] Infantry corps averaged around 100 men while cavalry corps were smaller, averaging around 50 with none below 40.[3] The basic yeomanry unit therefore approximated to regular army troop and company strength respectively. From April 1798 supplementary yeomen were attached to many corps as an unpaid un-uniformed reserve who offered to serve in an emergency or to fill vacancies in the regular corps.[4] As yeomanry numbers rose there were heavier local concentrations. Separate supplementary companies were organised, and existing regular yeomanry corps, limited to company or troop strength, spawned subsidiary companies. The Castlewellan Infantry, which started in 1796 as a single corps, had five separate companies by 1809.[5] Where three or more corps combined, these concentrations were considered as battalions while there were a few larger 'legions' at Cork, Derry city and Tyrone. The marquis of Abercorn's Tyrone Legion comprised over 1,200 men in 1803.[6]

1 Cooke to the 'Dublin Bar', n.d. Nov. 1796, N.A. R.P.620/26/94; Hardwicke to Hawkesbury, 4 May 1805, P.R.O. H.O.100/125/f. 15.   2 P.M. Kerrigan, *Castles and Fortifications in Ireland, 1485–1945*, p. 165.   3 Camden to Portland, 19 Oct. 1796, P.R.O. H.O.100/61/f. 164.   4 Circular, signed Castlereagh, 16 April 1798, Lurgan Yeomanry Detail Book, P.R.O.N.I. D3696/A/4/1.   5 Castlewellan Yeomanry Orderly Book, 1809–1820, P.R.O.N.I. Annesley Papers, D1854/8/4.   6 Abercorn to Hardwicke, 10

Yeomen enrolled for the 'protection of property and preservation of the peace' in the barony, city or town where an alarm post was stipulated in the commissions. All yeomen were to reside nearby in order to be mobilised easily.[7] The corps would decide on a defensible building as the headquarters for their duty area, often the captain's house. In Dublin the duty areas were city districts, protected by corps raised from the occupational or professional grouping whose business centred in that district. Thus in Dublin the Revenue Corps protected the area around the Customs House, the Lawyers around the Four Courts while the Bank of Ireland Yeomanry guarded College Green. However, in rural areas strategic defence did not necessarily tie in with civil divisions or, for that matter, suitable patterns of demographic settlement. Local dynamics such as the extent of the danger, the areas of landowners' influence, terrain, settlement patterns and proportions of cavalry and infantry simply would not fit centrally conceived templates. When it was accepted that infantry and mixed corps were necessary, the territorial demarcation of yeomanry corps pragmatically reflected the availability of local manpower rather than the legislation's territorial parameters.

As numbers grew, the tendency increased for duty areas to be based on smaller divisions, though still with a strategic underpinning. In 1797, on the Hertford estate near Lisburn, Derriaghy parish alone had three infantry corps. Another was just approved for Glenavy village, but it was considered that the wider parish of Glenavy was much more in need of one, as it bordered the parish of Killead, a United Irish stronghold.[8] In the Tyrone barony of Omagh West, two corps took the parish titles of Urney and Longfield. In other areas one finds purely baronial corps, usually cavalry. In Waterford, where there were fewer yeomanry, the territorial distribution of corps remains more reminiscent of the original plan, with the Middle and Upper Third baronies each having separate cavalry corps.[9] Yeomanry corps usually took their name from their duty area, though there were sometimes colourful local nicknames. These unofficial titles often vividly convey the ethos of a corps. At Mount Nebo in Wexford, Hunter Gowan's supplementaries became notorious as 'The Black Mob'. Sometimes the sobriquets were less sanguinary, though no less apposite. Michael Banim, the Kilkenny novelist, fondly remembered one antiquarian corps which paraded in the churchyard and earned immortality as the 'Tombstone Rangers'.[10]

Aug. 1803, P.R.O.N.I. Abercorn Papers, D623/A/81/65.   7 Yeomanry Plan, enclosure in Camden to Portland, 22 Sept. 1796, P.R.O. H.O.100/61/f. 112.   8 Smyth to [?] Downshire, 6 April 1797, N.A. R.P.620/29/190.   9 1797 Yeomanry List, N.L.I. Ir355 a10.   10 Quoted in the introduction to M. Banim, *The Croppy* (Dublin, 1828).

CONTROL

Although overall control of the yeomanry was centrally organised, individual corps had their own systems of internal government by elected committees which regulated discipline, membership and, to an extent, finance. The disciplinary aspect of this will be examined later. The Cookstown Cavalry committee had eight members together with a president who was to be an officer and to have a casting vote. It needed a quorum of six plus the president for decisions. Membership was rotated, with three members changed quarterly. The committee handled new admissions. A prospective yeoman needed at least a two-thirds majority. This was standard practice. The committee of the Doneraile Cavalry, in county Cork operated on exactly the same basis.[11] Yeomanry corps were expensive to establish and equip. From the government allowance of two guineas per man the corps were expected to acquire a uniform and present a military appearance. The captain and officers would engage a local tailor to produce uniforms to a standard pattern and then reimburse him when the Treasury paid the allowance, which was often later rather than sooner. Frequently the allowance was insufficient for even the least fashion-conscious corps and had to be supplemented by subscription from within the corps, or from the local magnate, or from gentlemen with adjoining estates to pay for protection.[12] This could take the form of an 'association' which balloted its subscribers for those who were to serve, with the more wealthy able to buy substitutes in lieu of personal service. Cavalry corps were particularly expensive, given the multiplicity of equipment they needed. The agent for the Shirley estate, county Monaghan, wrote to the absentee proprietor in Worcestershire: 'Our Irish yeomen not being so rich as yours, I must ... call on you for a subscription ... towards defraying such expenses as the two guineas per man will not effect. The exceedings cannot amount to less than £400 ... our subscriptions ... not more than £100'. When the yeomen themselves could contribute the cost was heavy. The Devlin and Farhill Cavalry, county Westmeath, had to lay out 13 guineas per man. If prospective yeomen had not their own horses the cost soared further. Downshire paid 150 guineas for three substitutes in the Cooleystown and Warrenstown Cavalry on his King's county property, including 40 guineas for 'a pair of blacks.'[13] The Cooleystown and Warrenstown yeomen served without pay but enrolled some dismounted men unable to serve gratis who were paid from the stock purse. James Stewart's Cookstown Cavalry, as ex-Volunteers, deliberately shunned official allowances, preferring to equip themselves at their own expense.[14]

11 Resolutions of the Cookstown company, 14 Nov. 1796, P.R.O.N.I. Stewart of Killymoon Papers, D3167/2/127; J. Groves White, *The Yeomanry of Ireland*, p. 28. 12 J. Groves White, ibid., p. 24; Galbraith to Abercorn, 11 Nov. 1796, P.R.O.N.I. Abercorn Papers, D623/A/108/6. 13 Steele to Shirley, 1 July 1797, P.R.O.N.I. Shirley Papers, D3531/A/92; Smyth to Downshire, 12 Jan. 1797, P.R.O.N.I. Downshire Papers, D607/A/522B; Everard to Downshire, 17 Oct. 1796, 3 Dec. 1796, D607/A/514,520; Hatch to Downshire, 12 Jan. 1797, D607/A/523. 14 Association of subscribers, n.d. [post 22 Oct.

Ultimate formal control of the yeomanry rested with the lord lieutenant, who had the power of issuing commissions in the King's name. This was markedly different from the situation in contemporary Britain, where the county lieutenancies issued commissions. Given the volunteering precedent and the fact that many ex-Volunteers became yeomen, the government continued to exercise tight control. In March 1797 Camden extended his powers to include dismissal of officers, against the opinion of the attorney general.[15] When the yeomanry did permanent duty as a military body, they were under military discipline and obeyed the commands of the commander-in-chief and his district generals. However, the civil administration still retained overall control, as the force could only be put on permanent duty by vice-regal warrant. In practice, to save time-consuming administrative entanglements, when permanent duty was required from small numbers of corps to deal with localised problems, the government gave district generals blank warrants. The force was administered centrally from the Yeomanry Office in Dublin Castle, a branch of the Irish War Office, part of the chief secretary's department. The routine administration devolved to the military under-secretary. Although the Act of Union amalgamated the Irish and British military establishments, yeomanry and militia remained under Castle control. When the chief secretary attended at Westminster, the entire yeomanry business became the military under-secretary's responsibility.[16]

Pay was the key to the administration system. The corps in the localities were disciplined and linked to the Yeomanry Office by a system of paid exercise parades and monthly inspections. Originally there were two weekly exercise days when they were drilled by their permanent sergeant, but this could be modified to take account of the force's level of training or the state of public finances. Yeomen received the regular rate of two shillings a day for cavalry and one shilling for infantry. The system involved printed forms being sent to all corps for return after each monthly inspection with the numbers attending parade and their state of discipline certified by the captains. These doubled as pay vouchers which could be drawn at the Treasury by the captain or an agent. In the early nineteenth century, exercise and inspection pay returns were calculated quarterly, to reduce administration.[17] While in their local role assisting the magistrates they answered to their captain or the magistrate but when engaged in military operations, the yeomanry captain became part of the chain of command devolving down from the district general. This could cause friction and much depended on the tact and sensitivity of the individuals involved. The irascible General Lake anticipated problems from yeomanry captains when he or-

1796], P.R.O.N.I. Stewart of Killymoon Papers, D3167/2/126. **15** Camden to Portland, 24 March 1797, P.R.O. H.O.100/67/f. 156. **16** Littlehales to Castlereagh, 25 May 1803, *Castlereagh Corrs.*, iv, pp. 281–3. **17** 37 Geo. III, c. 2, sect. i; Circular, 1 Dec. 1796, P.R.O.N.I. Lurgan Yeomanry Detail Book, D3696/A/4/1-2; Exercise and Pay Returns [Blank, watermark 1803], in private possession, Dr A.F. Blackstock.

dered them to report to his divisional commanders in March 1797, yet his successor in the northern district, George Nugent, was known for his ability to smooth relationships between the professional and amateur aspects of his command.[18]

OFFICERS AND MEN

Each corps had a minimum of two commissioned officers: a captain and lieutenant. Except in special cases, no corps under 60 was allowed more than a captain and a first and second lieutenant while those over 80 could have two captains, though in practice this rarely happened.[19] After the initial excitement and ostentation of raising yeomanry, the commitment of captains to the day-to-day running of the corps was an individual matter. Emergencies aside, yeomanry business took its place along with parliamentary or estate matters. An absentee, like Downshire, would often nominate his agent as captain. Some resident gentlemen retained the position nominally but let responsibility devolve to the first lieutenant. Others were more scrupulous. Lord Mountnorris of Camolin in Wexford, made sure that he was kept minutely informed of every detail, even when in Dublin on business. Similarly, the earl of Annesley took his Castlewellan yeomanry extremely seriously, viewing the position like his other law and order responsibilities.[20] When augmentations led to heavier concentrations, or when a number of corps were within the influence of an extensive landowner, the magnate could take the title of Captain Commandant while individual corps under him each had a captain commanding. Yeomanry captains were usually within the influence of a larger patron and had to meet criteria of loyalty and respectability. When William Jones resigned his command of the Drogheda Infantry in 1805, the customs collector, Edward Hardman informed his patron, Speaker Foster, of a dearth of people 'safe and respectable' to succeed. The second-in-command could not be promoted, since he was only a printer but, eventually, and doubtless beneficially, Hardman suggested Lancelot Fisher, who though 'not in point of fortune what I would wish for ... is a man whose education was good and he is a gentleman, steady, loyal and active'.[21] In urban corps based on occupational groupings influence was translated to professional and social standing within the group. William Saurin, a prominent spokesman for the Irish Bar and later attorney general, captained the first company of the Dublin Lawyers' Yeoman Infantry.[22]

The selection of captains was usually not an issue, provided the usual criteria were met. However some Dublin corps extended the principle of electing their of-

---

18 Lake to [?Knox], 25 Dec. 1796, N.L.I. Lake Papers, MS56/f.5.   19 Standing Orders for the Yeomanry Corps of Ireland, 15 May 1798, N.L.I. Ir355a3 (hereafter: Yeomanry, Standing Orders, 1798). 20 Camolin Cavalry Detail Book in Wheeler and Broadley, *The War in Wexford*, Castlewellan Yeomanry Detail Book, P.R.O.N.I. D1854/8/4.   21 Hardman to Foster, 14 Nov. 1805, P.R.O.N.I. Chilham Papers, T2519/4/304.   22 1797 Yeomanry List, N.L.I. Ir355a10.

ficers to election of captains. Sir George McCartney was elected to the Attorneys' Corps in 1796, though with government's sanction. This was an exception, however; the normal position was that adopted by the duke of Richmond in 1807 when he stopped the Bellisle Yeomanry exercising a similar right.[23] Despite Camden and Portland's wish to keep the yeomanry clear of county electoral politics, wherever a corps was within a magnate's influence, recommendations for vacant captaincies were made through him to the viceroy. Where the corps were 'independent' the natural successor to the vacancy applied directly. Alexander Taylor, probably the agent, who superintended the Headford estate in Galway while it was in minority, successfully applied for captaincy of the Headford Cavalry.[24] However, even here control was not abdicated as all new captains were vetted for their suitability to command not by the county governors, as in England, but by the district general.[25] By contrast, the selection of lieutenants was a delicate and sometimes contentious matter. Recommendations for commissions came from individual yeomanry captains,[26] but realistically, where the captains owed his position to a magnate, it would have been foolhardy for, say Daniel Mussenden, to recommend anyone Downshire disliked.

Lieutenants often handled the day-to-day command and hence had to wield sufficient local influence. Typically they were substantial farmers or minor gentry figures. However captains had to consider their men's feelings over recommendations for officers. Ballots were officially frowned on, as smacking of 'democratic' volunteering, but they were common. In areas with strong volunteering traditions, yeomanry simply would not have appealed to men if they had been denied this right. James Stewart's Cookstown Cavalry appointed Stewart captain and elected both officers and men by ballot.[27] Sometimes elections provoked social tension. In county Down Castlereagh and his father initially accepted officers proposed by the Newtownards and Comber Cavalry but when they tried to superimpose the agent, Cleland, as first lieutenant, resistance in the ranks forced the formation of a second corps to avoid the embarrassment of Cleland's resignation.[28] Although stopped in Britain by the Volunteer Consolidation Act of 1804, this right of election continued in the Irish Yeomanry.[29] Stopping it in Ireland would have been untenable, as the potential for disorder and disaffection was greater and the materials to counteract them more limited. Indeed, given government's fears about recreating the Volunteers, election of officers was part of the trade-off for central control. Leonard

23 Memorial of the Attorneys' Corps, 2 April 1814, P.R.O. H.O.100/170/ff. 8–9; Wellesley to the earl of Enniskillen, 1 June 1807, *W.S.D.*, v, p. 72. 24 Taylor to Littlehales, 13 Aug. 1806, N.A. O.P.232/3/42. 25 General Floyd's remarks on inspecting the yeomanry, 8 Sept. 1801. B.L Hardwicke Papers, add. mss. 35924 ff. 95–9. 26 Yeomanry Standing Orders, 1798. 27 Resolutions of the Cookstown company, 14 Nov. [1796], P.R.O.N.I. Stewart of Killymoon Papers, D3167/2/127. 28 Londonderry to Cleland, 3 Jan. 1797, Castlereagh to Cleland, 29 June 1798, P.R.O.N.I. Castlereagh Papers, D3030/J/1A, 8A-C; Yeomanry lists, 1798, 1805. 29 A. Gee, 'The British Volunteer Movement, 1793–1807', preface, p. ix. 30 'J.W.' [Leonard McNally] to Cooke, 14 Sept. 1796, N.A. R.P.620/36/227.

McNally praised the government's wisdom in relinquishing the nomination of officers in Dublin.[30]

The non-commissioned yeomanry officers were sergeants and corporals.[31] Every corps had a permanent sergeant, initially an ex-regular or seconded soldier employed to hammer rudimentary discipline into the yeomen. He also carried a heavy administrative burden, being responsible for the distribution of arms, ammunition and pay. The latter was a particularly onerous task as it involved the maintenance of pay and attendance registers and administering stoppages of money for non-attendance or indiscipline. As the yeomanry became a well-established feature of Irish life, the position of permanent sergeant tended to be filled by local men who rose through the ranks. John Harrow, permanent sergeant of the Mullaghglass Yeomanry, county Armagh, served for the entire duration of the institution. He entered in October 1796, serving two years as a private, then a further two as corporal and eight as sergeant, before being promoted to permanent sergeant, a position he held over twenty-three years. Henry Newton of the Aughnahoe Infantry, county Tyrone, served twenty-nine years as a yeoman, all but five as permanent sergeant. Venerable figures like this had great local influence. The longer a corps existed, the more indispensable the permanent sergeant's store of local knowledge became to his superior officers. The detail book of Annesley's Castlewellan Infantry reveals that the practical direction of all five companies was undertaken by permanent sergeants, with the commissioned officers, who had other occupations, merely enjoined to check the men at their convenience. However, intimate local knowledge and informal status could be a double-edged sword. George Douglass, permanent sergeant of the Lurgan Infantry was, like nine tenths of the corps, an Orangeman and 'an independent, willful old fellow' to boot, who knew little and cared less about yeomanry legislation.[32]

Other full-time, permanently paid, members were a drummer for infantry and a trumpeter for cavalry.[33] They assisted the sergeant with drill and called the men to arms in emergencies. Like the permanent sergeants, they were also ex-regulars at first, but soon became local men. During Sir Arthur Wellesley's chief secretaryship, adjutants were appointed as permanent staff where corps which normally acted together under the same captain commandant, were concentrated in battalions of 300 upwards. They were to be men 'of good character' who had served as commissioned officers or in the rank of sergeant major for a minimum of four years in the line, the East India Company, the fencibles or militia.[34] Adjutants were initially ap-

31 Pelham to Brownlow, 31 Oct. 1796, P.R.O.N.I. Lurgan Yeomanry Detail Book, D3696/A/4/1; *Commons Jnls.* (Ire.), xvii, appx. cccliii.   32 P.R.O.N.I. Mullaghglass Yeomanry Detail Book, D359; Crossle to Stanley, 22 Feb. 1831, P.R.O.N.I. Crossle Papers, D1927/40; 16 May 1831, P.R.O.N.I. Richardson of Drum Papers, D2002/C/17/21; P.R.O.N.I. Annesley Papers, D1854/8/4; P.R.O.N.I. Lurgan Yeomanry Detail Book, D3696/A/4/2.   33 37 Geo. III, c. 2, sect. ii.   34 Wellesley to Richmond, 16 Mar 1809, *W.S.D.*, pp. 608–10.

pointed to assist captains with increasing administration but from 1809 their primary role was to improve discipline, using their military experience to monitor drilling, ensure arms and ammunition were well kept, arrange the detail of military duty and certify pay returns. This meant *de facto* overseeing the permanent sergeant, for which the adjutant held the rank of lieutenant.[35]

DISCIPLINE

Yeomanry committees levied their own fines from the yeoman's pay for absenteeism and not keeping their weapons clean. This procedure was sanctioned by the Yeomanry Act, but in other aspects corps operated idiosyncratic informal discipline codes more in keeping with a fraternity or lodge. Indeed some corps operated like rudimentary friendly societies. The Ardress Infantry, county Armagh, lent James Alexander £1 2s.9d., probably against his exercise pay. They could also be unfriendly if a yeoman's performance was sub-standard. On 24 December 1796, with no seasonal allowances, Edward Armstrong was 'dismissed for stupidity'.[36] Membership was often seen as a status symbol. Michael Banim mocked the antics of the Kilkenny yeomen but noted perceptively that they enrolled to publicly identify themselves with the *status quo*.[37] Given that a yeomanry corps was a desirable, sometimes fashionable place to be, social acceptance tacitly underscored informal discipline codes. As membership was by consensus only the chosen could participate and conformity to norms of behaviour and politics was expected and could be enforced. Yeomanry corps were therefore self-regulating to a large extent in matters of discipline. On the face of it, discipline by elected committees seems very radical, but in practice, as in many other aspects of the yeomanry, it operated as a kind of compromise with traditional expectations of paternalism and deference. The captain would usually determine policy on discipline and behavior but this would have to be agreed either by the members or their committee. The Lurgan Infantry regulations were devised by their captain, William Brownlow MP, but proposed to the ranks as resolutions to be agreed. Here the sanctions ranged from fines (some pretty onerous such as the half-crown penalty for wearing uniform off duty), to the public disgrace of dismissal for non-attendance or misbehaviour, which carried the additional humiliation of having the names of those involved pinned to the church door. The Lurgan regulations were originally posted in the guardroom, but by 1831 were issued to every member in a printed booklet.[38]

Disciplinary matters were executed by yeomanry courts of enquiry or courts

35 Hamilton to Anderson, 29 April 1809, P.R.O.N.I. Belfast Yeomanry Detail Book, D3221/1/89, ff. 90–1.   36 P.R.O.N.I. D.296.   37 Banim, op. cit., introduction.   38 12 Nov. 1799, 9 Sept. 1801, P.R.O.N.I. Lurgan Yeomanry Detail Book, D3696/A/4/1; Printed Rules, 1 Mar. 1831, P.R.O.N.I. Brownlow Papers, D1928/Y/2.

martial. Caution needs to be exercised, as the terms were used without precision in a yeomanry context. Courts of enquiry were used for investigating allegations. This could be a simple internal matter for determining on disputed cases. Melvyn Milligan of the Castlewellan Infantry was cleared of stealing his lieutenant's geese by a 'court of enquiry'. However the term also applied at county brigade level, where the conduct of a yeomanry officer or an entire company was investigated by a court of enquiry, composed of officers from other corps. The findings of the enquiry would be sent to the Yeomanry Office for final determination by the lord lieutenant. Captain Swanzy of the Ballyhaise Infantry, county Cavan, was investigated by such a court when some of his men complained that he was retaining their pay to meet his personal debts.[39] Where internal investigations were involved, the principle of honour was of paramount importance as the ultimate unofficial sanction. A yeomanry corps, when not on permanent duty, was technically a voluntary association of citizens. In this context, yeomanry courts functioned as a means of dealing with problems in a way that served the interests of the corps, without resorting to the normal processes of civil law. Such internal inquiries *de facto* involved a man being judged by his social peers and were understandably kept private. Lord Donoughmore apologised to Pelham because the affairs of the Cork Legion became public, after a yeomanry court expelled three members whose behaviour in a heated dispute over voting money to the government for defence led to the second captain's resignation and accusations of disloyalty.[40]

For corps on permanent duty, courts of enquiry could lead to yeomanry courts martial. However, this term was also used imprecisely. The Lurgan Infantry grandiosely convened 'court martials' for minor infringements like non-attendance at parade. However, properly used, the term 'court martial' applied to yeomen doing permanent duty, who had voluntarily put themselves under the Mutiny Act. The Yeomanry Act provided for these courts which could be ordered by yeomanry captains, assembled by warrant of the lord lieutenant or a general officer and composed solely of yeomanry officers.[41] They dealt with serious matters like desertion, which was potentially punishable by death. Deserters from yeomanry corps were executed in 1798 but, as time passed, the severity of the punishment for such desertion lessened, and the presence of fellow yeomen on the courts cushioned miscreants from the full rigour of military law. In 1799 a yeomanry court martial successfully sought and received Cornwallis' sanction that deserters would surrender themselves and join the army for overseas service. Considerable discretion was used and allowance made for the fact that yeomanry service, by its nature, was performed near the men's homes. The drummer of the Castlewellan Infantry was arrested for desertion when

---

39 20 Feb. 1813, P.R.O.N.I. Annesley Papers, Castlewellan Yeomanry Orderly Book, D1854/8/4; Proceedings of Court of Enquiry into the pay of the Ballyhaise Infantry, 27 July 1807, N.A. O.P.232/4/19. 40 13 Mar. 1798, N.A. R.P.620/36/9. 41 9 Sept. 1801, P.R.O.N.I. Lurgan Yeomanry Detail Book; 37 Geo. III c.2, section vi.

his corps was on permanent duty in 1812. Annesley could have court martialled him, but agreed, in conjunction with the district general, that the matter would be better resolved by letting the drummer return to his post following a public reprimand at the head of the corps.[42]

Corporate indiscipline and misbehaviour was punishable by 'breaking' the entire corps. Disbanding was sometimes done at a county level on the recommendation of a court of enquiry.[43] The yeomanry was a status-conscious organisation and, even if internal affairs were private, yeomanry service was pre-eminently a public activity. A broken corps put the mark of Cain on the individuals concerned and reflected adversely on its captain's local standing. It was therefore usually an effective sanction. Where landowners took an active interest in their corps, the damage to their local reputations counted more in their eyes than fears that disbandment might besmirch their honour in a more general sense. Mountnorris was livid when some members of the Camolin Legion misbehaved on permanent duty in Ferns in 1799. By misbehaviour he meant drunkenness, losing equipment, fighting among themselves and refusing to salute superior officers. Mountnorris dismissed three men and admonished the whole corps, saying he was 'mortified that any of my tenantry, who were always so respected, should behave in a manner that degrades human nature'. Breaking carried the additional stigma of disloyalty. Mountnorris utilised this and warned them of the example of the Rathfarnham corps, disbanded during the rebellion. In 1812, Annesley carried out what Mountnorris threatened by breaking his entire third company describing as 'mutiny' their 'disorderly and unsoldierlike manner' before him on parade.[44]

CLOTHING, ARMS AND EQUIPMENT

The government wanted the yeomanry to be as different as possible from the Volunteers, who had been criticised for having no regularity in uniform, arms or drills. Consequently it was originally intended that yeomen should all wear the same uniforms and carry the same arms.[45] The uniforms were to be cheap and serviceable. A pattern was produced at Pelham's meeting in October, for a 'red jacket that buttoned close from the chin to the breeches, blue standing collar and cuffs, no facing, not to be esteemed so much for its elegance as its comfort'.[46] James Arbuckle had something similar in mind when he hinted to the aristocratic Downshire that cav-

42 Littlehales to Lieut. Gen. Dundas, 12 Feb. 1799, P.R.O. H.O.100/86/f. 95; 6 Aug. 1812, P.R.O.N.I. Castlewellan Yeomanry Orderly Book, D1854/8/4. 43 Abbott to Hardwicke, 31 Dec. 1801, B.L. Hardwicke Papers, add. mss. 35711. 44 Mountnorris to Smyth, 22 May 1799, quoted in Wheeler and Broadley, *The War in Wexford*, p. 291; 12 Mar. 1812, P.R.O.N.I. Castlewellan Yeomanry Orderly Book, D1854/8/4. 45 *F.J.*, 5 Nov. 1796. 46 Shannon to Boyle, 20 Oct. 1796, P.R.O.N.I. Shannon Papers, D2707/A3/3/22.

alry clothing should be on 'a plain and frugal system', using a cheap blue jacket and waistcoat plus the leather breeches most horse-owners had anyway.[47] No general list of yeomanry dress regulations has been found, but the standard infantry uniform was a plain red jacket with blue collars and cuffs and white breeches while cavalry coats were either dark blue or red. Infantry wore cocked hats or caps similar to those worn by regular light infantry. Caps were recommended by government.[48] Cavalry sometimes wore 'Tarleton' helmets, called after a British commander in the American War. The Ennis Cavalry of Clare wore a Tarleton with a black fur crest and a leopard skin turban fastened at the back with a crimson rosette and gold tassels and white metal chains and mountings. A helmet of the Armagh Cavalry's on display in the Armagh County Museum, is similar to the Ennis one but with a horsehair plume like a Greek warrior's. The Caledon Cavalry were less classically minded, or perhaps more frugal, as they confined themselves to a more prosaic and, given the Tyrone climate, decidedly more practical glazed cap.[49]

However, despite plans for regularity, in practice there was considerable variation in yeomanry uniforms. Like the Volunteers, many yeomen, particularly cavalrymen, saw their uniform more as a means of distinguishing themselves than distinguishing them from an enemy. Lord Shannon disapprovingly noted the desire of cavalry captains to clothe their corps in a flamboyant manner and their irritation at government's attempts to enforce a standard serviceable uniform.[50] Urban professionals also liked ostentation. Daniel O'Connell, as an impecunious yet ambitious young lawyer, was desperate to join a yeomanry corps to avoid the militia ballot and 'the disgrace of being forced to march as a common soldier'. He modestly opted for the Lawyers' Artillery, whose blue uniform coat cost a mere £4, almost twice the official allowance of two guineas for the entire dress, assuring his uncle this was significantly plainer and cheaper than that of the Lawyers' Infantry, 'all bedaubed with lace' at £9.[51] The sartorial elegance of the Dublin Bar paled beside the full dress uniform ordered by the Loyal Dublin Cavalry in February 1797: 'a scarlet coat, collar and cuffs blue, turnbacks white ornamented with blue and a blue heart; red wings and chain epaulettes, to be looped with silver twist ... sugar-loaf buttons ... breeches white leather ... boots black military ... light dragoon helmet, leopard turban, cloak dark blue with scarlet cape'.[52] This may not have made many croppies lie down but it certainly must have set some fortunate tailor up.

Freedom of choice of uniform therefore, like election of officers, became an-

47 11 Oct. 1796, P.R.O.N.I. Downshire Papers, D607/D/230.   48 Lurgan Yeomanry Detail Book, P.R.O.N.I. D3696/A/4/1.   49 F. Glenn Thompson, 'The Flags and Uniforms of the Irish Volunteers and Yeomanry', *Bulletin of the Irish Georgian Society*, xxxiii (1990); C.C.P. Lawson, *A History of the Uniforms of the British Army*, iii, p. 173; 16 Dec. 1796, P.R.O.N.I. Caledon Papers, D2443/C/2/9.
50 Shannon to Boyle, 20 Oct. 1796, P.R.O.N.I. Shannon Papers, D2707/A3/3/22.   51 D. O'Connell to M. O'Connell, 3 Jan. 1797, M. R. O'Connell (ed.), *The Correspondence of Daniel O'Connell*, i, pp. 26–8.   52 C.C.P. Lawson, ibid., iii, pp. 173–4.

other part of the compromise the government struck. Allowing the citizen soldiers to indulge themselves, within reasonable limits, with whatever idiosyncrasies appealed to their *esprit de corps*, certainly appealed to old Volunteers, but the government's decision not to ram standardisation down local throats helped ease the transition between the two organisations while still maintaining overall control. Also like the Volunteers, yeomanry corps readily proclaimed their identity and political sentiments by incorporating motifs on their equipment. The government permitted yeomanry to use private devices, unlike the regular army which had to stick to the regulation official heraldry and emblems. Yeomanry motifs ranged from prosaic slogans on infantry cross-belt plates to gorgeously worked pennants and colours. Cavalry corps carried a guidon, a swallow-tailed pennant made of silk and lavishly embroidered. Most yeomanry guidons followed the regular army convention of having the white horse of Hanover emblazoned on the corner. The guidons also contained depictions relating to the locality of the corps and their *raison d'être*. The Londonderry Cavalry guidon, in the Ulster Museum, bears the civic coat of arms and the motto 'Pro Aris et Focis' (For Hearths and Homes). Most yeomanry guidons bore standard loyal slogans. The Coleraine Cavalry had the royal cipher on one side and the arms of Coleraine on the obverse with the motto 'Pro Rege et Patria' (For King and Country) while the Lower Iveagh Cavalry (Second Troop) eschewed Latin and unfurled 'For our King, Laws and Constitution' in the face of revolution.

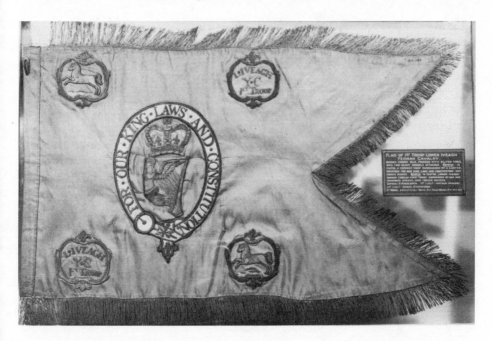

Guidon (Pennant) of the Lower Iveagh Yeoman Cavalry (county Down)

Cross-belt plate of the Glenauley Yeoman Infantry (county Fermanagh)

Cross-belt plate of the Belfast Merchants' Infantry

Not all yeoman infantry could afford lavish colours. Those that could, like the Belfast Infantry, usually followed the regular convention and carried two: the king's colours (the Union flag) and the unit colour. The Templepatrick Infantry's king's colour in the Ulster Museum has the royal arms in the centre of the union flag on one side and the arms of the captain, the earl of Templeton, centred on the other. Yeomanry flags were superficially like Volunteer flags but the political sentiments and symbols expressed on them reflected the radically different conditions in which the yeomanry existed, being more conformist to the British connection. Even those Volunteer flags which placed a crown above the harp, used the old Irish spiked 'Milesian' crown whereas yeomanry flags always depict the rounded imperial crown.[53] Yeoman infantry cross-belt plates are in the same *genre* as Volunteer belt plates, though again the sentiments depicted on them are markedly different. In addition to the standard emblems and expressions, they sometimes also contain raucous slogans of popular loyalism. The Glenauley Infantry cross-belt plate (Fermanagh) unambiguously proclaims 'Croppies lie down'; a far remove from the mystic and masonic-like symbolism of the Volunteers. Belt-plates like these symbolise the union of necessity between popular, parochial loyalism and a wider loyalty to king and empire. Despite much initial yeomanry opposition to legislative Union, particularly in Dublin and Ulster, this was not reflected on their standards. I can find only one example of an attempt at this, by Dublin's Liberty Rangers, who were prevented replacing their regimental colours with a flag bearing the legend 'For our King and the Constitution of Ireland'. Indeed yeomanry corps were quick to adopt the post-1801 Union flag and to incorporate the rose and thistle alongside the shamrock.[54]

Yeomanry were armed with the standard weapons for regular soldiers. In 1796 cavalry corps were provided with saddle and holster, bridle and collar, sword and pistol, sword-belt and cartridges. The pistol was an accessory to the main cavalry weapon: the slightly curved, one-edged light dragoon sabre. In 1798 some got short horse muskets or 'carabines' which were held in bucket holsters. By 1801, 2,000 of the 12,000 cavalry had carabines in addition to their swords and pistols. Experienced military men expressed doubts about carabines. According to General Floyd, they were cumbersome and rarely effective, except in expert hands 'for which reason' he sniffed 'the yeomen are better without it'. Yeomen infantry carried a musket and bayonet, a belt and a cartridge box containing twelve rounds of ball cartridge. Infantry sergeants carried pikes.[55] The musket was the standard short land pattern flintlock, the Brown Bess, with an effective range of around 100 yards. The arms were supplied from the Ordnance in Dublin and conveyed, often under yeomanry

53 I am grateful to Tom Wylie of the Ulster Museum for this information.   54 Castlereagh to Portland, 19 Jan. 1799, P.R.O. H.O.100/85/f. 130; G. A. Hayes-McCoy, *A History of Irish Flags*, pp. 102–8.   55 Abbot to Addington, 2 Nov. 1801, Abstract of general remarks made by Lt. Gen. Floyd, 5 Sept. 1801, P.R.O. Colchester Papers, 30/9/123/19, 30/9/172/65; Circular, 29 Oct. 1796, P.R.O.N.I. Lurgan Yeomanry Detail Book, D3696/A/4/1,2.

escort, to important garrison towns like Cork, Athlone and Newry. They were then distributed to military strongpoints where local corps collected them. The arms supply and distribution system was initially unable to cope with demand. There were frequent complaints about delays, especially from Ulster, where the need was greatest. By January 1797 only 14,000 out of 24,000 yeomen were armed.[56] Even when arms were received the complaints continued. The Aghalarg and Clonoe Infantry of Tyrone had ten useless guns, insufficient ammunition and could not exercise wearing their cartouche boxes.[57] There was little tolerance of such shortcomings by men who were impatient to appear in arms, however, they did not realise that this put them on an equal footing with most regular infantry units whose arms, for most of the eighteenth century, were frequently unserviceable and often unsafe.[58]

There were also problems with cavalry equipment. The Prosperous Cavalry had swords as badly tempered as their captain, who begged his brother in Dublin 'for God's sake do something about exchanging our swords ... nine of them are already broken and the others will fly like glass at the first stroke'.[59] Yeomen originally kept their arms at home for self-protection. This had a political dimension, as Catholics had been unable to hold guns under the Penal Laws and the holding of firearms was still controlled by the 1793 Arms Act. If this made Protestant yeomen feel special, it also made yeomanry guns special targets for arms raiders. The official policy was to gather the arms centrally for easier protection. Human instinct being what it is, the yeomen were never happy with this arrangement, and the problem remained. In 1806, the captain of the Drumkeerin corps, county Leitrim, was unable to persuade his men to deposit their arms and ammunition at the permanent sergeant's house.[60] This issue symbolises the enduring tension in the yeomanry between its official role as a centrally controlled, militarily integrated body and its local role as a territorial force, ready to respond to danger in a practical way without being ham strung by regulations dreamed up in the safety of the chief secretary's office.

56 Macan to Charlemont, 24 July 1797, H.M.C. *Charlemont*, ii, p. 305; Belfast Yeomanry Orderly Book, 1803–1810, P.R.O.N.I. D3221/1; T. Knox to Govt., n.d. [Nov. 1796], N.A. R.P.620/26/83; Lake to Gen. Knox, 28 Dec. 1796, N.L.I. Lake Papers, MS56/f. 10; Unsigned memo, 10 Jan. 1797, 620/28/81a.   57 McReynolds to Pelham, 9 Aug. 1797, N.A. S.O.C.1016/47.   58 J.A. Houlding, *Fit for Service: The training of the British Army, 1715–1795*, p. 152.   59 Trench to R. Trench, 1 June 1798, N.A. R.P.620/38/14.   60 Lindsay to Pelham, 4 April 1797, N.A. S.O.C.1016/44; Gen. Afflech's report, 17 Sept. 1806, P.R.O. H.O.100/138/f. 42.

NUMBERS AND DISTRIBUTION

The Irish Yeomanry was a numerically and geographically extensive institution. At its peak, of around 80,000 men, it was roughly the same size as the Volunteer movement. However, as an official body, much more statistical information is available on the yeomanry, enabling its overall dimensions to be described with reasonable accuracy while, at the same time, regional and structural patterns can be isolated and compared. This said, there are still problems with sources. Even the official records were incomplete. In 1808 a retrospective inspection return contained the caveat that the Yeomanry Office could provide no returns earlier than March 1803. The complete loss of Yeomanry Office records means we must rely on irregularly occurring parliamentary returns and fill the gaps with figures trawled from the mass of official correspondence in the Home Office papers and elsewhere. This introduces distorting factors which must be noted. Sometimes figures occur frequently enough for monthly changes to be plotted, at other times longish periods elapse without information. Moreover there were discrepancies between the establishment total at the Yeomanry Office and the actual inspection returns. This was not always due to absenteeism. Fraud will be examined later, but there were undoubtedly paper soldiers in the ranks. Idiosyncrasies in the inspection protocol also distorted the figures because not all the returns were received together. Another problem is that the official correspondence does not always stipulate whether the figure is for all ranks or omits officers. In such cases, I have assumed that the general total refers to the entire establishment. However, the margin for error is insufficient to upset the overall impression. The December 1803 figures show 7,000 officers, from a general total of 83,000.[61] The following table provides a numerical profile of the yeomanry establishment. It gives yearly figures for the critical early period from late 1796 to 1807, when the danger of invasion had lessened and the Catholic Question replaced law and order on the political agenda. Thereafter the returns, which are chronologically incomplete anyway, have been selected at intervals to convey a general impression. As the yeomanry was largely moribund after the end of war in 1815, it can be reasonably assumed that there was little variation in the missing years. Where the official figures distinguish between the establishment total and the effectives on parade, I have quoted both for comparison.[62] Where a choice of figures is available for any one year, I have selected the latest as the parliamentary returns were usually taken in December. The figures have been rounded up or down to the nearest thousand.

---

61 *Commons Jnls.*, 63, appx. 12, 59, appx. 11, p. 503.   62 Effective yeomen were defined as those who attended eight days in the preceding four months or sixteen within the preceding eight months, to gain exemption from the militia ballot. Source: J. Groves-White, *The Yeomanry of Ireland*, p. 11.

Table 1:   Yeomanry Numbers[63]

Date	establishment	effectives	Date	establishment	effectives
Dec. 1796	21,000		May 1807	69,000	61,000 (Dec.)
Dec. 1797	35,000		Apr. 1808	80,000	75,000
May 1798	50,000		Mar. 1810	85,000	
n.d. 1799	66,000		Dec. 1815		45,000
n.d. 1800	54,000		May 1817	45,000	
Nov. 1801	52,000		Mar. 1820		31,000
June 1802	51,000		n.d. 1824	32,000	
n.d. 1803	83,000	70,000 (Dec.)	Mar. 1828	37,000	20,000
Nov. 1804	70,000	64,000 (Dec.)	n.d. 1830	25,000	
Dec. 1805		70,000	n.d. 1831	29,000	
Apr. 1806	82,000	64,000 (Dec.)	n.d. 1832	31,000	

These figures reveal a general impression but they also hide much. Due to factors of control and cost, the establishment was initially pegged at 20,000, but the shock of the near-landing at Bantry Bay stimulated augmentation. The establishment continued to rise as Ireland remained unsettled and the invasion threat persisted. The Commons Secret Committee reported the figure at 50,000 during the rebellion but this disguises the last-minute scramble to get extra yeomanry raised. A more detailed breakdown is necessary for the critical years 1796–8 and for the period 1802–3, when the short-lived Peace of Amiens produced great fluctuations.

Table 2:   Yeomanry Numbers 1796–98[64]

Date	Number	Date	Number
Oct. 1796	7,000	Dec. 1797	35,000
Dec. 1796	20,000	Apr. 1798	43,000
Jan. 1797	25,000	May 1798	50,000
Feb. 1797	30,000		

63 1796: Camden to Pitt, 15 Nov. 1796, P.R.O. Chatham Papers, 30/8/236/104–5. 1797: J.F. Maurice (ed.), *The Diary of Sir John Moore*, p. 270. 1798: *Commons Jnls* (Ire.), xvii, appx. dccxxix; 1799: n.d. [late 1799, N.A. R.P.620/48/56. 1800: Cleary, *The Orange Society*, p. 261. 1801: Abbot to Addington, 2 Nov. 1801, P.R.O. Colchester Papers, 30/9/123/19. 1802: 28 June 1803, H.R.O. Wickham Papers, 38M49/ 5/33/35–44. 1803: *Parl. Papers*, H.C. 1803–4 (10), xi, p. 100. 1804: Littlehales to War Office, 15 Nov. 1804, P.R.O. H.O.100/121/f. 253; *Commons Jnls.*, 63, appx. 12, p. 618. 1805: Ibid. 1806: Bedford to Spencer, 3 April 1806, P.R.O. H.O.100/135/f. 106; *Commons Jnls.*, 63, appx. 12, p. 618. 1807: Richmond to Hawkesbury, 12 May 1807, P.R.O. H.O.100/114/f. 312; *Commons Jnls.*, 63, appx. 12, p. 618. 1808: 1 April 1808, P.R.O. H.O.100/144/f. 322. 1810: 24 March 1810, P.R.O H.O.100/155/ff. 176–7. 1815: 5 Jan. 1816, P.R.O. H.O.100/189/ff. 14/6. 1817: *Parl. Papers*, H.C. 1817 (309), viii, pp. 467–78. 1820: *Parl. Papers*, H.C. 1821 (306), xix, pp. 178–86. 1824: *Parl. Debs.*, second series, x, p. 291. 1828: *Parl.*

The April 1798 returns do not include supplementary yeomen. In April 1798 Castlereagh wanted 5,000 un-uniformed supplementaries organised by the captains of the various Ulster corps. They were not to be paid and only to receive arms and act in the event of an insurrection. As the crisis deepened, it was determined to make arms available for loyalist civilians. The distinction between these and supplementary yeomen was a blurred one, as epitomised by the gang wearing white hat bands and calling themselves 'supplementaries' who descended on Ballynahinch for two days after the battle armed with rusty guns and bayonets.[65] Castlereagh obtained 7,500 muskets for loyalists in the Belfast area in June 1798, 4–5,000 for mid-Ulster and 2–3,000 for Enniskillen.[66] Therefore it is reasonable to deduce the figure for the loosely-organised supplementaries in Ulster alone stood at somewhere between 5–10,000. Similar civilian levies were also organised in other parts of Ireland. With 50,000 regular yeomen and an unknown but obviously large number of supplementaries and civilian volunteers, the popular reaction against the United Irishmen in 1798 was very considerable. Official figures for supplementaries only begin when yeomanry were reorganised in 1803. At that stage they were not conceived as civilian levies but as a stationary reserve to the regular yeomanry if the main force was 'brigaded' and moved from their districts in the event of invasion or insurrection. Figures for supplementary yeomen are less readily available since, as they were unpaid, the returns were more *ad hoc*. There were approximately 9,500 supplementaries in 1804 and 8,000 in 1808. The last figures available show the supplementary establishment completely moribund by 1810. From a nominal total of almost 4,500, only 678 were present at a general inspection.[67]

Table 3: Yeomanry Numbers 1802–3[68]

Date	Number	Date	Number
June 1802	51,000	Aug. 1803	64,000
Mar. 1803	48,000*	Sept. 1803	65,000
June 1803	48,000 **	Dec. 1803	83,000

* includes officers   ** excludes officers

Papers, H.C. 1828 (182), xvii, pp. 247–51. 1830: *Parl. Debs.*, third series, viii, p. 1038. 1831: Memo on the Yeomanry of Ireland, n.d. 1831, D.U.L. Earl Gray Papers, Box 65, file 3, No. 6. 1832: *Parl. Debs.*, third series, xiv, p. 800.   **64** 1796: Yeomanry Office memo, 7 May 1802, B.L. Hardwicke Papers, add. mss. 35924 ff. 224–5; Camden to Pitt, 15 Dec. 1796, P.R.O. Chatham Papers, 30/8/236/104–7. 1797: Yeomanry memo, 10 Jan. 1797, N.A. R.P.620/28/81(a); Memo on the defence of Ireland, 21 Feb. 1797, P.R.O. W.O.30/66/28; J.F. Maurice (ed.), *The diary of Sir John Moore*, p. 270. 1798: Numerical strength of the Yeomanry n.d. c. April 1798, N.A. R.P.620/48/56; *Commons Jnls.* (Ire.), xvii, appx. dccxxix.   **65** *McComb's Guide to Belfast*, p. 137.   **66** N.A.M. 6807/174/ff. 473–5, Nugent Papers, Castlereagh to Nugent, 24 June 1798.   **67** Littlehales to War Office, 15 Nov. 1804, P.R.O. H.O.100/121/f. 253; Richmond to Hawkesbury, 12 May 1807, H.O.100/114/f. 312; Abstract of inspection reports, 24 March 1810, H.O.100/155/ff. 176–7.   **68** 1802: Memo on Reduction, 28 June 1803, H.R.O. Wickham Papers,

During the respite offered by the Treaty of Amiens, moves were afoot to reduce the yeomanry as, like the militia, they were only legally embodied during wartime. Two plans were mooted. Firstly, all corps were circularised and invited to offer for regular army service. Most offered to serve anywhere in Ireland; some anywhere in the British Isles, rather like fencibles.[69] This plan was shelved, and arrangements devised for a reduction which would break suspect corps and keep the better ones on unpaid stand-by. However the problem was solved by the long-expected resumption of war in May 1803. As in Britain, large infantry augmentations followed. The gross total of 83,000 seems large in Irish terms, but can be put in context by comparing it to the figures for the British yeomanry and volunteers, which rose to 380,000. The statistics also make it possible to distinguish between cavalry and infantry. Although government compromised on the original plan, cavalry formed a large proportion of the force in the early years. However the proportion of cavalry to infantry declined after 1798, as they proved unsuitable during the rebellion. The contrast between the figures for 1798 and 1799 shows this very clearly. The other reason was expense. Cavalry were more costly due to their equipment and higher pay. The following table gives an impression of the relative proportions of each. The figures quoted should be taken as rank and file only, as the official figures never distinguish between cavalry or infantry officers. The largest figure for each year is used.

Table 4:   Cavalry and Infantry Numbers[70]

Date	Cavalry	Infantry
Dec. 1796	10,000	10,000
Dec. 1797	18–20,000	15–17,000
May 1798	15,000	21,000
n.d. 1799	13,000	53,000
Oct. 1801	10,000	40,000
Dec. 1803	9,000	57,000
Dec. 1804	7,000	52,000
Dec. 1805	8,000	58,000
Dec. 1806	6,000	53,000
Dec. 1807	7,000	50,000
Mar. 1810	9,000	71,000
Dec. 1815	100	43,000

38M49/5/33/35–44. 1803: Littlehales to Shee, 31 March 1803, P.R.O. H.O.100/112/f. 104; Flint to Shee, 14 Aug. 1803, H.O.100/112/f. 232; Hardwicke to Yorke, 2 Sept. 1803, H.O.100/111/f. 166; *Commons Jnls.*, 59, appx. 9.   69 N.A. Calendar of Official Papers not extant.   70 1796, 1798: Yeomanry Office Memo, 30 Oct. 1801, B.L. Hardwicke Papers, add. mss. 35924 f. 121. 1797: Sir J. F. Maurice (ed.), *The Diary of Sir John Moore*, p. 270; 1799: Numerical Strength of the Yeomanry, n.d. 1799, N.A. R.P.620/48/56. 1801: Yeomanry Office to Abbot, 31 Oct. 1801, P.R.O. Colchester Papers, 30/9/124/

The yeomanry was a truly national institution with corps enrolled from every county and city and most major towns in the autumn of 1796. The following provincial tables are based on a selection of the best available figures using either key dates or otherwise taking the figures in roughly five-year intervals. The tables are supplemented by national distribution maps for the years 1797, 1803 and 1827 for ease of comparison. The figures are general totals of all ranks and are for the total enrolled establishment. I have used the establishment totals for the county/provincial tables on the assumption that those who were enrolled as yeomen, whether they attended well or not, constituted the potential strength and influence of the movement. Some minor idiosyncrasies occur between these figures and the rounded national totals because the largest and latest totals for 1797–9 in table 1 came from sources which give no county breakdown, while for 1810, a marginal note in the original source explained that around 2,500 men on the establishment were unrecorded.

Table 5:   Ulster Yeomanry Numbers[71]

County	n.d. 1797	n.d. 1798	n.d. 1799	Dec. 1803	March 1810	May 1817	n.d. 1827
Antrim	1,789	2,050	2,872	5,383	5,844	4,128	3,639
Armagh	1,879	1,879	2,684	3,028	3,531	2,065	1,970
Cavan	1,323	1,427	3,251	2,971	3,454	2,850	2,742
Donegal	1,300	1,375	1,868	2,820	3,605	2,553	1,903
Down	2,161	2,261	3,813	5,373	5,662	3,947	3,188
Fermanagh	1,071	1,262	3,237	3,537	4,075	3,876	3,653
L'derry	1,177	1,284	1,437	3,159	2,854	2,432	2,089
Monaghan	701	765	1,501	2,161	2,683	2,182	1,890
Tyrone	2,889	3,247	5,887	6,206	5,074	4,239	2,858
Totals	14,290	15,550	26,550	34,638	36,782	28,274	23,932

227. 1803–16: *Commons Jnls.*, 63, appx. 12 p. 618. 1810: Abstract of Inspection Reports, 24 March 1810, P.R.O. H.O.100/155/ff. 176–7. 1815: Abstract of Inspection Reports, 5 Jan. 1816, P.R.O. H.O.100/189/ff. 14–16.   71 Provincial Tables: 1797–9: Numerical Strength of the Yeomanry, n.d. 1799, N.A. R.P.620/48/56. 1803: *Parl. Papers*, H.C. 1803–4 [10], vol. xi, p. 100; 1810: Abstract of Inspection Reports, 24 Mar. 1810, P.R.O. H.O.100/155/ff. 176–7: 1817: *Parl. Papers*, H.C. 1817 [309], vol. viii, pp. 467–8; 1827: *Parl. Papers*, H.C. 1828 [182], vol. xvii, pp. 1–31.

Table 6:   Leinster Yeomanry Numbers

County	n.d. 1797	n.d. 1798	n.d. 1799	Dec. 1803	March 1810	May 1817	n.d. 1827
Carlow	425	653	770	1,272	1,176	581	561
Dublin Co				2,379	1,379	147	144
Dublin	3,294	4,299	6,746	4,637	4,444	245	19
Kildare	848	1,029	1,157	1,017	934	335	231
Kilkenny	563	694	722	1,339	1,203	240	243
King's	785	892	1,303	1,874	1,612	763	600
Longford	559	559	871	868	1,271	942	887
Louth	708	708	1,335	1,538	1,053	623	301
Meath	1,021	1,227	1,329	1,668	1,567	386	295
Queen's	1,155	1,155	2,006	2,029	2,115	1,164	1,057
Westmeath	507	569	1,175	1,286	1,419	710	426
Wexford	1,008	1,372	1,884	2,904	3,402	1,664	1,485
Wicklow	1,124	1,267	1,688	3,051	2,772	1,492	1,320
Totals	11,997	14,424	20,986	25,592	24,347	9,292	7,681

Table 7:   Munster Yeomanry Numbers

County	n.d. 1797	n.d. 1798	n.d. 1799	Dec. 1803	March 1810	May 1817	n.d. 1827
Clare	717	727	932	937	764	500	326
Cork Co.	2,799	3,916	5,231	4,839	5,930	859	699
Cork				*1,641			
Kerry	439	439	536	793	1,223	650	811
Limerick	819	1,289	1,726	1,998	1,805	420	188
Tipperary	1,206	1,977	3,145	3,787	3,133	699	419
Waterford	712	757	1,179	1,741	1,527	88	88
Totals	6,692	9,105	12,749	15,735	14,382	3,216	2,531

* Only in 1803 is Cork City shown as separate

Table 8:   Connacht Yeomanry Numbers

County	n.d. 1797	n.d. 1798	n.d. 1799	Dec. 1803	March 1810	May 1817	n.d. 1827
Galway	1,728	2,002	2,131	2,070	1,556	462	Nil.
Leitrim	552	552	1,028	1,243	1,273	959	719
Mayo	473	473	928	1,410	2,083	1,323	999
R'common	568	568	702	870	869	79	Nil.
Sligo	554	554	1,008	1,124	1,307	826	793
Totals	3,875	4,149	5,797	6,717	7,088	3,649	2,511

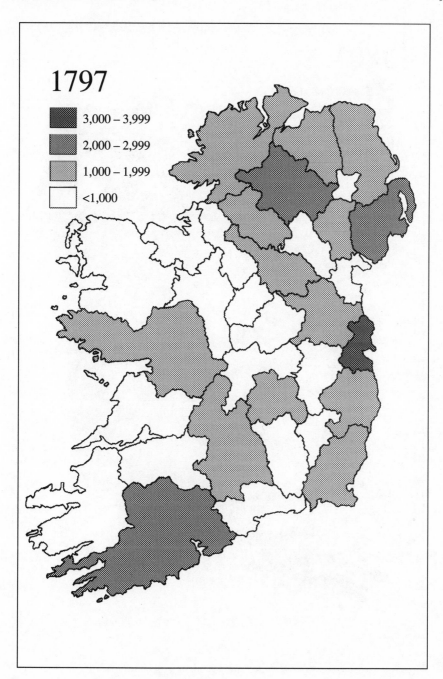

1797

	3,000 – 3,999
	2,000 – 2,999
	1,000 – 1,999
	<1,000

County density of Yeomany corp

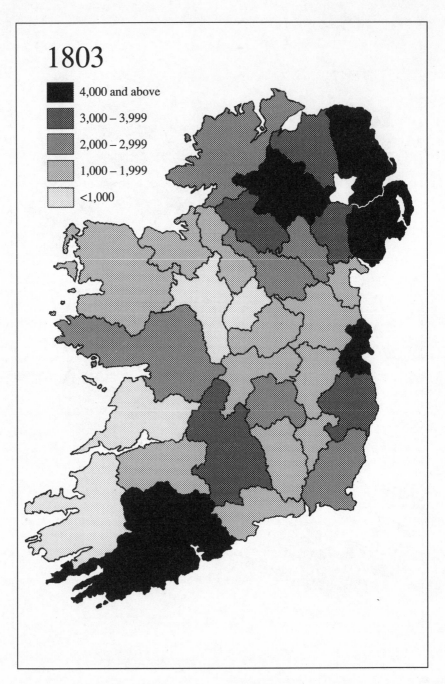

1803

- ■ 4,000 and above
- ■ 3,000 – 3,999
- ▦ 2,000 – 2,999
- ▦ 1,000 – 1,999
- □ <1,000

County density of Yeomany corp

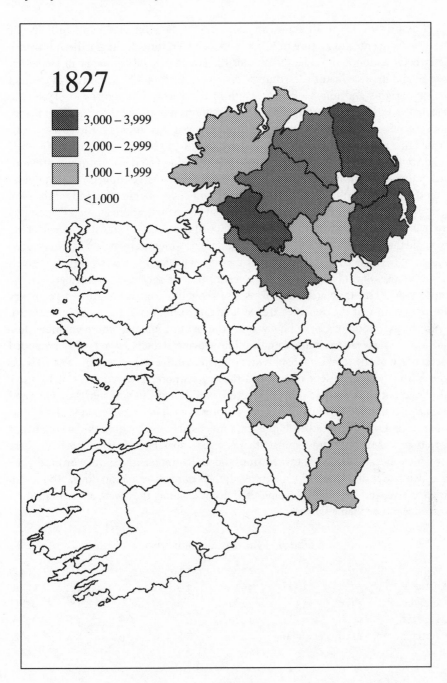

County density of Yeomany corp

The provincial spread shown in these figures calls for comment. Initially the heaviest concentrations were in Ulster and Leinster, though the northern province later became dominant. The reasons for the abundance of yeomanry in Ulster are varied and include historical, strategic and social factors. The Volunteer movement had its origins and much of its strength in the north. The figures for Tyrone in particular reflect the prominence of Dungannon in both Volunteer and yeomanry movements and the influence of the loyal associations. In 1801 Richardson estimated that the barony of Dungannon alone had 3,037 yeomen exclusive of officers.[72] The strategic need was also greatest in Ulster, being the most disturbed province when the yeomanry was formed in 1796. Also it had a larger non-Catholic population than the other provinces. With the selection of yeomen in the hands of the local gentry, this usually meant a *de facto* Protestant yeomanry, where enough Protestants were available. Moreover, the preponderance of lower-class Protestants made it inevitable that most Ulster corps would be infantry, which were increasingly favoured after 1798. The accompanying county density maps for 1797, 1803 and 1827 give a visual impression of the northern concentration of the force, particularly in the latter years. The 1797 and 1803 maps also show the arbitrary nature of yeomanry formation, in that the densities are weak on large sections of the western seaboard, with the exception of Cork. This was in contrast to England, where volunteer formation was heavy in maritime counties. The provincial totals, expressed as a rounded percentage of the total establishment, confirm that the end of war in 1815 affected the Ulster yeomanry less than it did those elsewhere. The numbers in Leinster declined but they did not drop as severely as did those in Munster. As Ulster and Leinster contained the bulk of Ireland's Protestants, it is possible that Catholic yeomen were discarded quicker. However, a more likely explanation is that yeomanry coverage in Munster and Connacht, was always sparser and, when parts of these provinces became badly disturbed from the early nineteenth century onwards, the war being over and troop levels improved, the yeomen were stood down. Too few to be effective, and inevitably keeping their arms at home, they were an incitement to disorder rather than a deterrent.

Table 9:   Provincial Comparison

	1797	1798	1799	1803	1810	1817	1827
Ulster	39%	36%	40%	42%	45%	64%	65%
Leinster	33%	33%	32%	31%	29%	21%	21%
Munster	18%	22%	19%	19%	17%	7%	7%
Connacht	11%	10%	9%	8%	9%	8%	7%

72 Richardson, *Yeomanry*, pp. 40–1.

EXPENSE

Although some yeomanry corps were funded by local subscription and some even served gratis, the organisation as a whole was financed by parliamentary grant. In this respect, as in many others, it was very different from the British volunteers and yeomanry. English yeomen normally served without pay and equipped themselves, except for arms and accoutrements, while only some volunteer infantry were paid for two day's drill per week.[73] The arrangement in Ireland was that the Irish War Office submitted an estimate to parliament based on the projected expenditure for pay and equipment for the coming year. If part of the vote of supply was unused, the Treasury re-appropriated the surplus. As with the rest of the yeomanry administration, loss of financial records hinders attempts at reconstruction. Yeomanry finances are entirely under-researched both as regards cost to the public purse or the local economic benefits they produced. Peter Stoddart touched briefly on the subject in his ground-breaking thesis. Stoddart's necessary concentration on military strategy led him to consider the cost of yeomanry to be 'relatively inexpensive': 'throughout its existence the force was as economical as government wished to make it'.[74] However, he underestimated the expense, relative and absolute, and ignored the local nature of the force.

Though it is true that the yeomanry system gave government all the control it wanted over the force, this is not the same as control over the circumstances when it would be used. Herein lay the problem: yeomanry permanent duty was both expensive, extensive and unpredictable. In 1798, with permanent duty looming, William Elliot, the military under-secretary, remarked privately, 'it certainly cannot be called a cheap *defence of nations*.'.[75] However, Elliot was only saying what was already common knowledge. When examined in the context of the Irish government's financial situation, the yeomanry was a financial problem from the start. The first levy in 1796 came in the middle of a financial crisis, when sufficient funds could not be raised to meet defence costs, specie was dwindling and loans were sought from England. In February 1797, Camden had £198,000 available to meet military purposes, yet faced demands for £221,300 which included £25,000 for yeomanry pay since October 1796, but not the much heavier cost of clothing and equipping the force. The gravity of the crisis can be seen in Belfast, where General Lake had to eat humble pie and borrow money from local merchants to pay his regular troops. The yeomen simply had to wait. Many corps were late in receiving their arms and equipment; others almost bankrupted their captains who had equipped them and advanced pay on the strength of the promised government allowances.[76]

73 I.F.W. Beckett, *The Amateur Military Tradition*, pp. 76, 82. 74 Stoddart, 'Counter-Insurgency and Defence in Ireland, 1790–1805', p. 77. 75 Elliot to Knox, 10 April 1798, N.L.I. Lake Papers, MS56/ f. 153. 76 Camden to Portland, 25 Feb. 1797, P.R.O. H.O.100/71/f. 134; Note: The figures cited in the text are in Irish currency, except were noted, up to 1817 when the treasuries merged. Thereafter they are in Sterling

The cost of yeomanry was spread over clothing and equipment allowances, exercise and permanent duty pay for the men and daily pay for the permanent sergeants, drummers and trumpeters. Clothing was a heavy expense, though, being predictable (a yeomanry uniform lasted three years) it was more easily budgeted for than permanent duty, the need for which fluctuated according to the state of the country. The first full estimate of £500,000 was for March 1797 to March 1798. It included £257,086 for exercise, £147,379 for clothing and £95,534 for estimated permanent duty.[77] Not surprisingly, further enlistment was stopped for financial reasons. In a debate on internal defence, Sir Lawrence Parsons claimed that yeomen were cheaper than regulars because, serving voluntarily, no levy money was paid. However, the government was not impressed by such arguments.[78] By late 1797 the yeomanry was a target area for retrenchment and the 1798 estimate was only £294,190.[79] This may have made financial sense, but from a defence perspective, it was soon proved wishful thinking. In April 1798, Castlereagh tried to lessen the potential cost of permanent duty by, for example, considering cavalry forage money as included in their pay and paying dismounted cavalry at the infantry rather than the cavalry rate.[80] However, the events of 1798 were to prove that saving on straw was indeed to clutch at straws.

The final figures for 1798 are unavailable, though permanent duty during the rebellion was reckoned at a staggering £60,000 per week.[81] The estimates for 1799 confirm the yeomanry's soaring cost: £687,485 was estimated for 52,274 yeomen, an average of over £13 per man. This was based on a projection of only one eighth of the entire force on permanent duty, which Castlereagh felt inadequate, given the invasion threat.[82] As early as 1799 moves were being made to regulate the cost of permanent duty without diluting the force's defence potential. During an invasion scare only those corps unable to be quickly assembled were put on permanent pay until the fleet's destination was ascertained. The monthly cost of keeping the whole establishment on duty was reckoned at £150,000. Some idea of the proportionate cost within the Irish military establishment can be had from figures which Cornwallis sent Portland in 1800. Out of a total military expenditure of £4.4 million, the yeomanry cost £626,000. This can be put in perspective by comparisons: the militia cost £775,000, yet they were full-time and, at 27,000, only about half the size.[83] Administrators regarded yeomanry as a potentially uncontrollable expense. The problem became much more acute after Union. The force expanded rapidly while the causes for permanent duty remained undiminished. The shift to Westminster

77 *Commons Jnls.* (Ire.), xvii, appx. xcv.   78 Clare to Trench, 18 Mar. 1797, P.R.O.N.I. Trench Papers, T3244/5/4; *Parl. Register*, xvii, part ii, p. 350.   79 Camden to Pelham, 20 Dec. 1797, P.R.O. H.O.100/70/ff. 367–9; Supply Memo., 9 Feb. 1798, H.O.100/75/f. 79.   80 Circular, 12 April 1798, P.R.O.N.I. Lurgan Yeomanry Detail Book, D3696/A/4/1.   81 Wellesley Pole to Mornington, 24 August 1798, B.L. Wellesley Papers add. mss. 37308 f. 167.   82 J. Groves White, op. cit., p. 10; Castlereagh to Pitt, 29 Mar. 1799, *Castlereagh Corrs.*, ii, pp. 243–6.   83 Castlereagh to Wickham, 28 May 1799, P.R.O. H.O.100/86/f. 437; 4 Mar. 1800, H.O.100/95/f. 161.

moved the problem centre-stage before a less sympathetic audience. Not only did it highlight the disordered state of the country, but also made the debates on the army estimates the grounds of potential conflict between Irish and British interests. The desire to avoid embarrassment underlies the remarks of Isaac Corry, the first post-Union Irish chancellor, when he advised the chief secretary, Charles Abbott, to 'lean lightly' on the exchequer for the payment of yeomanry clothing warrants. Whenever expense exceeded the vote of supply, as happened in 1802 and 1803, the options were either to submit new estimates or, if parliament objected, to draw on Army Extraordinaries.[84] The pattern of yeomanry cost can be seen in the following table for the post-Union period. The accounting system changed when the treasuries merged in 1817, after which the amounts actually paid to the force are not given. However, as the cost had stabilised by this stage, numbers reduced and frequency of duty lessened, it can be safely assumed that the sum granted and amount paid were around the same.

Table 10:   Yeomanry Expenditure[85]

Year	Granted	Paid	Year	Granted	Paid
1801	£IR460,567	£IR288,265	1818	£31,541	
1802	£IR224,567	£IR196,836	1819	£21,668	
1803	£IR172,433	£IR172,433	1820	£69,500 [inc. clothing]	
1804	£IR1,398,115	£IR622,615	1821	£19,023	
1805	£IR541,666	£IR312,462	1822	£61,319	
1806	£IR770,040	£IR310,790	1823	£19,384	
1807	£IR899,493	£IR268,073	1824	£19,343	
1808	£IR694,944	£IR273,978	1825	£19,305	
1809	£IR732,680	£IR356,862	1826	£19,271	
1810	£IR641,842	£IR274,201	1827	£18,126	
1811	£IR351,749	£IR175,008	1828	£17,890	
1812	£IR348,300	£IR223,945	1829	£17,977	
1813	£IR288,300	£IR212,629	1830	£17,807	
1814	£IR123,833	£IR123,725	1831	£19,291	
1815	£IR67,473	£IR52,233	1832	£19,861	
1816	£IR47,667	£IR39,010	1833	£12,335	
1817	£51,665	N/A	1834	Nil.	

The financial implications of the end of war in 1815 are clearly noticeable. Previously, the Irish Yeomanry had consumed £3,864,055, giving an average yearly cost

84 11 Nov. 1801, P.R.O. Colchester Papers, 30/9/123/83; Memo on the Yeomanry Establishment, 13 May 1802, B.L. Hardwicke Papers, add. mss. 35924 ff. 276–7; Littlehales to Wickham, 16 July 1803, H.R.O. Wickham papers, T38M49/5/33/79. 85 *Commons Jnls.*, vols. 57–90.

of £257,603. The post-war reduction reflects the decrease in numbers but also shows that permanent duty was severely curtailed when more regulars were available for peacekeeping and, from Peel's time, the introduction of new police forces, which took over much of the yeomanry's role. The other striking feature about yeomanry expense is that it far outstripped the cost of its British equivalents: the volunteer infantry and yeomanry cavalry. During war-time, certain years were exceptionally costly. The huge estimate and grant for 1804 stands as a testimony to the continuing problem of permanent duty. At £1,290,567 (Sterling) it swamped the grant for the British volunteers which stood at £730,000. In the army estimates debate in December 1803, Charles Yorke, secretary-at-war, tried to defend this by claiming the British estimate was inaccurate, that it did not include clothing and that, as was true, the Irish figure was projected on proposed augmentations which were shelved. However, no amount of muddying the waters obscured the crystal-clear truth that Irish yeomen were far more expensive than their British counterparts.

Official returns in December 1803 gave the total of the Irish force as 82,941, whereas the combined British voluntary force was 380,193, giving a British per capita average for 1804 of just £1.9 whereas in Ireland it was £15.5 (Sterling).[86] The continuing high cost of the Irish Yeomanry began to erode patience at Westminster. To some extent the different composition of the two forces accounted for this. Mounted yeomen on permanent duty cost three times as much as infantry, and, notwithstanding the run down in cavalry since 1798, still existed in significant numbers. There were 12,000 cavalry allowed for in 1804, giving a permanent duty cost of £216,000 for the privates alone, compared with £480,000 for 80,000 infantry privates.[87] However, this aside, the big difference was the amount of permanent duty done by the Irish force. In a letter accompanying the 1805 estimates, Littlehales, the military under-secretary, noted that the permanent duty component of the 1804 estimate had been £839,850, which equated to 17 weeks duty, whereas for 1805 they merely asked £626,807. The high component of permanent pay reflected the reality that Ireland was much more disturbed than Britain, though this fact seems to have been taken less seriously in London than in Dublin. Indeed, there are indications the Irish government asked for more than they used, just in case it was needed. The total sum required by the Irish War Office for 1805 was £918,865, but parliament dug its heels in at £541,666.[88] Eventually the heavy cost of permanent duty was partially ameliorated by rotating detachments of corps rather than having the whole establishment on duty at once. This made sense economically and strategically, as it could be done without losing the potential of having the entire force at hand.

Such large amounts of money being distributed into the Irish countryside must have had an effect on local economies. It is outside the scope of this work to investi-

---

86 *Commons Jnls.*, lix, appx. vii.;. xi, p. 100; *Parl Debs.*, i, p. 1677.   87 *Commons Jnls.*, 59, p. 469.   88 Hardwicke to Hawkesbury, 16 May 1805, P.R.O. H.O.100/126/f. 62.

gate the impact but the effect must have been considerable, especially as yeomen did not have to forgo their normal occupations to serve (the harvest season was often the signal to put them off duty). Moreover, as cavalry were much more likely to serve gratis, the heavy increase in infantry numbers after 1798 can only have further boosted local economies by spreading wide the benefits of yeomanry pay. Indeed, as numbers rocketed in 1803, in an entirely accidental but nonetheless important way, yeomanry pay provided a sweetener after Union. Even so, human nature being as it is, some wanted more than their share.

Yeomanry administration relied heavily on a captain's honesty and social standing but the system was ripe for fraud and presented irresistible opportunities for the less scrupulous. There were many avenues for deception. Even in the midst of the 1798 rebellion, some Wexford captains exploited the confusion and charged for non-effective men in their permanent duty returns. Another notorious abuse was for captains using their monopoly of local knowledge and information to have their corps put on permanent pay under false pretenses. In October 1799, the Fethard county Wexford, corps tried this on the basis of a fictitious assassination attempt on one of its members. In a rare Treasury comment, Sir George Shee noted 'abuses of a very scandalous nature prevailed in the returns'.[89] One of the brigade major's functions was to watch out for such graft, but it continued as long as the yeomanry did. In 1807 Arnold Cosby, the entrepreneurial captain of both the Shercock and Killenkere corps in county Cavan, was amazed when the brigade major investigated him for drawing double pay, which he had been happily doing apparently in the belief that paying one captain for two corps was no different than paying two for one each.[90] Cases like this made their way into the official records because they were investigated. Although similar incidents doubtless went undetected, there is no indication that the level of fraud was any higher than would be normal in similar institutions. A recent study has shown that charging for non-effective men was winked at in the eighteenth-century British Army.[91] Although Shee complained of abuses, he did not suggest their correction as a mode of economy; rather he looked to a reduction in the number of exercise days. This was one of the main methods used to control expense. Yeomanry exercise averaged two days per week, but was dropped at times to one day. For example, in September 1797 exercise was cut to one day per week. The circular said that it was because discipline had improved, and applauded the zeal of the yeomen. However, a much more plausible reason was the severe financial crises the Irish government was facing. During the Peace of Amiens exercise was kept up voluntarily, but no pay was given. At other times exercise was reduced to one day per week in the winter, reverting back to two in the summer. Although summer exercise duty could clash with the busy time in the agricultural

89 Wheeler and Broadley, *The War in Wexford*, p. 274; Burrowes to Marsden, 12 Oct. 1799, N.A. R.P.620/56/44; Shee to Castlereagh, 22 Aug. 1800, P.R.O.N.I. Castlereagh Papers, D3030/1432.   **90** Cosby to Littlehales, 4 Apr. 1807, N.A. O.P.232/4/5.   **91** A Guy, *Oeconomy and Discipline*, p. 109.

year, it was felt that exercising in winter weather meant even greater inconvenience. In 1809, savings were made by cutting exercise duty to one day per fortnight for the winter. By 1815, exercise days had been reduced to one per month.[92]

The post-war reductions coincided with Robert Peel's chief secretaryship. A thoroughgoing and frugal administrator, Peel set about yeomanry retrenchment with relish, telling the Home Secretary that he would slash the cost in 1816 to £34,000, one twenty-fourth of the 1807 figure. He refused the Yeomanry Office permission to include £105,000 for new clothing, saying those who would not serve without new uniforms could resign. In the event, £47,000 was voted, but Peel prudently cut exercise days right back to six days in the year, arguing that the saving of £13,500 could be held against possible permanent duty. He also combined the districts of brigade majors, losing five in the process, and cut back Yeomanry Office staff and pay agents.[93] From that time to the final disbandment of the yeomanry in 1834, the institution was largely moribund from a financial as well as an operative point of view. Any comment in the estimates debates was motivated more by politics than by serious concern at its comparatively innocuous expense, which ran at around £20,000 per annum. There were some exceptions. For example in 1822, permanent duty (£42,242) and a slight augmentation in yeomanry numbers in response to the Rockite disturbances in Munster pushed the vote to just over £60,000, though by the following year it reverted to its usual amount.[94]

RELIGIOUS COMPOSITION

Contrary to what some historians imply and the United Irishmen claimed, when the yeomanry was being raised there was no official policy against Catholic or Presbyterian membership. Camden advised Downshire to include trustworthy Catholics and Dissenters and told Lord Waterford that it was unwise to refuse Catholics.[95] Yet the conclusion that the yeomanry was overwhelmingly Protestant is inescapable to anyone familiar with the period. In Monaghan Lord Blayney explained to Pelham that although there was no material religious distinction in his area, 'the Protestants being the most to be depended on they are accordingly ... in the returns'. In September 1796, John Beresford unambiguously described enlistment to Lord Auckland as 'the arming of the Protestants, who can be depended on'.[96] Moreover, the

92 Circular, W W. Pole, 18 Nov. 1809, P.R.O. H.O.100/152/f. 248; Peel to Palmerston, 20 Feb. 1816, B.L. Peel Papers, add. mss. 40289 f. 83.   93 Peel to Sidmouth, 16 Dec. 1815, P.R.O. H.O.100/189/ff. 3–6; Peel to Littlehales, 16 Feb. 1816, B.L. Peel Papers, add. mss. 40290 f. 86; Peel to Palmerston, 20 Feb. 1816, add. mss. 40289 f. 83; Peel to Littlehales, 6 Apr. 1816, add. mss. 40290 ff. 194–6.   94 *Commons Jnls.*, 78, p. 804; ibid., 79, p. 775.   95 S. Palmer, *Police and Protest*, p. 160; n.d. [c.30 Aug. 1796], P.R.O.N.I. Downshire Papers, D607/D/142; Camden to Waterford, 14 Sept. 1796, K.A.O. Pratt Papers, U840/0174/15.

initial tardy enlistment and low Volunteer-yeomanry continuity in Down and Antrim, areas of heavy Presbyterian settlement, points to the *de facto* exclusion of Dissenters in eastern Ulster. The fact that Camden had to give directions to the various magnates shows that Catholic and Presbyterian participation was a contentious issue. Moreover, with Fitzwilliam's conception of a largely Catholic, middle-class yeomanry as a benefit of emancipation, it is not surprising that Camden's government, dead set against further relief, encountered problems in this area. The parliamentary opposition and the Catholic Committee both tried to discourage Catholic enlistment. This had some effect, yet Camden could tell Portland that, despite the efforts of Grattan and Keogh, in many areas Catholics were 'fairly coming forward and joining in association with the Protestants'.[97] He needed to hear this: Fox's whigs would have eagerly seized on a blatantly sectarian yeomanry to attack Pitt and Portland's policy of coercion. However, the evidence suggests that it was more than wish-fulfillment on Camden's part.

A definitive denominational breakdown is impossible. In a pre-census age such information was not readily available. Even had it been, it is highly unlikely such statistics would have been gathered, given their explosive political potential. Complete yeomanry muster rolls are rare, as a result of the Four Courts fire, though some do turn up in private papers. Where they exist they offer two possibilities. If roughly contemporary local parish records survive, an attempt can be made to try to match surnames. This is necessarily problematical. It is difficult to get parallel contemporary survivals for the three main denominations and similar surnames can turn up, particularly in Anglican and Presbyterian records. Muster rolls offer an alternative opportunity to play the typically northern Irish game of deducing religion from name. For historical purposes either method can only be used as a rough guide in default of the means of clearer analysis. There are pitfalls as the example of James O'Hara of Newry shows. If his name appeared on a muster roll, its typically Irish form would make it appear he was a Catholic. However, as secretary of the Glenvale corps he drafted a resolution to Downshire headed 'We the Protestant yeomen of Glenvale'.[98] Given the patchy survival of yeomanry muster rolls and the difficulty, even where lists can be contemporaneously matched, in locating names with certainty on parish registers, this can only provide a broad impression and must be supplemented with reportage from private and official correspondence.

At Newry, Downshire considered Catholic offers to serve as both cavalry and infantry. He refused the 120 prospective infantrymen, 'staved off' many more from outlying districts, yet accepted a similar offer from Protestants. However, the higher social standing of cavalry corps made a difference and some 'very respectable and loyal papists' were enrolled in the Newry cavalry.[99] The same pattern appears in

96 4 Sept. 1796, *Beresford Correspondence*, ii, p. 129; 15 Nov. 1796, N.A. R.P.620/26/54. 97 14 Oct. 1796, P.R.O. H.O.100/65/f. 41. 98 2 Jan. 1797, P.R.O.N.I. Downshire Papers, D607/E/4.

parts of Monaghan where the Farney Cavalry had sufficient Catholics to be the focus of United Irish propaganda.[100] This introduces the first point to be made about Catholic membership. The government's criterion was trustworthiness rather than religion, but they delegated the power of judging the level of trust to the landed gentry in the localities. It made sense to rely on local knowledge but this method of selection meant that a complex of social, demographic and political factors entered the equation. Catholic yeomen tended to exist in areas where Catholics had land, where there were few Protestants, or where there was a background of good relations between religious groups. There is no evidence of Catholic yeomen in Armagh or Tyrone at this stage, though this did not necessarily mean disaffection. On Charlemont's Tyrone estate, between 140 and 200 of his Catholic tenants offered as yeomen, while a further 450 took the oath of allegiance, but all were happy to put themselves under the protection of a Protestant loyal association provided it was led by gentlemen of property.[101] At Maralin, where Down bordered Armagh, Captain Waddell drew up resolutions offering infantry service in December 1796. These were signed by around 700 Protestants but, despite their being presented to local Catholics, only around 30 signed despite having three chances to do so.[102] It seems that in areas where the Dungannon resolutions were adopted, the resultant loyal associations were solely Protestant. Whether this was by intent or default depended on local circumstances.

County Londonderry is exceptional, in that not only do early muster rolls survive for the county but some of these have been marked to indicate religious persuasion. They suggest a correlation between Catholic membership and *concentrations* of native Irish surnames. Out of the 53 privates in Connolly McCausland's Banagher Cavalry, 14 were marked as Catholic, all with native Irish surnames. However, three of the other eight corps named have clusters of more than five native Irish surnames. The religion of the dismounted privates in McCausland's corps is not marked but there are 81 native Irish surnames from a total of 82. The Faughan Glen Infantry roll shows a mixed corps with Catholics outnumbering Protestants by 34 to 18 in 1798, and by 33 to 8 in 1800. It is impossible at this distance in time to be sure whether this was merely a representation of the available manpower, or an attempt to reflect the local distribution of religious groupings, though it is notable that no surnames of the Londonderry (city) Cavalry are of the native Irish type.[103] The other possibility is that Catholics were considered more trustworthy than Presbyterians. In neighbouring Donegal there is simultaneous evidence of openness towards Catholic participation and wariness of Presbyterians. The 1835 Select Committee on Orange lodges heard that there had once been a 'good many' Catholic yeomen in

99 Downshire to Pelham, 25 Nov. 1796, P.R.O.N.I. Downshire Papers, D607/A/77.   100 Handbill, 24 Mar. 1797, P.R.O.N.I. Shirley Papers, D3531/A/5/91.   101 Lindsay to Pelham, 5 Jan. 1797, N.A. R.P.620/28/43; Lindsay to Charlemont, 11 Jan. 1797, H.M.C. *Charlemont*, ii, pp. 292–3.   102 Waddell to Cooke, 29 Dec. 1796, N.A. R.P.620/24/173.   103 P.R.O.N.I. Derry Muster Rolls, T1021/3.

Donegal. The Rebellion Papers confirm this, showing the pre-conditions for Catholic yeomen. In early 1797, following the Bantry invasion attempt, the Reverend Hamilton of Raphoe could get almost as many Catholics (110) as Anglicans (120) to take the oath of allegiance but, in this area of substantial Presbyterian settlement, only 19 reluctant dissenters, 'on pains of broken heads and banishment'. Hamilton was murdered by the United Irishmen shortly afterwards, but as yeoman cavalry were raised for the barony of Raphoe, it is most likely they included fair numbers of the wealthier Catholics.[104]

There is contradictory evidence about Catholic membership in the Dublin yeomanry. William Parnell, a liberal Protestant supporter of emancipation, claimed that the principal Dublin Catholics were rejected to a man by all except the Lawyers' Corps.[105] The Lawyers' Corps certainly contained Catholics, most notably Daniel O'Connell, but Parnell's claim of otherwise total exclusion does not square with government policy. Camden would not permit Dublin Catholics to join the yeomanry *en masse* and form exclusive corps but was perfectly happy to let them enlist individually in existing corps.[106] There may well have been resistance, but other evidence shows there was considerable Catholic enlistment both in various city corps and in the province of Leinster generally. Again this evidence must be qualified by the knowledge that political arguments were being constructed. Musgrave estimated that over 2,000 Catholics tried to join Dublin corps in the six weeks preceding the 1798 rebellion. On the same tack 'An Orangeman', probably John Giffard, gave figures claiming there were 22 Catholics in one company of the Rotunda Infantry, others in the Merchants' and St Sepulchre's Corps. In the rural areas of Leinster which suffered in the rebellion, there is more politically-tinged evidence of Catholic participation. Musgrave implied there were many Catholics in the Leinster corps. In Wexford, he claimed 24 Catholics in Colonel Le Hunt's Shelmaliere Cavalry, 16 in the Coolgreany Cavalry, 46 in the Castletown Cavalry, a majority of the Wexford Infantry, and one-third of the Clane Cavalry in Kildare. He also mentions Catholic yeomen in Wicklow and county Dublin, highlighting the Rathcoole Infantry as having 42 Catholic privates and 3 officers, with similar concentrations in the Coolock and Rathdown Cavalry corps.[107]

Although these statistics were provided to prove United Irish infiltration and argue the rebellion was a Catholic conspiracy, they cannot be discounted as evidence. Professor Cullen has noted recently that Musgrave 'cannot be dismissed out of hand'.[108] For one thing, he had access to contemporary information. The author

---

104 *Parl. Papers*, H.C. 1835 [377], xv, p. 358; Hamilton to Marshall, 14 Jan. 1797, N.A. R.P.620/28/99; 1797 Yeomanry list.   105 W. Parnell, *An Historical Apology for the Irish Catholics* (Dublin, 1808), p. 173.   106 Camden to Portland, 3 Jan. 1797, P.R.O. H.O.100/69/f. 24.   107 Musgrave, *Rebellions*, pp. 268–9; BL8146cc30, 'An Orangeman' [? John Giffard], 'Orange Vindicated in a reply to Theobald McKenna Esq.'; this pamphlet refers to a 1799 pamphlet by Musgrave under the pseudonym 'Veridicus' which refers to Catholic yeomen in rural corps, pp. 55–6.

of 'Orange Vindicated' unashamedly drew on Musgrave in a bitter pamphlet controversy with Theobald McKenna, who government considered very able and well-informed. If Musgrave's figures were inaccurate it could have been easily proved; indeed the author throws out this very challenge. Moreover, evidence from private correspondence encourages the same conclusion. The duke of Leinster, who commanded the Athy Cavalry, complained to Camden that an infantry corps was being formed in the town which would be entirely Protestant, therefore making distinctions between the denominations. This implies that cavalry corps here followed the pattern of mixed religious membership seen elsewhere.[109] During the rebellion Lord Aldborough told William Elliot that his corps was the only 'executive' one in that part of Kildare and submitted a list of around 40 native Irish surnames from corps around Athy, Narramore and Castledermot. In King's county, the captain of the Dunkeerin Cavalry admitted the presence of 19 Catholics.[110] In Meath, John Pollock convened a meeting of the principal inhabitants of the barony of Morgallion, consisting of 25 landed gentry and about 175 wealthy farmers, to consider a yeomanry. Pollock reckoned about three quarters of the audience was Catholic, and wanted to try their sentiments to test the effect of Grattan's remarks in parliament. Although he had found great differences about the admissibility of Catholics, and potential problems from the minor Protestant gentry, who threatened to withdraw their support for the raising of yeomanry corps if they were not all made officers, the matter was resolved by having two corps under the largest landowners in the barony. The Catholic peer Lord Gormanston was asked to take command of a cavalry troop of 40 Catholics, and Thomas Bligh invited to lead an infantry corps of the same number for Protestants. Pollock was so satisfied with the outcome that he boasted to Pelham that if government wanted Grattan, Keogh, Bond and Jackson put in Newgate, he could march 'fifty papists from here who would arrest them or lose their lives in the attempt'.[111] Myles Byrne admits that the United Irishman tried to enlist Catholic yeomen in Wexford in 1797, and there were purges of Catholic yeomen that year on suspicion of disaffection.[112] However, as this evidence suggests there were still significant numbers of Catholic yeomen in Leinster by 1798, there must have been even more at the first levy.

The sources reveal little about the force's religious composition in Munster or Connacht. As these provinces had less Protestant settlement than the others, logically one would expect to find more Catholic yeomen. In 1803, Sir Edward Littlehales, under whose direction the Yeomanry Office came, dismissed possible objections to a Catholic yeomanry brigade major for Kerry because 'whatever corps are formed in that county, they must in a great degree be composed of Roman Catholics'.[113]

108 L. Cullen, 'Late eighteenth-century politicization in Ireland', *Culture et Pratiques Politiques en France et en Irlande*, p. 148.   109 25 April 1798, K.A.O. Pratt Papers, U840/182/35.   110 n.d. [*c*.5] June 1798, N.A. R.P.620/38/51; Rolleston to Castlereagh, 19 May 1798, 620/37/106.   111 18 Oct. 1796, N.A. R.P. 620/25/176.   112 S. Gwynn (ed.), *The Memoirs of Myles Byrne*, pp. 11–14.

Littlehales spoke retrospectively, as the main issue under consideration was the increase of yeomanry after the renewal of war. There is probably a connection between the paucity of evidence and the fact that United Irish organisation was more rudimentary there than in the north and east. These is evidence of the composition of the yeomen in Cork city, but this emanated from the electoral rivalry of the Donoughmore and Westropp interests. Lord Donoughmore's Cork Legion was the largest yeomanry body in the city, and reflected his liberal political stance by including many wealthy Catholics, in spite of the Catholic Committee, who sent Richard McCormick to Cork in 1796 to try to prevent them joining.[114] There were certainly sufficient Catholic yeomen in Cork to attract Musgrave's attention, which, in turn prompted a reply from Thomas Townshend, MP, a supporter of Edmund Burke, who was adjutant in Westropp's corps before and during the 1798 rebellion. Townshend admitted that his corps had been almost totally Anglican but defended the Legion's 'considerable number' of Catholic gentry against Musgrave's assertions of disloyalty. The Donoughmore papers offer confirmation. In 1799 the Legion published an anti-Union address, showing a clear majority of native Irish surnames.[115] Similarly, when yeomanry corps were first raised in the heavily Catholic province of Connacht, lack of evidence of Catholic enrolment is more likely to be indicative of the absence of conditions for commenting on it. Some early evidence exists for Leitrim, where in August 1796 the Mohill Cavalry offer had 6 Catholics from 41 while the Carriglen Cavalry had 7 from 52. Another unnamed Leitrim barony had 12 Catholics in a cavalry offer of 57.[116]

What broad conclusions can be drawn from this evidence? First, the United Irishmen's claims in 1796 that the Castle was deliberately levying a denominationally exclusive force do not stand up: socially exclusive would have been nearer the truth, as the initial levy shows a strong correlation between Catholic membership and social and economic eligibility for cavalry corps. Although infantry corps were more likely to be exclusively Protestant, the evidence from parts of Ulster and Leinster shows that this was by no means always the case, whereas infantry in the cities of Dublin and Cork reflected the rise of a Catholic merchant and professional class. Catholics had recently been allowed to practise law, and O'Connell's obsessive need to cut a figure in the Lawyers' Corps bespeaks not only a rising young man but one very aware of the social significance of what he was doing. For the young Catholic lawyer, turning out in uniform with his colleagues confirmed the acceptance of himself and his co-religionists into a key profession. Given the vitality of the Catholic interest in Galway city, it is very likely that there was a significant level of partici-

113 Littlehales to Wickham, 3 June 1803, H.R.O. Wickham Papers, 38M49/5/33/7.   114 'J.W.' to Cooke, 28 Sept. 1796, N.A. R.P.620/36/227.   115 'W.F.' to [Cooke], 24 Feb. 1797, N.A. R.P.620/28/ 295a; T. Townshend, 'Part of a letter to a noble Earl ... vindicatory of the Yeomanry and Catholics of the City of Cork' (Dublin, 1801); 13 Feb. 1799, P.R.O.N.I. Donoughmore Papers, T3459/D/6/6.
116 n.d. [c. 30 Aug. 1796], K.A.O. Pratt Papers, U840/0157/10/1; Jones to Cooke, 4 Sept. 1796, N.A. R.P.620/25/12.

pation in the yeomanry. Moreover, key figures among the remaining Catholic peers and landowners were permitted to raise their own yeomanry corps. In Kerry Lord Kenmare commanded the Killarney Cavalry. In Meath, in addition to Gormanston, the earl of Fingall headed the Skreen Cavalry; though a Protestant himself, he was from a Catholic family and a member of the Catholic Committee. It is reasonable to conclude that, despite pre-existing political and social tensions and campaigns against Catholic enlistment, the government's wish for the force to represent property and loyalty had a measurable effect. Inevitably there was an element of tokenism. On Downshire's Edenderry estate in King's County, John Everard admitted to his patron that he 'would not have enrolled any papist but that Mr Pelham's speech in p[arliament] disavowed making any objection to them'.[117]

Any estimate of the numbers of Catholic yeomen in the first year of the institution must therefore be a cautious one. At the end of 1797 the yeomanry stood at about 35,000 with 14,000 of these in Ulster. Given that the proportion of Catholics identifiable in cavalry corps is usually above 10 per cent, that the bulk of cavalry corps were in the south, and that there were certainly Catholics in some Ulster corps, an estimate of between 2,000 and 3,000 probably errs heavily on the side of caution. This notional figure does not overturn the reality of the yeomanry's heavily Protestant composition, especially as Protestants were a demographic minority on the island, but it does show that wealthier Catholics were significant minority. Catholic membership of the yeomanry changed over time, indeed the evidence shows there were three distinct periods – 1797–8, 1803 and 1814 – when purges were initiated to remove Catholics, or steps taken to prevent their joining the force. As these were politically driven, they will be examined in a later chapter. Suffice it to say for present purposes that from 1798 the force generally took on an even greater Protestant profile, but that some Catholic yeomen remained among the scattered Munster and Connacht corps until the yeomanry was disbanded in 1834.

The question of Presbyterian membership in the northern yeomanry is an important one with a wider historical reference. However, in this case estimating numbers is even more difficult. The sources do not distinguish Presbyterians, or give figures even to the limited extent that they do for Catholics. The only numerical estimate comes from Musgrave, who claimed that the 14,000 yeomen in Fermanagh, Tyrone, Derry and Armagh in 1798 were mostly Orangemen and three-quarters Presbyterian. He was rather more specific on Tyrone, where he asserts that 4,200 of that county's 5,000 yeomen were both Presbyterian and Orange.[118] This would give a figure of about 10,000 Presbyterians in these counties alone, leaving aside Antrim and Down, and counties like Monaghan which had substantial Presbyterian settlement. However, Musgrave must be treated with caution as it was as

---

117 17 Oct. 1796, P.R.O.N.I. Downshire Papers, D607/A/514.   118 Musgrave, *Rebellions* (1801 edition), p. 194.

much in his interests to underplay Presbyterian disloyalty as it was to highlight Catholic treachery. On the other hand, he could have been contradicted at the time, since he used contemporary information.[119] In the absence of other figures, Musgrave's computation may be used as a working hypothesis, to test against the circumstantial evidence, in order to allow more informed speculation about the extent and timing of Presbyterian support for the yeomanry. The first point to be made is that it is difficult to believe that 84 per cent of Tyrone's yeomen were Presbyterian, given the Dungannon Association's close association with the Anglican clergy. For example, Thomas Knox's own Killyman Infantry were very likely all Anglicans: the 1831 census figures for the parish show only 205 Presbyterians, as opposed to 3,499 Church Protestants.[120] Certainly, with Fermanagh's heavy Anglican settlement, it is impossible to believe that three quarters of its yeomanry were Presbyterian. The only official return giving county numbers for 1798 is undated but it gives a total of only around 7,600 for the counties in question. Musgrave says his claims come from the period when the rebellion broke out so that it is possible the overall numerical discrepancy was not so great when new-raised and supplementary corps were included. The 1799 figures for these counties were just over 13,000.

However, leaving aside the question of broad numerical accuracy, Musgrave's implication of significant Presbyterian involvement in the yeomanry outside Down and Antrim is supported by evidence gleaned from reports to government. In the north of county Tyrone and the south of county Londonderry, Richardson reported that 'several Presbyterian gentry (individuals formerly factious enough) at least as forward as the old loyalists'. In September 1796, James Buchanan of Omagh proposed the yeomanry plan to 2,000 Presbyterians at their meeting house.[121] Although outside Musgrave's area, Monaghan presented similar conditions for Presbyterian membership as Armagh and Tyrone, having a substantial Presbyterian population and being an area of recent United Irish expansion. Happily the 1798 muster list for Hamilton Dacre's Monaghan (town) Infantry Yeomanry can be matched against Anglican records for 1802, and the 1821 congregational census for First Monaghan Presbyterian church. From the 126 surnames on the muster roll, 43 are identifiably Presbyterian, 30 are Anglican, seven turn up in both churches and the remainder cannot be located, though they do not appear to be Catholics. This would tie in with the position in rural Monaghan, where the barony of Farney yeomanry also included Presbyterians.[122] Moreover, although the United Irishmen were ecumenical

119 Musgrave, *Rebellions* (1802 edition), i, p. 237.   120 *Parl. Papers*, H.C. 1835 (45) First Report of the Commissioners of Public Instruction, vol. xxxiii.   121 Richardson to Abercorn, 2 Feb. 1797, P.R.O.N.I. Abercorn Papers, T3541/1B3/6/5; Buchanan to Cooke, 16 Sept. 1796, N.A. R.P.620/25/133.   122 List displayed in Monaghan County Museum; P.R.O.N.I. MIC1/248/A/1; MIC1P/199A/1; Printed handbill: to the Farney Yeomanry, 24 March 1797, P.R.O.N.I. Shirley Papers, D3531/A/5/91.

in their infiltration policy during 1797 in Tyrone and Armagh (the Killyman corps were under suspicion) when they went the length of encouraging declarations, these were anti-establishment in content. It is hard to imagine James Hamilton Junior's Tyrone corps being Anglicans, as they declared for reform and emancipation.[123] Given this clear evidence of Presbyterian involvement west of the Bann from 1796 onwards and considering the large numbers of supplementary yeomen raised in central Ulster from April 1798, Musgrave's figures must be given some credence, without discounting the element of propaganda. There was certainly an element of wishful thinking in Musgrave's assertion of concurrent Presbyterian involvement in the Orange Order and the yeomanry. Although there was definite, but as yet unquantified, Presbyterian involvement in the early Orange movement,[124] it is highly unlikely to have reached the levels Musgrave claims, much less to assumed the high degree of correlation with the yeomanry. To take the example of county Londonderry, the Hill family's opposition to Orangeism in Derry city and the presence of Catholics in rural corps in the county, make Musgrave's claims clearly exaggerated. However, given the wide range of General Knox's investigations into infiltration in 1797, and allowing for the influx of new corps and supplementaries in mid-1798, there must initially have been significant numbers of Presbyterian yeomen in central and western Ulster, certainly in excess of 5,000, plus some in the east as well. As will be seen later, Presbyterian involvement in eastern Ulster jumped forward in two stages following the insurrections of 1798 and 1803.

OCCUPATIONAL AND SOCIAL COMPOSITION

Camden's original wish for a yeomanry cavalry on the English model, composed of country gentlemen and respectable horse-owning 'yeoman' farmers, fell on stony ground in Ireland. It soon transpired that there simply were not enough individuals of this type to make up a strategically viable force. William Brownlow complained that he could not raise cavalry on his Lurgan property as only between 15 and 20 people there could afford to keep horses. In north Antrim, Edmund McNaughton's Dunluce Cavalry were '*very loyal* but in general not *very rich*'. Lord Londonderry thought one of his cavalrymen, Cumming, was exceptional, being like 'a real English yeoman ... worth at least £6,000'.[125] Financially, and to an extent socially, this made the Irish Yeomanry less like their English counterparts and more like the English volunteer infantry, who mostly received pay for exercise and actual duty

---

123 Hamilton to Abercorn, 4 Apr. 1797, P.R.O.N.I. Abercorn Papers D623/A/89/21; Knox to Pelham, 17 May 1797, B.L. Pelham Papers, add. mss. 33104 ff. 77–8.   124 Senior *Orangeism*, pp. 49, 69; F. Holmes, *Presbyterians and Orangeism, 1795–1995*, pp. 2–5.   125 T.H and J.E. Mullan, *The Kirk and Parish of Ballyrashane*, p. 80; Brownlow to Pelham, n.d. Jan. 1797, N.A. R. P.620/28/73; Londonderry to Camden, 28 Feb. 1797, 620/29/3.

while the English Yeomanry were only paid for duty, a right frequently waived. However, this only reflected differences in social and economic structures: the general principle that property equated to loyalty and trustworthiness was the same in both countries. Local pride often made up the financial shortfall, as it would have been embarrassing for a landowner to admit to the government that his estate would not produce a 'respectable' force. In Tyrone, Abercorn's law agent James Galbraith raised a troop of cavalry around Drumquin, composed of farmers who, despite being 'very respectable' could not afford to clothe themselves even on the government allowance of two guineas each. Galbraith noted other similarly circumstanced gentlemen applying for subscriptions to neighbouring landowners.[126]

Though subscriptions and the infantry option meant that loyalty was not sacrificed on the altar of respectability, there was a well-defined social pecking order within the force, with cavalry corps seen as superior to infantry. Prospective members of the Dromore Cavalry snobbishly determined to 'serve only if allowed to associate with persons of some respectability' and their honour remained unsatisfied until 'one or two inferior tradesmen' were rejected.[127] The aristocratic marquis of Downshire reluctantly accepted infantry offers in county Down, though he complained to Camden that many 'would join for the sake of getting a suit of clothes'. In 1802, when the government was considering reducing yeomanry exercises to maintain the force during the financial retrenchment of the Amiens 'peace', it was noted that the 'more respectable' cavalry could do without exercise pay but many infantrymen 'could not afford to lose a day's work'.[128] The economic and social gap between cavalry and infantry was mainly a rural phenomenon. Urban infantry corps were different. The functional need for infantry was perceived as greater in towns and cities, and in large conurbations these corps were often raised on an occupational basis. Dublin's various professional corps, of lawyers, attorneys, merchants, and revenue officials were at least the social equals of rural cavalry corps. The lawyers were the first to receive commissions and considered themselves the premier Irish yeomanry corps. Jonah Barrington, a member of the Lawyers' Infantry, relates an anecdote which conveys the affluence of some of these metropolitan corps. He describes how elderly gentlemen patrolled Merrion Square in a leisurely manner on fine evenings before stopping for tea and whist, while in inclement weather they were carried in sedan chairs with their muskets poking out the windows. There were also some urban cavalry corps such as the Dublin Merchants' Cavalry. However, the Merchants' Infantry were in no way their inferior being commanded by Arthur Stanley, a director of the Bank of Ireland. The two Cork city yeomanry groupings, Lord Donoughmore's Cork Legion and Westropp's Cork Volunteers,

126 Galbraith to Abercorn, 11 Nov. 1796, P.R.O.N.I. Abercorn Papers D623/A/108/6.   127 Bishop of Dromore to Downshire, 4 Nov. 1796, P.R.O.N.I. Downshire Papers, D607/D/283.   128 4 Nov. 1796, K.A.O. Pratt Papers, U840/0160/8; Hardwicke to Wickham, 19 April 1802, H.R.O. Wickham Papers, 38M49/5/10/30.

contained city freemen, freeholders, merchants, principal manufacturers and trad-ers.[129] Narcissus Batt's Belfast Infantry reflected middle-class mercantile aspira-tions: they employed a full-time sergeant major in 1803 to ensure that their drills and manoeuvres reflected their self-esteem and offered a salary of £50 per annum, more than double the government allowance, raised from a officers' subscription. Similarly they raised £80 for regimental colours and over £100 for a yeomanry band.[130]

A detailed occupational analysis of the Irish Yeomanry would be impossible to achieve, as the few surviving muster rolls do not give this information. However it is still possible to obtain a reasonably accurate overview from the contemporary com-ments of administrators, generals and landowners. Given the largely agricultural nature of the Irish economy, it would be a truism to say that many yeomen were employed on the land. However, the extent to which this was the case can be gauged from the fact that the authorities considered the agricultural cycle as a factor when-ever they contemplated calling the force out on duty. When the French fleet sailed from Brest in May 1799 the yeomanry did permanent duty despite, as Castlereagh noted, it being the potato planting season in Ulster.[131] The contemporary predilec-tion for ascribing behaviour to occupation or social class reveals a more detailed breakdown of the composition of the force without overturning its largely agricul-tural basis. In 1801, General Floyd surveyed the yeomanry and reckoned the best types should be the tenantry of the country, 'husbandmen, manufacturers and shop-keepers'; the more wealthy he thought should be cavalry. The Yeomanry Office en-dorsed his report 'it is composed exactly as the Lieutenant General recommends'.

The following year the chief secretary, William Wickham also made a tripartite division, distinguishing some corps as being composed almost entirely of gentle-men of fortune, others of farmers under their landlords, and still others of shop-keepers and inhabitants of towns.[132] He considered the farmers as the best type, with the propertied yeomen loyal but ineffective, and the townsmen lazy and liti-gious. Other rural occupations were represented. The Dunlavin Cavalry in Wick-low included the various employees of the landowner who raised them, namely serv-ants, masons, a blacksmith and a slater. Weavers feature in many Ulster infantry corps, sometimes comprising the whole corps, as in the Lurgan Infantry and all corps in the Moneymore, Coagh, Arboe and Stewartstown area of south Tyrone. In other areas they served alongside farmers. Alexander McMullan, a Downshire aco-lyte, listed 30 men from the parishes of Annahilt, Hillsborough and Drumbo will-

129 C. Maxwell, *Dublin under the Georges*, p. 44; Stanley to Pelham, 8 July 1797, P.R.O. H.O.100/70/ff. 45–6; 13 Feb. 1799, P.R.O.N.I. Donoughmore Papers, T3439/D/6/6.   130 Belfast Yeomanry Orderly Book, 1803–1809, P.R.O.N.I. D3221/1.   131 Castlereagh to Wickham, 11 May 1799, P.R.O. H.O.100/86/f. 349.   132 Abstract of general remarks, 8 Sept. 1801, B.L. Hardwicke Papers add. mss. 35924 ff. 95–9; Yeomanry Memo, 24 Mar. 1802, H.R.O. Wickham Papers, 38M49/5/10/14.

ing to serve as infantrymen, 25 of whom were farmers four weavers and one a linen draper.[133] This probably was a higher than average social mix for infantry corps. There was considerable variation within the force. John Stewart told Abercorn that three quarters of the yeomen in west Tyrone 'have not ten pounds worth in the world to protect', but as he wrote in November 1803, he may well have been referring to the large numbers of supplementaries raised that year.[134] The general rule of thumb regarding the social class of yeomen, cavalry or infantry, was that all had something to defend. Their economic connection with the establishment, however tenuous, was also recognised by their opponents. In late 1797 Camden told Portland that the Cork United Irishmen were withholding trade from those who had enrolled as yeomen.[135] A considerable economic gap, with social and religious parallels, existed between even the yeoman infantryman and the poorest members of Irish society. Indeed, the yeoman was usually of a higher social and economic group than those who would normally join the regular army. Lord Rossmore summed it up in 1799, noting, 'our infantry yeoman is composed of much better material than the common soldier'. A recent study of the British Volunteer Infantry makes exactly the same point.[136]

The Irish Yeomanry emerges as a force which belies its previously scanty historical treatment. The Irish government took the control of the yeomanry seriously, compromises over issues like election of officers and the existence of committees are best seen as flexible modifications of original plans designed to keep control by being responsive. Yeomanry numbers were extremely significant, equalling and probably exceeding the highest total ever achieved by the Irish Volunteers and maintaining it for much longer. This meant that the cost of the force was high, an expense less easily tolerated by the Westminster parliament after Union. The impression of an overwhelmingly Protestant force remains, but it is modified by evidence of regionally substantial Catholic participation, especially before 1798. Presbyterian involvement was also initially substantial in western Ulster and became general throughout the province after the rebellion. Socially, the yeomanry represented a wide variety of groups from peers and landowners to weavers, tradesmen and even labourers. However, although the common denominator for most yeomen was that they had something to defend, property defence was only one aspect of the force's remit. The deepening security crisis from the near-invasion at Bantry Bay in 1796 dictated that a wider, more militarised role would come sooner rather than later.

---

133 Ash to Castlereagh, 11 July 1798, N.A. S.O.C.1017/36; McMullan to Downshire, 28 Nov. 1796, P.R.O.N.I. Downshire Papers, D607/D/356.   134 Stewart to Abercorn, 15 Nov. 1803, P.R.O.N.I. Abercorn Papers, D623/A/142/23.   135 Elliot to Pelham, 30 Oct. 1797, N.A. S.O.C.1016/27; 15 Nov. 1797, P.R.O. H.O.100/66/ff. 59–64.   136 Movements for light infantry well adapted to the yeomanry of Ireland, 2 Feb. 1799, P.R.O.N.I. Rossmore Papers, T2929/32/56; A. Gee, 'The British Volunteer Movement, 1793–1807', p. 134.

6

'Convince them you think they are good soldiers, and you will make them such'[1]

General John Knox used this adage in 1799, when he was formulating plans to utilise part of the northern yeomanry as an anti-invasion force. However, three years earlier, when the new yeomanry force was finally on foot, the question was not about their utility as soldiers but whether they could be useful to soldiers. Militarily the Irish government faced an unenviable dilemma in formulating its defence policy. Basically, the problem was about how to meet the strategically antithetical demands of providing local protection against the depredations of United Irishmen and Defenders, which necessarily involved small scattered detachments, while at the same time retaining the ability to gather sufficient force, 'concentration' in contemporary parlance, to meet an invading army.[2] The yeomanry's remit was to relieve the army by providing domestic peacekeeping and the potential for garrison duty to allow the regulars to concentrate during invasion or insurrection.[3] As each eventuality was quintessentially unexpected, advance planning was of the first priority. However the first official consideration of how this was to be achieved did not come till late November 1796 when Camden calmly informed Portland that 'we are considering in what manner the different corps ... can be most advantageously employed in order to leave the army more at liberty to act'.[4] The appearance of French ships in Bantry Bay on 21 December rudely interrupted Camden's considerations, revealed an appalling state of unreadiness on the part of the military commanders, and thrust the yeomanry into action for the first time. Given that the force was recently raised and no emergency contingency plans were determined, the overall response must be judged successful. Yeomen took over town garrisons and guard duty at gaols to free the regulars up to oppose the anticipated landing, and used their local knowledge to keep communication lines open and convey expresses. They took up the task with an ostentatious patriotism reminiscent of the heady days of volunteering.

---

1 Richardson, *Yeomanry*, p. 48. 2 For a full discussion see P.C. Stoddart, 'Counter-insurgency and Defence in Ireland, 1790–1805', see also T. Bartlett, 'Defence, counter-insurgency and rebellion: Ireland, 1793–1803' in T. Bartlett and K. Jeffrey (eds), *A Military History of Ireland*, pp. 247–93. 3 37 Geo III, c. 2. 4 28 Nov. 1796, P.R.O. H.O.100/65/f. 136.

William Stephenson of Clonmel encapsulated the enthusiasm gripping the southern yeomen on their first taste of danger, when he wrote of being 'up to the saddle-skirts in snow at the head of a party of yeomen impressing horses for the artillery'. Shannon told Camden how men of £3–4,000 a year were escorting baggage and carrying expresses. Even the affluent banker John La Touche rode twenty-five miles on a foul night with an express.[5] Obviously there was an element of new-fangled enthusiasm and self-importance in this which may have disappeared had the French landed. Thrashing through the Christmas snow was an exhilarating diversion from the tedium of estate or commercial business and the sense of danger and comradeship no doubt added spice to many a punchbowl. Yet the threat was real: had the full contingent landed, over 14,000 seasoned French troops plus artillery would have struck at Ireland's badly-organised defences. Cork would undoubtedly have fallen. Carhampton reckoned that only 8,000 troops could have been assembled to oppose the French there.[6] The problem of concentrating the troops was a matter of high military policy and strategy. The yeomanry successfully freed up regulars, allowing them to be concentrated, and in consequence were highly valued by the government. The experience underlined advantageous aspects of yeomanry service, in particular the utilisation of local knowledge. Mr White of Seafield House, Bantry, commander of a local yeomanry corps, organised outposts on the cliffs and kept the government minutely informed of developments. Accurate information was vitally important, as at this stage it was not clear if the Bantry appearance was a diversion to draw off the Irish army while the main landing occurred elsewhere. White and his yeomen were considered to have done such essential service that he was subsequently elevated to the peerage as Lord Bantry.[7]

Though the yeomanry had been successful in their own terms during the invasion scare, and were excluded from the subsequent criticism heaped on the military hierarchy, the shake-up in Ireland's military defences following the Bantry crisis had important ramifications for their future role. There were two alternative proposals on how best to improve defence. The first was to station large bodies of troops near areas thought to be in danger from invasion, and at key centres such as Cork and Dublin. This approach, favoured by Carhampton, would shorten response time by allowing quicker concentration. Prior to invasion, this arrangement would combine surveillance with peacekeeping whereas, if a landing occurred, the force nearest would harass and delay the French to give the remainder time to concentrate. Dalrymple, the southern district commander, proposed an alternative: to maintain a separate standing field army of 14,000 men ready to seek and destroy the invader.[8] Dalrymple's was the military idealist's textbook solution, presupposing unlimited resources. In reality the problem facing the government and its generals was how to

5 4 Jan. 1797, Stephenson to Pelham, N.A. R.P.620/28/34; Camden to Portland, 10 Jan. 1797, P.R.O. H.O.100/69/f. 62.   6 Stoddart, op. cit., p. 133.   7 Lecky, *Ireland*, iii, p. 531.   8 Stoddart, op. cit., pp. 138–62.

maximise the resources it had. From this point onwards, under-utilisation of the yeomanry's military potential becomes a constant theme in the government's defence strategy. The aftermath of the Bantry fiasco saw the first move to integrate the yeomanry into contingency plans against invasion and insurrection. Following its good performance during the crisis, which included offers of general military service from many yeomen, plans were laid for the force to assume garrison duties in an emergency and provide volunteers for a body of 'irregular cavalry' to act in a guerrilla-type harassing role and slow up the French advance.

This introduced another problem. The southern yeomen who leapt on their horses at Christmas did so in the knowledge they faced no real threat from United Irishmen or Defenders. This was far from the case in Ulster where there had been problems raising yeomen in Down, Antrim and parts of Tyrone. Those that were raised faced frustrating delays waiting for their arms while they endured a rapidly growing system of intimidation. Lake set up arrangements for magistrates throughout the northern district, including Thomas Knox himself, to apply to the divisional generals for troops.[9] The harsh reality of Ulster in early 1797 dictated that military protection was needed to protect the yeomen and enable the struggling corps to become firmly established before they could be of utility either to the magistrates or the generals. At this stage opinion was split on the degree of assistance the yeomen could provide for the army. Carhampton and Pelham thought a combination of peacekeeping and a limited anti-invasion role was possible. General Knox, and presumably his superior Lake, thought the force was numerically sufficient for 'police' duties but had 'great doubts' about their fitness for the line.[10] The result was a compromise.

Before Bantry Bay, yeomanry activities were confined to drilling and providing *ad hoc* assistance to magistrates in cases where they were strong enough to do so. With the Bantry precedent in mind, a military policy for the entire force was determined and its implementation tailored to what was possible both in terms of local yeomanry strength and the local security situation. The Dublin corps were felt to be equal to the task of the garrison duty in the city by January 1797. In March, with the United star still in the ascendant, all corps were ordered to extend their peacekeeping duties by establishing local guards, piquets and cavalry patrols for night duty, in co-operation with the regular general commanding in each district.[11] Lord Aldborough's response in county Wicklow is illustrative, although his enthusiasm made him act in anticipation of the official instructions and arrange deployment in advance of the district general's approval. Aldborough put 20 cavalry and 20 infantry on duty, established a guard house from which he threw out a network of cavalry to patrol the approaches to Baltinglass, with sentry boxes also placed at strategic

9 Lake to Pelham, 5 Jan. 1797, B.L. Pelham Papers, add. mss. 33103 ff. 51–2.   10 J. Knox to Abercorn, 25 Feb. 1797, P.R.O.N.I. Abercorn Papers, D623/A/156/6.   11 Circular, 5 Mar. 1797, P.R.O.N.I. Lurgan Detail Book, D3697/A/4/1.

points. The remit of the patrols was to seize and disarm all 'idle and suspicious' persons, and bring them to the guard house for questioning by an officer or magistrate.[12] In Ulster, where the United Irish threat was greater, the piquets and guards were more defensive and designed to protect vulnerable property, particularly the homes of magistrates and yeomen, where the presence of arms made them a target rather than a deterrent. Such guards usually consisted of one officer and six men.[13] Around the same time, because of the shortage of regulars, some yeomen were used in arms searches in parts of Ulster. Both piquet duty and arms searches were considered as 'occasional duty', as distinct from permanent duty. This compromise drew a more militarised service from the yeomanry without interfering with its basically civilian nature. The yeomen were paid at regular army rates, but were not subject to military discipline, an anomaly which caused problems, as a raw civilian force was launched into duties that even hardened regulars found extremely problematic. The logistics of arms searches necessitated surprise, and small, mobile detachments. The yeomen were under the direction of the district generals but commanded by their own officers. The government näively considered that zeal would compensate for military discipline, but in practice the enthusiasm was often for sectarian score-settling rather than disinterested public service. The poor ratio of officers to men, the lack of training and discipline and in some cases the absence of a magistrate was a headache for the authorities and there were frequent complaints about indiscipline.[14] The use and effect of yeomanry in arms searches had a long-term impact on the wider Irish law and order issue and will be discussed more fully in due course. The government publicly fostered the view that the more militarised role was successful. Camden ordered a general inspection by the district generals in April 1797 and in July praised the yeomen in parliament for improvements in discipline. Privately the Castle admitted that control of the yeomanry on duty was difficult and the cost high: once the immediate security risk lessened, piquets were discontinued in August 1797, with discretion for local guards left to the generals.[15] The United Irishmen in Ulster had been damaged, though Lake felt, correctly, as June 1798 was to show, that disaffection was 'smothered but not extinguished'.[16] The counter-insurgency/national defence problem similarly waited for the next crisis to cause it to flare up again.

The appointment of Sir Ralph Abercromby as commander-in-chief to replace Carhampton in November 1797, brought Irish military affairs to a crisis. A career soldier with a very considerable reputation, Abercromby had a doctrinaire approach

12 Aldborough to Pelham, n.d. March 1797, P.R.O.N.I. Aldborough Papers, T3300/13/2/13.   13 Caledon to Pelham, 14 Apr. 1797, N.A. R.P.620/29/256; Lindsay to Pelham, 22 Apr. 1797, N.A. S.O.C.1016/45.   14 Circular, 5 July 1797, P.R.O.N.I. Lurgan Detail Book, D3696/A/4/1.   15 Copy of Camden's Speech, 3 July 1797, P.R.O. H.O.100/72/ff. 70–1; Elliott to Knox, 19 Aug. 1797, N.L.I. Lake Papers, MS56/92, Circular, 25 Aug. 1797, P.R.O.N.I. Lurgan Detail Book, D3696/A/4/1.   16 Lake to Pelham, 27 Jan. 1798, B.L. Pelham Papers, add. mss. 33105 f. 336.

to military matters and was clear about the division between the army's civil and military role. He was particularly worried about the bad effects of having so many troops dispersed on peacekeeping detachments at the request of the magistrates both in Ulster and elsewhere. This approach, on top of the usual professional jealousy, meant inevitable conflict within the military hierarchy. Abercromby immediately ordered Lake's troops to be drawn in from peacekeeping and posted to stations along a natural defensive line from the Bann through Lough Neagh and the Blackwater to Lough Erne and eventually to Ballyshannon. The idea was to prevent movement by the disaffected in the event of invasion and eliminate one of the preliminary stages of concentration should the regulars have to move. Potentially this threw the full peacekeeping burden on the yeomanry. Abercromby referred Lake to the circular of August 1797, directing him to put the yeomen back on piquet and patrol duty to compensate for the regulars.[17]

By January 1798, however, the plans were modified, probably in response to objections from Lake and Knox. The main change was structural. Pre-arrangements were to be made for the yeomanry to amalgamate in larger bodies than their usual self-sufficient corps and be moved to defensive 'stations' along the same line as that proposed by Abercromby. A stiffening of regulars, one cavalry regiment and 3,000 infantry, was to remain with the yeomen and army officers appointed to supervise the various yeomanry brigades and determine the station on strategic grounds, 'as many of the [yeomanry] captains would wish to make their own home their head quarters'. The possibility of utilising some of the 14,000 Ulster yeomen as light troops against the French was left as an additional option.[18] The idea of superimposing a military structure on the naturally scattered and separate yeomanry corps appears to have come from John Knox whose correspondence gives a strong impression of a restlessly innovative mind at work. In September 1797 he secured Pelham's approval for a plan which would enable the army to concentrate together in the event of invasion.[19] Though unstated at the time, this most likely involved gathering the yeomanry in brigades; indeed, it may have been an extension of his wish to raise fencible regiments earlier in the year, the refusal of which almost led to his resignation. At any rate, in January 1798, details of all yeomanry stations in Ulster were transmitted to the Castle by Knox, rather than Lake who commanded the district.[20]

Lake and Knox differed in their views of the yeomanry as an aid to the military, with the latter's Irish gentry background and local connections making him much more positive. Lake told Knox that he was initially 'fumed out of my life and almost mad' at the idea of leaving Ulster to be defended by its yeomanry, which he feared would 'undo everything we have done', and the stiffening of regulars was undoubt-

17 Abercromby to Lake, 13 Dec. 1797, P.R.O. W.O.30/66/f. 194.   18 N.A.M. 6807–174/f. 333, Nugent Papers, Orders to Ulster Yeomanry, n.d. Jan. 1798.   19 Pelham to Knox, 28 Sept. 1797, N.L.I. Lake Papers, MS56/98.   20 Elliott to J. Knox, 24 Jan. 1798, N.L.I. Lake Papers, MS56/125.

edly at his insistence.[21] However, the yeomanry brigade plan had Pelham's approval and was to be implemented throughout Ireland. The tension between the Castle, the northern generals and Abercromby was almost palpable. Lake gleefully told Knox that, 'between ourselves, Pelham and the chief are by no means on good terms', while Abercromby himself, on a tour of the southern district, began to revert to his original assessment of the yeomanry's emergency role. Writing from Cork, he told Camden that he was 'nearly convinced it would be bad to bring them [the yeomanry] together and appoint officers to command them'; that they would be better employed as guides and intelligence gatherers. Ironically, though Lake detested Abercromby, his objections to the military use of yeomanry were, like his chief's, those of the soldier. As it was government policy Lake had to warm to the idea, though he worried about control of large yeomanry brigades not under regular military discipline and insisted nothing be done at this stage other than pre-arrange the stations.[22]

Abercromby's criticism of the Irish army, and his implication that the gentry were not doing their job of keeping the localities quiet, had outraged Ascendancy opinion, to the extent that his resignation was inevitable. However his sacrifice on the altar of gentry pride did nothing to placate the coming storm. Abercromby was replaced by Lake as commander-in-chief, but his analysis of Ireland's defence strategy remained. The yeomanry needed to provide support to let the regular army gather in strength. The worsening situation and the coming of Castlereagh to the chief secretaryship saw further refinement of Knox's plans, which took on board many of Lake's concerns. General Knox was called to the Castle to help Castlereagh and Camden adapt the yeomanry brigade concept for the whole country. Basically Knox saw the military deficiency in the territorial organisation of yeomanry. Separate baronial, parish or town corps might meet the purposes of local peacekeeping but were militarily unmanageable for larger operations. To make it possible for scattered corps to act in unison, Knox saw the necessity of pre-arranging a strategically placed, defensible common rallying point which was acceptable to the yeomen themselves. Knox met yeomanry captains in Fermanagh, Cavan, Monaghan, Armagh and Tyrone, to fine-tune the new arrangements.[23] To facilitate assembly, a system of alarm posts was pre-arranged for the yeomen to gather in an emergency, prior to marching to the yeomanry stations for permanent duty.[24] Each district general was given an allocation of yeomanry brigades composed of the corps from surrounding baronies. In Derry city, Brigadier General, the earl of Cavan had responsibility for

21 Lake to Knox, 7 Jan. 1798, N.L.I. Lake Papers, MS56/121.   22 Abercromby to Camden, 23 Jan. 1798, K.A.O. Pratt Papers, U840/0166/10; Lake to Knox, 26 Jan. 1798, N.L.I. Lake Papers, MS56/126.   23 Castlereagh to Knox 23 April 1798, N.L.I. Lake Papers, MS56/155; Knox to Lake, 20 May 1798, Castlereagh Correspondence, i, pp. 195–8.   24 Return of the yeomanry corps on duty in Dublin, n.d. [June 1798], P.R.O. Colchester Papers, 30/9/133/6; Goldie to Brownlow, 5 July 1798, P.R.O.N.I. Lurgan Yeomanry Detail Book, D3696/A/4/1.

the yeomanry of some of the baronies of Donegal and Tyrone, and all those of county Londonderry. At Enniskillen, Knox had the remainder of Tyrone and Donegal, plus Armagh, Monaghan, Fermanagh and Cavan in six yeomanry brigades, while Nugent directed the brigades in the east of the province from Blaris Camp near Lisburn.[25] In total the yeomanry of the Northern District provided eleven brigades. As provided for in the Yeomanry Act, new offers were invited for yeomen to go on permanent duty and put themselves under the Mutiny Act. Each district general was allocated their brigades, new control structures devised, and a reserve of supplementary yeomen and armed civilian volunteers organised for emergency duty. Yeomanry brigade majors were appointed on a county basis to inspect the corps and check pay returns. Although they did not hold commissions they were to have military experience and functioned as liaison between the district generals and the yeomanry captains. Standing orders were issued to regulate administration and ensure smooth integration into the military system.[26] These Irish arrangements were designed to counter the expected rebellion but in their form they were consonant with contemporary military thinking in Britain, where invasion was the dominant fear. The British volunteers and yeomanry were also given a more militarised role, with offers for service wider than the locality of the corps being solicited, inspecting field officers were appointed (a similar official at this stage to the Irish brigade major) and unpaid armed associations (like the Irish supplementaries) organised to take over local peacekeeping if the corps should move.[27]

Although these new arrangements would be the nearest the yeomanry force came to full military duty – Lake grimly ordered that all corps in Knox's district have the Yeomanry Act read to them, 'to let them know what they had to expect [military discipline] under the circumstances'[28] – in reality there was still room for compromise. The overriding objective was to extract the maximum possible military benefit from the yeomanry institution without pushing civilians to the point where they would resign, as they were perfectly entitled to do. In Carlow, those corps who refused permanent duty were converted to supplementaries who could continue to exercise and be ready for any emergency.[29] In Ulster Camden privately assured Charlemont, who apparently saw the hand of arbitrary power behind every Yeomanry Office circular, that his yeomen could do permanent duty without being under military law as, in this instance, he would construe the act according to its voluntary 'spirit'.[30] Not all yeomen volunteered for permanent duty in 1798, but most saw service in the rebellion, whether acting as a military corps under the Mutiny Act, or serving voluntarily. The Hillsborough Cavalry had an officer and 30 men on

25 N.A.M. 6807–174/ff. 433–4, Nugent Papers, Plans for yeomanry division by baronies, 22 May 1798. 26 Standing Orders for the Yeomanry of Ireland, 1798, B.L. 8827 AAA 43; Nugent to Castlereagh, 21 June 1798, P.R.O.N.I. Dublin Letters, MIC67/f. 64.   27 A Gee, op. cit., p. 284.   28 8 April 1798, N.L.I. Lake Papers, MS56/152.   29 1 April 1798, N.A. R.P.620/36/110, Rochfort to Pelham.   30 3 April 1798, H.M.C. *Charlemont*, ii, pp. 318–9,

permanent duty in June 1798, with a further 40 serving as volunteers and a further 40 available for relief duty.[31]

The numbers and deployment of yeomanry on permanent duty was the concern of the district generals. Whole corps, or detachments of corps, could be used. The regulations governing control and pay were strict. If 50 men from a corps were put on permanent duty, a captain had to go on duty with them. If 20 men were involved, a subaltern would suffice. Cavalry captains were paid fourteen shillings and six pence per day, first lieutenants nine shillings, sub-lieutenants eight shillings and privates two shillings. Infantry captains got nine shillings and four pence, first lieutenants five shillings and eight pence, sub-lieutenants four shillings and eight pence and privates one shilling. The returns were 'considered upon honour' and there was a fine of £200 for false returns. An interesting point about permanent pay is that it was paid in advance, unlike exercise pay which was retrospective. As soon as a corps went on permanent duty, the general officer signed a certificate for the number of men and estimated duration and sent it to the War Office, whereupon pay was issued.[32] This indicates that many yeomen could not afford to be away from their normal occupations for long periods. However there is also the tacit implication that yeomen were more controllable, or possibly less uncontrollable, when in the government's debt, rather than the other way around. The yeomanry brigade system was still being integrated into the military structure when events overtook planning and the long dreaded insurrection put these arrangements to the acid test.[33]

A BLOODY SUMMER: THE 1798 REBELLION

The Irish Yeomanry's role in the 1798 conflict has often been misunderstood and sometimes misrepresented. Hayes-McCoy claimed that the yeomen were 'soldiers only in name'; more like a 'Home Guard' or the Ascendancy's 'political police'.[34] This is consonant with the received popular opinion of the force, which highlights their role in martial law activities – house burnings and arms searches – preceding the rebellion, and their indiscriminate ferocity in mopping up afterwards, but passes over their role in the actual fighting. Atrocities undoubtedly happened in the crucible of the Leinster rising, which saw outrages by both sides in a conflict where the founder United Irishmen's non-sectarian ideal disappeared under old animosities and atavistic fears. However, this is not a good starting point to assess the yeomanry's role. In the dire emergency of 1798, the yeomanry's performance must be evaluated in the context of the 'new arrangements' just described. Did they cope well in a situation where variations of all possible scenarios rapidly developed? Contempo-

31 Stephenson to Downshire, 6 June 1798, P.R.O.N.I. Downshire Papers, D607/F/200.   32 Yeomanry Standing Orders, 1798.   33 Lake to Gen. Knox, 30 May 1798, N.L.I. Lake Papers, MS56/f.168.   34 Hayes-McCoy, *Irish Battles*, p. 274.

raries felt they did cope well. The period between May and September 1798 witnessed large-scale insurrection in Leinster and Ulster and a French landing in Connacht. Both required direct action from local yeomanry and both meant military relief duties elsewhere. Even Cornwallis, incorrigibly hostile to the yeomanry, admitted that, despite exceeding the militia in licentiousness, brutality and plundering, they had 'saved the country'.[35]

In practice Knox's 'alarm posts' and 'stations' became a series of small outlying garrisons in towns and villages, with more substantial defences for larger and more strategically central towns. Once these garrisons had been established, detachments of yeomanry, particularly cavalry could patrol the outlying countryside. This strategy was designed to give earliest notice of United Irish mobilisation and to secure key positions until sufficient force could be brought to bear. Given the reality of few regular troops, in relation to the possible numbers the United Irishmen could muster in Ulster and elsewhere, it was accepted that parts of the countryside would have to temporarily abandoned. This contingency was covered by planning. Fall-back positions were pre-determined should the outlying garrisons be faced with overwhelming force. The Castlewellan Infantry were dispersed in town guards in Ballynahinch, Rathfriland and Bryansford, as well as in Castlewellan itself, with Newry as the fall-back. Those in north Antrim and parts of county Londonderry were to retire to Coleraine.[36] These strategically significant, defensible garrison towns functioned as a last resort to be defended at all costs, and a haven where forces could gather to counter-attack. In Ulster these included Blaris camp (near Lisburn), Belfast, Downpatrick, Coleraine, Derry city, Portglenone, Armagh, Portadown and Newry. Sometimes the garrison would be composed entirely of yeomen, as in Enniskillen; others were mixed, with detachments of regulars, fencibles or militia. A similar integrated defence system operated elsewhere in Ireland. The Camolin Cavalry Detail Book shows garrisons and defence posts in Wexford.[37] The system was adaptable for urban corps but still embodied the principles of early warning and defence.

Waterford was left largely to the defence of the yeomen during the rising.[38] Dublin too had sufficient yeomen (over 3,000) to take much of the garrison duty. Major General Myers prearranged a system of emergency alarm posts. The Merchants' Infantry and Stephen's Green division gathered at Stephen's Green, the Lawyers at the parliament house, the Attorneys at the Four Courts, the Rotunda division at Essex Bridge and the Revenue corps at the Custom House. The 400-odd cavalry from various corps were split between two centres, one at College Green and the other at the lower end of Sackville Street. From these meeting points daily guards

35 N.A.M. 6602–45–3f. 5, Cornwallis Papers, Cornwallis to Ross, 24 July 1798.   36 Knox to Hewitt, 31 May 1798, P.R.O.N.I. Dublin Letters, MIC67/f. 39; Cavan to Lake, 9 June 1798, P.R.O. H.O.100/77/f. 139; Nugent to Lake, 10 June 1798, N.A. R.P.620/38/121.   37 Wheeler and Broadly, *The War in Wexford*, passim.   38 Mrs Frazer to Portland, 29 June 1798, P.R.O. H.O.100/66/f. 142.

and patrols were mounted by detachments of the corps. The cavalry guarded both sides of the river, Beresford's Riding House in Gloucester Street, and Leinster House. A detachment of one captain, one subaltern officer and fifty men patrolled each side of the Liffey from 9 p.m. till 9 a.m., when they were relieved by another detachment. Infantry corps mounted similar guards using detachments thrown out from a central defensible guard house.[39] The general intention was first to secure key buildings, thus seizing the initiative; then to restrict movement and stop crowds gathering, making it difficult for any co-ordinated action by the United Irishmen. In Belfast a similar strategy was adopted. The alarm post of Lord Donegall's cavalry was at the front of the White Linen Hall where they could command an intersection of wide streets.[40]

In the event of an insurrection both numerical advantage and, potentially the key element of surprise rested with the United Irishmen. The degree to which this natural advantage could be exploited depended on local United Irish organisation, the intelligence available to the authorities and the yeomen's quick response. The bureaucracy of intelligence-gathering might mean that although the government knew a rising was coming they could be taken by surprise by the precise moment at which it burst into flame. The rapidity of mobilisation in Antrim and Down was unstoppable by the yeomanry. McCracken's plan, to seize Antrim town as the magistrates met, was as simple as it was effective. It could be argued that the garrison, comprising Lord Massereene's yeomen, some citizens and a detachment of regular dragoons, was ineffective, but in reality Nugent had so little force at his disposal, and so wide an area of potential danger to cover, that he was inevitably going to be vulnerable to a concentration of force against any of the weaker points in his defence network. Similarly in Wexford the same lack of troops was apparent. Gordon, an historian of the Wexford rising, estimated the number of regulars and militia in the county at no more than 600, leaving the defence of the county *de facto* to yeomen and supplementaries. Here too the speed and size of the United Irish mobilisation on the night of 26 May caught the government forces, including yeomanry, by surprise, and there was no significant response for ten hours. Most of the yeomanry units were stationed in towns like Gorey, Ferns, Enniscorthy and Newtownbarry, with the result that the United Irish mobilisation in the countryside proceeded virtually unhindered.[41]

Where the United Irishmen were less well organised, the yeomanry brigade system worked well. When news of the Leinster rising reached Cork, General Brownrigg ordered all yeomanry brigades to assemble at their stations and threw out cavalry patrols to keep communications open in the countryside. Good intelligence and poor United Irish organisation helped the scattered yeomanry guards and patrols

39 Return of the yeomanry corps on duty in Dublin in June 1798, P.R.O. Colchester Papers, 30/9/133/6.   **40** Belfast Yeomanry Detail Book, P.R.O.N.I. D3221/1/89.   **41** Lecky, *Ireland*, iv, pp. 354–5; Gordon, *History of the Rebellion in Ireland*, pp. 86–8; D. Gahan, *The People's Rising*, pp. 32–4.

prevent coordinated action by their opponents. In Leitrim a poorly organised, partial rising occurred near Mohill, but was easily suppressed by the local yeomanry.[42] At the vital river crossing of Portglenone in county Antrim, the townspeople turned out along with the local yeomanry and thwarted the insurgents, who planned to capture this vital crossing between Antrim and Derry.[43] In Knox's district the arrangements successfully met the strategic objective of preventing the spread of insurrection into western Ulster. Detachments of corps in north Armagh were ordered into Lurgan and Portadown under the command of Joseph Atkinson of the Crowhill Infantry, where, in conjunction with fencibles and regular dragoons, they were to barricade the bridge over the upper Bann, prevent 'improper communication' from the county Down side, and stop all passage across the river between Portadown and Lough Neagh. Knox considered Atkinson's duty to be of 'the greatest consequence', as he himself moved a large force of yeomanry towards Toomebridge to seal the northern gateway to western Ulster.[44] When intelligence came of an intended rising to his south in Cavan, Knox immediately mustered a mixed force, consisting of the light company of the Essex regiment, two cannon, 200 infantry and 75 cavalry of the 'remarkably good' Fermanagh yeomanry, before marching from Enniskillen to link with the Cavan yeomanry brigades and ensure that the rising stopped before it started. Indeed, Knox's yeomanry brigade system was so effective and their numbers so considerable that in mid-June Lake considered using them in the southern conflict. (Nothing came of this, presumably because regular reinforcements arrived soon afterwards.[45]) The system also worked very well in Dublin, where the confined, more easily observable urban conditions and the strength of yeomanry numbers led to the United Irishmen losing the vital element of surprise. Viewed from a government perspective, this strategy was outstandingly successful, as seizure of the capital was central to the United Irish plan. Camden praised the speed with which Myers implemented his system.[46] It was arduous duty. One yeoman, Robert Johnston, complained he was on duty four times a week for over twenty six hours at a stretch.[47]

The system of fall-back positions worked better in Ulster than in the south-east. When the Down rising broke, the small garrisons of yeomanry and fencibles at Saintfield, Comber and Newtownards (the latter after a successful defence) fanned back to Belfast, putting the Lagan between themselves and the disaffected barony of Castlereagh. The system was flexible and allowed for on-the-spot decisions reflecting prevailing conditions. When the Castlewellan detachment at Ballynahinch

42 Brownrigg to [? Lake], 28 May 1798, P.R.O.N.I. Dublin Letters, MIC67/f. 34; Camden to Portland, 1 June 1798, P.R.O. H.O.100/81/f. 1.   43 Hudson to Charlemont, 19 June 1798, H.M.C. *Charlemont*, ii, p. 325.   44 Goldie to Atkinson, 10 June 1798, P.R.O.N.I. Atkinson of Crowhill Papers, T2701/2/8; Nugent to Knox, 10 June 1798, P.R.O. H.O.100/77/f. 135.   45 N.A.M. 6807–174 ff. 465–9 Nugent Papers, Knox to Nugent, 17 June 1798. Hewitt to Knox, 15 June 1798, N.L.I. Lake Papers, MS56/f. 153.   46 Musgrave, *Rebellions*, p. 261; Camden to Portland, 4 June 1798, P.R.O. H.O.100/81/f. 13.   47 Johnston to Downshire, 6 June 1798, P.R.O.N.I. Downshire Papers, D607/F/202.

was overwhelmed by incoming United Irishmen on the Saturday before the Battle of Ballynahinch, seven were captured but the rest withdrew to Hillsborough rather than Newry.[48] (Hillsborough was nearer and would involve less crossing of dangerous country in a confused and rapidly changing situation.) However, such was the weight of numbers involved in Wexford that even major towns could not be held in the early stages of the conflict. The Camolin cavalry were forced to abandon their post on 27 May and fall back on Gorey, together with all the loyal inhabitants of Camolin.[49] Gorey was defended by the earl of Courtown's yeomanry, and had to be abandoned in turn, with the entire government force and miscellaneous refugees falling back to Arklow. In other parts of the south the yeomen did better. Musgrave claimed the yeomanry garrison of Monasterevin repulsed an attacking force of over 1,300.[50]

The system was basically defensive, but allowed for detachments of yeomanry to counter-attack along with the regulars, while still retaining enough manpower to hold the base. The defence of Dublin was so successful, that Myers was able to march a force of 500 yeomen, with two cannon and 100 Fermanagh militiamen, against a reported gathering of rebels on Lord Powerscourt's Wicklow estate, although without the authority of Cornwallis, the new commander-in-chief.[51] The Armagh yeomanry garrisoned the town when a detachment of the 22nd. Light Dragoons was suddenly rushed to the fighting in Antrim.[52] General Nugent waited at Belfast until he had gathered sufficient force before venturing out to Ballynahinch to apply the *coup de grâce*, leaving the town garrisoned mainly by yeomen and civilian volunteers. Downpatrick provided the rest of the government force which defeated the Down rebels. It had been garrisoned by the Argyle Fencibles and various neighbouring local yeomanry corps, but was left entirely to the Downpatrick Infantry and civilians when the bulk of the garrison marched to join Nugent at Ballynahinch.[53]

However no amount of contingency planning would ensure the yeomen would fight if and when the conflict came. Questions had been raised about yeomanry loyalty north and south in 1797. The United Irish campaign of infiltration was generally related to Presbyterian or Catholic membership, though there were some instances in Ulster of Anglican yeomen being suspected of disloyalty. Despite purges in 1797 and 1798, this campaign, which Myles Byrne describes, evidently had some effect, and doubts lingered about whether the force would fight. There were reports of desertions in some corps in counties Wexford, Kildare and Dublin. One county Dublin corps, the Rathcoole Infantry, proved disaffected to a man, with the excep-

48 Lane to Downshire, 10 June 1798, P.R.O.N.I. Downshire Papers, D607/F/221.   49 Gordon, op cit., p. 104.   50 Musgrave, *Rebellions*, p. 307.   51 Ross to Downshire, 24 June 1798, P.R.O.N.I. Downshire Papers, D607/F/271.   52 F. Gervais to P. Gervais, 10 June 1798, P.R.O.N.I. Gervais Papers, T1827/3/14.   53 McKey to Downshire, 10 June 1798, P.R.O.N.I. Downshire Papers, D607/F/219; *Down Recorder*, 9 June 1838.

tion of their captain and two privates. By way of example, their lieutenant was tried by court martial and executed. Disaffection was also reported in county Cork and in the North around Dungiven. Some prominent individual desertions occurred. The United Irish leader at Arklow, Anthony Perry of Inch, was an ex-yeoman.[54] In Down, Lake had entertained doubts about Matthew Forde's Kilmore yeomanry because of Forde's own liberal politics. United Irish intimidation of yeomen, yeomanry involvement in the government's campaign of counter-terror, and perceived Orange and Defender links, had already created mutually antagonistic parties nursing subjective grievances. As local residents, both the loyalists and their opponents had a stake in the territory they fought over. The rebellion did not test yeomanry loyalty so much as it uncovered the failure of the infiltration campaign. Nugent's dispatch following the Battle of Ballynahinch scotched the suspicions about Forde's yeomen by expressly mentioning how well this corps had fought. Castlereagh admitted that 'some few [yeomanry] corps ... and but very few in that vast military establishment, have been corrupted'.[55] 'Hearths and Homes' certainly was a strong motivation to fight, but the local context of the conflict could prove a double-edged sword. With both parties activated by potent mixtures of fear and revenge, the problem was not getting the yeomen to fight but making them stop.

The determination of the rebels drew comment even from their opponents and clearly their *ad hoc* tactics had no precedent in the military experience of those commanding or comprising the government forces. With the regulars severely depleted and reinforcements uncertain, yeomanry along with fencibles and militia would inevitably be in the thick of a conflict which would not be played by the rules. In some aspects of their composition and deployment the yeomen had advantages over their opponents, in others they were disadvantaged. The potential advantages the United Irishmen held over the government forces were surprise, strength of numbers and local knowledge. From an army commander's viewpoint, having detachments of local yeomanry in his force rendered the latter aspect less of a problem. The Camolin Cavalry Detail Book shows the extent that military commanders used the yeomen's local knowledge to its best advantage in reconnoitreing, carrying expresses and providing guides and escorts.[56] The numerical disadvantage was considerable. The Wexford yeomanry stood at 1,884 *after* the rebellion, whereas the insurgents were able to assemble 10–15,000 for the attack on New Ross. This imbalance was to some extent counteracted by the yeomen having defensible positions in towns, often the market house, plus the availability of good firearms and being trained in their use. In the Wexford rising it has been noted that attacks on defended build-

54 Marshall to Pelham, 2 June 1798, B.L. Pelham Papers, add. mss. 33105/ff. 368–9; Cooke to Wickham, 3, 4 June 1798, P.R.O. H.O.100/81/ff. 3–9; Roberts to Castlereagh, 7 June 1798, N.A. R.P.620/38/83; Hamilton to Abercorn, 9 June 1798, P.R.O.N.I. Abercorn Papers, D623/A/90/20; Hayes-McCoy, op. cit., p. 290.   55 Castlereagh to Wickham, 12 June 1798, *Castlereagh Corrs*, i, pp. 219–20; Nugent to Lake, 13 June 1798, N.A. R.P.620/38/129.   56 Wheeler and Broadley, *The War in Wexford*, passim.

ings were the most costly and least effective of the types of action engaged in by the rebel forces.[57] The structure of market houses was both their strength and weakness: as two-storey stone buildings with slate roofs, they gave height for musketeers in a commanding central position and protection against assault by fire; however, with the ground level necessarily kept open, for trading, they were vulnerable to fires being started with straw. The garrisons of Randalstown and Ballymena were smoked out in this manner and taken prisoner. At Portaferry Captain Matthews, who commanded the local yeomen, had prior military experience and learnt the lessons of Randalstown and Ballymena by blocking up the archways of the market house.[58] Here the attackers were repelled by a combination of musketry from the market house and cannon fire from a revenue cruiser in the harbour. Having inflicted heavy casualties, the yeomen withdrew safely to their fall-back position across the lough to Strangford, itself within reach of the heavily defended town of Downpatrick. Much depended on the resolution of the United forces. If they were prepared to face fire and take heavy losses to get close enough, they were generally successful due to weight of numbers. Small yeomanry garrisons at, for example, Newtownards and Monasterevin, were able to repel attacking forces of 1–2,000 but at Enniscorthy at least 6,000 insurgents cleverly split their force for simultaneous attacks and used the age-old but bluntly effective tactic of driving cattle in advance of their charge to panic the defenders.

From the United Irishmen's perspective, the element of surprise offered the best conditions for success. Not only could they seize the initiative but also have the best chance of exploiting their opponents' weaknesses. Given that the army was largely composed of militia, fencibles and yeomanry, men who had never seen action, the major weakness was inexperience. Of all the government forces, the yeomen had the least military training and experience. Fencibles and militia were at least full-time soldiers and used to garrison life, whereas yeomen had only been on permanent duty for a matter of weeks. Inevitably this inexperience saw some bad decisions, sheer panic and a foolhardiness which ranged from misplaced bravery to arrogant underestimation of their opponents.[59] At Enniscorthy the yeoman infantry detachment drawn up to defend the main gate, underestimated the danger and moved out too far from cover, thinking this would scatter the oncoming assault, whereas their cavalry reserve blindly launched a headlong charge at the massed rebel ranks, only to be mauled by pike and musketry. The underlying mind-set here was a relic of the earlier eighteenth century, when the sight of a red coat had usually been enough to cow agrarian mobs. At other times inexperience led to overestimation. At Antrim Lord Massereene's yeomen panicked and ran, on the first volley from their opponents. However such inexperience should be seen in the context of the conflict: the nature of the fighting in 1798 was largely unfamiliar to the regular officers

57 D. Gahan, op. cit., p. 121 and passim.   58 A.T.Q. Stewart, *The Summer Soldiers*, p. 190.   59 Gahan, op. cit., pp. 48–9; Ross to Downshire, 9 June 1798, P.R.O.N.I. Downshire Papers, D607/F/212.

and men, with the possible exception to those who had served in America. Moreover, like all government forces, the yeomen were facing an unpredictable enemy who were themselves pragmatically making up their tactics as best suited their numbers, their arms and the country they fought in. Put succinctly, in the initial fighting neither side had the measure of the other. At Antrim regular cavalry, the 22nd Light Dragoons, paid the same price as the Enniscorthy yeoman cavalry had done for charging a column of pikemen which held its ground.[60] In these circumstances, given that in the initial conflict the insurgents often held the advantage of surprise, the yeomen clearly performed as effectively as any other arm of the government forces.

When the conflict moved from its initial phase of speedy, unpredictable strikes, to large-scale predictable confrontations, the United Irishmen were playing the game according to rules the government's generals understood. County Down affords the best example of this. At the start of the Down rising the Battle of Saintfield saw a mixed government force of fencibles and yeomanry ambushed and forced to retreat with heavy casualties, whereas the climactic battle at Ballynahinch several days later, saw a planned, patient response. Nugent was able to bring separate forces to bear on the rebels from different directions, putting their larger army on the defensive and paving the way for victory. Both attacking forces were supported by yeomanry and both had yeomen guarding their bases, Belfast and Downpatrick, when Nugent chose the moment to begin the offensive. Though there were occasions when circumstances meant yeomen tackled the insurgents unassisted, they mostly fought alongside regulars, militia or fencibles, under regular army commanders. This compensated for the necessarily uneven quality of their own leadership, being a civilian force raised by men whose criteria for service was social influence rather than military ability. Integrated service improved the overall efficiency of the force. Gordon noted that 'yeoman infantry, supported by regular troops fought steadily against the foe'.[61] Although integration in the army obviously helped the yeomen, the process was not all one-way. In parliament Castlereagh praised all government forces for their role in suppressing the rebellion, but highlighted the yeomen for voluntarily marching with the army: 'without these services ... it would have been impossible for the other branches of the public force to have saved the country'.[62] General Needham, whose force of 1,500 at the Battle of Arklow included 280 yeoman cavalry and 80 infantry, told Camden that 'the zeal and spirited conduct of the yeomanry corps were everything I could wish'. At Ballynahinch, Nugent told Lake, who had previously criticised the yeomanry, of their 'extreme steadiness and bravery' and confided to Castlereagh that they were 'equal to the best troops' in such actions. Gordon expressed the generally accepted view that yeoman cavalry, though good for reconnaissance, were less effective in the actual fighting due to the broken na-

60 Stewart, op cit., p. 112.   61 Gordon, *A History of the Rebellion*, p. 63.   62 Quoted in J. Groves-White, *The Yeomanry of Ireland*, p. 8

ture of the countryside. He also noted that their higher social status made them less deferential than the infantry having a total 'want of proper subordination'.[63]

The yeomanry were therefore at their most effective in two related circumstances: when they were integrated with the army, and when the danger was greatest. In the first weeks of June thousands of regular reinforcements, plus fencibles and English militia, poured in and the initiative swung away from the insurgents both in Ulster and Leinster. Once the rebellion was defeated in the field, the task of the army reverted to restoring tranquillity as soon as possible. This was hindered by the eagerness of the yeomanry to keep up the conflict by attacking everyone they suspected of having been involved with the rebels. When the immediate danger lessened, yeomanry discipline broke down in many areas which had been the scene of fighting. This post-conflict indiscipline was not confined to the yeomanry. Cornwallis, who succeeded Lake as commander-in-chief on 20 June, noted the propensity of all those in arms to cut down 'anyone in a brown coat' after battles, and that in the Irish forces this was not confined to the private men. The Irish militia were notoriously undisciplined. Nugent had great problems restraining members of the Monaghan regiment from wrecking Lord Moira's house after the Battle of Ballynahinch, whereas Castlereagh received complaints from Waterford that 'friends or foes are all the same to them and they will plunder indiscriminately advancing or retreating'. Cornwallis recognised this, but made a distinction between the militia and the yeomanry, whom he compared in type to American loyalist militiamen but in character 'a thousand times more ferocious'.[64] One of Cornwallis' generals, Sir John Moore, whom even the United Irishmen considered a humane commander, perceptively noticed that this was more than post-conflict indiscipline. Moore realised the influence of local residence and connections and that some of the yeomen he commanded had had their houses burnt and friends or relations murdered by the rebels and were bent on revenge.[65] However, on permanent duty the yeomanry were a military force and, from a military viewpoint, such actions were hugely counter-productive. With the Ulster rising already crushed, and in the south the initiative firmly with the army following Vinegar Hill and the re-capture of Wexford town, Cornwallis' strategy was to stabilize the conflict-zones by getting the inhabitants to return to their homes as a first step in a return to normal conditions. With the enemy defeated, he wanted to end the war, or prevent an ongoing '*petite guerre*' or guerilla war, by ending warlike conditions. Yeomen engaging in vendettas prevented a beginning being made on the slow road back to tranquillity. The polarisation was such that the assumption was made that anyone who was not a loyalist was a rebel. The

63 Gordon, ibid., p. 63; Needham to Camden, 10 June 1798, P.R.O. H.O.100/73/f. 21; Nugent to Lake, 13 June 1798, N.A. R.P.620/38/129; Castlereagh to Pelham, 16 June 1798, B.L. Pelham Papers, add. mss. 33105/ff. 439–40. 64 Cornwallis to Portland, 28 June 1798, P.R.O. H.O.100/77/f. 200; Cornwallis to Ross, 24 July 1798, *Cornwallis Correspondence*, ii, p. 371, Anon. to Castlereagh, 29 Aug. 1798, *Castlereagh Correspondence*, i, p. 342. 65 Maurice (ed.), *The Diary of Sir John Moore*, p. 302.

infamous case of Hugh Wollaghan, a Wicklow yeoman who shot an unarmed man on suspicion and later claimed he was acting on orders, became a *cause célèbre*.[66] However, there were many other similar incidents. At Baltinglass General Duff reported that 'the yeoman patrols are doing much mischief by firing at every person they meet in the fields, which deters many of them from returning to their habitations and convinces them that they cannot escape death'.[67] Notwithstanding orders from Cornwallis and the best efforts of his staff, the yeomanry in the areas of recent fighting proved less amenable to discipline once the danger lessened. Despite issuing a proclamation at the end of June, on 26 July Moore recorded in his diary that he was still 'constantly obliged to reprove [yeomanry] violence ... to gratify their revenge and ill humour on the poor inhabitants'.[68]

The yeomanry in action in 1798 could therefore be characterised as a mixture of loyalty and licentiousness. However, balanced judgments are the luxury of a later age. Contemporaries were unambiguous in their praise or condemnation. Mary Ann McCracken described the yeomen, some of whom had just arrested her brother, as 'those worst destroyers of their country'. John Patrickson, writing from Dublin at the height of the rising, claimed before reinforcements arrived that: 'the yeomanry ought to be immortalised and if the country is saved, it will be due to them'.[69] Such unrestrained language testifies to the major role the force played in the conflict. Yet arguably their participation in the actual fighting, while very important, obscures their equally significant role in making possible the defensive network of garrisons which, though broken in places by the initial onslaughts, nevertheless contained the rising in well-defined areas and bought valuable time until reinforcements arrived. Moreover, this duty was national and helped prevent outbreaks in other parts as well as enabling the movement of regular troops towards the fighting. Castlereagh's praise in parliament noted that the flexibility of yeomanry service was critical in the suppression of the rising and 'in estimating the public force, they had not been looked to for anything beyond mere local service'.[70] Without General Knox's system of yeomanry brigades this would have been impossible. This system was to be soon tested again.

The yeomanry were put off permanent duty in July 1798 but their respite was cut short on 23 August by the arrival of a small French expeditionary force under General Humbert at Killala, county Mayo. The western yeomen had no experience in combat, as their activities earlier in the summer had been confined to garrison duty. Although the landing was small (1,099 officers and men) the situation was serious. These were seasoned troops, correctly believed to be the harbinger of more, who carried arms for the United Irishmen. The situation deteriorated on 26 August

---

66 The trial of Hugh Wollaghan, T.C.D. MS872.   67 Duff to Lake, 28 June 1798, P.R.O.N.I. Dublin Letters, MIC67/f. 69.   68 Maurice (ed.), op. cit., p. 309.   69 M.A. McCracken to F. McCracken, n.d. July 1798, T.C.D. McCracken Papers, MS 873; Patrickson to Downshire, 6 June 1798, P.R.O.N.I. Downshire Papers D607/F/199.   70 Quoted in J. Groves-White, *The Yeomanry of Ireland*, p. 8.

when, having gained a foothold in Killala, about 700 French troops, with United Irish support, scattered a larger force in what became known as 'The Races of Castlebar'. This scenario contained all the potential military roles for the yeomen: confronting the French at the point of landing; countering the concurrent insurrection; taking on garrison duties; and sending detachments to join regular brigades moving against the invader.

The first resistance the French met was a mixed force of Killala yeomen and loyal citizens. They bravely marched out to meet the invaders but their inexperience soon showed, as Humbert had landed a detachment further along the coast who were able to attack the small yeomanry contingent from behind, killing three and dispersing the rest. Thirty Ballina yeomen and some townspeople ventured towards the French positions but soon realised the impossibility of their task and fell back to the town. The pre-arranged system of alarm posts and stations was severely tested in Mayo. As the Ballina yeomen were endangering themselves, about fourteen rural yeomanry corps, mostly cavalry, fell back into the town. A small force of detachments from each corps then ventured out, only to be driven back by discharges of musketry and grapeshot.[71] In the circumstances such a hastily gathered, inexperienced force could not be expected to succeed against well-led experienced regulars who, in the context of the landing, also had the advantage of numbers and firepower. The foolhardiness of some yeomen, in venturing from defensible positions against a superior force, brave though it was, must be balanced by the fact that the emergency assembly procedure worked locally, and also that corps from other districts were able to supplement the overall military response, both actively and as a reserve.

The entire yeomanry went on permanent duty on 29 August. Baronial brigades quickly gathered in towns according to plan. The numbers were sufficient (between 40 and 50,000) for garrison duties and, in some cases, joining the regular brigades sent against Humbert. As earlier, the garrison of Dublin was left almost entirely to its yeomanry. At any time there were around 700 infantry and 100 cavalry on duty. The Belfast yeomanry 'immediately re-assembled' following their stand-down and took the town's garrison duty.[72] The abundance of yeomen in Tyrone and Fermanagh allowed both garrison duty and mobile detachments, *de facto* the harassing role of light troops. General Taylor was ordered to assemble a brigade at Sligo and march to join Lake at Boyle, county Roscommon, where they were to follow the French until Cornwallis himself arrived with massive reinforcements to give battle. Taylor's force of 2,500 included almost 950 yeomen, mostly detachments of Fermanagh corps who had been hurriedly marched down. Taylor left Sligo in the hands of a mixed garrison of fencibles, militia and local yeomanry. Yeomanry had a key role against any possible move north by Humbert, garrisoning Belturbet and Ballyshannon.

71 Sandford to Graham, 24 Aug. 1798, P.R.O. H.O.100/78/ff. 177-80.   72 Ross to Downshire, 30 Aug. 1798, P.R.O.N.I. Downshire Papers, D607/F/375; Craig to Hewitt, 31 Aug. 1798, P.R.O.N.I. Dublin Letters, MIC67/f. 128; Pollock to Wickham, 26 Aug. 1798, P.R.O. H.O.100/81/f. 339.

Drawing the lesson from earlier events, Nugent's policy for yeomanry garrisons included a residue of more experienced troops: 'the yeomanry shall be as well organised as possible and mixed with the more regular troops so as to be of the greatest service'.[73] These arrangements were carried out efficiently and quickly. General Urquhart, who commanded the yeomanry brigades of the Donegal baronies of Tyrhugh and Boylagh, said they assembled within two hours of receiving Taylor's order. Taylor himself noted that the Sligo yeomen came in 'as fast as possible'. Besides garrison duty, the yeomanry again proved their worth in counter-insurgency. In districts which lay along Humbert's line of march, yeomanry brigades mobilised to prevent further local insurrections and were in readiness to march against the French if necessary, while the Longford yeomanry completely routed a large force of United Irishmen at Granard.[74]

The success of the yeomanry in this campaign was undeniable, though it must be added that the regular army was no longer in a depleted state following the augmentations in June. The response was altogether much less *ad hoc* than it had been earlier in the year and their speedy musters were particularly praiseworthy given that the invasion came at the harvest time. Even Cornwallis, who disliked the yeomanry as (in his view) a viciously partisan, amateur force, conceded that they had 'rendered the greatest services' during the campaign. However, though his praise was not faint, it was equivocal enough to damn him in the eyes of loyalists, as it included complimenting them for 'not having tarnished that courage and loyalty ... by any acts of wanton cruelty towards their deluded fellow subjects'.[75] Against an irresistibly larger force, Humbert's inevitable surrender came at Ballinamuck on 8 September. When the dust of battle and campaigning settled, Cornwallis began to plan a new defence system, building on the existing arrangements and, despite his instinctive aversion, still allocating a major role to the yeomanry.

HOME DEFENCE, 1798–1815

Although the insurrection was rapidly crushed and its leadership broken, the danger of invasion remained, and the experience in Connaught showed that, even without good local organisation, the appearance of the French could spark concurrent risings among the 'disaffected'. Moreover, Humbert's lengthy perambulation highlighted the danger a substantial invasion force would present. In other words, despite advances in defence planning during 1798, the basics of the problem remained: how to launch enough force to crush an invasion speedily yet at the same time guard

73 P.R.O.N.I. T3516/2; Taylor to Castlereagh, 25 Aug. 1798, P.R.O. H.O.100/81/f. 325; Nugent to Hewitt, 30 Aug. 1798, H.O.100/78/f. 308.   74 Urquhart to Castlereagh, 25 August 1798, P.R.O.N.I. Dublin Letters, MIC67/f. 122; Taylor to Castlereagh, 25 Aug. 1798, P.R.O. H.O.100/81/f. 325; Nugent to Lake, 5 Sept. 1798, H.O.100/78/f. 306.   75 General Orders, 9 Sept. 1798, P.R.O. H.O.100/82/f. 60.

against insurrection. Cornwallis' strategy was to divide the army in each of the five military districts into stationary and moveable brigades. For example, in the Northern District, which consisted of the Province of Ulster plus parts of Sligo and Leitrim, there were six stationary and two moveable brigades. All brigades were to be engaged on normal garrison and peacekeeping duties but their dispersal was preplanned, so that those constituting the moveable force could, on news of an invasion, concentrate rapidly and march on the French, while the stationary force secured the country from any attempts to exploit the situation. It was reckoned that this system could bring 20,000 men against the French within five days, no matter where the landing occurred. The yeomanry were considered as part of the stationary force, and each brigadier-general could call out the whole of the force in his area on news of a landing.[76]

The actual detail of how the yeomen were to slot into this system seems largely to have been based on the assumption that the 1798 arrangement of yeomanry brigades would apply for the new arrangements. The prominence of John Knox is shown by the fact than Cornwallis urgently recalled him from England, where he had been on the point of embarking for St. Helena, when news came of the sailing of the Brest fleet in spring 1799. Knox was ordered north immediately on arrival and hoped to get overall command of the yeomanry from Nugent.[77] In all military districts generals were ordered to become fully conversant with the local yeomanry and establish strategically important places to 'guard against insult and surprise'; especially, remembering Humbert's progress, to control 'the great roads to the capital'. Each yeomanry brigade was to comprise infantry battalions, usually 3–4 corps, and cavalry squadrons of 1–2 troops. For example, Cavan had two yeomanry brigades: the first had 1,226 officers and men made up from three battalions and five squadrons. Each corps was to assemble at its usual place of array and then proceed to a battalion alarm post. The system was designed to ensure that pre-arranged clusters of yeomanry would assemble at the nearest strategic strongpoint and allow the regular army to move. The county brigades were under the overall direction of the county yeomanry brigade major, who relayed the regular brigadier-general's commands. As in 1798, one yeomanry captain was pre-selected for each alarm post to command the battalion assembling there. Belturbet was the post for the first battalion and first and second squadrons of the first Cavan yeomanry brigade, consisting of the Swanlinbar, Belturbet and Castle Saunderson Infantry corps and the Belturbet and Ballyconnell Cavalry troops. The choice of alarm posts was strategic. Belturbet is itself a crossing point on the river Erne and was considered as a centre

---

76 K.P. Ferguson, 'The Army in Ireland from the Restoration to the Act of Union', pp. 180, 192; General Order, 12 Sept. 1798, P.R.O. W.O.30/66/f. 213; P.C. Stoddart, op. cit., pp. 340–5.   77 Circular, Adjutant General Hewitt, 22 April 1799, P.R.O. H.O.100/83/f. 368; Bishop Knox to Abercorn, 5–6 May 1799, P.R.O.N.I. Abercorn Papers, D623/A/157/12; Richardson, *Yeomanry*, p. 48.

from which yeomanry detachments could cover outposts at Castle Carrigan and Ballyconnell and guard crossings on the Woodford River.[78]

As in 1798, it was accepted that general plans were capable of local adaptation at the discretion of the district generals. Nugent's plans show that the Ulster yeomanry were of greater military potential than those elsewhere because of their numerical strength, with the exception of Dublin. According to General Dundas there were insufficient yeomanry in Kildare for 'anything else than to allocate them the most secure stations in their own baronies'. Clearly he saw these stations as protecting the yeomanry rather than the other way about. Kildare had only 536 yeomen in 1799 whereas Tyrone had 5,887.[79] The northern yeomanry's defence potential can be seen in context when it is realised that in October 1800 the regular stationary force in the northern district was 4,500. The previous year the Ulster yeomanry, which could support the stationary brigades, stood at 26,550. Munster, roughly equivalent to the southern district, had 5,660 in its regular stationary force, whereas its yeomanry in 1799 totaled 12,749.[80] Such numerical discrepancies underlay different interpretations of the degree of military duty which could be realistically expected from the yeomanry in an emergency.

Cornwallis considered yeomanry unfit for field service with the regulars against the French, but Nugent's 1799 arrangements reveal that he used his discretion to pre-arrange for some yeomen to join the moveable brigades. Lisburn's yeomanry battalion of 97 men was considered sufficient to provide detachments to march with the 22nd Light Dragoons. At Hillsborough and Banbridge the respective yeomanry battalions of 375 and 268 were confined to keeping communication open on the main Dublin road and guarding arms depots.[81] A third option, favoured by Knox, was to use larger bodies of yeomanry as 'light' troops. Light troops were a development dating roughly from the American war. Their role was as skirmishers and intelligence-gatherers in the *petite guerre* of the frontiers rather than as troops for set-piece battles. In the Revolutionary and Napoleonic wars, the French used *tirailleurs* (sharpshooters) to great effect. These were large bodies deployed in irregular order to cover the advance or retreat of regular battalions and harass the enemy with ambushes. However, the British army had allowed their American experience to slip. A number of training developments saw Britain eventually develop effective light infantry by the time of the Peninsular campaign, amongst which were Sir John Moore's experiments with light infantry training in Ireland between 1798 and 1799.[82] Arguably, the experience of the 1798 rebellion had an input in this as

78 N.A.M. 6807–175 f. 188, Nugent Papers, Arrangement of Yeomanry Corps, 11 Aug. 1799. 79 N.A.M. 6807–175 ff. 251–6, Nugent Papers, Defence plan for the Central District, 10 Apr. 1800; Numerical strength of the Yeomanry, n.d. 1799, N.A. R.P.620/48/56. 80 Nugent to District Generals, 24 Oct. 1800, P.R.O. H.O.100/94/ff. 189–90; Numerical strength of the Yeomanry, n.d. 1799, N.A. R.P.620/48/56; Circular, Castlereagh, 4 Nov. 1800, P.R.O.N.I. Lurgan Yeomanry Detail Book, D3696/A/4/1. 81 N.A.M. 6807–175 ff. 125–7, Nugent Papers, Proposed distribution of Brig. Gen. Drummond's brigade 29 April 1799. 82 J.A. Houlding, *Fit for Service*, pp. 222,-3, 251–2; P.J. Haythornthwaite, *The*

well as wider European military developments. Certainly, henceforth there were moves to capitalise on the experience of the yeomanry in 1798. When Knox arrived in Ulster in May 1799 he visited each county to establish its effective yeomanry strength and see how many could do emergency service as light troops. Nugent agreed that it would 'give great spirit' to employ some yeomen this way, but urged caution. He conceded there were sufficient yeomen in Fermanagh, Cavan and Tyrone to have a surplus as light troops, but the important maritime county of Antrim had only enough to function as part of the stationary force of guards and garrisons. Knox's arrangements were strongly based on his 1798 strategy. He planned a light brigade of 3,500 yeomen raised from Fermanagh, Cavan, north Armagh and the barony of Dungannon, comprising detachments of up to half the strength of individual corps but not including supplementaries. This force would move to the north coast on the first sign of invasion, to be joined by 500 yeomen from whatever county was threatened. He saw their role as typically that of light troops, in skirmishing and delaying the invader by using their local knowledge to harass and obstruct until a large regular force could be brought up.[83]

Nugent's caution was not only about numbers. Antrim had been disturbed in the winter of 1798 and there was a real danger to the homes and villages of rural yeomen if they moved either to join Knox's column or the yeomanry brigades in towns. Neither eventuality was put to the test, but clearly there were fears that home-defence could mean neglecting the yeoman's *raison d'être*, the defence of his own home. Nugent's papers show revised arrangements for the northern district in April 1800. These make no mention of light brigades but show evidence of unease with the proposed stationary role. As before, battalions composed of clusters averaging 3–4 corps, were pre-arranged to occupy strategic strongpoints, bridges, passes and arms depots in the event of the regulars moving. However, this time not all corps were to be organised in battalions. Others were 'to be left in their own quarters for ... peacekeeping, driving cattle etc.'.[84] Another invasion scare in 1801 showed that unease had not been assuaged. Resistance was shown in Ulster towards proposals to gather the yeomanry in large brigades in the towns. George Knox reported to the chief secretary, Charles Abbott, that his elder brother Thomas felt the corps were of more use staying in their own districts watching and overawing the disaffected who, he feared, might use their removal to attempt a rising. These objections were listened to, and circulars were issued emphasising that it was a measure of last resort; that only portions of corps would move; and that the men had the option of joining the brigade most convenient to their homes.[85] Although during 1798 the yeomanry in Ulster and elsewhere did more or less what was proposed in 1801,

Armies of Wellington, p. 95. 83 Richardson, *Yeomanry*, pp. 44–9; Nugent to Knox, n.d. [c. 6] May 1799, N.L.I. Lake Papers, MS56/205. 84 N.A.M. 6807–175 ff. 288–90, Nugent Papers, 23 Apr. 1800. 85 4 Aug. 1801, P.R.O. Colchester Papers, 30/9/123/ff. 170–3; Marshall, Circular, 31 July 1801, P.R.O.N.I. Lurgan Yeomanry Detail Book, D3696/A/4/1.

from the yeoman's perspective emergency service primarily meant guarding his own home and immediate neighbourhood during conditions of heightened tension. From a military perspective, the yeomen responded better to reality than theory. From the government's perspective, having generals on the staff like Nugent and Knox who were aware of local dangers and sensitive to local feelings meant that contingency plans could be modified and therefore kept in place should theory become reality. Whatever their detrimental effects, the crises of the 1790s ensured that central government was better informed about the country. The responsiveness necessitated kept the yeomanry brigade system intact.

This responsiveness was severely tested in 1803 by a new set of proposals which came from Britain. Following the collapse of the Amiens 'peace' the voluntary forces in Britain and Ireland were heavily augmented and, though the commander-in-chief of the army, the duke of York, had no formal authority over them he decided they should be given better military training and organisation. The augmentations were used to invite offers of more extended emergency service. In Britain inspecting field officers were appointed in September 1803, to supervise and organise between ten days and a month's intensive military training in large brigades.[86] The duke of York's 'brigade system', as it became known, was criticised in both Britain and Ireland. William Windham claimed in parliament that it was impossible to ever make regulars of volunteers who by their age, height, family ties, and occupations were naturally local and stationary. Charles Yorke, secretary-at-war, defended the augmentations and brigading, saying they were intended to assist the regulars in the event of invasion by acting as a flanking or rearguard force and to convey an impression of numbers. The general idea, according to Pitt, was to improve the military capability of the force as far as possible towards the ideal of the regulars.[87]

This system was considered for the Irish Yeomanry so that it could be divided into stationary and moveable brigades, like Cornwallis' division of the army. The sources are no longer extant which would detail how this would have sat alongside Cornwallis' system, still the core of defence thinking, but presumably the proposed new yeomanry brigades would have functioned as the light arm of their regular equivalents. The big problem with this proposal was that it was British volunteer policy superimposed on the Irish Yeomanry, a different force which faced different challenges. The British volunteers were first and foremost an anti-invasion force whereas, the Irish yeomen, though they had a similar role, were mainly concerned with insurrection. With these differences in mind, the commander-of-the forces, Sir William Cathcart, toured Ireland in October 1803 in order to establish how many yeomen in each province could be arranged in stationary and moveable brigades. By early November Wickham, the chief secretary, realised the plan for moveable brigades must be confined to Ulster, where a 'limited number' might be formed,

---

86 I.F.W. Beckett, *The Amateur Military Tradition*, p. 106.   87 *Parl. Debs.*, i, pp. 1686–1705.

whereas brigade training should be shelved for 'future consideration'. There were differences of opinion between the government and the military authorities about how to go about brigading the Irish Yeomanry. By July 1804 Cathcart had accepted that the Irish yeomen could not be brigaded like English volunteers, due to the much greater danger of insurrection or domestic disorder, and were thus better left 'independent and baronial'. Cathcart also realised that the Irish Yeomanry's different structure mitigated against possible large-scale co-operative action, not being under the control of county governors and having no rank higher than captain.[88] The viceroy, Lord Hardwicke, agreed, and added that the difficulty was compounded by regional variations in density. Apart from the urban yeomanry in Dublin and Cork, which were *de facto* brigades already because of their numbers, compact location and organisational structure, the yeomanry of Munster, Leinster and Connacht should remain a stationary force, composed of separate corps who could secure their districts from insurrection. The 'zeal, spirit and superabundance' of the Ulster yeomanry could potentially provide some moveable brigades. Even here Hardwicke was cautious. He needed to be: concerns in 1801 about yeomanry brigades leaving rural districts unguarded had been vindicated in the eyes of the gentry by Robert Emmet's rising in July 1803, which caught the Castle. Hardwicke offered a tactful compromise for Ulster. As a first step, he wanted separate companies formed from selections of young single men of suitable occupations, from corps in areas thought safe enough to be secured by the remainder. These he proposed would eventually amalgamate in battalions of 3–600 which would combine to give brigades 1,200–1,800 strong, but he conceded that even this tactful, gradualist approach, might upset the gentlemen. Littlehales, his military under-secretary, circularized the main Ulster gentry figures to test opinion. The result was not encouraging. Abercorn was typical. He went through the motions of finding suitable yeomen in his area of Tyrone but felt that most were 'too poor to leave their occupations yet not poor enough to consider pay as either inducement or equivalent'.[89] The eventual outcome was a delicate balancing act between the lord lieutenant, who commanded the yeomanry, and the duke of York who commanded Cathcart. This involved giving the yeomen some proper military training and provision for joint action which stopped short of English-style brigading. Clearly the Irish authorities, both civil and military, were unenthusiastic about brigading but wanted to appear to follow Union principles. There was, however, no lack of enthusiasm in appointing additional staff for brigading, the brigadier generals of yeomanry and inspecting field officers, as they were a welcome boost to Castle patronage.[90]

---

88 Cathcart to Wickham, 28 Oct. 1803, H.R.O. Wickham Papers, 38M49/5/34/73; King to Wickham, 4 Nov. 1803, P.R.O. H.O.100/114/f. 153; Wickham to Cathcart, 11 Nov. 1803, H.O.100/111/f. 285; Cathcart to Littlehales, 16 July 1804, H.O.100/121/f. 32.   89 Hardwicke to Hawkesbury, 20 July 1804, P.R.O. H.O.100/121/f. 12; Littlehales to [several northern gentlemen], 28 July 1804, H.O.100/122/f. 344; Abercorn to Littlehales, 5 Aug. 1804, P.R.O.N.I. Abercorn Papers, D623/A/82/41.   90 Cathcart

The brigading proposal petered out in a fudge, which tried to keep the principle afloat for the future while giving the yeomanry some field training for the present. Hardwicke intended that the training arrangements were not 'to go to the *avowed* object of brigading' which should be 'gradual and progressive' even in Ulster.[91] The compromise was to improve yeomanry training while tentatively setting up the machinery for brigading in Ulster. In reality though, unlike the untried British volunteers and yeomanry, the Irish yeomen had proved in 1798 that they could provide emergency assistance for the army both in garrison and field duties. Though it is obviously never stated, one gets the definite impression that this knowledge underlay and simultaneously undermined all attempts at a wider military role for the force. In this respect, 1798 was the high-water mark of the yeomanry's military utility. Notwithstanding, the 1803–4 brigading proposals did precipitate a review of yeomanry training.

As would be expected with a hastily-raised civilian force, training was a difficulty from the beginning. A yeomanry captain's commission obliged him to train and discipline his men, but the task fell in practice to the permanent sergeant, who was originally a retired or seconded soldier. The yeomen were supposed to be given the basics of standard training for regular horse and foot. This consisted of five basic elements: the Manual Exercise, the Platoon Exercise, Evolutions, Firings and Manoeuvres. The Manual Exercise included learning the sequence of loading, presenting and firing the musket, and bayonet practice. The Platoon involved synchronized volley firings under command, while evolutions were the basics of field exercise such as marching and turning in rank and file. Cavalry corps did the basic sword exercise, standard throughout the army since 1796. The Firings and Manoeuvres were complex movements for larger linear formations, designed to give controlled fire along an extended front. However, only the first three exercises could be undertaken by small dispersed companies like yeomanry corps. It took regular recruits anything from several weeks to a number of months full-time practice to master these basics. Given that the Manual exercise alone was *reduced* to 24 separate operations in 1756 and that the yeomen only trained twice weekly, it is very likely the fitness for service of many corps was questionable to say the least. Not surprisingly, the district generals were given a supervisory role from early on. Typically, John Knox was to the fore, supervising yeomanry training around Dungannon from December 1796.[92]

The experiences of 1798 revealed serious flaws in yeomanry training and turned the minds of General Knox and others to the potential of the yeomen as light troops. Lord Rossmore considered they might suffice as light infantry *in extremis*, but that it was possible to instruct them in the musketry aspects of light service. This in-

to Hardwicke, 18 Aug. 1804, B.L. Hardwicke Papers, add. mss. 35719.   91 Circular, 22 Oct. 1804, N.A. O.P.232/2; Littlehales to Hardwicke, 18 Oct. 1804, B.L. Hardwicke Papers, add. mss. 35721.   92 J.A. Houlding, op. cit., pp. 160–2, 259; J. Knox to A. O'Connor, 26 Dec. 1796, N.A. R.P.620/15/3/8.

volved selecting sharpshooters for skirmishing and training the rest in progressive aimed fire by sections rather than the standard volley fire which, he felt, had proved disastrous against a charge of pikemen. He used a most poignant example by referring to Major Lombard of the North Cork Militia, whose company had loosed one general unaimed volley 'and was immediately piked by the rebels' at the Battle of Oulart Hill. Rossmore advocated aimed partial fire backed by skirmishing marksmen so 'the company is always firing but never unloaded' for 'what could his [Lombard's] bayonets avail against pikemen'.[93] Given the localised and independent nature of the yeomanry and the liberal discretion of generals it is very likely some corps tried to adapt their exercises at this time. There were differences of opinion in both Britain and Ireland as to whether the voluntary forces would be better trained as light troops or whether they should continue to receive the standard training, based on the Prussian model.[94] Aimed musketry (as opposed to volley-firing) was the basis of light infantry training. In 1803 a concerted attempt was made, with the aid of the new yeomanry inspectors, to instruct the yeomen in 'priming and loading quick, firing quick, as far as may be consistent with tolerable aim and on preparing themselves to be enabled to act on occasions singly and independently'.[95] In September 1803 the entire force was put on permanent duty in response to an invasion scare and to improve their training. New drills for musket firing were issued to all corps.[96]

Formal light infantry training was a complex affair. The 1803 drill manual of the Belfast Yeomanry sets out no less than 18 separate manouevres.[97] Inevitably these attempts foundered against the rock-solid reality that the yeomanry was a force composed of civilians who could never experience the grinding daily routine whereby the regular army gained the most of its basic training. In 1805 General Floyd, commanding the Southern District, thought such exercises 'of little use against the enemy', and that it was better to substitute something more simple. Floyd's concept of light troops echoed Knox's 1799 proposals and were based on Irish realities rather than the British drill manual. Floyd saw the yeomanry role as a mixture of guerilla force and peacekeeping detachment, best suited to 'worry them [the French] to death day and night' and 'suppress any partial rising of the disaffected'. In 1807 Arthur Wellesley endorsed this view. Wellesley brought the professional soldier's knowledge and objectivity to the post of chief secretary. In considering Ireland's defence capabilities and weaknesses, he had a very good opinion of the yeomanry in general but resisted giving them 'parade discipline' as 'attempting too much'.

93 Movements for Light Infantry well adapted to the Yeomen of Ireland, 2 Feb. 1799, P.R.O.N.I. Rossmore Papers, T2929/32/56. 94 I.F.W. Beckett, op. cit., p. 106. 95 Circular, Littlehales, n.d. July 1803, H.R.O. Wickham Papers, 38M49/5/33/81. 96 John Foster to Wickham, 7 Sept. 1803, H.R.O. Wickham Papers, 38M49/5/39/55; 19 Sept. 1803, Lurgan Yeomanry Detail Book, D3696/A/4/1; Wickham to Fox, 13 Sept. 1803, P.R.O. H.O.100/113/f. 111; Orders for the Infantry Brigades of the City of Dublin, B.L. 1608/3464. 97 Printed Directions, Belfast Merchants' Infantry (Belfast, 1803), L.H.L. BPB18031.

Wellesley felt they were better left in their localities, retaining the potential for emergency light duty.[98] Attempts at improving yeomanry training were an ongoing feature throughout the force's existence. In 1810, a Castle circular noted that 'permanent sergeants of the yeomanry corps having been in general reported to be so deficient in their knowledge of drill and exercise as to be unequal to the duties of their situations'. They were all ordered to the nearest garrison town for a month's intensive instruction in the basics of the Manual, Platoon and Sword exercises, and in simple field manouevres. Obviously if the trainers were having to be trained, the competency of the men must have minimal.[99]

As brigading proved impossible even in Ulster, the additional staff recruited to implement it, the brigadiers and inspecting field officers, were in an anomalous position. The original functions of yeomanry brigade major included supervising military training. However, by the early nineteenth century, their role was seen as civil, more like that of a commissary. When the yeomanry were off permanent duty, their functions were financial and administrative, involving monthly inspections of arms and accoutrements and handling pay and clothing returns. However, the line between inspecting the condition of a corps and inspecting their drills was a fine one, and in practice the monthly field officers' inspections became an expensive replication. Yeomanry inspectors were discontinued in 1806 but resurfaced under Wellesley with a redefined area of responsibility, as the military-yeomanry link in each of the six military districts, and continued until the end of the war.[100] By their permanent presence they also provided reassurance to the district generals that, if and when the yeomanry became his responsibility on permanent duty, a command structure could immediately be slotted into place and so avoid delay or confusion.

Although the large-scale brigading envisaged in 1803–4 was a non-starter, the military ideal of co-operative, co-ordinated action which Knox saw so clearly in 1798 remained. So did the flexible, pragmatic approach which had been so successful in 1798. In June 1805, Cathcart drew up contingency plans in the event of regulars having to move to meet invasion. Cathcart saw the yeomanry's role as 'principally for local security against invasion', except in certain areas where large bodies of yeomanry could gather both to provide local security and assist the army in the field, but later cautioned against too much reliance being placed on the yeomanry in the case of 'a vigorous invasion'.[101] In 1807, Arthur Wellesley adopted a similarly pragmatic approach in his contingency planning, which gave the Dublin and Ulster yeomanry a more major role than those elsewhere. Wellesley planned to concentrate

---

98 Floyd to Long, 18 Nov. 1805, N.L.I. Kilmainham Papers, MS1218; Floyd to Elliott, 1 Jan. 1807, P.R.O. H.O.100/141/f. 7; Wellesley to Hawkesbury, 7 May 1807, *W.S.D.*, v, pp. 28–36.   99 Circular, W.W. Pole, 1 Nov. 1810, P.R.O.N.I. Annesley Papers, D1854/8/4; Houlding, op. cit., p. 269.   100 Bedford to Spencer, 3 April 1806, P.R.O. H.O.100/135/f. 106; Wellesley to Gordon, 8 Dec. 1807, *W.S.D.*, v, p. 215.   101 Cathcart to Littlehales, 29 June 1805, N.L.I. Kilmainham Papers, MS1218; Cathcart to Hardwicke, 14 Aug. 1805, B.L. Hardwicke Papers, add. mss. 35719.

his forces in four stations: Galway, Cashel, Cork and Dublin. The troops from the North were designated for Galway along with those from Connacht and the upper Shannon. The Ulster yeomanry, in their county divisions were to occupy strategic towns and vulnerable features when the garrisons moved. For example, the Londonderry yeomanry were to occupy Derry city and the entrances to Loughs Swilly and Foyle. In some cases, where there were particularly heavy concentrations of corps available, part of the force would serve outside their home county with a reserve left to hold it. Of Down's 4,500 yeomen, 1,000 were to hold the county while the rest were to be posted to Leinster too act as a reserve for local corps there. Castlereagh, mindful of the gentry nervousness caused by any advance yeomanry arrangements other than pure local defence, agreed totally with Wellesley's proposed deployment, but cautioned him against telling the yeomen more than general details until the moment they were to come into effect, as 'at the moment of danger and exertion you may rely on them for any sacrifice ... but till that moment comes more ought not to be announced to them than the points at which they are to assemble within their own counties'.[102]

Pragmatism also informed Wellesley's views on yeomanry training. Clearly his approach was non-doctrinaire and intended to make the best possible use of local yeomanry manpower without imposing systems impossible to implement. In 1808 he and Richmond decided that yeomen could be trained and exercised for eventual service in battalions of 300 and above, comprised of contiguous corps. The consent of the yeomen was solicited and received and by June circulars went out to all brigade majors to implement the arrangements. To 'render the arrangement permanent and avoid confusion in emergency' the battalions of each county were numbered sequentially. To avoid the hurdles of local yeomanry pride and gentry rivalries, the most northerly battalion in each county became the first battalion and so forth, working southwards. This was pragmatism at its best: maximising the possible without the sacrifices the impossible would have meant. No one's nose was put out of joint. Those corps who did not volunteer to exercise in battalion were left to exercise singly as before.[103] This did not always mean tardiness, in parts of the south and west the physical distance of corps made this impossible. Although similar battalions were part of invasion contingency planning since 1798, it was an innovation to have the normal weekly training conducted in such formations. The plan was a success. By March 1809 there were around 100 such battalions operating with permanent adjutants appointed to each.[104] However it did not mean a departure from the localized nature of the force. The expanded size of the yeomanry (standing at 75,000 effectives in 1808) meant that local corps could often form second and third companies and become a battalion without difficulty. The Castlewellan Infantry, for

102 Wellesley to Harrington, 1 Dec. 1807, Castlereagh to Wellesley, 28 Dec. 1807, *W.S.D.*, v, pp. 201–10, 279–83.   103 Memo: Wellesley to Littlehales, 23 June 1808, ibid., pp. 458–61.   104 Wellesley to Richmond, 16 March 1809, N.L.I. Richmond Papers MS58.

instance, comprised five companies at this time. The eventual arrangement met
Wellesley's earlier judgment that the best disposition of the force was 'in detached
companies of various strength throughout the country'.[105] Wellesley's system remained intact until the end of war in 1815.

Windham had famously slated the British volunteers as 'painted cherries which
none but simple birds would take for real fruit' and Knox may have needed to convince the Irish yeomen they were soldiers who could face the French, but 1798
proved they could actively face insurrection and the contingency plans of shrewd
military thinkers like Cornwallis and Cathcart ensured that the yeomen had a role in
home defence which was no less important for its turning out to be a passive one.[106]
The main feature of the yeomanry's strength as a military force was its localised
nature. This ensured they had a vested interest in suppressing insurrection, because they themselves would most likely become the first victims of any uprising. In
1803 a United Irish informer told how Thomas Russell envisaged the first step in
the proposed Down insurrection as attacks on the various yeomanry posts 'with no
quarter to be given to loyal yeomen or Orangemen'.[107] The fact that yeomen were
permanent, local residents was also of advantage in that it gave intimate knowledge
of the district they served in, and made them readily available for rapid mobilisation
during invasion scares.

However, this position of local strength paradoxically contained the yeomanry's
greatest weakness as a military force. It was fine so long as the location of the problem they faced coincided with an area containing plenty of yeomen. However, when
the south and west of Ireland became seriously disturbed by agrarian combinations
from about 1806 onwards, the full potential of the force could never be utilised, as
most yeomen were concentrated in Ulster. The rapid demise of Presbyterian disaffection, and the rise of Orangeism in the north, as well as Ulster's large Protestant
population ensured that yeomanry numbers were heaviest where they were least
needed. Various plans to make the force more mobile ran into the obdurate reality
that the yeomen themselves saw their role as local and were reluctant to move from
home. Large-scale moveable yeomanry brigades never existed outside the minds of
military strategists. Wellesley's more realistic system of battalions was the best compromise available between the demands of the military authorities for flexibility and
mobility and the yeoman's need to feel his home was secure. The yeomanry dealt
best with insurrection or overawing the country during invasion scares. It therefore
achieved its maximum military potential in the years 1796 to 1805. The danger of
organised rebellion was effectively ended with the Battles of Vinegar Hill,
Ballynahinch and Ballinamuck in 1798, while the Battle of Trafalgar in 1805 ended
the worst of the invasion scares by fatally damaging French naval power. Apart from

105 Wellesley to Hawkesbury, 7 May 1807, *W.S.D.*, v, pp. 28–36.   106 Quoted in: I.F.W. Beckett, op.
cit, p. 107.   107 Beatty to Dublin Castle, 17 Aug. 1803, P.R.O. H.O.100/112/f. 404.

such emergency service, most yeomanry duty consisted of offering the army as much help with domestic peacekeeping as their structural limitations would allow. The consensus of opinion among military men was that the yeomanry were inefficient for all but emergency service, and some generals showed the greatest reluctance to use them at all. This led to disagreements between the military hierarchy and the government. The generals saw everything in terms of functional utility but successive governments recognised that the yeomanry force had important political dimensions as well. It is to this subtle and less obvious aspect of the yeomanry that we now turn.

7

The foundation of a useful plan to strengthen government[1]: the Castle and the Yeomanry

When Camden's government were considering yeomanry in the summer of 1796, they were insistent that the proposed force was kept clear as clear as possible from the entanglements of Irish politics by making its structure of control different from that of the Volunteers. Power was centralised to minimise the risk of political interests aggrandising the patronage offered by the yeomanry and destabilising the country further by raising the temperature at elections. However, it soon became clear that yeomanry, as well as being an addition of civil and military force had also, a very important political aspect. This importance comes from the broad range of political contexts the yeomanry influenced, ranging from the political relationship between Dublin and London, parliamentary politics in College Green and Westminster and the critically important relationship between Dublin Castle and the Irish gentry.

The Irish government was vulnerable to criticism from Britain over its defence policy, because this involved British as well as Irish interests. Put bluntly, the military capability of Ireland was a cause for concern. The militia were ill-disciplined and suspected of disaffection; the large number of soldiers on scattered peacekeeping detachments militated against an effective anti-invasion strategy. The worsening internal state of Ireland also meant that more and more troops were tied up there. Moreover, the poor quality of generals on the Irish staff was symbolised by the office of commander-in-chief. General Cunninghame, who held the post from 1793, was old and had long wanted to retire. Camden procrastinated over a replacement until August 1796. When his first choice, Sir Charles Grey, refused, Camden had to accept Carhampton as the only available substitute. Carhampton's pedigree was not particularly impressive: he had served in Ireland as adjutant-general and in England as lieutenant-general of the ordnance.[2] Camden had difficulty demonstrating to his political masters that Irish defence would not be a liability. The evidence suggests that the Irish government used the yeomanry measure to ward off criticism from London as well as to placate its political supporters at home. Castlereagh,

---

1 Camden to Portland, 12 July 1796. P.R.O. H.O. 100/60/f. 261.   2 K.P. Ferguson, 'The Army in Ireland', pp. 150–1.

always close to Camden, hinted as much to Pitt, noting that there were wider benefits to be had from yeomanry than the immediate objects of opposing foreign and domestic enemies. It would, he claimed, stop Ireland being a drain on the sister kingdom and enable her to contribute offensively to the war effort.[3]

The overall interests of government and the Irish gentry met in the yeomanry insofar as both needed the rule of law to survive. Beyond this, each had different conceptions of the necessity for the measure. Lord Clare doubtless spoke for many, seeing yeomanry as a defence of the Protestant Ascendancy against 'the treason of one set of men (Presbyterians) and the barbarism of another (Catholics)' and considered that the measure's success depended on catching the spirit of Irish Protestants as it rose rather than making them feel that their offers were subject to their not offending Catholic opinion.[4] Although Camden's administration was committed to 'rallying the Protestants' after the combined shocks of 1793, Catholic relief, and Fitzwilliam,[5] the relationship between Camden and his Irish supporters was by no means an easy one. There were a number of flies in the ointment. Camden dreaded the very spirit that Clare wanted to catch, fearing it would prove uncontrollable. Not all landowners supported government: some, like the duke of Leinster, supported the opposition, and their demands for reform and Catholic relief. As an English landowner, Camden privately doubted the ability of the Irish gentry to administer law and order. When his plan to extend the Baronial Police failed in 1795, he accused the country gentlemen, who had reneged on promises of support, of worsening the state of the country by neglecting their duties as colonisers, to maintain proper bonds between landlord and tenant.[6] With no satisfactory police established, in 1796 he was forced to rely on these same people to confront the United Irishmen.

Small wonder then, that Camden trod warily at first, eager to avoid the political storms his new measure could unleash. The government's political manoeuvring in the early stages of the development of the yeomanry is well worth investigating. To summarise, the political problems facing government over yeomanry were that first, they had to delegate power to a volatile gentry who were losing control of their tenants; and second, any new initiative in the area of defence or law and order, gave opportunities for the opposition in England and Ireland to attack Pitt's war policy and press for reform, by representing yeomanry as a sectarian force enforcing coercion in place of proper policies. Camden's wary attitude regarding yeomanry underwent a dramatic conversion soon after the yeomen were actually embodied. By January 1797 he was praising them to the skies.[7] Although the road from Bantry accounted for some of his zeal, there were other reasons too. The yeomanry system was proving that it could be politically useful, by giving government better control

---

3 Castlereagh to Pitt, 17 Oct. 1796, P.R.O. Chatham Papers, 30/8/327/ff. 11–12.   4 Clare to Camden, 7 Sept. 1796, K.A.O. Pratt Papers, U840/0183/8.   5 Bartlett, *Fall and Rise*, pp. 203–27.   6 Camden to Portland, 25 Sept. 1795, P.R.O. H.O. 100/58/f. 334.   7 Camden to Portland 10 Jan. 1797, P.R.O. H.O. 100/69/f. 62.

over the gentry. Checks were built into the system to ensure the power delegated to the localities would circulate back to the Castle and not be diffused among political factions. Though designed to stop a Volunteer revival, the system proved a political trump card in Camden's pack.

By insisting that landowners submit their offers directly to the Castle rather than the county governors, as in England, the government retained the ultimate veto and made the yeomanry function as an additional channel of communication between centre and localities. Magnates like Downshire were listened to; captains could recommend officers; but only government could accept.[8] Raising yeomanry attached local landowners to government, and the system of pay and inspections kept them there. As we have noted, the pay system in Ireland differed from England, where the yeomanry were mostly financed by county subscription. Deliberate deviation from the English precedent meant that the Irish Yeomanry was an expensive measure, but, from a governmental viewpoint, the cost was more than compensated for by fact that the yeomanry system perpetuated strong central control and gave the Castle a linkage to gentry of various political views. By a flexible, sensitive, implementation of the system, government attached important elements of the old northern Volunteers to the yeomanry at a critical period when they could have gone either way. Obligations of pride and pay, plus the increased danger from showing their colours, forged the link permanently.

A couple of examples illustrate how Camden utilised the yeomanry as an aid to governing. The Yeomanry Office was established in 1796, but all proposals for corps were screened first by the chief secretary. Although this increased his workload, it militated against yeomanry working against government, giving instant visibility and a chance to nip problems in the bud. In early 1797 different political groups tried to harness the yeomanry to their own ends, but were 'spotted'. In Dublin the Catholic Committee tried to get its supporters enrolled in a distinct corps, as did pro-reform old Volunteers. Pelham told both that no new corps could be allowed, but permitted the prospective recruits to enlist individually in existing corps.[9] The government thus broke up dangerous aggregations and avoided setting precedents, yet still acted within the law, as the original levy was complete. Moreover, the government was able to deflect the attempt, especially the Catholics' attempt, while still covering themselves against accusations of partiality, without alienating well-intentioned Catholics or old Volunteers. It was clever politics. Small wonder that Camden's attitude became benign: the yeomanry, once a worry, were promising to be a political godsend at a time of crisis. Grattan, remembering Fitzwilliam's promise of a yeomanry to follow emancipation, had dubbed the new institution an 'Ascendancy army', and was trying to link this accusation with the general discontent over defence policy after Bantry Bay. Pelham had already made a speech disavowing

8 Yeomanry Standing Orders, 1798.

a denominationally exclusive yeomanry; now government could counter by accusing Grattan of trying to prevent Catholics joining.[10] By establishing control early on, and being able to limit proposals, government could also expand the movement where necessary. Concurrent with the 'sieving' of the Dublin proposals, Pelham delegated authority to General Knox to augment whatever northern corps he thought fit.[11] The system's adaptability was turning out to be well suited to Ireland's kaleidoscopic problems. This flexibility of administration, only possible because of government's absolute control, is particularly well illustrated in the case of Charlemont.

The selection of those magnates and landowners who would raise yeomanry in each county was necessarily a practical rather than a political choice, being based on individual influence, status and the ability to raise men. A yeomanry raised solely by government supporters would have been politically indefensible, even in the 1790s, as well as strategically disastrous. However, once the 'constitutional' imperative of eclectic raising was established, there were opportunities for politicking. Charlemont, as commander-in-chief of the Ulster Volunteers, had consistently taken a whiggish, reforming line in politics. Not surprisingly, Camden initially flinched when Charlemont offered to raise infantry but Pelham soon convinced him that Charlemont's proposal was 'particularly suited to reconcile those who were eager promoters of the Old Volunteers'.[12] Charlemont had undoubted influence in Ulster and on previous occasions, as in the disturbances following the snubbing of Irish peers at George III's coronation, had proved that, in a crisis, his loyalty outweighed his radicalism.[13] As we have seen, Camden was eager to assist Charlemont in putting loyalty first on this occasion by letting him enlist his old Volunteers in a separate corps. This helped advertise the yeomanry to other ex-Volunteers, but also had the important political effect of keeping an influential whig on board to maintain the appearance of consensus. This indulgence of Charlemont was very significant. He was a key figure whose co-operation could unlock a large deposit of manpower to government's account and allow them to mix consensus with coercion as the crack-down on the United Irishmen began in earnest. Indeed this readiness to accommodate Charlemont's sensitivities established a pattern which was to continue.

In November 1796 it was proposed to proclaim Armagh under the Insurrection Act. Charlemont, his whiggish instincts aroused, assessed the politics of the situation correctly and played his highest card first, threatening resignation from the yeomanry. Camden responded instantly, and excepted Armagh city from the proclamation, rather than risk a 'very detrimental' step.[14] Indeed, so keen was Camden so keep

---

9 Camden to Portland, 3 Jan. 1797, P.R.O. H.O. 100/69/f. 24.   10 *Parl. Reg.* (Ir.), xvii, pp. 13, 165; Everard to Downshire, 17 Oct. 1796, P.R.O.N.I. Downshire Papers, D607/A/514; Camden to Portland, 18 Oct. 1796, P.R.O. H.O. 100/62/f. 272.   11 Pelham to Knox, 31 Dec. 1796, N.L.I. Lake Papers, MS56/f. 14.   12 *D.N.B.*, Lord Charlemont iii, pp. 235–6; Camden to Portland, 3 Sept. 1796, P.R.O. H.O. 100/62/f. 208; 22 Sept. 1796, H.O.100/66/f. 106.   13 *D.N.B.*, ibid.   14 Charlemont to Johnson, n.d. [c. 20 Nov. 1796], Camden to Charlemont, 22 Nov. 1796, H.M.C. *Charlemont*, ii, pp. 288–9.

Charlemont's influence in the yeomanry that he obliged Gosford, Charlemont's political rival and a Castle supporter, to waive his own opinion on the matter.[15] More indulgences followed after the Bantry scare when all corps were circularised to see how many would march from their own areas. This brought a predictably prickly response from Charlemont, sensitive to the distinction between citizens defending their property and being ordered around the country by government. Although the Yeomanry Act provided for remote service if corps volunteered for permanent duty, Camden quickly reassured him that government had no such intentions.[16] In May 1797 General Knox feared, with reason, that some northern corps had been infiltrated by United men who had disingenuously taken the oath of allegiance. He devised a further 'test' oath to combat this, whereby the yeomen would declare that they were not, nor ever had been, United Irishmen. Charlemont's yeomen were outraged, construing a slur on their loyalty. Again government responded favourably. Pelham directed Knox to except Charlemont's corps saying, 'I cannot help wishing to indulge as respectable an old man as Lord Charlemont'.[17] Hard politics underlay this apparent charity. Charlemont's influence and name were needed even more, since the yeomanry were beginning to be used in arms searches which had all the appearance of that whig anathema: martial law.

The issue of disarming marked the next instalment of official balm for Charlemont's irritation. Some tenants complained to him that over-zealous, ultra-loyalist yeomanry captains were taking the law into their own hands and terrorising them. Charlemont's outrage was the trigger for Camden to order Lake to ensure no more gratuitous disarming.[18] In many respects Charlemont was being used cynically to preserve a gloss of constitutionalism to ward off criticism in Britain and in Ireland, where Grattan's whigs had withdrawn from parliament in protest against the policy of coercion. Pelham had already told Lake that he could use troops and yeomanry to disarm without the presence of a magistrate, which was *de facto* martial law.[19] When government requested offers for permanent duty in April 1798, Charlemont again recoiled at the prospect of yeomen being under the Mutiny Bill. Camden pointed out that the circular directing the corps to take a more military role was not superseding their original offer, and that they could still undertake the more military duty and be excepted from the Mutiny Bill if they so wished.[20] This was not in the Act, which stated that 'if any such troop or company shall ... voluntarily offer to act as a military corps' they would be subject 'to the like military disci-

15 Camden to Gosford, 26 Nov. 1796, K.A.O. Pratt Papers, U840/0173/6; Gosford to Camden, 30 Nov. 1796. U840/0173/7. 16 37 Geo. 111, c.2, section 5; 7 Jan. 1797, H.M.C. *Charlemont*, ii, p. 292.
17 Pelham to Knox, 20 May 1797, N.L.I. Lake Papers, MS56/f. 7; Pelham to [Knox], 14 June 1797, MS56/f. 88. 18 Livingston to Charlemont, 8 Nov. 1797, H.M.C. *Charlemont*, ii, pp. 310–11; Camden to Charlemont, 18 Nov. 1797, Charlemont to Camden, 19 Nov. 1797, K.A.O. Pratt Papers, U840/177/9, 10. 19 Lake to Pelham, 16 April 1797, B.L. Pelham Papers, add. mss. 33103 ff. 361–3. 20 Camden to Charlemont, 3 April 1798; Charlemont to Camden, 4 April 1798; Charlemont to Johnston, [?5] April 1798, H.M.C. *Charlemont*, ii, pp. 318–19.

pline as his Majesty's regular and militia forces'.[21] These examples show Camden's first instinctive reaction to the Dungannon Association as 'the foundation of a useful plan to strengthen government' was being fulfilled in the yeomanry in a political as well as a military sense.[22]

Other key magnates were similarly indulged. Lord Downshire was handled very diplomatically over his blinkered insistence that county Down should raise only cavalry. Similarly his desire for a completely subscription-raised force was not stopped. Government were sensible enough not to interfere and wait till reality dawned. Abercorn occupied a similar position of vast influence in Tyrone, but was hostile to the Camden administration. At first he opposed the raising of corps, claiming the state of the country was due to bad government. His relations with Hardwicke were better and he was indulged to the hilt by being allowed to raise his own yeomanry legion in Tyrone of 1,200 men, by an administration eager to conciliate opinion in the wake of Union.[23]

The political potential of the yeomanry extended beyond securing and extending government influence amongst landowners. The existence of a voluntary, property defence force was used to justify an increasingly coercive policy. The Insurrection Act, giving magistrates power to proclaim districts disordered, impose a curfew, and call in troops, had been on the statute book since February 1796. Its powers had been held in reserve, partly for prudence sake and partly due to the political dangers of acting outside the 'constitution'. By late 1796, the strategic necessity for the Insurrection Act increased but the political dangers remained. The Irish Yeomanry were in the same voluntary military tradition as the militia, and could be presented as citizen defenders, the antithesis of a standing army, to point up the 'constitutionalism' of governmental policy. A proclamation was issued in November 1796, threatening the Insurrection Act because yeomen were being intimidated. The same reason was given as a pretext for Lake's disarming of Ulster in March 1797.[24] Camden told Portland that he expected the order to Lake, which he felt obliged to explain to both Lords and Commons, would engender 'all the [obloquy] which is usually bestowed upon those acts which are not strictly within the law' and highlighted the intimidation of actual and potential yeomen as a prime justification. The order specified that yeomen would assist the troops in disarming and so 're-store to the Civil Power its constitutional authority'. Pelham felt that the severity of the problem put the severe remedy within the spirit of the constitution.[25] Government were utilising the voluntary military tradition, now with parliamentary sanc-

---

21 37 Geo. III, c.2, section 5.　22 Camden to Portland, 12 July 1796, P.R.O. H.O. 100/60/f. 261. 23 Abercorn to Galbraith, 18 Nov. 1796, P.R.O.N.I. Abercorn Papers, D623/A/80/25; Abercorn to Hardwicke, 10 Aug. 1803, D623/A/81/65.　24 6 Nov. 1796, P.R.O. H.O. 100/65/f. 109; Report of the Secret Committee of the House of Commons, *1798, Commons Jnls.* (Ir.), section viii, xvii, appx. dcccxxix.　25 [?18] March 1797, P.R.O. H.O. 100/71/f. 187; Camden to Portland, 21 March 1797, H.O. 100/69/f. 162.

tion, as a political defence for exceeding the letter of the law by making the free operation of yeomanry the benchmark beyond which lay anarchy.

This interpretation was artificial. The United Irishmen would have gone on ahead, yeomanry or not. Moreover, Carhampton had been sent to visit northern magistrates to orchestrate calls for the Insurrection Act, in order to make it seem they arose spontaneously.[26] Indeed, the impulse behind government policy was not as defensive as the ministers tried to make it appear. John Claudius Beresford, responding angrily to Grattan's criticism of the disarming, declared that he wished the United Irishmen in open rebellion so they could be faced.[27] He was only saying publicly what others said in private. Camden admitted to Portland that he would 'not lament the attempt at insurrection. It will enable us to act with effect'.[28] Government made much political capital of the constitutional aspect of yeomanry. In June 1797 the Dublin yeomen took up guard duty. Camden delightedly reported not only the strategic benefits, but that 'they have also given a very advantageous tone to the measures of government'. In March 1798 the official order to disarm the south used as a pretext attacks on legally established yeomen.[29] This political use of yeomanry as constitutional stooges also had its disadvantages as the Abercromby affair showed.

Sir Ralph Abercromby, Carhampton's replacement as commander-in-chief, was a military reformer, who had supported the American colonists and purposely stayed in Ireland during that conflict. There was no love lost between him and the conservative Irish gentry. He was disgusted by the state of the Irish army, dispersed as it was on peacekeeping duties, and issued a general order in February 1798 heavily criticizing it.[30] Abercromby claimed that the job of the yeomanry was policing, which was taken as a slight by the gentry. No doubt this would have happened anyway, as the commander-in-chief's desire for a more conciliatory policy put him out of kilter with gentry opinion. Nevertheless, by publicly equating the free enrolment of yeomanry with the maintenance of good order, government had narrowed the scope for constructive criticism, and at the same time opened the way for reactions of unlimited outrage whenever anyone did. In other words government were compromised by their public praise. Camden respected Abercromby as a soldier but had to give way to gentry and 'cabinet' pressure and permit him to resign. The Abercromby affair pointed to a truth that was to become more apparent in the Cornwallis administration: the political ramifications of yeomanry were not all benign.

Cornwallis arrived on 20 June, after the northern rising had been crushed and when the initiative in Wexford had passed to government. As Camden advocated, Cornwallis' viceroyalty combined the offices of commander-in-chief and viceroy.

26 Pelham to Carhampton, 10 Nov. 1796, B.L. Pelham Papers, add. mss. 33102 ff. 321–4.   27 *Parl. Reg.* (Ir.), xvii, p. 146.   28 10 May 1797, P.R.O. H.O. 100/69/f. 291.   29 Camden to Portland, 12 June 1797, P.R.O. H.O. 100/69/f. 402; Elliot to Abercromby, 14 March 1798, H.O.100/75/f. 241.   30 Lord Dunfermline, *Sir Ralph Abercromby*, passim.

Though apolitical in a conventional whig-tory sense, he personally favoured Catholic relief, was liked by Pitt and had a first-rate reputation as a soldier. He was considered one of the best British generals in the American war, and had military and administrative experience in India, where he had been Governor General between 1786 and 1792.[31] His policy followed two main lines: a markedly more conciliatory approach to the disaffected and, of paramount importance, the attainment of legislative Union. The latter objective was an ill-kept secret which had the corollary of putting the Catholic question back on the agenda because Catholic attitudes would have an important bearing on its passage.[32]

Although Cornwallis had vastly more 'colonial' experience than Camden, he also found Ireland difficult. A successful viceroy had to strike a delicate balance between English and Irish interests. Neither Camden nor Cornwallis did this. Camden's inexperience and personality led him to be rather overpowered by his Irish advisers, though the yeomanry formation process shows him not totally bereft of ideas. Cornwallis' previous experience moulded his attitudes in such a way as to make clashes with the Protestant gentry inevitable. He was contemptuous of those he considered colonials, and especially disliked local self-defence forces, such as he had encountered in America.[33] The treatment of Abercromby, an admirer of his, confirmed Cornwallis' prejudices. He considered this as improper interference in military affairs by the Irish 'cabinet'. Cornwallis thus cut himself off from those advisers who would not support his policies, most notably Speaker Foster, whom he politically ostracised.[34]

Ironically, Cornwallis arrived after the sting had been drawn from the rebellion by the types of troops he most disliked: yeomanry, militia, and fencibles. To the rebels he held out in one hand overwhelming force, and in the other the possibility of terms. A deal was worked out with the state prisoners, whereby these United Irish leaders were offered the lesser sentence of transportation in return for a statement declaring that their plans were French-inspired and separatist and the sparing of the life of one of their number, Oliver Bond, currently under sentence of death.[35] Many Irish Protestants, with the smoke of rebellion still in their eyes, would gleefully have hanged every one of them. The stage was set for friction between the new viceroy and an important section of his Irish subjects. Robert Ross conveyed to Downshire the mood of Dublin Protestants: 'I understand from everybody that none of the old cabinet are consulted. That body is now composed of English or Scottish generals who can know little of the disposition of the country or its inhabitants'. Cornwallis' dislike of amateur soldiers became apparent the day after his arrival. He asked Castlereagh for a return of the number of northern loyalists armed

---

31 Foster, *Modern Ireland*, p. 280.   32 Bolton, *The Passing of the Irish Act of Union*, p. 61; Bartlett, *Fall and rise*, p. 252.   33 N.A.M. 6602–45–3 f. 5, Cornwallis Papers, Cornwallis to Ross, 24 July 1798.   34 A.P. W. Malcomson, *John Foster*, p. 75.

as supplementary yeomen, and stopped the embodiment of any more supplementaries.[36]

This must have seemed a declaration of intent. Not surprisingly, after less than a fortnight Cornwallis complained that 'the life of a Lord Lieutenant of Ireland comes up to my idea of perfect misery, but if I can accomplish the grand object [Union] ... I shall be sufficiently repaid'. He noted that his plans for conciliation were being compromised by the violent attitudes of the government's Irish supporters, and the gratuitous ferocity of his native troops.[37] The rapidity with which these mutual animosities were struck shows how, in the frantic atmosphere engendered by the rising, opinion ran strongly against conciliation, compromise or even the benefit of the doubt. Disgustedly, Cornwallis complained, 'any man in a brown coat who is found within several miles of the field of action is butchered without discrimination' and ominously noted this ferocity 'in the Irish corps at least, is not confined to the private soldiers'. His contempt for both these forces and their gentry commanders rattles through his correspondence, but his hardest cuts were reserved for the yeomanry, who satisfied his presuppositions. They were, he said, like the loyalists of America, 'only much more numerous and powerful and a thousand times more ferocious' and even exceeded the militia in 'murder and every kind of atrocity'.[38] As the fighting in the field ended the stage was set for political conflict between the Protestant gentry and their governor.

The deal over the state prisoners was the first time gentry resentment could be concentrated on one issue. His opponents brought their pressure to bear via the yeomanry. Rumours were widely circulated in Dublin that they would lay down their arms if Oliver Bond was reprieved from sentence of death.[39] Although this opposition relaxed when it became known that Clare supported the deal, the fact that yeomanry was being used as a channel for political opposition boded ill for the future. It should be noted *en passant* that Grattanites, who also raised yeomanry, were highly in favour of Cornwallis and what they perceived his policies to be at this time. Sir Lawrence Parsons believed the furore over the prisoners was a smokescreen from an Ascendancy fearing Cornwallis' integrity threatened their dominance in Irish affairs.[40] The wind that brought the French to Mayo in August 1798 blew Cornwallis' criticisms of yeomanry back in his face, as he was forced to use them again. However, to a pragmatist, here was an opportunity to repair relations with the government's Irish supporters. The invasion was far from Dublin and small enough to ensure its failure. Cornwallis, later described as 'consummately stubborn

---

35 M. Elliott, *Wolfe Tone*, p. 390.   36 Circular, 2 July 1798, P.R.O.N.I. Lurgan Yeomanry Detail Book, D3696/A/4/1.   37 Elliot to Knox, 21 June 1798, N.L.I. Lake Papers, MS56/f. 202; Circular, 2 July 1798, P.R.O.N.I. Lurgan Yeomanry Detail Book, D3696/A/4/1; N.A.M. 6602–45–3 f. 2, Cornwallis Papers, Cornwallis to Ross, 1 July 1798.   38 Cornwallis to Portland, 28 June 1798, P.R.O. H.O. 100/7/ f. 200; N.A.M. 6602–45–3f. 5, Cornwallis Papers, Cornwallis to Ross, 24 July 1798.   39 , N.A.M. 6807–174 ff. 491–5, Nugent Papers, Corry to Nugent, 28 July 1798.   40 Parsons to Charlemont, 27 July 1798, H.M.C. *Charlemont*, ii, p. 330.

and intractable', slammed the door of reconciliation shut with an ineptitude rivalling the blundering of his generals at the 'Races of Castlebar', thanking the yeomanry for not disgracing themselves by 'wanton cruelty' against Humbert's Irish followers.[41] Understandably, this unbelievably tactless public remark was interpreted as a snub, implying reasonable behaviour was so unusual as to warrant comment.[42] However there was no shortage of genuine snubs.

On 5 October 1798 Cornwallis ordered a *fue de joi* in Phoenix Park for the evening, but suddenly brought it forward to the afternoon without informing the city yeomanry. As a result there was little fire and still less joy. He re-scheduled it for the following day but, the yeomen were so angry that some corps were half-empty while others were totally so.[43] Yeomanry continued to be the battleground for conflict between Cornwallis and the Ascendancy. The case of Hugh Wollaghan was redolent of the submerged political manipulation that underlay the mutual antagonism. Wollaghan was a Wicklow yeoman, court-martialled in October 1798 for killing a man because of perceived United Irish sympathies. Wollaghan claimed he was acting in obedience to an order. The court, presided over by the earl of Enniskillen, acquitted him.[44] Cornwallis was livid and sent a thundering letter to the Adjutant General of the Eastern District, Sir James Craig, condemning the acquittal, dissolving the court, dismissing Wollaghan from his corps and barring him from entering any other. Cornwallis ordered the letter to be read in open court, then banned those who sat on the Wollaghan court martial from ever sitting on another one. Enniskillen, who had influence with the Orangemen, resented this treatment and remained personally and politically hostile to Cornwallis for years.[45] Robert Ross told Downshire that Cornwallis was making the yeomen and Orangemen make common cause, and that his nickname had changed from 'Cornywallis' to 'Croppywallis'.[46]

On the surface, the Wollaghan affair looks an archetypal example of an enlightened governor being met by brutish intransigence and violence from Irish Protestants. When examined more closely, it belies any such simple interpretation. William Elliot, the civil under-secretary, told Castlereagh he 'cannot help attributing it [the verdict] to some party or political motive'.[47] Elliot was in a position to know. If true, it represents another example of yeomanry being used to pressurise the viceroy, a bait he would always rise to. In this analysis, Cornwallis' political opponents calculated that his response would be taken as an attack on the honour of the yeomen, and that the outrage would reach national Protestant opinion via the national yeomanry network. Given that his intentions regarding Union had been leaked, it is likely this device was used to prepare opposition in advance. Such an interpretation explains a

41 A. Knox to Hill, 16 Nov. 1798, P.R.O.N.I. Hill of Brook Hall Papers, D642/A/10/25; General Orders, 9 Sept. 1798, P.R.O. H.O.100/82/f. 60.   42 Johnston to Downshire, 13 Sept. 1798, P.R.O.N.I. Downshire Papers, D607/F/407.   43 Ross to Downshire, 6 Oct. 1798, P.R.O.N.I. Downshire Papers, D607/F/449.   44 The trial of Hugh Wollaghan, T.C.D. MS.872.   45 Taylor to Craig, 18 Oct. 1798, *Castlereagh Corrs.*, i, pp. 424–5. Bolton, op. cit., p. 64.   46 29 Oct. 1798, P.R.O.N.I. Downshire Papers, D607/F/502.   47 2 Nov. 1798, *Castlereagh Corrs.*, i, pp. 421–2.

letter from Castlereagh's secretary Alexander Knox to Sir George Hill. Knox told Hill, a yeomanry captain, strong Protestant and active magistrate, that 'voluntary compliance with murderous directions is of course *murder*'.[48] Obviously Castlereagh was trying to limit the political damage by preparing influential people in the north in advance of rumours. The strength of Cornwallis' reaction compromised Castlereagh's ability to placate his fellow countrymen. Indeed, Castlereagh had tried to placate his master also. Camden, sure of his nephew's sentiments, secretly told Castlereagh that, although he agreed the violence of some 'partisans of the Protestant interest' should be repressed, he believed condemnation of them 'will infinitely hurt the English interest in Ireland', and noted perceptively, 'the great question of Union will be hurt by this measure'.[49] Castlereagh was in an awkward position, given that his Ascendancy background conflicted with his career prospects, his past with his future. A semi-legible, unpublished letter to Camden showed that having tried without success to convince Cornwallis of the political implications, Castlereagh was uncomfortably resigned to doing his duty.[50] Bolton sees the Wollaghan incident as contributing to the deteriorating relationship between the Irish gentry and Cornwallis.[51] No doubt this was true, yet there was another court martial scandal involving the acquittal of a militia lieutenant who killed a yeoman suspected of being a United Irishman.[52] This case attracted nothing like the same attention. Why did yeomanry strike a sensitive chord with both the viceroy and the gentry?

Cornwallis' problem was that yeomanry were militarily essential. This reluctant dependency sickened and angered him. It struck deep at the psyche of the professional soldier and injected spleen into his correspondence: 'these men [the yeomanry] have saved the country, but now they take the lead in rapine and murder'.[53] As the need to rely on the yeomanry became more and more obvious, with actual invasion and periodic invasion scares, Cornwallis' resentment increased *pro rata* until he became fixated, an irritable old warrior oblivious to the political problem he was creating for himself.

There are many reasons why yeomanry became special to many Protestant Irishmen and represented more than their functional role. Some of these reasons could be applied to other aspects of the Irish Protestant experience: the need to be recognised and supported as the 'garrison' in times of danger was always reassuring for a demographic minority. More immediately, yeomanry were raised and paid for by their newly 'independent' parliament and had fought and bled in suppressing what was commonly perceived as a Catholic rebellion. This interpretation reawakened memories of 1641 and 1690 and appeared to have the sanction of government, mediated via the yeomanry. The anger and confusion when policy changes shattered

48 n.d. [Nov. 1798], P.R.O.N.I. Hill of Brook Hall Papers, D642/A/10/1.   49 4 November 1798, *Castlereagh Corrs.*, i, pp. 424-6.   50 Castlereagh to Camden, n.d. [early Nov. 1798], P.R.O.N.I. Castlereagh Papers, D3030/355.   51 Bolton, op. cit., pp. 63–5.   52 C. Ross (ed.), *Cornwallis Corrs.*, ii, p. 423.   53 Cornwallis to Ross, 24 July 1798, *Cornwallis Corrs.*, ii, pp. 370–1.

the illusion can be well imagined. Camden, more perceptive since he left Ireland, summed the feeling up well: 'the insinuation thrown out against the yeomanry [Cornwallis's claim that they had provoked the rebellion] could not be otherwise construed by the friends of that institution than as a disapprobation of that conduct they had been allowed to pursue before'.[54] Camden's warning that the Wollaghan case would damage the prospects for Union proved prophetic.

The storm clouds gathering around the proposed legislative Union broke on the last day of November 1798. Castlereagh nervously informed Portland that 'what was apprehended ... has happened: Captain Saurin of the Lawyers' Corps, this day in the Four Courts ordered them to assemble ... to take into their consideration a question of the greatest national importance'. The proposal was nothing less than that the Lawyers' corps should call on the entire Irish Yeomanry to oppose Union.[55] The anti-Union campaign involving the yeomanry is worth describing in some detail as it not only illuminates the political potential and limitations of the institution, but also puts to the acid test Camden's fears of re-creating the Volunteers. Saurin, a leading anti-Union activist, tried to use his position as yeomanry captain to broaden and publicise the campaign. Cornwallis saw what was happening, calling it an attempt 'to commit the public ... against the measure, as subversive of the constitution' by claiming the Union proposal violated the yeoman's oath to 'support and maintain the *constitution of this kingdom as by law established*'.[56] The lawyers' meeting was intended to set an example to be followed by the country gentlemen. In the event the majority of the corps decided it was inappropriate 'for an armed assembly to discuss a to discuss a parliamentary measure' and they decided to meet instead in their civil capacity.[57] The distinction was a fine one, as the same message could go out to yeomanry captains in their civilian capacity. That message was basically that the political and constitutional *status quo*, established by the gentry using the Volunteers, was threatened and should be resisted. The fact that, in key areas, the yeomanry was often built on the same networks as the Volunteers meant that the message did not have to be formally expressed at armed parades to have the same resonance. Charlemont, horrified at the prospect of Union, urged James Stewart to call a Tyrone county meeting, and eagerly awaited a favourable result from the lawyers to set the tone for more meetings.[58]

Although cooler heads saw the danger of yeomen taking up political subjects in their military capacity, the prospect of such interference was taken seriously enough to reach Whitehall. Portland ordered Saurin's removal from his legal and yeomanry offices, but Cornwallis, in a rare demonstration of political skill, decided against

---

54 Camden to Castlereagh, 11 April 1800, *Castlereagh Corrs.*, iii, pp. 271–4.   55 Castlereagh to Portland, 30 Nov. 1798, P.R.O. H.O. 100/79/f. 204; D. Plunkett, (ed.), *The life, letters and speeches of Colonel Plunkett*, i, pp. 117–18.   56 Cornwallis to Portland, 5 Dec. 1798, *Castlereagh Corrs.*, ii, pp. 34–7.   57 Plunkett, ibid., pp. 117–18.   58 8 Dec. 1798, P.R.O.N.I. Stewart of Killymoon Papers, D3167/1/75.

creating a yeoman martyr.[59] The attempt overtly to mobilise the yeomanry on a political issue was nipped in the bud. Another Dublin corps, the Liberty Rangers, had planned to parade with a flag replacing their regimental colours, bearing the legend 'For our King and the Constitution of Ireland'. They were stopped, with Saurin's help, on threat of being disarmed.[60] However, Saurin's contrition was only apparent. Having failed to cast the yeomanry in an overtly political, Volunteer-like role, anti-Unionists switched to scare-tactics by circulating rumours that the yeomen were prepared to lay down their arms over Union.[61] Active yeomanry opposition to Union was not confined to Dublin. Lord Donoughmore's Cork Legion published an anti-Union address in February 1799 and the Ulster yeomanry were reported as 'much dissatisfied'.[62] In the event, the Union proposal was defeated, not by mutiny, but by votes in parliament and the support of political heavyweights like Foster. However, 'out of doors' pressure also played a part. John Beresford and Lord Clare, both supporters of Union, noted that the relative absence of formal yeomanry protests had not prevented their opponents working on the feelings of yeomen and linking the Union proposal with Cornwallis' unpopularity amongst most Irish Protestants. The 'public clamour' against the measure, they said, 'was quadrupled by the bad treatment which the yeomanry conceived they had received'.[63]

Government policy dictated that the Union measure would be tried again. No time was lost by its supporters and opponents in marshalling their resources. There is evidence that some Union supporters tried to wrong-foot their opponents by getting their corps to support Union. Possibly with the Cork address in mind, Cornwallis prevented the Castle Otway corps raising a pro-Union declaration in August 1799, fearing 'the danger of the precedent and of the handle that might be made of it'.[64] Major northern anti-Unionists, like Downshire, had no difficulty in persuading local yeomanry against it. Their opposition was already bespoke, emanating from fear that Catholic emancipation would follow Union. Although official Orange policy was to stay neutral, many Orangemen opposed Union as individuals. Many of Downshire's infantry were Orangemen, as were those of his neighbour, Richard Annesley. In January 1799, Downshire's agent Lane reported that Union was 'unpalatable' to local yeomen, while Annesley's yeomen were so disgusted at Cornwallis and the proposed Union, he doubted whether they would undertake any duty.[65] This resentment was apparent when Cornwallis toured the north in the au-

---

59 Cornwallis to Portland, 5 Dec. 1798, *Castlereagh Corrs.*, ii, pp. 34–7, [Portland] to Cornwallis, 10 Jan. 1799, P.R.O. H.O. 100/85/f. 35; Cornwallis to Portland, 16 Jan 1799, H.O. 100/85/f. 85. 60 Castlereagh to Portland, 19 Jan. 1799, P.R.O. H.O. 100/85/f. 130. 61 Patrickson to Downshire, 1 Jan. 1799, P.R.O.N.I. Downshire Papers, D607/G/l. 62 13 Feb. 1799, P.R.O.N.I. Donoughmore Papers, T3459/D/6/6; Anon. to Castlereagh, 3 July 1799, N.A. R.P.620/47/77. 63 Beresford to Auckland, 6 Feb. 1799, *Beresford Corrs.*, ii, pp. 208–11; Clare to Camden, 16 Feb. 1799, K.A.O. Pratt Papers, U840/CIO3. 64 Castlereagh to Portland, 5 Aug. 1799, P.R.O. H.O.100/87/f. 89. 65 5 Jan. 1799, P.R.O.N.I. Downshire Papers, D607/G/4; Annesley to Downshire, 12 Jan. 1799, D607/G/16.

tumn to gather support for Union but wisely declined inspecting any northern yeomanry except in places of his own choosing.[66]

As Union came before parliament again in January 1800, its opponents reverted
to intimidation. Their campaign had some effect, but had the air of desperation
about it. Castlereagh told Portland that 'our timid and wavering friends' were alarmed
'as the yeomanry, principally composed of (Dublin) shopkeepers and tradesmen,
are amongst the most intemperate of our opponents'. A few days later Cooke noted
that they were 'almost wild' and 'ready for mischief. Cornwallis took the threats of
yeomanry mutiny seriously enough to order 1,000 extra troops into Dublin to
strengthen the garrison.[67] In parliament, the anti-Union coalition of reformers and
conservatives drew deeply on their common Volunteering roots to produce rhetoric
reminiscent of the 1780s.[68] Grattan, in a bizarre but heavily symbolic gesture, returned ghost-like to College Green, dressed in full Volunteer uniform. However,
neither the words in parliament nor the agitation outside were sufficient to prevent
the well-established procedure of bargaining for political property allowing the passage of Union.

How serious was the yeomanry's opposition to Union? Government's treatment
of the anti-Union yeomen shows the danger was significant enough. An interesting
comparison can be made between the reluctance to make a martyr of Saurin, and
the eager strike at Downshire when he tried to use his position as colonel of the
Down militia to raise an anti-Union petition. He was removed from his command
and from his civil posts as county governor and privy councillor.[69] There was a
personal element in this: Cornwallis detested Downshire as a 'pampered borough-
monger', who typified the venal Ascendancy. As a soldier, Cornwallis would equally
have hated Saurin's misuse of the military system, yet Downshire was broken while
Saurin was allowed to remain. The reason is that yeomanry had far greater potential
for political action than militia and required much more adroit handling, because of
their connections with all levels of the Protestant community and the respect in
which they had been held by that community since 1798. Militia, because their rank
and file was generally Catholic, and also because of their largely unjustified reputation for disloyalty, were not the darlings of the Protestant interest in the same way as
yeomanry. Criticism of the yeomanry, meant *de facto* criticism of the gentry, and this
was what the anti-Unionists played on. Moreover, the fact that militiamen served
outside their own counties lessened their political potential on an issue like this
where kin and patronage linkages into the local communities would have been the
means by which opinion was prepared against Union. Yeomanry, on the other hand,
were territorially rooted and yeomen were civilians when off permanent duty and

---

66 Nugent to Gosford, 30 Sept. 1799, P.R.O.N.I. Gosford Papers, D 1606/1/1/220B.   67 29 Jan 1800,
P.R.O. H.O. 100/93/f. 56; Cooke to King, 3 Feb. 1800, P.R.O. H.O. 100/95/f. 66.   68 *Debate on the
Proposed Union*, 5–6 Feb. 1800, (J. Moore, Dublin, 1800), passim.   69 Castlereagh to Portland, 7 Feb.
1800, P.R.O. H.O. 100/93/f. 84.

consequently less amenable to direct military discipline than militiamen. Therefore, notwithstanding the government's ultimate control over the yeomanry, as over
the militia, there were more political impediments to this being exercised to its full
potential in the former. This was another important reason why the anti-Unionists
tried yeomanry first in their campaign. Downshire's attempt to harness the Down
militia came later and had a feeling of desperation about it. Similarly, yeomanry
could be used to 'prove' the Irish gentry could defend Ireland, having broken the
rebellion before Cornwallis' reinforcements arrived. This was a blatant exaggeration, as militia and fencibles also played a major part. Nevertheless, it was used
politically because it neatly undermined the strategic argument for Union, that Ireland ultimately relied on Britain for protection. Ultimately though, with the 1798
rebellion fresh in their minds, the yeomen needed the government more than the
government needed the yeomen.

This was the fatal flaw in the campaign. When the measure passed, the mutiny
threats proved unfounded. Cornwallis' reinforcements were not needed. Camden's
Volunteer nightmare, though briefly given substance by Grattan's nocturnal visita-
tion, faded in the dawn of the new century. Not all yeomen opposed Union, and
those who did were less able to defend Grattan's parliament than the Volunteers had
been in establishing it. The yeoman's potential for political action was compromised by his *raison d'être* in a dangerously disturbed country bearing scant resem-
blance to the Ireland of the 1780s. By way of emphasis there is evidence that the
remnants of the United Irishmen tried to resurrect their cause by attaching it to the
discontent against Union. A pamphlet by 'Eunomous' started by quoting Blackstone
on the right to have and use arms when every other means of preserving the constitution had failed. The constitutional argument was maintained until the conclusion, which was pure United Irish propaganda. This asked that should government
subvert the constitution by first goading the peasantry to rebellion, then destroying
the parliament by corruption, 'Yeomen of Ireland, could you be silent?'[70] With support like this what yeoman would make an enemy of the government?

This is not to say the yeomen of Dublin and elsewhere were not genuine in their
opposition to Union so much as saying that they could not push their resistance to
its logical conclusion. Indeed, it would be easy to overestimate the reaction of the
yeomanry generally on the basis of the available information. The danger of a military body involving itself in politics means that yeomanry opposition, particularly
of the type engendered in Dublin, inevitably found its way into the sources and may
consequently assume greater importance in retrospect than it had at the time. It is a
useful corrective to note that yeomanry corps everywhere quickly adopted the new
post-Union flags and motifs into their colours.[71] The anti-Unionists found that,
despite their advantage of having a politically naive viceroy, an angry yeomanry and

70 'Eunomous', 'An argument addressed to the yeomanry of Ireland' (Dublin, 1800), B.L. 8145d27.   71
G.A. Hayes-McCoy, *A History of Irish Flags*, pp. 102–8.

the Catholic bogey, the most they could achieved with the yeomanry was to impede and restrict government's management of policy; they could never emulate Volunteers and change policy. They yanked at the sleeve of government whereas the Volunteers had had ministers in an armlock.

Camden found that yeomanry could be an asset to governing, Cornwallis proved this was only true when government policy was perceived to be in the interests of the constituency which produced the yeomanry. Cornwallis' experience was therefore entirely different from Camden's. To some extent, this was conditioned by personality, but the abrupt change in policy, with its perceived ingratitude, played a larger role. Camden's utilisation of the political potential of yeomanry to bind diffuse elements of the 'well affected' created a more politically homogenous institution, a process made irreversible by the rebellion. Ironically, this phenomenon, which originally worked greatly to Camden's advantage, was the main reason why the yeomanry had the power to impede, but not reverse, Cornwallis's policy. However, the potential to be a useful tool in the business of government still remained, to be availed of when policy changed again. This happened when Pitt resigned in 1801 because the king refused to allow emancipation to follow Union.

Philip Yorke, third earl of Hardwicke, became viceroy under Pitt's successor, Addington. Hardwicke took over the government of Ireland in the context of the political outworkings of Union. An entirely different political animal from Cornwallis, he had much more in common with the Irish gentry. He was a Cambridgeshire landowner, one-time member for and lord lieutenant of his county, with responsibility for raising yeomanry. With the Catholic question off the agenda, his major concerns were with the ramifications of Union. This brought with it much uncertainty. For one thing, the status of the office of viceroy was ill-defined. Also, more urgently, much Irish opinion remained unreconciled to the measure. In both cases yeomanry were to play an important role.

Hardwicke saw himself as a peacemaker, whose job it was to placate the anger over Union.[72] The continuing invasion threat meant that his relationship with the yeomanry had to be established quickly. He put out feelers, by arranging a review in Phoenix Park to see if the yeomen would do duty once more. Saurin again caused trouble, choosing to interpret this as government trying to humiliate the Irish Bar by catching them unawares, and threatened to resign his commission.[73] This petty action was in the continuing context of the yeomanry being used for political pressure. Nevertheless, it put Hardwicke in an awkward position. His remedy shows acute awareness of the yeomanry's political potential. He told Alexander Marsden, his civil under-secretary, that the yeomanry force was too important for him not to show consideration to its supporters, and ordered him to discourage Saurin's resignation, explaining that he wanted the review to get acquainted with the yeomen.[74]

72 M. MacDonagh, *The Viceroy's Postbag*, pp. 8–10.   73 Lindsay to Abbot, 23 June 1801, P.R.O. Colchester Papers, 3/9/115/ff. 5–9.   74 16 June 1801, B.L. Hardwicke Papers, add. mss. 35776.

This was untrue. Hardwicke wanted to assess their reliability after Union. Honour satisfied, Saurin kept his commission. Hardwicke's private secretary, Charles Lindsay noted the significance of the affair, saying that many Dublin corps were 'not yet reconciled to the Union' and that if Saurin resigned, the rest would follow.[75]

After the review the yeomanry captains were lavishly entertained at the vicere-gal lodge. A sumptuous banquet was provided where the bitter taste of Union was obliterated by 'an abundance of turtle, turkey and venison and a hogshead of good claret broached from the wood'. Diplomacy and drink mingled. There were ninety-six yeomanry officers present, symbolically marking the foundation year. Hardwicke spared no trouble to make his point. At the climax of a long series of toasts, the sated yeomen saw Charles Abbot suddenly appear in the uniform of a light horse volun-teer and Reginald Cocks in that of a Worcestershire yeoman. Behind the bonhomie was hard political reality. Hardwicke told his brother Charles, the secretary at war, that he intended the carefully cultivated good spirit of the Dublin yeomanry to radi-ate throughout the country.[76] If yeomanry were to do duty again, they would need to be re-clothed. This gave another opportunity to stitch up the damage caused by his predecessor. Re-clothing was costly and opened up a delicate issue, of whether to re-clothe the entire establishment, at that time 54,000, or confine it to the most needy. The Home Office was unresponsive, but Hardwicke, like Camden during the formation period, acted unilaterally and ordered the re-clothing in advance of the parliamentary grant, rather than snub the Irish gentry.[77]

Hardwicke worked hard at cultivating good yeomanry relations to maintain a favourable political climate. In August 1802 there were attempts in Wicklow and Antrim to start legal proceedings against yeomen involved in killings in 1798. In both instances the yeomen involved memorialized Hardwicke. The Antrim memo-rial was accompanied by a subscription list, headed by the governor, Lord Donegall, and including most members of the county establishment, civil and military.[78] Rather than arbitrarily stop proceedings by the attorney general's power of *noli prosequi*, Hardwicke wanted the grand jury to dismiss the case. However, he emphasized that if this was the start of a campaign by the disaffected, he wanted indemnifying legis-lation considered.[79] With Catholics disappointed, Protestant opinion and Protes-tant votes were all the more vital to government. Here again Hardwicke showed that he saw yeomanry as the key to that opinion.

The post-Union status of the viceregal office was complex and multi-dimen-sional. There were three main problem areas, involving a variety of relationships:

75 Lindsay to Abbot, 23 June 1801, P.R.O. Colchester Papers, 3/9/115 ff. 5–8.   76 Hardwicke to Yorke, 31 July 1801, B.L. Hardwicke Papers, add. mss. 35701.   77 Hardwicke to Portland, 1 June 1801, P.R.O. WO/35/21/ff. 24–6, Hardwicke to Pelham, 31 July 180 1, P.R.O. H.O.100/103/f. 305.   78 Memorial of T. Hamilton, n.d. [July 1802], P.R.O. H.O.100/110/f. 242.   79 Hardwicke to Pelham, 4 Aug. 1802, P.R.O. H.O. 100/109/f. 157, H.O. 100/110/f. 240; Eldon to Pelham, 4 Aug. 1802, H.O. 100/110/f. 248.

between government and gentry, between the viceroy and the commander-of-the-forces (as the Irish commander-in-chief was known after Union) and between Dublin Castle and the Home Office. The gentry problem was the most urgent. Apart from placating anti-Unionists, there was the difficulty of governing with reduced patronage at a time when more was needed because of the post-Union reduction of seats. The Union 'engagements' had removed most of the viceroy's civil patronage, while military assimilation sent Ireland's military patronage to the duke of York. This brought more friction between the viceroy and the commander-of-the-forces, a relationship which had been growing increasingly uneasy since the later eighteenth century. The military hierarchy had moved out to Kilmainham and begun to kick against its subservience to the civil administration.[80] However, the raising of militia and yeomanry had reasserted the Castle's position. Ireland's law and order problems continually thrust the rival authorities into forced co-operation and exposed the professional antipathy between soldiers and civil administrators. Post-Union military assimilation put a new edge on an old problem, as it gave an opportunity to redraw the boundaries. The third problem concerned the relationship of the Irish lord lieutenancy with the British government. After Union this was left ill-defined. The cabinet was divided. Addington and Pitt supported Hardwicke exercising the office in a similar manner as before Union but with a reforming brief. Pelham, now at the Home Office, wanted to seize for his own department most of the viceregal powers by reducing the governor of Ireland to the status of a county lord lieutenant.[81] Addington stopped Pelham, but rancour and rivalry remained.[82] Pelham was joined by some Irish politicians, such as Clare, who lost out under Abbot's reforms, and Cooke, whose designs on the chief secretaryship had been thwarted. As Camden had found to his advantage, and Cornwallis to his cost, yeomanry had become an integral part of governing Ireland, kept high on the political agenda by its frequent and expensive usage. Yeomanry was to prove an important component in the working out of all three areas outlined above. How this happened can best be seen by examining two of the major issues Hardwicke faced: the ramifications of the Peace of Amiens, and Emmet's rebellion.

The prospect of peace in late 1801 presented both governments with a dilemma. Financial difficulties, and, in the case of militia and yeomanry, legislation, demanded military reductions; yet nobody seriously believed peace would last. Hardwicke was faced with the unpleasant prospect of European considerations destroying a force he had used to advantage in the governing of Ireland. Although disbandment was *prima facie* a financial and legal matter, it had strong political undercurrents. It presented Pelham with a golden opportunity to undermine fatally the power of the viceroy. Hardwicke got in first and pressed for partial retention, basing his argu-

80 K.P. Ferguson, op. cit., pp. 65–6. 81 T. McCavery, 'Finance and Politics in Ireland, 1801–17', p. 37 and passim; Lord Colchester (ed.), *Diary and Correspondence of Charles Abbot* (hereafter: *Abbot, Corrs.*), i, pp. 277–8. 82 Malcomson, *John Foster*, p. 442.

ment on the reputation of the yeomanry, the likelihood of domestic trouble, and injured gentry feelings.[83] Despite having military opinion in his favour,[84] Hardwicke's request for a Home Office ruling on partial retention was deliberately ignored. Hardwicke dreaded losing an institution over which he had complete control, which gave him some patronage to offer the gentry and which kept security and defence policy within his ambit.

Hardwicke played his cards carefully. Abbot prepared a detailed memorandum proposing to reduce exercise days to one per fortnight, keeping in reserve the possibility of one per month. Hardwicke could thus acknowledge the financial realities, while still keeping the political power yeomanry gave him. Anticipating Pelham's reaction, he pointedly asked that 'this very important matter' be decided by the King. Hardwicke carried his point and obtained Pelham's reluctant sanction to make exercise fortnightly and use his own discretion on further retrenchment.[85] In March 1802 peace became a reality, and speculations about yeomanry reductions had to be translated into policy. Amazingly, it was belatedly realised that the 1796 Yeomanry Act made no provision for peacetime retention. Marsden, the civil under-secretary, tried to force an interpretation of yeomen as volunteers who could still assemble, and argued that the act merely regulated and paid them. Hardwicke was not swayed by this rash counsel, realising that he would fatally compromise the institution this way by leaving it wide open to parliamentary attack, as illegal, and that he would lose much of its patronage potential with the gentry. He asked Pelham to get the Irish Act extended for six months, reiterating his discretion over 'state of the country' needs. Hardwicke was understandably pessimistic about the outcome. Littlehales drafted letters instructing the yeomanry captains and brigade majors on the procedure for complete disbandment.[86] There was much difference of opinion as to the utility of auxiliary forces in Britain. Pitt's secretary-at-war, William Windham, criticised the English yeomanry and volunteers as an expensive and largely wasted military resource. Hardwicke's brother Charles was considered a poor replacement at the War Office and, given this and Pelham's antipathy, Irish yeomanry disbandment was a distinct possibility.

The issue of auxiliary forces came up in the debates on militia disbandment on 12 April 1802. The opposition claimed it was unconstitutional to have yeomanry and volunteers in peacetime. Addington rejected this, and Yorke announced his intention to use the peace to consolidate defence. He intended the English yeomanry to make offers of voluntary, unpaid service and the volunteers to be reduced, except

83 Hardwicke to Pelham, 14 Oct. 1801, B.L. Hardwicke Papers, add. mss. 35771; Hardwicke to Pelham, 16 Oct. 1801, P.R.O. H.O. 100/104/f. 203.   84 Abbot to Addington, 16 Oct. 1801, *Abbot Corrs.*, i, pp. 373–4.   85 Hardwicke to Wickham, 31 October 1801, H.R.O. Wickham Papers, 38M49/5/10/24, Pelham to Hardwicke, 16 Nov. 1801, 38M49/5/10/30.   86 Hardwicke to Wickham, 6 April 1802, B.L. Hardwicke Papers, add. mss. 35771; Marsden to Littlehales. 7 April 1802, H.R.O. Wickham Papers, 38M49/5/11/21; 8 April 1802, 38M49/5/11/22; 7 April 1802, P.R.O. H.O.100/109/f. 57.

in large cities.[87] This left a number of doors dangerously open through which the Irish Yeomanry could be pushed. Firstly, being predominantly infantry, they could be construed as 'volunteers' and be subject to reduction. Secondly, the possibility of service without pay would have robbed the Irish government of an important political instrument. In Westminster, Irish yeomanry pay was expense; in Dublin Castle it was control by means of honour or indebtedness and patronage. Wickham acted quickly. The following day he got Addington to rule that both Irish militia and yeomanry would be maintained and that the condition of Ireland, rather than the European situation, would determine to what extent. Shortly afterwards Wickham triumphantly told Hardwicke, 'I trust the yeomanry will be at your Excellency's disposal, and indeed this is all I had aimed at with respect to them'.[88] Wickham was wrong. He had misunderstood the danger of a new Yeomanry Bill, framed under British dynamics, yoking the Irish force to its cross-channel counterparts under the Union principle of military assimilation. Littlehales prepared the way by imploring Wickham to emphasize that, in Ireland, yeomanry business was 'a political question of great magnitude' and 'a matter of serious state policy'. Previous to the military reduction debate, Hardwicke had hoped, as a last resort, to retain one third of the Irish yeomanry with arms but no pay. This would at least have left him with something to build on later. However, when a new Yeomanry Bill was being prepared, Littlehales, who had drafted a reduction plan, was instructed not to publicise it till the draft bill could be studied.[89]

Pelham was poised to exploit the Irish companion to the new Bill. Hardwicke described his conduct as an intolerable 'personal affront'.[90] Hardwicke's own behaviour left much to be desired, as he went to any length to defend his yeomanry. He told Pelham of an incident at Ferns in county Wexford earlier in June, claiming that loyal yeomen had been attacked by people involved in the 1798 rising, yet the actual incident had been reported as a dispute amongst countrymen, in which some yeomen voluntarily got involved and after which both parties became friendlier following the usual fairday dialogue, of 'many heads ... broken on both sides'.[91] Hardwicke deliberately misrepresented the incident as one familiar to Pelham from his days in Ireland, to emphasize that Irish yeomanry were indispensable, European peace or not. The Irish Bill was a sensitive affair. Wickham reported that it 'was drawn with great care and well considered, but it was necessary to use great caution, and to word the clauses in such a manner as that the Bill might pass through the house with the least *possible* observation'.[92] In the event, on 22 June 1802 the new Irish

---

87 *Parl. Debs.* xxxvi, p. 535.   88 Wickham to Hardwicke, 13 April 1802, 21 April, 1801, B.L. Hardwicke Papers, add. mss. 35713.   89 Littlehales to Wickham, 3 May 1802, 21 May 1802, H.R.O. Wickham Papers, 38M49/5/11/48, 58. 90 Hardwicke to Wickham, 24 May 1802, H.R.OI. Wickham papers, 38M49/5/30/21.   90 Hardwicke to Pelham, 11 June 1802, P.R.O. H.O. 100/109/f. 144; Gen. Grose, Wexford to Littlehales, 9 June 1802, H.O. 100/109/f. 148.   92 Wickham to Hardwicke, 6 June 1802, B.L. Hardwicke Papers, add. mss. 35713.

Yeomanry Act passed parliament along with an Act enabling the British Yeomanry and Volunteers to be continued in peacetime.[93] The critical difference between the two was that pay continued for Irish yeomen. Moreover, a large degree of viceregal control remained intact. The Act provided for reducing and disarming corps, but left it to the viceroy's discretion. The Irish Yeomanry's distinct character, which had been conceived in response to local conditions, was preserved. Hardwicke succeeded in keeping a force which not only maintained viceregal power but gave the Irish government the prestige necessary to govern. He celebrated shortly after the Act passed, justifying the lavish entertainments to Addington on the solid political ground of demonstrating that the Castle's 'style' was unaltered.[94]

Hardwicke did not rest on his laurels. He realised the Irish Yeomanry were vulnerable in a climate of financial retrenchment, because they would inevitably have to do permanent duty for local disorders due to reductions in the regulars. He arranged for the responsibility of communicating with the magistrates and putting yeomanry on duty to be transferred to the generals commanding military districts, along with all the administration involved, thus formalizing the existing arrangement. Hardwicke made it clear that all communications from the district generals would by-pass the commander-of-the-forces and go straight to the military undersecretary at the Castle, because permanent duty in peacetime was different from that in wartime.[95] Hardwicke probably took advantage of the fact that the commander-of-the-forces, Sir William Medows, was well into his sixties and had not Cornwallis' military reputation, to push this scheme.[96] Medows referred it to the duke of York, who was furious, fearing an attempt to undermine the authority of the army commander. The issue ended in stalemate, as Hardwicke pledged, rather evasively, that nothing would be done regarding yeomanry without 'direct concert and co-operation' with the commander-of-the-forces.[97] This was to be the first shot in the resumption of the old rivalry between the Castle and the military hierarchy at Kilmainham.

In early 1803, with war again looming, the policy of military reductions was replaced by measures designed to improve Britain's capability to meet the new European style of conflict. The French *levee en masse* of 1793 had ushered in an age of huge armies and less formally organized battle formations. Speed, flexibility and surprise replaced the rigid manoeuvring of the old Prussian system. Britain's response took a number of different forms, including, as we have seen, giving the voluntary forces more military training. In addition to this there was a confusing plethora of new legislation to raise more men for home defence.[98] Hardwicke knew

93 42 Geo. III, c.68 [Ir.]; 42 Geo. III c.66 [G.B.].   94 22 July 1802, B.L. Hardwicke Papers, add. mss. 35704/ff. 298–9.   95 Hardwicke to Pelham, 7 Aug. 1802, P.R.O. H.O. 100/109/f. 173.   96 *D.N.B.* xiii, pp. 206–7.   97 Duke of York to Pelham, 26 July 1802, B.L. Hardwicke Papers, add. mss. 35773; Hardwicke to Pelham, 7 Aug. 1802, P.R.O. H.O. 100/109/f. 173.   98 There were no less than 21 separate Acts in 1802–3: I.F.W. Beckett, *The Amateur Military Tradition*, p. 92.

he had to scrutinise these new British defence measures, to monitor their implications for the Irish Yeomanry. His situation was difficult. He could not impede imperial policy, yet by implementing it to the letter, he was again in danger of losing the political advantage yeomanry gave him. Fearing the ramifications of the new legislation, he told his brother that yeomanry and militia were the only defence measures the Irish government could take of its own accord, and unequivocally declared his own preference: *'entre nous* the former is the best force for Ireland'.[99]

The kaleidoscopic policy changes over levying additional defence forces in Britain made Hardwicke's task of preserving the Irish Yeomanry in its existing form difficult and uncertain. With the restart of war, he had planned to augment by 8,000 yeomen, but had to shelve this in anticipation of his brother's latest brainwave: the Army of Reserve, a scheme to raise men by parochial levy to train as replacements for the regulars. Ireland's quota was to be 10,000. Whichever way Hardwicke turned there was potential political danger. By canvassing for the large-scale augmentations necessary to put Ireland back on a defence footing, he risked offending those loyalists he had to refuse, since to have accepted every offer would have made him vulnerable to attack at Westminster over cost. On the other hand, the Army of Reserve threatened to drain-off much Castle power to Kilmainham. There was an added complication. Charles James Fox's younger brother, General Henry Fox, was now commander-of-the-forces. Moreover, he promised to be a more significant obstacle than Medows. Fox was highly regarded by the duke of York and was a royal favourite, having once been the king's aide-de-camp. Inevitably Fox took his master's line and strongly supported the Army of Reserve, rather than yeomanry augmentations as the latter locked-up manpower from the army. Statesman-like, Hardwicke agreed to implement the measure before further augmenting the yeomanry. His chief secretary, Wickham, was less tactful, complaining that the 1802 Yeomanry Act gave the viceroy all the power he needed for defence preparations.[100] The Army of Reserve represented a very significant threat to the yeomanry, not just because of the alteration in the balance of power between civil and military authorities, but because the Irish levies were intended to be interchangeable with those raised in Britain. This was similar to the parochial levy scheme of 1796, which was unpopular in Ireland. The identity of endangered interests, which bound Castle and gentry so close together in the yeomanry in 1796–8, was recurring less than three years after the Union. Arguably, the existence of yeomanry helped put the gentry even more in the Castle's pocket after Union. An augmented yeomanry offered patronage to compensate for that lost with the Irish parliament and the threatening innovations from Westminster made the gentry more reliant on the Castle, as yeomanry were a comforting link to pre-Union Ireland.

---

99 Hardwicke to Yorke, 14 March 1803, B.L. Hardwicke Papers, add. mss. 35702. **100** 43 Geo. III c. 82; Littlehales to Wickham, 28 June 1803, H.R.O. Wickham Papers, 38M49/5/33/35; Wickham to [?Yorke], 17 July 1803, 38M49/5/20/2.

The Army of Reserve issue re-opened the Castle-Kilmainham rivalry but on the night of 23 July something happened in the Liberties of Dublin which fanned the feud into a major political battle. In military terms, Robert Emmet's abortive rebellion was little more than a skirmish. However, it caught the Irish government by surprise and caused acute embarrassment. To deflect criticism, both at home and at Westminster, the blame was pinned squarely on General Fox.[101] His ill-concealed dislike of the yeomanry and the association with his brother Charles, who opposed the war, made him an ideal scapegoat. The Castle claimed that, when an informer advised of the likelihood of trouble, the authorities told Fox to order the garrison accordingly and ordered the yeomanry not to assemble, as this would cause alarm. However, Fox did not alert the garrison and there was panic as the yeomen gathered at the Castle looking for their arms which had been removed by Fox's instructions. Messengers were sent to the Ordnance, where it was presumed the yeomanry guns were, but instead found an obtuse officer who had apparently lost the key. Significantly, the yeomanry arms had been removed from the Castle without Hardwicke being notified.[102] However, the government itself was not without blame and Hardwicke knew it: when some of Emmet's powder blew up in Patrick Street on 16 July, there was no reaction from the Castle. Worse still, in the eyes of Irish loyalists, Hardwicke had been following a conciliatory law-and-order policy. Martial law had been allowed to lapse and some loyalists were beginning to contrast the security provided by a Union parliament with that which they had been used to receive from College Green.[103] Hardwicke's administration was in crisis. Under attack from different fronts, the Castle deflected the blame onto Fox, and allowed popular Protestant misconceptions about the rising to go unchallenged. Yeomanry featured in both evasions.

Fox was more than a scapegoat for Emmet's rising; he was a thorn in the government's flesh because he embodied the military hierarchy's new administrative assertiveness and had antagonised the yeomanry. The duke of York's reforms had produced a similar power struggle between the British military hierarchy at Horseguards and the British War Office, which had resulted in the commander-in-chief winning more control over military affairs.[104] Fox saw himself in the same position *vis-à-vis* the Irish War Office. His campaign against the civil administration's control over military matters was conducted on the issue of the yeomanry, as the events of 23 July showed all too clearly. Because of the deleterious effect on Protestant public opinion of any criticism of that force, Hardwicke could assume there was consensus for Fox's removal. Wickham presumed too much when he toyed with the notion that outrage against Fox would mean the yeomen would accept

101 Wickham to Abbott, 12 Aug. 1803, *Abbott Corrs.*, i, pp. 438–9.   102 Statement made to Hardwicke, *Castlereagh Corrs.*, iv, pp. 316–24; Wickham to Abbott, 12 Aug. 1803, *Abbott Corrs.*, i, pp. 438–9.   103 Malcomson, *John Foster*, p. 440; Hardwicke to Yorke, 29 July 1803, B.L. Hardwicke Papers, add. mss. 35702.   104 S. Watson, *The Reign of George III*, p. 415.

Cornwallis back in a purely military capacity.[105] The latter's support of emancipation had put the mark of Cain on him, nevertheless it is indicative of government's thinking that they believed yeomanry opinion meant loyalist opinion. The popular belief that Irish Catholics were at best ambivalent about Emmet was also given credence in government circles, to the extent that Wickham questioned Dr Troy, the Catholic archbishop of Dublin and the chancellor, Redesdale got involved in an acrimonious correspondence with the Catholic peer, Lord Fingall.[106] Had the Irish government caught the neurosis of some of its Protestant subjects, or was there more afoot?

Allowing a new conspiracy to gestate undetected certainly obliterated the credit gained for soothing feelings wounded by Union or honouring compensation agreements for damaged pockets. Hardwicke needed to reach out to Irish Protestants and re-identify his government with their interests. Recent history dictated that the best way to do this would be through the yeomanry. Immediately after Emmet's rebellion, the whole establishment was put on permanent duty, and Hardwicke pushed for a huge yeomanry augmentation in the face of Fox's support for the Army of Reserve. Hardwicke was obliged to try out the Army of Reserve, though he did not want it to succeed, knowing its unpopularity with the gentry (a county could be fined if it failed to produce its quota of 300 men). Predictably, the measure flopped. Tyrone was one of the best counties, producing 172 men, while Donegal had only 20.[107] The fact that the Army of Reserve, as a parochial levy, possibly to be raised by ballot like the militia, could be represented as a 'Catholic' measure worked in the government's favour. In Cavan, Lord Farnham spoke for Protestant and Orange opinion, saying the county preferred an increase in yeomanry, and noting that any other levy would give offence as 'our yeomanry being *almost* all of a certain description (i.e. Protestants)'.[108] One thing was sure: Protestant opinion demanded that the yeomanry augmentation would not include Catholics. Wickham told Castlereagh they must either reject the services of loyal Catholics or create new, solely Catholic, corps which would, he predicted, meet with strong opposition throughout the country.[109] Hardwicke did permit some Catholic supplementaries in Tipperary but this was the exception to the general rule.

Fox's removal did not finally come till October, but his days were numbered as he blundered on, presenting Hardwicke with grand opportunities make conciliatory gestures to Protestants. Fox had issued orders forbidding regular sergeants from drilling the yeomanry on permanent duty. This was taken as a gratuitous in-

---

105 Wickham to Addington, 9 Aug. 1803, H.R.O. Wickham Papers, 38M49/5/45/26; Lady Hardwicke to Mrs Abbott, 10 Sept. 1803, *Abbott Corrs.*, i. pp. 439–44.   106 Bartlett, *Fall and Rise*, p. 276; Malcomson, *John Foster*, p. 439.   107 Hardwicke to Pelham, 24 July 1803, P.R.O. H.O. 100/1 12/f. 131; Hardwicke to Yorke, 2 Sept. 1803, H.O.100/111/f. 166.   108 Farnham to Wickham, 21 Aug. 1803, H.R.O. Wickham Papers, 38M49/5/39/44.   109 Wickham to Castlereagh, 14 Aug. 1803, *Castlereagh Corrs.*, iv, pp. 294–8.

sult by the yeomen and allowed Hardwicke to claim loftily that 'the intention was certainly unfavourable to the yeomanry and ill-judged', and insist it was revoked. A typical Hardwicke gesture followed soon afterwards. Twenty thousand people watched a grand yeomanry review in Phoenix Park, a public display of favour and gratitude which was rounded off by a sumptuous private dinner which, like the 1801 bonanza, had a guest list of ninety-six yeomanry captains and 'grandees'. There was one notable absentee. Fox apparently had a boil on his thigh.[110]

Hardwicke had again shown his aptitude for hitting the right spot with Irish Protestants and heading off the resentment which had been growing since 23 July. The yeomanry institution was proving to be a half-way house, an inn where the landlord could treat the regulars to a free night if custom was beginning to decline. In early September 1803 Hardwicke was able to report that the Irish Yeomanry had risen to 65,000, the highest total so far and an increase of 17,000 since June. He noted soberly, 'for various reasons which are particularly applicable to this country, it will be necessary to avoid carrying out this plan (the Army of Reserve) to too great an extent'.[111] Hardwicke had turned the Emmet crisis to his advantage, scoring a political hat-trick by getting rid of Fox, sidestepping criticism at Westminster and conciliating the gentry (through playing the Protestant card for all its worth). Yeomanry were an important feature in all three aspects. Arguably, Robert Emmet did more for the Irish government in Thomas Street than he did for Ireland.

Fox's replacement was Sir William Schaw Cathcart, a soldier with distinguished service in America, where he had commanded Scottish volunteers, and in the Netherlands.[112] The announcement of Cathcart's appointment drew comment from the anti-Hardwicke faction in London. Cooke, hypocritically carping to Camden about Hardwicke and Redesdale discouraging Catholic yeomen, eagerly smelt blood: 'I do not know that Lord Cathcart is a very cool man ... and I should not be surprised if the Castle and the Hospital (Kilmainham) shall still be like Protestants and papists'.[113] Cathcart arrived on 18 October to a viceroy determined that he should not have the latitude of his predecessor. Armed with the chancellor's legal opinion, Hardwicke asserted that the 'supreme government', civil and military, was a viceregal responsibility. As an apparent token of better relations, one of Cathcart's first orders was to continue yeomanry permanent duty by another month.[114]

The proposed introduction from August 1803 of the 'brigade system' carried the potential for more conflicts of authority, not to mention gentry problems. Hardwicke directed Cathcart to assess its viability. Any increased militarisation of the force was viewed uneasily by the Castle, yet it was imperial policy and had to be tried. Another weighty consideration was the question of how the yeomen themselves would react. There was a world of difference between sending in loyal offers to

110 Hardwicke to Yorke 11 Aug. 1803, B.L. Hardwicke Papers, add. mss. 35702; Lady Hardwicke to Mrs Abbott, 10 Sept. 1803, *Abbott Corrs.*, i, pp. 439–44.   111 Hardwicke to Yorke, 2 Sept. 1803, PRO H.O. 100/111/f. 116.   112 *D.N.B.*, iii, pp. 1196–8.   113 13 Sept. 1803, K.A.O. Pratt Papers, U840/C/104/5.   114 Hardwicke to Yorke, 18 Oct. 1803, B.L. Hardwicke Papers, add. mss. 35704 ff. 20–5.

serve anywhere in Ireland, and the practicalities of their having to drill together with the corps of other gentlemen who may have been political rivals. Even if they were not rivals, decisions on who would have overall command of battalions or brigades would soon make them so. Hardwicke was cautious and suggested that brigading had most chance of succeeding in Ulster where there was an abundance of corps.[115]

One can detect from the correspondence concerning brigading a better working relationship between the civil and military authorities. Cathcart concurred with Hardwicke's doubts on its feasibility anywhere except Ulster, and noted the political difficulties even there.[116] As we have seen, there was considerable gentry unease caused even by the consideration of a plan which would remove the yeomanry from their 'natural' role of protecting their farms and villages. Yet Hardwicke had to try the plan. Adept at getting the best of all worlds, Hardwicke covered himself just in case brigading went ahead, by ensuring the Irish government got what patronage was going in the new yeomanry inspectors and distributing it judiciously. Hardwicke sent to the duke of York a list of his recommendations of 'persons connected with the country … whose influence makes them useful'. These included Lord Rossmore, who was highly recommended by virtue of his former army service and current position as Monaghan brigade major. Abercorn also saw the political potential if the plan went ahead, recommending Lord Mountjoy, John Stewart and Mr Sinclair. In practice, brigading was watered down to suit the yeomanry captains by putting a quarter of each corps on permanent duty for training with adjacent corps on four successive days each month, instead of putting whole county establishments on extended training duty.[117] Brigading, like the Army of Reserve, was handled pragmatically by Hardwicke. He got Cathcart's agreement that brigading was not feasible, even in the north, and should be effectively deferred by being considered 'gradual and progressive'.[118] Relations with the military hierarchy were improving. Co-operation over brigading and a realistic approach from Cathcart helped, but probably the biggest factor was less yeomanry permanent duty. Civil-military relations were always worst when yeomanry duty forced their respective hierarchies into co-operation. Symbolically a joint yeomanry-military review was held in Phoenix Park for the King's birthday. The entire left wing was given to the yeomanry, and the formalised celebrations were minutely and successfully coordinated by Cathcart.[119] The contrast with Fox was unmistakable. By 1805, the new chief secretary, Charles Long could praise the new understanding with Kilmainham, quoting Augustus on the alteration of Rome, 'I hear on all sides it was very bad, it is now excellent'.[120]

115 Hardwicke to Yorke, 27 Oct. 1803, P.R.O. H.O. 100/111/f. 257.   116 Cathcart to Littlehales, 16 July 1804, P.R.O. H.O. 100/121/f. 32.   117 Hardwicke to Hawkesbury, 23 Aug. 1803, P.R.O. H.O. 100/123/f. 16, H.O. 100/121/f. 75; Abercom to Littlehales, 5 Aug. [1804], P.R.O.N.I. Abercorn Papers, D623/A/82/41; Hardwicke to Hawkesbury, 17 Dec. 1804, P.R.O. H.O. 100/121/f. 229.   118 Littlehales to Hardwicke, 18 Oct. 1804, B.L. Hardwicke Papers, add. mss. 35721.   119 Hardwicke to Hawkesbury, 5 June 1804, P.R.O. H.O. 100/124/f. 220.   120 Long to King, 1 Dec. 1805, P.R.O. H.O. 100/128/f. 313.

Looking across the crucial administrations of Camden, Cornwallis and Hard-wicke, the overall picture which emerges is that the political dimensions of the yeo-manry institution were extremely significant. The Irish Yeomanry had proved to be a governing tool with various applications ranging from giving control over the Irish gentry, through patronage, pay and service predicated on honour, to helping Dublin Castle maintain its authority in the face of Home Office encroachment as both Irish and British governments adjusted to the ramifications of the Act of Union. How-ever, the political role of the yeomanry could also be double-edged, and limits had been set during this period. Although yeomanry opposition to Union had re-awak-ened much of the rhetoric and some of the physical threat of the Volunteers, 1798 had shown the reality that the yeomen needed the government more than the gov-ernment needed the yeomen. Despite this, the fact that the yeomanry functioned as a link between the government and the wider Protestant community remained the most significant political aspect of the force. As will be seen later, this legacy was handed down to future administrators as the yeomanry inevitably became involved in the politics of the Catholic Question. We must first turn to their impact on those who raised and commanded them: the Irish gentry.

8

The Anglo-Irish and the Yeomanry

In March 1797 William Brabazon, earl of Meath, was shot dead in a duel with another member of the Anglo-Irish elite, fellow Wicklow landowner Robert Gore of Delgang. Duelling was common in eighteenth-century Ireland but the circumstances of this notorious affair most certainly were not: they fought about the yeomanry. Both men wanted to start yeomanry corps in north Wicklow and Brabazon accused Gore of falsifying yeomanry resolutions to 'poach' his tenants.[1] This affair is a measure of how seriously the nobility and gentry took their involvement in the yeomanry. They had good reason.

This chapter address the question of how the Anglo-Irish Ascendancy responded to the formation of yeomanry, and what effect the continued existence of that force had on the position of this relatively small group of propertied Irishmen in their relationships with their tenants, with each other and with the government. The definition used in the most important recent work on the Anglo-Irish is adopted here: that they were a social rather than an ethnic elite.[2] This is especially true when it came to raising yeomanry. Catholic peers, such as Lord Kenmare, had the same power to raise as the marquis of Downshire. However, the events of the seventeenth century had ensured that this elite was predominantly, if not exclusively, Anglican. Though numerically small, there was much social diversity within the Anglo-Irish, and the term, as used here, is intended to comprehend this diversity, which included peers, country gentlemen, local magistrates and clergy.

Before assessing the importance of yeomanry to this group, it is essential to establish their contemporary position. The eighteenth century opened with the ramifications of the Williamite wars: the land settlement and the Penal Laws. Had it ended with 'Grattan's Parliament', the Linen Board and the great upsurge in the construction of classical public buildings and private houses in a confident style rivaling London or Bath, it could properly be called the century of the Anglo-Irish. But it did not. In the closing decade, Ascendancy in all its dimensions came under threat from the United Irishmen, while, locally the rule of law was additionally

---

1 J. Kelly, *That damn'd thing called Honour: Duelling in Ireland, 1570–1860*, p. 209. 2 Malcomson, *John Foster*, intro. xvii.

challenged by a resurgent sectarianism. There are different views as to the origin of this crisis. It is generally accepted that the 1793 Act giving Catholic relief, along with the Act of Union, were crippling blows to the Anglo-Irish.[3] The main arguments do not see 1793 as a single cause. One line of debate holds that 1793 Catholic relief fractured the 'moral economy', the bond of co-operation between landowner and tenant, made possible by accepted vertical ties of paternalism and deference. This destruction came about, so the argument goes, by revitalising the ordinary Catholic's distrust of the Ascendancy. The 1793 Militia Act was seen as victory thwarted because it conscripted by ballot and reinforced the more negative attitude shown by their landlords since the Relief Act.[4] Another cogent argument, referring specifically to the Munster gentry, but capable of national extension, claims that the Anglo-Irish were deeply flawed as a group due to congenital insecurity, and that cracks were in evidence well before 1793.[5] However, by 1796, the Anglo-Irish were a group whose social, political, economic, emotional and physical well-being was under increasing pressure from a variety of directions. Anglo-Irish confidence was undermined by a combination of the influence of the French Revolution and the indigenous and deeper-rooted problems of Ireland, which more than offset Camden's pro-Protestant policies. Every aspect of a typical landowner's life must have become more difficult. His property was less secure and his tenants harder to control. Generally he must have felt his influence, with tenants and with government, was dissipating. The extent of these difficulties should not be under-estimated, nor should they be considered as applying to the Ulster gentry alone. Munster was considered to be surprisingly loyal when invasion threatened in 1797. However, recent research has shown the prospect of invasion made it harder to collect rents.[6]

Moreover, the Anglo-Irish were being viewed more and more critically by government. The uneasy relationship, described as a loveless marriage of convenience,[7] deteriorated further. Successive administrations, faced with the deepening law and order problems of the 1790s, began to question the ability of the Anglo-Irish to conduct local government. Fitzwilliam found 'the whole texture of government very weak', complained of multiple governors in counties, reflecting different political connections, and of inadequate supervision of magistrates, whose appointment, he believed, was conditioned more by jobbery than public service.[8] The fact that 'party', coming from the personal nature of politics and fuelled by competition for patronage, also existed in Britain seems to have been ignored. The crucial difference was that the landed elite in Ireland was so small that fragmentation was potentially disastrous to such a limited power-base. Camden even blamed landowners for degen-

3 Malcomson, ibid., p. 110; Bartlett, 'An end to moral economy', p. 48.   4 Bartlett, ibid., passim.
5 L.M. Cullen, 'The 1798 rebellion in its eighteenth-century context', in P.J. Corish (ed.), *Radicals, Rebels and Establishments*, pp. 110–11.   6 L.J. Proudfoot, 'Urban patronage and estate management on the Duke of Devonshire's Irish estates', p. 252.   7 Malcomson, ibid., p. 384.   8 Fitzwilliam to Portland, 10 Jan. 1795, P.R.O. H.O.100/56/f. 57.

erating from English standards of influence over their tenants. Historians have ana-
lysed the problems facing the Anglo-Irish rather than the available remedies. In
fact, their ability to respond was deeply compromised. Their doubts about militia
meant this force became part of the problem rather than part of the answer. The
1793 legislation suppressing the Volunteers deprived them of the other traditional
method of reasserting control. Therefore, in this context of insecurity and self-
doubt, one would expect an eager response to the opportunity to raise yeomanry.

The rapid passage of the Yeomanry Bill, debated in a committee of the whole
House, seems to indicate virtually unanimous gentry support. However, an analysis
of the way the measure was received in the localities reveals a much more complex
and interesting picture and shows how these complexities conditioned the form the
new force eventually took. In some northern counties the response was very mixed,
which seemed to substantiate Portland's doubts about the Irish gentry's ability to
raise a yeomanry. There were, he said 'so many parties, religious and political, and
such a variety of interests, besides so many speculations, so much refinement, so
much jealousy, notwithstanding so little skill and ability in managing and conducting
parties that, without care, instead of effective yeomanry 'you will get a collection of
people ... employed in promoting ... the power and influence of the person to whose
troop they belong ... and made subservient to election purposes'.[9]

In June 1796, Captain Waddell, whose property lay in west Down, noted that
'the gentlemen here, like our neighbouring county, (Armagh) do not draw together'.[10]
In Armagh, the sheriff, John Ogle, complained to Cooke that 'those who have the
largest stakes in the country allow themselves to be blinded by their partial views
and prejudices, to their true interests and the safety of the state'.[11] Both spoke primarily of Orange-Defender problems, but the principle held good for anything involving landowners as local guardians of law and order. Division meant that events
or measures needing co-operation could easily degenerate into 'issues'. This was
especially true for yeomanry, which promised to be lucrative in terms of patronage
and prestige. Awareness of its potential for divisiveness lay behind government's
decision to change the original plan from an English-style county yeomanry, raised
by parish quota, to separate, baronial corps and for Camden to sign the commissions, rather than the county governors. The difference was subtle but important;
the power being delegated to the localities was easier managed if fragmented into
smaller administrative units which would militate against political aggrandisement
by county interests. He explained to Downshire, 'you know what problems that
would cause in counties having several governors'.[12] Although this system meant
firm central control, the following local studies show Camden had not underestimated the disruptive potential of levying yeomanry.

9 29 Aug. 1796, P.R.O. H.O.100/62/f. 200.   10 Waddell to Ross, 14 June 1796, N.A. R.P.620/23/174.
11 14 Aug. 1796, N.A. R.P.620/24/113.   12 n.d. [c 30 Aug. 1796], P.R.O.N.I. Downshire Papers, D607/
D/142.

Down was a key county in the raising of yeomanry. Landlords elsewhere watched the progress of its yeomanry meetings as an indicator of the overall viability of the measure. Lord Hertford saw it as the test county for yeomanry.[13] This was due to a number of social, demographic and political factors, as well as the United Irishmen's strong support in the east of the county. Down was populous and wealthy, with a large electorate and a broader than normal social hierarchy. A substantial considerable class of smaller gentry stood between the large landed families and the tenants. It had also been politically volatile, with the Downshire domination being opposed by the Stewarts, who were in turn supported by a substantial 'independent' interest.[14] Down's political divisions, as much as the strategic imperative emanating from the extent of disaffection, promised to make the raising of yeomanry there both essential and problematic. It thus merits in-depth analysis and makes it necessary to have some idea of how many people could theoretically have raised corps. An unsigned memorandum amongst the Camden papers shows that when the initial fencible county cavalry plan was being considered, it was thought that Lord Downshire, Lord Londonderry, and the Newry Revenue could all raise troops.[15] When government's thinking switched to separate baronial corps, especially when they accepted the need for infantry corps which could be levied from even smaller territorial units, the responsibility for marshalling the offers was delegated down to individual landowners of sufficient influence, with the major magnates getting what can best be described as a superintending role. It is difficult to compute accurately how many of these gentry figures could potentially raise yeomanry. The wealth and influence of individuals could fluctuate over time, according to idiosyncratic factors such as the bad leasing policy of a predecessor or mismanagement and indebtedness. However, an impression can be gained from an 1812 survey, showing almost 100 landlords with a sizeable tenantry,[16] a figure which equates with the list of magistrates for 1796, bearing 121 names.[17] Amongst the major landed interests, Downshire was the largest, with over 63,000 acres in 1793.[18] He was governor and also a great borough-owning magnate, with nine seats at his disposal at this time, including one of the county seats.[19] The other seat was held by the Stewarts, who had about half the Downshire acreage.[20] The other major families were the Fordes, who had a rental of £16,000 in 1812, the Blackwoods, with about the same; the Wards, with estates in Bangor and Castleward; and the Annesleys of Castlewellan. Other major owners were absentees: Lord Moira, whose estate was at Ballynahinch; and Lord de Clifford, much of whose extensive Downpatrick estate was badly let and in practice out of his

13 Hertford to Downshire, 2 Sept. 1796, P.R.O.N.I. Downshire Papers, D607/D/147. 14 P.J. Jupp, 'County Down Elections, 1783-1831', *I.H.S.*, xvii, 70, Sept. 1972, pp. 177–206. 15 n.d.[Aug. 1796], K.A.O. Pratt Papers, U840/0157/11. 16 E. Wakefield, *An account of Ireland, statistical and political*, i, p. 20. 17 *Stewart's Almanack*, (Dublin, 1796). 18 Except where otherwise noted, I am grateful to Dr A.P.W. Malcomson of P.R.O.N.I. for information relating to the size of the major Down families.
19 Malcomson, *John Foster*, p. 197; 'The parliamentary traffic of this country', in Bartlett and Hayton (eds.), *Penal Era and Golden Age*, p. 155. 20 Jupp, op. cit., p. 189.

influence. Therefore, in a county whose aggregate population was around 200,000, those with sufficient influence to raise yeomanry were a small, socially elite group.

From a governmental viewpoint, the reality was that the troop-raising potential of a landowner was the same thing as his political interest. Their difficulty was not only how to keep the two things separate when they were naturally linked, but to do so in a way that did not insult the landowner and discourage him from raising. The more important the landowner; the greater the difficulty. Downshire was a political conservative, whose good disposition government was keen to retain. Camden summoned him over to Ireland in the early autumn of 1796 to deal with the worsening state of Down and canvass for yeomanry. Downshire's conduct of the yeomanry canvass is revealing. Not for him the tentative, sensitive assessment of opinion that was happening elsewhere at this time. Lord O'Neill, governor of Antrim, canvassed the general opinion of the county, both among those gentlemen serving in its militia and those still resident and arrived at the balanced judgment that the difficulties outweighed the advantages, and requested extra troops as a better option.[21] Antrim did raise yeomanry, as will be shown later, but the difference in the reactions of the different governors is significant.

The *Northern Star* bears smug testimony to the critical importance of raising yeomanry in Down by honouring its yeomanry meetings with its choicest satire. The governor was described as 'Don Downe'; and his 'state-of-the-country' assessments like Quixote's windmills.[22] Downshire was to co-operate with the Stewarts, which probably explains why he chose Newtownards, in the heart of Stewart territory, for a meeting of magistrates and gentlemen of property to discuss the raising of a county cavalry force. However, this 'alliance' did not mean an end to problems. For one thing, Downshire planned a yeomanry force which was very different from that envisaged by the government. He wanted a county regiment of 500, financed by subscription, like yeomanry raised by English aristocrats. Camden warned him that, to prevent 'difficulties' over applications, it was better to raise separate cavalry troops by baronies, rather than as an aggregate county force.[23] Dr Haliday, Charlemont's friend and fellow whig, correctly predicted difficulties of a different sort.[24] The feeling was that some of the gentlemen in the independent interest, whigs who looked to Grattan and Lord Moira, would use the meeting as a platform for their political views. In the event Downshire did not arrive from England in time for the Newtownards meeting. Perhaps it was as well, as Haliday's predictions were proved accurate. Gawen Hamilton complained that the proposed yeomanry force reflected the state of the county in an unmerited light, and that the proposals should be for the 'prevention of crime' not 'the punishment of guilt'. What Hamilton meant was

21 O'Neill to Camden, 8, 28 Aug. 1796, K.A.O. Pratt Papers, U840/0130A.   22 *N.S.* 12–16 Sept. 1796.   23 Lane to Reilly, 31 Aug. 1796, P.R.O.N.I. Downshire Papers, D607/D/139A-B; Camden to Downshire, 7 Sept. 1796, D607/D/155.   24 Hertford to Downshire, 2 Sept. 1796, P.R.O.N.I. Downshire Papers, D607/D/147; Haliday to Charlemont, 7 Sept. 1796, H.M.C. *Charlemont*, pp. 278–9.

that tranquillity would be more readily restored by conciliation, in other words
parliamentary reform, rather than coercion. Others were less diplomatic and talked
openly and loudly of reform and redress of grievances previous to the consideration
of defence and one, Arthur Johnston, produced a counter-proposal which one observer considered little short of revolutionary.[25] Such stances probably owed as much
to county politics as they did to political ideology. Yeomanry, as a government measure and with Downshire eagerly involved, presented reformers with a ready-made
body of discontent which could be exploited politically with a general election coming the following year. Whatever the cause, this opposition seemed to show one of
Camden's major worries coming to fruition: yeomanry meetings being used to ar-
ticulate grievances.

Despite the opposition Downshire was determined. He arranged a second meeting, this time in Hillsborough, probably because his influence would be most effectively felt in his own territory. Camden, nervous of county meetings, warned him
not to offer any specific plan to ensure that the yeomanry looked like the crown
measure it was, rather than Downshire's own, and hoped the resolutions would be
sufficiently general and innocuous not to compromise governmental control.[26] The
Northern Star reported that the meeting consisted of 'nearly all the beneficed clergy
of the dioceses of Down and Dromore, and several from Connor ... four or five
peers, about 50 revenue officers and half as many country squires but we saw nothing of the yeomen'. Downshire told this gathering that the government had a general defence measure in mind and therefore all he wanted was a commitment to arm
when the time came.[27] Although the *Star* was naturally opposed to raising yeomanry,
the report ties in with what Camden had requested of Downshire and can be taken
as accurate. It is clear from Downshire's behaviour and Camden's comments that
the marquis saw the opportunity to repeat the dominant role he had taken in the
raising of militia in 1793 by raising his own yeomanry regiment. However, though
baulked in this by Camden's insistence that his remarks be general, Downshire persisted in trying to maintain control of whatever force was raised, by insisting on a
county subscription scheme, organised by himself as governor. Camden tactfully
told him it was 'difficult to reconcile your plan with that which has been circulated'
and that, as some might find the cost restrictive, government 'should hold out the
temptation some pay and some clothing to those who would accept it'. Subscribing,
as we have seen, carried the danger of Volunteer-like independence. Downshire's
influence was so important and necessary that Camden dare not snub him. The
viceroy permitted voluntary subscriptions, but made subscribing optional, fearing
problems in counties with multiple governors. However, Camden made it clear that
he would have preferred Downshire to waive his subscription scheme, as doing so

25 Arbuckle to Downshire, 11 Sept. 1796, P.R.O.N.I. Downshire Papers, D607/D/159.   26 Camden
to Downshire, 11 Sept. 1796, P.R.O.N.I. Downshire Papers, D607/D/160.   27 *N.S.*, 16–19 Sept. 1796.
28 24 Sept. 1796, P.R.O.N.I. Downshire Papers, D607/D/200.

would facilitate raising separate (baronial) corps.[28] Downshire did not compromise; indeed, he persisted to the extent of hampering the raising of a workable mixed yeomanry in a county where raising was going to be difficult in any case. The omens were not good: the United Irishmen, strong in the populous Presbyterian districts of east Down, had successfully harnessed the pre-existing Volunteer structure; the radical gentry were trying to use the issue to make political capital; and now the leading conservative was determined to plough his personal furrow apparently oblivious to the consequences.

The plan revealed at the Hillsborough meeting was to raise 500 cavalry for the county to be paid for by church and laity.[29] The scheme certainly was costly. In November 1798, Bishop Percy complained to his wife of his heavy expenditure including 'at least' £50 for the Dromore Yeomanry 'besides the £100 paid last year'.[30] By the end of October 1796 it was becoming clear that the flagship county for yeomanry was in danger of being unable to raise any significant force at all. Cleland, Lord Londonderry's agent, sourly told Downshire that yeomanry could only be raised with unanimity amongst landowners, but that 'disunion, private schemes and jealousies has [sic] rendered it ... impracticable'.[31] Some of Cleland's bitterness probably came from the fact that Lord Londonderry's first attempt to raise yeomanry failed. For his part, Downshire doggedly persisted with his plan for subscription-raised county cavalry well after government and landowners elsewhere accepted the necessity of infantry and of separate corps. Indications came in from all quarters that things were going badly. James Arbuckle of Donaghadee tactfully suggested some infantry must be considered, as the aggregate cavalry scheme meant, when divided over the county, as little as 6–10 men per parish, leaving them open to intimidation.[32] For those hungering for loyalty and defence an immediate helping of oatmeal and potatoes was preferable to a long and uncertain wait for venison. Downshire's insistence on his own version of yeomanry was creating panic amongst its supporters who were under threat from the United Irishmen. The strain was unbearable.

With the rapid shifts in official thinking on the yeomanry measure, Downshire's extreme interpretation of the property-based yeoman cavalry idea was now anachronistic. Since the beginning of September, the alternative line of thought, infantry associations, had been given official approval. In areas where social and demographic conditions favoured infantry, either pure infinity or mixed horse and foot yeomanry corps were permitted. The structures for these corps were often based on 'loyal associations' which been in existence, in some cases, since 1795. In some cases, as on the Hertford estate, the associations had links with the Orangemen; in others, such

---

29 Pelham to Downshire, 2 Oct. 1796, P.R.O.N.I. Downshire Papers, D607/D/213.   30 Bishop Percy to Mrs Percy, 7 Nov. 1798, B.L. Percy Papers, add. mss. 32335 ff. 98–101.   31 25 Oct. 1796, P.R.O.N.I. Downshire Papers, D607/D/253.   32 4 Nov. 1796, P.R.O.N.I. Downshire Papers, D607/D/282.

as Waddell's district near Maralin, attempts were made to include Catholics, with little success.[33] With the raising of yeomanry hindered by Downshire's scheme, and as the United Irishmen continued their spread into the west of the county, popular pressure built up for some form of local defence.

Matters came to a head in November 1796 at a meeting in Newry held to discuss the proclamation of the county under the Insurrection Act. This emergency legislation would give the magistrates extensive new powers to arrest people on suspicion of disaffection, to impose curfews and to search for arms. This meant more force had to be available to them and, with the army depleted owing to the European war and the loyalty of the militia under suspicion, more yeomen were needed. The commander-in-chief, Lord Carhampton, was sent north to stress the troop shortages and encourage the raising of yeomanry. Camden told Downshire the limit was lifted for the number of yeomanry in disturbed counties.[34] Under pressure now from both the government and his own conservative supporters, Downshire boasted he would soon have 'respectable' cavalry corps in the baronies of Upper and Lower Iveagh, Castlereagh and in Newry and, if government wanted it, he had received infantry offers, and could turn out 500 in a fortnight. However, Downshire left Camden in no doubt of his disapproval, snobbishly complaining that 'proper officers would be hard to find and many [privates] would join for the sake of getting a suit of clothes'.[35]

Downshire was livid when he discovered that some gentlemen had taken the initiative and acted on their own. Lord Annesley and Savage Hall enrolled people willing to serve in infantry corps, and applied directly to Pelham to have them gazetted. Presumably they used government's policy change over infantry to excuse their non-conformance with the cavalry plan. Downshire berated Pelham about finding 'several corps of infantry added in county Down when I am doing all I can to prevent them from being established in my neighbourhood'. He had already seen his aristocratic neighbour in Antrim, the marquis of Hertford, allow infantry along the border with Down. Hertford had kinship-links with the Stewarts and had earlier declined to support the Down subscription. Downshire had refused infantry offers in west Down and now felt these tenants, seeing their Antrim neighbours enroll, would question his influence as a paternalist and with government. Enraged at Hall and Annesley, he thundered at Pelham, 'If I am to have anything to do in this county, pray do not let others act without my knowledge'. Pelham was suitably apologetic, claiming he thought Downshire knew of Annesley's actions. Annesley himself tried to placate the angry aristocrat by telling him that some of his own tenants were in the infantry corps.[36] Pelham affected innocence, claiming that he thought 'the

33 Higginson to [?Cooke], 22 August 1796, N.A. R.P. 620/24/156; Waddell to Cooke, 29 Dec. 1796, 620/24/173.   34 29 October 1796, P.R.O.N.I. Downshire Papers, D607/D/263.   35 Downshire to Camden, 27 Oct., 4 Nov. 1796, K.A.O. Pratt Papers U840/0160/5,8.   36 Downshire to Pelham, 24 Nov. 1796, N.A. R.P.620/26/77; 26 Nov. 1796, P.R.O.N.I. Downshire Papers, D607/D/345; 19 Dec. 1796, D607/D/414.

wish of the county was to accept as many offers as could be trusted'.[37] But the reality was that everyone knew Downshire was out of step except the marquis himself. Eventually Downshire was persuaded by Carhampton to accept infantry offers, despite his having 'different ideas on the subject'.[38]

Why did Downshire persist so stubbornly when it must have been obvious his scheme was counter-productive? Was it personal, the rooted intransigence of a proud aristocrat, or were there deeper reasons? The main answer to emerge from this analysis is that Downshire's eager but idiosyncratic response to the opportunity to raise yeomanry was much more than an aristocrat looking nostalgically back to a time when property defended itself without assistance from the lower orders or pay from government. The answer is to be found in Irish county politics. Reverend Richardson reckoned that Downshire's 'personal qualities and private friendships' prevailed against three-fifths of the property and the whole of the dissenting interest in the county.[39] Downshire's yeomanry plan echoed his response to the 1793 militia levy with this difference: as a new measure, the precise form yeomanry would take was still uncertain and therefore represented a grand political speculation as domination of the county force could only increase his political interest in time. Camden's reaction shows he could see that allowing Downshire to monopolise the Down yeomanry financially was an aggrandisement of political influence even greater than if he had been allowed to issue commissions like an English county lord lieutenant. Downshire, had he succeeded, would have put himself in a position to determine who did what *before* commissions were issued and could have given out positions at his pleasure. Indeed, his control over finances would ensure the various yeomanry captains were effectively in his debt. Downshire's opposition to infantry certainly came from social snobbery and fear of having to depend on the lower levels of Protestant society, the levels that were producing Orangemen. However, consideration of the political dimension makes possible an additional interpretation of Downshire's stance. For one thing, despite their public co-operation, the rivalry with Castlereagh was still there. In the summer of 1796 Castlereagh had tacitly supported the loyal associations infantry offers from the Hertford estate by transmitting them to Camden.[40] Moreover, to have freely allowed infantry would set a precedent for reformers like Matthew Forde, who supported Lord Moira, and depended heavily on the 'dissenting interest'. Most Presbyterians would have been of the social and economic level that produced infantry. Thus Downshire, playing on his strength with government, was resisting the final form yeomanry took because the county cavalry prototype better suited his political needs.

Downshire's reluctant acceptance of infantry corps did not mean an end to the

---

37 Pelham to Downshire, 26 Nov. 1796, P.R.O.N.I. Downshire Papers, D607/D/345.   38 Carhampton to Pelham, 8 Nov. 1796, B.L. Pelham Papers add. mss. 306–9.   39 22 Feb. 1796, P.R.O.N.I. Abercorn Papers T2541/1B3/6/5.   40 Rev. P. Johnston to Hardwicke, n.d. July 1804, in M. MacDonagh (ed.), *The Viceroy's Postbag*, pp. 24–7.

political jousting; it merely took another form. The first yeomanry vote for 20,000 men meant that the number of corps any county could raise was limited. When the territorial logic of the yeomanry shifted from county regiments to self-contained baronial corps with the inclusion of infantry, smaller parish or village units were possible because of the greater demographic density of those eligible to serve. This was a highly significant development for the character and subsequent ethos of the force. However this narrowing of the territorial definition of corps, coupled with the parliamentary limitation, had a very definite political context which informed the response of the Anglo-Irish in county Down to the actual formation of corps, both cavalry and infantry. The critical point is that the yeomanry divisions, being civil and ecclesiastical, could not be easily married to the boundaries of a landowner's influence. Indeed they could fall between the areas of influence of political rivals. The formation of yeomanry corps therefore sees a scurry of political opportunism, compromises and arrangements. To see this development the lens needs to be adjusted to examine local areas in close-up.

Between Dromore and Maralin there were two important landowning families, the Waddells and the Dowglasses. Captain Waddell of Islanderry was in the Downshire interest: a Down militia officer and a frequent correspondent of Downshire's political protégé, Robert Ross of Rosstrevor, one of the members for Newry. Waddell was also a magistrate and when on leave, took a very active interest in the state of the locality, as his frequent correspondence in the Rebellion Papers testifies. Dowglass was in the independent interest and had supported the Volunteer campaign for parliamentary reform.[41] The district was in a confused and turbulent state, with sectarian problems spreading from nearby Armagh, and a growing United Irish threat. Waddell favoured the Dungannon plan, which would have allowed him to make infantry offers from loyal tenants of his own choosing. However, being in the Downshire interest, and not having the social standing of Annesley or Hall, he was reluctant to take this preference any further. At the end of August, when Downshire's supporters were canvassing support for the Newtownards yeomanry meeting, Waddell was approached 'by some people of respectability', wanting him to take command of a cavalry corps 'to consider themselves as under the direction of Lord Downshire' and to have a George Dowglass 'concerned' with him. Waddell needed all the help he could get and referred the matter to Ross.[42] Superficially this looks like the standard canvas for yeomanry, but sources later in 1796 indicate deeper motives were involved.

This affair next surfaces in October when a Thomas Dowglass, who must either be the same person or of the same connection, gave a frosty answer to Downshire who had previously written twice, enclosing a copy of the Yeomanry Bill and offering command of the corps. Dowglass was unmoveable: 'there is not anything in the

---

41 Jupp, 'Down Elections', pp. 201–2.   42 22 Aug. 1796, N.A. R.P.620/24/144.

Bill to make me change my mind'.[43] Downshire did not give up. The following month the bishop of Dromore reported that Dowglass would take a corps, but only if he were elected to the captaincy by members of the corps in the manner of the old Volunteers. This was whitewash: clearly what Dowglass wanted was a corps consisting entirely of his own supporters. Three days later the real reason for this became clearer. The bishop told Downshire that Dowglass would not act against the wishes of Matthew Forde. Despite the bishop trying 'every argument to make him accept command', Dowglass would not budge.[44]

The early approaches make it look as though Downshire's supporters tried to secure an arrangement whereby Waddell's military experience could justify him heading the proposed corps, and that Dowglass would have the nomination of the subsidiary officers. When the attempt to get him to share with Waddell failed, Downshire offered him command but Dowglass made deliberately impossible conditions of acceptance. What was happening was that Dowglass knew he could not accept Downshire's invitation and remain in the whig-independent interest which was at best equivocal about yeomanry. This opposition was political and came from two sources. Locally the whigs would have naturally resisted Downshire's attempts at dominance and nationally they would follow Grattan's line on the yeomanry.

The *Northern Star* responded to the failed Down yeomanry meeting in Newtownards with a satirical poem entitled 'The Derry Downe Rout', written in feigned amazement at the apparent liaison between the Hill and Stewart families over the yeomanry, that:

> A Whig and a Tory's the same:
> For Hill waved his wand,
> and at his command
> to his congress they hastily came.[45]

However, the response from that meeting and the subsequent reactions of many county Down landowners in the whig-independent interest showed that they differed very much from their 'Tory' counterparts when it came to raising yeomanry. The tactics of the reformers at the Newtownards meeting had clearly been thought out in advance as they tried to hijack the resolutions at the first yeomanry meeting to make their own point. This anticipated Grattan's initial response in parliament when the yeomanry measure was being discussed. In an accurate paraphrase of the *Star*'s report on the Hillsborough meeting, he fulminated that 'an Ascendancy army won't do – a Revenue army won't do, no more than church militant'.[46] The move to Hillsborough had certainly lessened the influence of independents and reformers

43 25 Oct. 1796, P.R.O.N.I. Downshire Papers, D607/D254. 44 Bishop Percy to Downshire, 1, 4, 5 Nov. 1796, P.R.O.N.I. Downshire Papers, D607/D/275, 283, 286. 45 *N.S.*, 16–19 Sept. 1796. 46 *Parl. Register* (Ire.), xiv, p. 13.

for the second meeting. Only one, the advanced Belfast radical Eldred Pottinger made the journey and tried unsuccessfully to intervene with a resolution for reform and conciliation as the best defence.

Despite the *Star*'s claims, not only were whigs and tories different when it came to yeomanry, but whigs, or more correctly the amalgam of reformers and radicals of different hues which constituted the 'independent' interest, were divided among themselves over the issue even as much as the conservatives were about Downshire's stance on the raising of the force. Probably helped by the government's readiness to accommodate old Volunteers in the yeomanry, Grattan changed his stance on the force and raised yeomen himself as did other leading whigs. Lord Moira had pointedly refused to have anything to do with yeomanry, believing Downshire was already using militia patronage to 'communicate' with the Martins, a local family who were demonising Charles Hamilton, Moira's agent, as a United Irishman.[47] Forde supported Moira, yet broke ranks him and with the other 'independents' and raised had infantry corps at Seaforde and Kilmore, by early 1797. At this stage they were the only corps, aside from Lord Londonderry's Newtownards Cavalry, outside the Downshire interest. Forde, obviously taking the lead from Grattan, used the change of government policy over infantry to raise his yeomanry, keep his tenants from the United Irishmen and prevent a Downshire monopoly. Therefore Forde took the lead for the independents and reformers, though he made sure to appoint Moira's agent, Charles Hamilton as his first lieutenant in the Kilmore corps.

Downshire's response to Forde's raising of yeomanry shows that he tried to capitalise on the slow start of his political rivals. As county governor and Custos Rostolorum he had responsibility for the magistracy and law and order generally. This allowed him to try to organise corps wherever they were deficient. One such area was Strangford, near the Ward estate. Ward was also in the independent interest, and in December 1796, Downshire repeated his Maralin tactics by offering the captaincy to one of Ward's supporters, William Hoey of Bellville. If Hoey had accepted the captaincy, he would have put himself in a position where Downshire was the natural channel of communication with government on yeomanry business. However, Hoey politely refused, accepting instead a commission in Forde's yeomanry.[48] The 1797 list shows he rejected a captaincy for a lieutenancy in the Seaforde Infantry, rather than be responsible for upsetting the local political balance of power.[49]

Forde's adoption of yeomanry was politically far-sighted. By preventing a conservative monopoly, he could anticipate the argument that the independents were either traitors themselves or condoned treachery. The proclamation of martial law in May 1797 again brought the local political power struggle over the yeomanry to the forefront. Grattan resigned his position in the yeomanry and his followers with-

47 Moira to Pelham, 2, 11 Oct. 1796, N.A. R.P.620/26/10, 27.   48 Hoey to Downshire, 13 Dec. 1796, P.R.O.N.I. Downshire Papers, D607/D/397.   49 N.L.I. Ir355a10.

drew from the Irish parliament in protest against coercion.[50] This had local ramifications. On the eve of the proclamation of martial law, pro-reform gentlemen had tried unsuccessfully to hold a county meeting at Downpatrick to press for reform as an alternative means of quietening the country. Nugent moved troops to surround the town to prevent the meeting taking place.[51] Forde's instinct was proved correct. This left the 'independents' open to accusations of disloyalty, and, as a counter to such charges, they began to try to enrol yeomen, using a truncated version of the yeomanry oath. Their objective was two-fold. They could make a loyal gesture to spike the arguments of their opponents, while, at the same time, register a protest against coercion. Nugent reported that Eldred Pottinger, Gawen Hamilton of Killyleagh, Charles Hamilton of Ballynahinch, Edward Southern and Mr. Trotter of Downpatrick were all trying to administer a 'half oath', which swore loyalty to George III, but omitted the concluding section about defending the laws and the constitution.[52] The implicit point was that, with martial law and the Insurrection Act, there was no constitution to defend.

While this was going on, Downshire rushed in with accusations against Matthew Forde's Kilmore Infantry. Forde's corps had been on foot since early in the year and certainly did not owe their existence to the whig reaction to martial law. This made little difference as Downshire was determined to tar all whigs with the same brush. Downshire, as governor, could stop any disingenuous attempts to raise yeomanry and had access to the military authorities. He lost no time in striking at Forde. Lake reported that he had it 'on the best authority ... that Mr Forde's yeomanry are all sworn United men, except two'. Forde's isolated position, as the only 'independent' in the Down yeomanry, made him vulnerable. Pelham ordered Lake to disarm Forde's yeomen, if they turned out to be as bad as reported, but wisely advised him to speak to Forde beforehand, describing him as a 'very respectable man, much liked in the country' though 'a very likely man to take the popular side of the question, right or wrong'.[53] The eventual outcome was that Forde was put in the embarrassing position of having to solicit a loyal declaration from his men and have it published in the newspapers. Nugent, perhaps less inclined than Lake to listen to rumours, decided to 'put them to the proof by employing them with some of the Ancient British Light Dragoons in searching for arms'.[54] Despite the different stances over yeomanry, Forde still supported Moira: Camden described him as 'a particular partisan of Lord Moira's'. By July 1797, most Down gentlemen, including Lord Londonderry, Nicholas Price and Forde himself, agreed that there was 'a change for the better' in the state of the county. Downshire stood alone in

50 Lecky, *Ireland*, iv, pp. 64, 73.   51 Lane to Downshire, 19 April, 21 May 1797, P.R.O.N.I. Downshire Papers, D607/E/250, 262.   52 Lake to Pelham, 26 June 1797, B.L. Pelham Papers add. mss. 33104 ff. 288–9; Nugent to Pelham, 27 June 1797, 33108 f. 130.   53 6 June 1797 B.L. Pelham Papers, add. mss. 33104 ff. 185-8.   54 Lake to Pelham, 4 June 1797, Nugent to Pelham, 25 June 1797, B.L. Pelham Papers, add. mss. 33104 ff. 175-6, 271-2.

recommending a continuation of coercion, clearly keen to wring the maximum political benefit from the stance of his opponents. Camden detected a political motive,
noting that 'Lord Downshire had some other than a reason of state policy for his
opinion'[55] Forde's yeomanry therefore offered Downshire a golden opportunity to
attack Moira. The conservative monopoly of yeomanry in Down was not fully broken till the eve of the rebellion in 1798. By this stage, the earlier divisions within
conservative ranks over the social composition of the force the cavalry-infantry argument, had been patched up.

The offers of emergency manpower from the Orange Order in March 1798 and
the government's measured response through the organisation of supplementary
yeomen had an immediate impact in Down. Political divisions over the yeomanry
had militated against really effective action against the United Irishmen. A 'County
Down Committee of Secrecy' was established to respond to a situation described as
'nothing short of actual war'. Downshire was on the committee as were Annesley,
John Waring Maxwell of Finnebrogue and Holt Waring. Waring been involved with
early Orange associations around Waringstown, which tried to intervene in the sectarian disputes and enlist the men on the side of the magistrates, Annesley had
enrolled Orange, or proto-Orange yeoman infantry in November 1796 and Waring
had started a corps at Inch in February whose members concurrently established an
Orange lodge.[56] Downshire had a precedent for sinking his differences over infantry
as, since its move to Dublin, the Orange association was encouraged, as Camden
put it, 'by some very respectable persons'.[57]

Locally, these developments in early 1798 translated themselves into a need for
additional yeomanry. This caused a resumption of the political feuding. On the Ward
estate around Strangford, in default of the raising of yeomanry, the lower-class Anglican tenantry had organised themselves in Orange societies for protection against
the United Irishmen. The conservatives quickly took advantage of the situation and
harnessed these societies to raise new yeomanry corps, sometimes from amongst
the tenants of their opponents. Maxwell was prominent in this. James Verner MP,
brother-in-law to Thomas Verner, the Irish grand master, spoke to Castlereagh about
getting Maxwell permission to enrol his Ballyculter corps. Maxwell proposed raising another infantry corps in Downpatrick, both based on pre-existing Orange societies. Supplementaries were organised for Maxwell's Ballyculter Infantry. Fifty men
took the yeomanry oath and drew up a declaration: 'the above are Protestant men
who ever made publick [*sic*] profession of their loyalty'. Many of these men were
Ward's tenants. The proximity of rebellion and the unity of their opponents stung

---

55 Camden to Portland, 10 July 1797, P.R.O. H.O.100/70/ff. 41–4.   56 County Down Committee, n.d.
March 1798, P.R.O.N.I. Perceval-Maxwell Papers, T1023/146; Annesley to Downshire, 7 Nov. 1796,
P.R.O.N.I. Downshire Papers, D607/D/293, Senior, *Orangeism*, p. 37; 6 February 1797, P.R.O.N.I.
Perceval-Maxwell Papers, T1023/144; *An historical account of Orangeism in Lecale District* (Belfast,
1990).   57 Camden to Portland, 29 March 1798, P.R.O. H.O.100/75/f. 331.

the independents into action. Lord Bangor's brother, Colonel Robert Ward, came up from Dublin to raise yeomen. J.H. Reid, a Strangford Orangeman who held a commission in Maxwell's Ballyculter corps, attacked Ward's move in a similar way to Downshire's assault on Forde the previous year. It was 'strange', according to Reid, that Ward 'who had neither spirit nor inclination, not to give it a worse name' only applied to raise yeomen in the area when he heard that Maxwell was doing so, then, 'pops in and says he'll head them – why 'tis a humbug'. Echoing the local Anglican curate's opinion that Ward was trying 'to counter the loyal resolutions of the Ballyculter Boys', Reid added that any yeomen Ward would raise amongst his own supporters would be 'no doubt of every religious denomination and ... every man a rebel to his country'. Meanwhile, in Dublin, the campaign against Forde resumed. Verner urged him to recommend Maxwell's proposal to Camden. Claiming Forde 'ought to be materially interested in the success of such a spirit of loyalty and lay aside that dangerous opposition to government and partiality for a reform which has been the ground work of sedition and rebellion', in reality Verner was putting Forde in a position where he had to compromise his own liberal principles and recommend an Orange corps, or appear disloyal and leave himself vulnerable to more criticism. On 30 May Nugent told Maxwell that permission had been obtained for him to raise yeomen and supplementaries at Strangford and Ballyculter and that he, Nugent, proposed to disarm Forde's Kilmore yeomanry and use their guns to arm the two new corps.[58]

The evidence suggests that Ward was genuine about trying to raise yeomen, but wanted to put his own political stamp on it. The essential difference between Ward and the conservatives was that he did not agree that a partisan armament was necessary. One of Ward's supporters, Charles McCarthy of Strangford, tried to influence Castlereagh, giving his opinion that if the Orangemen were armed 'it will cause discontent and bickering in the barony of Lecale'. Instead, he advocated a yeomanry being raised, similar to that in Portaferry of which he was a member 'that is no distinction of religious sects'.[59] The government however had adopted a course of encouraging wavering radicals to join the yeomanry as part of the process of trying to detach the Presbyterians from the United Irishmen by playing on their atavistic fears of Catholics, as most potently demonstrated by Castlereagh's comment to Nugent that the arrest of Steel Dickson, reputedly the United Irish general for Down, was an exception to 'the policy of acting against the Catholic rather than the Presbyterian members of the Union.'[60] This was having an effect. Ward's response was consistent with that of other independents. Downshire's agent reported that Gawen Hamilton and Eldred Pottinger wished to put politics behind them and arm

58 Reid to 'Jack' [Martin], n.d. late May 1798, J. Verner to Maxwell, 23 May 1798, Nugent to Maxwell, 30 May 1798, P.R.O.N.I. Perceval-Maxwell Papers, T1023/148, 152–4. 59 McCarthy to Castlereagh, 17 May 1798, N.A. R.P.620/37/99. 60 N.A.M. 6807–174 ff. 457–8, Nugent Papers, Castlereagh to Nugent, 6 June 1798.

to defend the county.[61] The 1798 rebellion itself completed this process. The first yeomanry list published after the rebellion showed that Ward had his own corps at Castleward, Gawen Hamilton had one at Killyleagh, Dowglass captained the Maralin Infantry, Forde still had his two corps, plus another at Cumber Bridge near Ballynahinch.[62] Indeed, Forde's corps was one of the few to suffer fatalities at the Battle of Ballynahinch. Nugent, in a postscript to his report on the battle, allowed this reality to dispense with all the political propaganda surrounding the corps, telling Lake, 'bye the bye, the Kilmore yeomanry behaved most gallantly'.[63]

Political tensions amongst the Anglo-Irish were not the only factors which influenced the formation of yeomanry. The raising of corps in the half-barony of Mourne also shows personal and economic influences at work. There was also a political context in Mourne. It is difficult to identify all the interests involved, but there were reportedly five separate attempts to raise yeomanry.[64] The main landowners in the area were the Needhams of Mourne Park, though Downshire also was involved. Being the second largest owner in Newry, Downshire was the political rival of the Needhams, or, more correctly, of Isaac Corry, who had taken over one of the borough seats from his father, a member there with Needham support. Downshire nominated the other member, Robert Ross.[65] The Needham's were notorious for their apathy and neglect, with all estate affairs in the hands of an agent, Acheson Thompson, who was nominated to canvass for yeomanry.

The raising of the Mourne yeomanry shows the danger of using a single source. The Downshire papers contain what looks like a blow-by-blow account of the birth pains of the corps. The scenario mirrors that in other baronies where rival interests jostled over yeomanry. Downshire's supporters tried to out-manoeuvre and blacken Needham's agent. Gustavus Matthews of 'Loyalty Farm' told Downshire that Thompson was apathetic about raising yeomanry, and hinted that his principles were doubtful. Matthews reported an approach by 'some loyal men', who wanted him to lead them in an infantry corps to be called 'The Loyal Men of Mourne', the name of the old Volunteer corps in the area. He said that, as the barony was seventeen miles long, two corps could be justified and that Alexander Chesney could raise a corps in his (the southern) sector of the barony. Apparently Downshire saw problems here, probably because government was restricting the numbers of new yeomen to keep within the parliamentary grant. He asked Matthews to 'coalesce' parties and co-operate with Chesney. However this was not the end of the difficulties. Lucas Waring of Craigavad told Downshire that the corps embodied rather slowly and that Chesney had met opposition from 'many opulent farmers and favourites of Mr. Acheson Thompson, who on other occasions have implicitly obeyed

61 Lane to Downshire, 6 May 1798, P.R.O.N.I. Downshire Papers, D607/F/161.   62 1798 Yeomanry List, N.L.I. Ir. 355 a 4.   63 13 June 1798, N.A. R.P.620/38/129.   64 Chesney to Downshire, 24 Jan. 1797, P.R.O.N.I. Downshire Papers, D607/E/53.   65 A.P.W. Malcomson, *Isaac Corry, 1753–1813, an adventurer in the field of politics*, passim.

his orders ... and are [now] unfriendly to the institution'. He recommended that, if Downshire approved, Matthews could raise a good corps in the northern part of the barony. For his part, Chesney reported that his two lieutenants refused their commissions, claiming bad health and a wish to serve as cavalry, and noted that he had done the canvass in advance of Thompson and had the list ready to put in his hand when he came. Chesney apparently also had problems with local United Irishmen, who burnt the house of one of his yeomen. Matthews, with the apparent magnanimity of a fellow victim, noted that Chesney was 'too public-spirited to be intimidated'. Chesney was 'highly gratified' by the suggestion of co-operation with Matthews and wished 'the plan of putting the lists together had been adhered to, which could have been increased to 100 men, and then divided'.[66]

On the face of it, and going by the Downshire correspondence, the context here would appear to be Newry politics. Although not actually in the lordship of Newry, parts of the south of the barony of Mourne lay in Needham's estate. Newry was an open borough with a history of tempestuous politics and the scenario seems to have been that Downshire was trying to undercut Needham's interest, taking advantage of his opponent's personal or political equivocation by allowing two willing men to raise the barony.[67] Chesney was a revenue officer and Downshire intended revenue officials to be a central plank in his plans. The combination of factors – sharply contested local politics, an apathetic agent on an absentee rival's estate and a conveniently-placed revenue officer – make it impossible to dismiss the political context. It is too consistent with Downshire's methods elsewhere. However, there was another even more narrowly local context to the conflict. Chesney, in the privacy of his own diary, revealed that what was reported to Downshire was not necessarily the whole truth. Chesney was a newcomer to Mourne, whose family had lowly origins in Antrim. He had fought on the loyalist side in the American war, under Francis Rawdon, Lord Moira, but had returned to Ireland in a state of poverty. He then secured a revenue post on a coast notorious for smuggling, and was scraping a living from this and occasional pieces of 'salvage'. According to folk memory in the area, he made himself highly unpopular with established and more wealthy families who, it is said, resented his zeal against smugglers.[68] Chesney's diary reveals that, from 1795, he felt a 'connection' operated against him.[69] The entry for January 1797 mentions he had to raise the corps himself as Henry McNeilly and Thomas Spence had refused commissions. Both references to this in the Downshire Papers misrepresent the cause of this defection. Chesney himself said it was due to health problems or social snobbery. Waring attributed it to disloyalty and laid the blame on Acheson

66 Matthews to Downshire, 10 Jan 1797, P.R.O.N.I. Downshire Papers, D607/E/20; Downshire to Matthews, 14 Jan. 1797, D607/E/29; Waring to Downshire, 26 Jan. 1797, D607/E/60, Chesney to Downshire, 24 Jan, 1797, D607/E/53, Matthews to Downshire, 10 Feb. 1797, D607/E/91; Chesney to Downshire, 21 Feb. 1797, D607/E/117. 67 Carleton to Downshire, 25 March 1797, P.R.O.N.I. Downshire Papers, D607/E/224. 68 J.S. Doran, *My Mourne*, pp. 142–7. 69 Alexander Chesney's Diary, p. 50 and passim, P.R.O.N.I. D2260/15/59.

Thompson. However, an entry for January 1798, describing an unsavoury scramble over salvage rights over a grounded sloop, ironically named 'The New Loyalty', shows the entire affair in a different dimension. Obviously plunder could override politics. Chesney said the clique against him included Matthews, who had openly supported McNeilly's claim to the salvage. McNeilly's refusal of his commission in 1797 assumes its true proportions; as a newcomer on the make, Chesney was not going to play the game by its well-understood rules. Indeed the 'United Irishmen' who attacked Chesney's yeomen were likely more interested in the rights of salvage than the Rights of Man.

Beneath the politeness seen in the Downshire correspondence, Matthews and Chesney were in bitter personal rivalry over local patronage, but both were wary of losing all by appearing concerned about such things in troubled times. This rivalry predated the yeomanry and the natural corollary was that when corps were formed such rivalries would influence their formation. In this case, both men clearly saw yeomanry as an opportunity either to extend or consolidate their local influence. When it looked as though there would just be one corps, this rivalry took the form of competition for the controlling interest. Chesney resisted this and Matthews pushed for his own corps, which he eventually got in April 1797.[70] This did not satisfy him. Chesney's diary for August 1798, when all corps were still on permanent duty, shows Matthews tried to get an order from the brigade major to assume command over both Mourne Corps. Presumably Matthews wanted to snub his rival and discredit his influence, as it is inconceivable he could have expected co-operation from Chesney's yeomen. Chesney appealed to Castlereagh and got the order rescinded and established that Matthews' corps would rank after his, the usual practice for later-raised corps. The following year, Chesney had an opportunity for revenge.

Chesney sat on a yeomanry court martial which acquitted Matthews of irregular conduct. Possibly by this stage, his position was more secure, though he consoled himself self-righteously in his dairy by speculating on his rival's response in a similar position.[71] This example shows the effect of local personal rivalry amongst minor gentry families cannot be underestimated either in the way it drove and conditioned their response to the force or in the way yeomanry corps, even in the year of rebellion, were seen as legitimate bones to contend for. This however is not to say that electoral politics or graft was the prime motivation either of the Anglo-Irish elite or the gentry.

The responses of the governor and landowners in county Antrim contrasts interestingly with those of Down. Antrim had a smaller gentry population than Down with 68 qualified as magistrates in 1796 against Down's 121.[72] Lord O'Neill was

70 Matthews to Downshire, 6 April 1797, P.R.O.N.I. Downshire Papers, D607/E/244.   71 Chesney's Diary, 25 Aug. 1798, n.d. Oct. 1799, P.R.O.N.I. D2260/15/pp. 55–9.   72 *Stewart's Almanack* (Dublin, 1796).

governor. Other major landowners, Lord Donegall and the marquis of Hertford were absentees, whereas the earl of Antrim, who owned over 150,000 Irish acres in the east of the county, had lost control over most of his lands as they were granted away in perpetuity.[73] The situation was different from Down in that, unlike Downshire, O'Neill was not the largest landowner. He was also a different political animal, being a political 'independent', popular with the Presbyterians.[74] As we have seen, his approach was more cautious and consultative and less dictatorial than Downshire's. However, it is unlikely that this caution was politically motivated, as there were other more basic factors in operation: the danger of United Irish infiltration and the problems of actually getting a functional yeomanry.

Edmond McNaughton, an important north Antrim landowner, warned that there would be problems getting proper persons to serve in a yeomanry and in getting persons fit to command them.[75] Lower down the social scale, a magistrate's son, lieutenant Henry Irwin Stewart, told his commanding officer 'in Antrim, there actually are not those people who come under the description of yeomen ... they are chiefly manufacturers, people who are supported without cultivating so much ground as would enable them to keep a horse in the manner required', but that infantry corps could not be formed unless under the protection of troops, which rather defeated the purpose.[76] Unlike Downshire, O'Neill did not push for cavalry. However, allowance must be made for the difference in the social demography of the two counties. Stewart felt sure cavalry would work in county Down. Given that cavalry was numerically possible in Down, it is illegitimate to compare the responses of the two governors on this point, despite the fact they may well have had different views on the subject. However, a fruitful comparison can be made over their responses to infantry. Neither was keen, but for different reasons. O'Neill's political background meant that he could dismiss infantry much less lightly than Downshire. It is notable in his initial reluctant response to Camden that he felt associations would produce counter associations. As we have seen, in this context association meant infantry. His remarks to Camden about needing military protection to raise yeomanry, as Stewart's letter clarifies, applied to infantry. Unlike Downshire, he seriously considered this option of his own volition, but rejected it at first. O'Neill's initial response bespoke an uncomfortable reality for Antrim landowners: that the difficulties with yeomanry outweighed the advantages.

To understand why, it is necessary to look at the situation of the resident landowners. To levy infantry corps in this largely Presbyterian county, with its strong tradition of Volunteer radicalism and current high levels of United Irish support, would be asking for trouble. The different response from gentlemen on militia service indicates that landowners had relatively recently found it more difficult to de-

73 NB I am again grateful to Dr Malcomson for this information.   74 Malcomson, *John Foster*, p. 234.
75 McNaughton to [?Pelham], 10 Sept. 1796, N.A. R.P.620/25/2.   76 Stewart to Barber, 7 Sept. 1796, N.A. R.P.620/25/104.

cide where their tenants' Volunteer radicalism ended and support for the United Irishmen began. The evidence from Belfast some months later showed O'Neill's fears to be reasonable. Yeomanry were only raised after great difficulty in Belfast, and it is clear many of those who enlisted retained their radicalism. Martha McTier told Drennan that 'half the yeos in town' subscribed to a fund for people taken up under the Insurrection Act.[77] In this light, and given that Orange-linked magistrates from the Hertford estate were trying to get him to form associations for the rest of the county on the Dungannon model, O'Neill's initial hesitancy looks more like a prudent waiting game based on a recognition of danger signals. Small wonder that O'Neill was reluctant to recommend a measure which he felt would, if cavalry, fail through lack of numbers, or if infantry, further de-stabilise his county either by arming doubtful corps of ex-Volunteers or Orangemen. There is less evidence in Antrim of the self-interested political and social jostling that there was in Down, but that is not to say that the reactions to the proposed measure were all rooted in purely strategic concerns. Camden, echoing Foster's phrase, had cautioned O'Neill about the 'great delicacy' of the yeomanry proposal.[78] For instance, there would have been a prickly awkwardness about recommending a measure that Hertford, who owned more property than O'Neill, had not yet agreed to.[79] In the event, when government accepted the inevitability of a mixed yeomanry, and the measure was ratified in parliament, Antrim did patch together a yeomanry of sorts. The first yeomanry lists of 1797 show that 10 corps, were formed in the county, seven of which were infantry, including three on Hertford's estate.[80] As we have seen from the Volunteer comparison, this was well below the potential of the county. The response of the nobility and gentry in other Ulster counties was less reticent than in Antrim and less precipitate than Down, yet these other areas also reveal a combination of motives.

Given Downshire's role, the marquis of Abercorn would have been expected to follow a similar line in Tyrone. He was joint governor and owned a very extensive tract of property, which exceeded 26,000 Irish acres exclusive of his Baronscourt estate and around 10,000 in Donegal.[81] Despite this, and the fact that Abercorn was already a borough owning magnate who wanted to increase his political powerbase, he was notably tardy and unresponsive. When approached in November 1796 by his own law agent, James Galbraith, who was trying to raise a cavalry corps between Baronscourt and Drumquin, Abercorn's response is worthy of examination. Galbraith used the example of other landowners elsewhere who had applied to 'the noblemen and gentlemen who have adjoining estates' for financial support.[82] Abercorn, though well-disposed to Galbraith, claimed that, 'although armed corps

77 n.d.[c. April 1797], D.A. Chart (ed.) *The Drennan Letters*, pp. 253–4.   78 13 Aug. 1796, K.A.O. Pratt Papers, U840/0130A.   79 Malcomson, *John Foster*, p. 296.   80 N.L.I. Ir355a10.   81 A.P.W. Malcomson, 'A lost natural leader: John James Hamilton, first Marquess of Abercorn', *Proceedings of the Royal Irish Academy* v. 88, no.4, 1988, p. 68.   82 11 Nov. 1796, P.R.O.N.I. Abercorn Papers, D623/A/108/6.

of yeomanry might be of great service ... as it has been managed, I have thought the system very problematical, and therefore declined taking any step, and even holding out any encouragement, where I may be supposed to have influence', and expected 'most of the yeomanry corps will be nominal, or on paper: in some instances the money thrown away, in others embezzled'.[83] Abercorn also said that he could not, politically, subscribe to one corps and refuse another, but his real reasons ran deeper.

Around this time Thomas Knox was smugly telling government that yeomanry in Tyrone were going on 'very prosperously', that he had two corps himself, and had just inspected others under Lords Caulfield and Powerscourt in Tyrone and one under James Verner on the border with Armagh. However, Knox kept the bad news for the last, noting, 'unfortunately, from Dungannon to the Northern Ocean, with the exception of Stewartstown, there is not one corps likely to be raised'.[84] Abercorn's response arose from his row with Thomas Knox over Knox's resignation from the Tyrone militia. As Knox enthusiastically grasped and tried to mould the new measure, Abercorn just as eagerly poured cold water on it. It would be unfair to Knox to attribute his efforts, first with the Dungannon Association and then with yeomanry, to purely selfish political motives. Nevertheless, as an opportunist like Downshire, Knox was alive to the opportunities yeomanry presented to increase or re-coup political interest. He even suggested to Charlemont that he, Charlemont, should be made captain commandant of the entire yeomanry of Armagh and Tyrone. [85] This was surely a gross presumption on the part of an outgoing member to a an elderly and respected privy councillor, even given Charlemont's position with the old Volunteers. Charlemont wisely refused the bait, but Abercorn was in no doubt what Knox was about.

The Abercorn Papers do not overtly specify what lay behind his initial reluctance over yeomanry, but there is no doubt this was a major consideration. In March 1797 the government again briefly toyed with the idea of allowing gentlemen to raise fencible regiments to enlist time-expired militiamen. Typically, Knox was eager to raise one. Abercorn's reaction to this, and the grounds he gave, defines his earlier yeomanry standpoint clearly, given Knox's pivotal role in that force. He told John Stewart 'if a single man of mine should enlist with Thomas Knox (who after showing by his conduct in quitting our regiment that he considers everything merely as the job of the day) I really shall feel inclined to give up the point and have done'.[86] Therefore Abercorn's initial reluctance was both personal and political. The political aspect also had a wider dimension.

In his reply to James Galbraith, Abercorn blamed the poor state of the country on Camden's government.[87] Abercorn had entertained ambitions to be lord lieuten-

83 Abercorn to Galbraith, 18 Nov. 1796, Abercorn Papers, D623/A/80/25.   84 Knox to [?Camden], 27 Nov. 1796, N.A. R.P.620/26/83.   85 Charlemont to Stewart, 10 Sept. 1796, P.R.O.N.I. Stewart of Killymoon Papers, D3167/1/68.   86 [?4] March 1797, P.R.O.N.I. Abercorn Papers, D623/A/80/40.
87 18 Nov. 1796, P.R.O.N.I. Abercorn Papers, D623/A/80/25.

ant, and his antipathy to Camden was a by-product of his soured relationship with Pitt after the refusal of the viceroyalty. As a component of Abercorn's viceregal ambition, he had declared support for Catholic relief.[88] Abercorn must have felt in political limbo as wider events moved the Catholic question off the political agenda. The disenchantment was mutual. Camden denied Abercorn the nomination of a successor to the borough-carrying bishopric of Clogher, telling Portland that he did not want 'the parliamentary interest of Lord Abercorn to preponderate, more especially as he has a most decided opinion of the propriety of granting to the Roman Catholics those privileges which I was commanded hither to resist'.[89] However, Abercorn's granite-like reactions to Knox did not mean his attitudes to yeomanry were set in tablets of stone.

Abercorn's stance on the Catholic question had become equivocal by 1796–7 and this may have had a bearing on a *volte-face* over yeomanry by 1798 when men within his influence such as Galbraith and John Stewart had yeomanry corps, though his 'conversion' was more probably a result of the general acceptance of yeomanry and the deteriorating state of the country. The Reverend William Richardson tried hard to convert Abercorn to support the yeomanry in early 1797. Although involved with Knox as co-founder of the Dungannon Association, as a churchman and a magistrate, Richardson could represent the yeomanry without representing Knox. Richardson got a favourable response to a long letter in which he claimed that the yeomanry, which he said included the most law-abiding of the Orangemen, were the only defence against the United Irishmen.[90] By 1803 Abercorn's conversion to yeomanry was so comprehensive that he raised his own legion of 1,200 men.

The response of the major landowners in county Armagh was conditioned by county politics. Charlemont's dominant role in raising yeomanry in Armagh has been described. An anonymous United Irish pamphleteer described him as 'patron of the Yeomen-Soldiery of this county', and taunted him with the fact that Gosford had taken over of the governorship, in an attempt to stop Charlemont from raising.[91] This failed, but here again the dominance of one interest was offset by the reticence of a rival. Gosford was not fully involved until three months after yeomanry were first raised. In December 1796 he sheepishly told Camden that the delay was due to his tenants being 'stiff dissenters, who made so many difficulties and objections ... that I thought it more prudent to give them a little time to convince them of their error'.[92] Arguably, it was Camden rather than his tenants that Gosford was trying to convince. Charlemont's yeomen, raised on the basis of his Volunteering influence, were also bound to have contained many Presbyterians. It is far more likely that Gosford's pride was hurt because the man he had replaced as governor was given

88 Malcomson, 'A lost natural leader' (passim). 89 9 Nov. 1797, P.R.O. H.O.100/70/ff. 289–93. 90 22 Feb. 1797, P.R.O.N.I. Abercorn Papers, T2541/1B3/6/5; 17 March [1797], D623/A/80/41. 91 [9] Nov. 1796, N.A. R.P.620/26/32. 92 Gosford to Camden, 21 Dec. 1796, K.A.O. Pratt Papers, U840/0173/9.

preference over him. Like Abercorn, when it became clear that yeomanry were being successfully established everywhere, continued reluctance for local political or personal reasons would have been impolitic in terms of Gosford's reputation with government. Pelham tactfully accepted one of Gosford's nominees, Obins of Portadown, but had to refuse the others, from colonels Cope and Sparrow, because the yeomanry had reached its full complement.[93] There is the strong possibility that the reluctant nobleman could have damaged his support amongst the smaller landowning gentry by standing off.

The examples of Down, Antrim, Tyrone, and Armagh have shown how large a part local politics and the social and economic position of smaller and larger landowners could play in conditioning the response to yeomanry, and how this in turn could determine the actual form yeomanry took in an area, or the speed of the levy. These pre-existing considerations could condition attitudes differently according to the social and political balance of power in the area. Downshire's haughty pride and his desire to strengthen his interest impelled him strongly towards yeomanry, while the same instincts initially turned Abercorn away from it. However, it would be a mistake to attribute all the responses of the Anglo-Irish to these inherited and constant facts of life. There were also more immediate causes.

Reluctance to raise yeomanry could signify a simple inability to do so. This seems to have been the case in county Londonderry, though not in Derry city itself. Sir George Fitzgerald Hill raised the Londonderry cavalry but criticised the resident gentry in the county for not attempting to raise corps, not from disloyalty, but from 'an absolute want of spirit' and 'an ill-judged neutrality' to avoid antagonising the United Irishmen.[94] Hill put a negative construction on the inability of others to colour his own efforts more brightly. An enclosure in a letter from the governor, Thomas Conolly, shows the rural gentlemen were trying their best to form corps but their tenants were making all manner of excuses.[95] The truth was, as Richardson told Abercorn some months later, the tenants were all United Irishmen and no amount of influence would have worked.

Therefore this necessarily brief look at some responses from the Anglo-Irish in a variety of locations points strongly to the conclusion that yeomanry were not raised as easily as the speed of the levy and the support for the measure in parliament make it appear. The strength of the United Irish influence which curtailed the formation of yeomanry in county Derry was contemptuously attributed by Sir George Hill to the pusillanimity of other landowners compared, of course, to himself. Camden saw it differently, blaming the City of London companies for encouraging absenteeism by expecting exorbitant rates for the renewal of leases.[96] This begs the question of whether strong United Irish influence and weak gentry influence were the same

93 Pelham to Gosford, 13 Dec. 1796, P.R.O.N.I. Gosford Papers, D1606/1/1/190B.   94 Hill to [Pelham], 23 Nov. 1796, N.A. R.P.620/26/72.   95 McCausland to Conolly, n.d. [Nov.] 1796, N.A. R.P.620/26/61.   96 Camden to Portland, 3 April 1797, P.R.O. H.O.100/69/f. 176.

thing. From the tenant's point of view, the overriding dynamic determining his action may well have been to seek whatever combination offered the best local protection. No amount of deference would have worked if the tenants had lost confidence in their landlord's ability to protect them. In other areas, beneath the apparent ease of raising there was often a turmoil of conflicting interests and compromises. This is a feature more associated with the beginning of yeomanry because, as the total establishment was steadily increased by government, smaller 'territories' were possible, thus easing the potential for political friction. It is highly likely that further local studies for would uncover a similar range of locally-conditioned responses for and against the new force in southern counties, though the overall generalisation, that responses to yeomanry were generally favourable, still holds good.

A number of points emerge at this stage in the analysis. First, the delicacies and difficulties apparent at the initial raising of corps shows that the unanimous gentry support that historians sometimes take for granted was something the government of the day certainly did not. Camden has come in for justifiable criticism as a second rate politician, over-dependent on his advisers,[97] but the fact that yeomanry were established with relatively little trouble compared to what could have happened, redounds to the credit of his administration (if not to himself personally, though he made no bones about claiming it). The other significant point to emerge is that, as would be expected seven years after the French Revolution, the upper levels of the Anglo-Irish propertied elite dreaded anyone except themselves and the substantial gentry having any say in the force. The insistence on cavalry by Lord Downshire is representative of this tendency, as is the frequency of comments about the lack of proper officers.

Cost was another important factor which had a bearing in the responses of the Anglo-Irish. Despite government allowances, establishing a yeomanry corps could be an expensive business. The question needs to be asked as to whether the cost of having a corps put some off the idea. The allowance only covered the basics in terms of equipment and a plain, standardised uniform. Many corps wanted and got uniforms of their own choice. Lord Boyle's Midleton Infantry, wanting to distinguish themselves from his Imokilly Cavalry, had their captain order special 'red waistcoats and pantaloons'.[98] Receipts in the Caledon papers show the Caledon Cavalry went well beyond the basics. Among their requirements were 17 yards of fine blue cloth, 20 glazed caps and 30 stocks, while their agent had to acquire gold and silver braided lace at £2 14s.0d., a trumpet and cord at £3 16s.4d. and a drum and fife at £2 11s.1d.[99] Even where ostentation was not the order of the day, the fact that the first month's pay and the equipment cost had to be met by the captain *in advance* of reimbursement must have been a heavy expense to many, almost like a loan to gov-

97 Malcomson, *John Foster*, p. 71.   98 Godfrey to Boyle, 15 Feb. 1797, P.R.O.N.I. Shannon Papers, D2707/A3/4/17.   99 16 Dec. 1796, P.R.O.N.I. Caledon Papers, D2433/C/2/9; 24 April 1799, D2433/C/3/3.

ernment.[100] If we take an average cavalry corps as 50, with exercise at two shillings per exercise day twice a week, horse furniture at £4 11s.0d. and clothing at two guineas per man, even the most frugal captain would have to find £320 to set up his unassuming yeomen. In reality the cost was likely to be much higher. The Caledon Cavalry cost £195 15s.4d. in clothing alone for 1798, well above the government allowance of £150 3s.0d.[101] James Galbraith applied to Abercorn for assistance because the two guineas clothing allowance 'is so much under the difference [and] more than I can afford'.[102] This was not always the case, however. In some instances the yeomen opted to serve without pay, and to clothe and equip themselves. Sometimes wealthy magnates met the entire expense, like the earl of Courtown, who financed yeomanry around Gorey in county Wexford.[103] Not all the participants could afford this, which explains the proliferation of local subscription schemes (as opposed to Downshire's scheme which was organised on a county basis). The cost may have caused some men, who were not situated close to a wealthy magnate, or whose neighbours supported a different political interest, to think twice but it is more likely that they struggled on. John Rea of Letterkenny complained that the Raphoe yeomanry were financially supported by the bishop of Raphoe and two wealthy gentlemen, whereas his men had so long to wait for the parsimonious Treasury to pay them, and felt so aggrieved about the Raphoe men's apparent preferential treatment, that he had to advance the money himself.[104] Although the initial outlay for a gentleman was the heaviest expense, yeomanry were a recurring charge. James Stewart re-clothed his corps in accordance with the government directive of August 1801. By November he was still owed £207 to cover this. Also in November 1801, J.W. Maxwell of Finnebrogue, county Down was owed between £200 and £300 for pay arrears.[105]

The cost of yeomanry was therefore a major consideration to landowners. However, it is unlikely that it caused many negative responses. With the major Irish nobility and gentry behind the measure, most landowners would have preferred damage to their purses than their pride and standing in county society. Moreover, such reticence could easily be misrepresented by their political opponents as disloyalty. The financial impact was high, but in many respects, once the initial expense was past, yeomanry proved a sound investment. The address of the Irish House of Lords to Camden stated that yeomanry corps had a beneficial effect on the value of property.[106] Investment in yeomanry also opened up considerable patronage, that vital constituent in the various relationships which define the Anglo-Irish

100 1 Dec. 1796, P.R.O.N.I. Lurgan Yeomanry Detail Book, D3696/A/4/1–2.   101 Receipt, 21 Sept. 1798, P.R.O.N.I. Caledon Papers, D2433/C/3/1.   102 11 Nov. 1796, P.R.O.N.I. Abercorn Papers, D623/ A/108/6.   103 n.d.[post 22 Oct.] 1796, P.R.O.N.I. Stewart of Killymoon Papers, D3167/2/126, Gordon, *A History of the Rebellion*, p. 104.   104 Rea to Sackville-Hamilton, 27 March 1797, N.A. R.P.620/29/ 116.   105 11 Nov. 1801, P.R.O.N.I. Stewart of Killymoon Papers, D3167/2/158; 19 Nov. 1801, P.R.O.N.I. Perceval-Maxwell Papers, T1023/219–220.

as a social, political and economic grouping. In practical terms these relationships, in no particular hierarchy of importance, can be described as with their tenants; with other landowners; and with the Castle. Generally speaking, yeomanry bound gentry and government closer together, through ties of patronage, political expediency and mutual inter-dependence. But there was a cost to this. Downshire's dream of an aristocratic, semi-autonomous yeomanry in 1796 can be contrasted with the position in 1807, summarised by Arthur Wellesley: 'through the military department of my office we have the yeomanry completely in our hands'.[107] Yeomanry may not have revolutionised the 'loveless marriage' between government and gentry, but it provided an offspring both were responsible for. Did this new responsibility help with older ones?

As we have already seen, landowners faced increasing problems in keeping control over their tenants. Research has shown how the growth of the linen industry in Ulster gave rise to a multitude of small tenants by encouraging sub-division which removed the 'substantial farmer class'. The larger landowners could only control these small tenants at the price of compromising their paternalist authority.[108] By the time yeomanry were formed, landlord-tenant relationships in the north were undergoing a further buffeting by sectarian outbursts and throughout Ireland by the implications of the French Revolution and the ramifications of the Catholic question. These problems are the benchmark against which effects of the formation and continuance of yeomanry are to be measured. According to J.V. Beckett, social control in the late eighteenth and early nineteenth centuries had as its central feature the mutual bond between the paternalist landowner and the deferential tenant.[109] This bond, which had as its core, the landowner's role as landlord, was reinforced by his position as magistrate, as employer, educator, patron of the clergy and owner of the 'big house' which, along with the parish system, gave the locality its identity and pride. Beckett wrote primarily of England, but the Irish landowning gentry were of the same social group; indeed, many had kinship and property links with English landowners. The same expectations and assumptions regarding the relationship between landowner and tenant pertained in Ireland. Even a cursory glance at the Rebellion Papers confirms the bonds holding social control were at breaking point by 1796.

On 30 January 1796 the Reverend Andrew Newton reported that riotous tenants at Coagh, county Tyrone, were refusing to pay tithes and threatening the Anglican clergy. By August they were 'twenty times as bad', as a consequence of intimidated juries acquitting United Irishmen, and were erecting mock gallows.[110] From every Ulster county came reports of trees being cut down on estates. This was a double

106 n.d. [Jan.] 1797, N.A. R.P.620/28/118.   107 Wellesley to Hawkesbury, 7 May 1807, *W.S.D.*, v, pp. 28–36.   108 W.H. Crawford, 'Landlord-Tenant relations in Ulster, 1609–1820', *I.E.S.H.*, xi (1975), pp. 5–21.   109 J.V. Beckett, *The Aristocracy in England, 1660–1914*, Chap 10 (passim).   110 Newton to [Bourne], 30 Jan. 1796, N.A. R.P.620/23/7; Newton to Bourne, 15 Aug. 1796, 620/24/120.

stab at the old standards of deference and paternalism. Not only were the trees being used for shafting pikes, the international symbol of revolution, but, by felling a landowner's timber the tenants were committing as great a crime against property as if they had taken the land the trees grew on. Some, like Newton, were *in situ* to watch the strands of deference snapping one-by-one; to others, discovering the extent of the problem came as a shock. In October 1796 Mr Boyd of Letterkenny was astounded to find that his tenants openly refused to sign a moderate resolution to form a corps 'accompanied by expressions of impudent disloyalty, with a boldness I really believe arising from the expectation of an invasion'.[111] There is evidence the availability of yeomanry could benefit landowners who had been having problems controlling their tenants. In March 1797 General Lake told Pelham social control had broken down in parts of Ulster, quoting as his authority some gentlemen who, 'though strong for parliamentary reform are now frightened and say we have been the cause of this measure [disarming] originally, and now have no power over our tenants and labourers'.[112]

Raising yeomanry helped a landowner's influence over his tenants in a variety of ways. First, before a man's influence could be improved he needed accurately to assess how badly it had been damaged. By proposing to raise a yeomanry corps, thereby creating an alternative to the United Irishmen, a landowner could test the strength of his influence over his tenants in troubled and changing times. If successful in raising a corps, yeomanry gave the landowner both an accumulation of patronage and the opportunity to act like a paternalist. Yeomanry patronage, when channelled into the localities, helped larger patrons distribute benefits to supporters and individual yeomanry captains reinforce the links with their tenants by a plethora of rewards, favours and obligations. It made the influence and reputation of a major landowner a pearl of great price for smaller men who needed to use it to 'advertise', as it were, for members for their own corps. W.C. Lindsay became very upset when Charlemont gave his 'blessing' to Captain Evans' Castlecaulfield Cavalry, which he felt would impede his own intentions to raise yeomanry.[113] Lindsay eventually got his own cavalry corps, but with cavalry types so scarce there was obviously an element of competition for members and magnates could allow their name to be used as a favour to be repaid at election time.[114] From the tenant-yeoman's perspective there were two types of economic benefit to be had from being in a corps, which can be crudely defined as pay for exercise or permanent duty, and preferential treatment because of yeomanry service. The yeomen owed their existence to their captain, not the government, and, although their pay came from the public purse, it was obtained by the landowner and channelled through him for distribution or confiscation according to how well an individual was judged to have

111 J. Boyd to R. Boyd, 5 Oct. 1796, N.A. R.P.620/25/148.　112 13 March 1797, B.L. Pelham Papers, add. mss. 33103 ff. 224–5.　113 Charlemont to Stewart, n.d. *c*.Feb. 1797, P.R.O.N.I. Stewart of Killymoon Papers, D3167/1/69.　114 1798 Yeomanry List, N.L.I. ir355a4.

done his duty and behaved himself. Even in the most 'democratic' of corps this system of payment can only have enhanced the captain's influence since he was the sole intermediary between the men and government. The substantive nature of permanent pay obviously increased both the financial benefits a captain could confer and the enhanced influence he could expect. It proved too tempting for some. In 1802 Wickham noted the tendency of some captains to convey a misleading impression of local law and order to keep their corps on permanent pay, and complained the following year that 'the [yeomanry] system here is full of job, and that we cannot count on the numbers that we have on paper.'[115] Yeomanry service could carry with it the possibility of preferential treatment in tenancy and business matters. It seems to have been accepted that if a man gave good service in the yeomanry corps the landlord or the patron of the corps would reward him by 'helping him out' when necessary. When the owner of the Foljambe estate in Tyrone instructed his agent to restrict tenants to 21-year leases, because of his concern about sub-division, he made an exception for 'those yeomanry who stood forward with so much honour … in the late unnatural rebellion', offering them additional, individually calculated, terms.[116] When the captain of a corps looked to a larger patron, he could solicit aid for its deserving members. James McKay recommended a yeoman to Downshire for help 'on some contract business' with the telling injunction, *'he is an original member'*.[117] This kind of patronage, operating in the closed society of a yeomanry corps, went hand in glove with a revival of time-honoured traditions of paternalism.

The landlord was captain and the source of rewards or punishments, while the tenants could respond with traditional service at a time when many of the old familiar certainties were being eroded by war and political uncertainty. Moreover, raising a corps gave a landowner the opportunity to reinforce the bond of mutual obligation with that of military discipline. Some landowners took their paternalist obligations as yeomanry captains very seriously indeed. In Tyrone a Mr Maxwell was reported (during an invasion scare when his corps were on permanent duty) as 'again prevented from going to England, as he will not leave his yeomanry till this bustle is over', despite the fact that 'his health absolutely requires change of climate'.[118] On such permanent duty the yeomen and their captain were in closest contact. During the same emergency William Brownlow laid down the rules for his Lurgan corps with the strictness of a father to his wayward children. He made them all get their hair cut before he would distribute the new clothing government had allowed. Conversely, the paternalist-captain could reward as well as punish. Corporals Warren and Thompson were made sergeants 'for their good behaviour'.[119] Such evidence

115 Wickham to Lord Liverpool, 13 Dec. 1802, H.R.O. Wickham Papers, 38M49/5/3/10; 14 Aug. 1803, *Castlereagh Corrs.*, iv, pp. 294–8. 116 Foljambe to Speer, n.d. [c. 1800], P.R.O.N.I. Foljambe Papers, T3381/10/4. 117 10 Sept. 1798, P.R.O.N.I. Downshire Papers, D607/F/402. 118 Rev. Gervais to P. Gervais, 15 May 1799, P.R.O.N.I. Gervais Papers, T1287/3/74. 119 9 Sept. 1801, P.R.O.N.I. Lurgan Yeomanry Detail Book, D3696/A/4/1.

makes yeomanry appear a godsend to any landowner, maximising existing social control and proving a lifeline where traditional influence was wavering. Castlereagh made this point retrospectively to Wellesley in 1807, noting that 'the persons entrusted with the command of the corps are enabled to exercise a discretion in the selection of their men. The individuals are always of their immediate neighbourhood, and generally under their influence. If not perfectly to be depended on when first received ... they acquire better habits from their comrades'.[120] This reveals a limitation in the yeomanry's social control potential. The critical element was selection.

The yeomanry corps commanded by Castlereagh's father was a case in point. Lord Londonderry was initially unsuccessful in getting his tenants to take the oath of allegiance but, after pressure from Castlereagh himself, no less than 700 obliged, and any amount of recruits was to be had. Londonderry was understandably suspicious at swift conversions, and only selected those he was sure of.[121] Therein lies the point. Selection was necessary yet also had its drawbacks. The landowner risked alienating wavering tenants by excluding them. If they were potentially disloyal, it put them further out of his reach; if not, their loyalty and deference must have seemed ill-rewarded. A further problem existed in areas where cavalry were preferred. Even Downshire recognised how excluding his poorer tenants would damage his influence over them. By the selective nature of yeomanry, whether selection came because of suspicion on religious or political grounds, a preference for cavalry, or simply through having to keep within governmental limits, raising yeomanry naturally excluded more than it included. Even in the nineteenth century, when the initial levy had quadrupled to around 80,000, the general effect can only have been to define narrowly the constituency of tenants over which the landlords could have strong influence. Hardwicke recognised this in 1803 when he contemplated the risky and unpopular expedient of allowing Catholic supplementaries in Tipperary, in addition to the regular yeomanry, to be raised by Lords Ormond, Lismore, Mathew and Cahir. He hoped this would prevent their tenants from 'taking a wrong course', especially as they were 'ancient Irish families who are looked up to by the common people with less prejudice than many others'.[122]

Another factor militating against good control of tenants was the insistence of some corps (like James Stewart's Killymoon yeomen) on electing their officers and nominating their captain.[123] In this case it could be argued this practice was only continuing the pre-existing relationship, as both tenants and landlord were old Volunteers. Nevertheless, as many landowners joined the Volunteers to keep control over their tenants, the prevalence of this practice[124] meant a compromise in the

---

120 28 Dec.1807, *W.S.D.*, v, pp. 279–83.　121 Camden to Portland, 13 Dec. 1796, P.R.O. H.O.100/62/f. 368.　122 Hardwicke to Wickham, 5 Oct. 1803, H.R.O. Wickham Papers, 38M49/5/30/84.　123 14 Nov. [1796], P.R.O.N.I. Stewart of Killymoon Papers, D3167/2/127.　124 See, for example: The memorial of the Tullyhunco Yeomanry Infantry, n.d.[Dec. 1807], N.A. O.P.232/4/30.

landowner's control over the members of the corps. At the other extreme, a captain's power was open to abuse. Captain Blake of the Tully Rifles in Galway complained to Brigade Major Marshall that one of his yeomen was trying to leave the corps, and was hoping for protection from a middleman on Blake's estate, from whom he had taken a lease. Blake obviously felt a proprietorial interest in his corps, as he fumed, 'if those savages here, after being trained and drilled to the use of arms, shall be permitted when they please to give up ... there will be an end to most country corps'.[125] There is no record of whether Blake prevented his tenant from quitting, but he certainly tried hard. When a fine was refused, Blake distrained the man's cow, only for the tenant to break into Galway Pound and retrieve it. Paternalism in the yeomanry therefore operated within a consensus that was founded on a recognition that mutual interests were being involved. It allowed the kind of compromises between extremes of self-interest (which on the captain's part was absolute feudal control and on the yeoman's the right to resign as a volunteer) which kept things running relatively smoothly. Where the consensus broke down, as in the Galway example, the existence of yeomanry as something to resign from offered disgruntled tenants a platform to show how little control an overbearing patron had.

Orangeism was another important aspect of yeomanry which could help or hinder a landowner's relations with his tenants. There were early attempts by some gentlemen, notably Thomas Knox and James Verner, to gain control over their Orange tenantry by attaching them in the cause of local defence. This tendency ran beneath the surface of the Dungannon Association. Whenever the shadowy connection did surface publicly, the beneficial aspect of control was emphasised. Thus Richardson wrote, in trying to sell the idea of yeomanry to Abercorn, a man who disliked Orangemen and looked down on men like Verner: 'the best of them [the Orangemen] are in the yeomanry. The banditti who robbed in their name, follow their trade without that pretext'.[126] No doubt there was an argument to be made from expediency, with the country drifting towards rebellion, but, in spite of the strategic benefits of controlling both the disloyal and the ultra-loyal it was control at a price.

In August 1796, speaking about Verner's loyal resolutions, Mr. Bell of Warrenpoint told Pelham, 'I see flaming and very strange, exaggerated accounts of Mr. Verner and his thousands ... if they were in shoes [sic] what men of principle or property would be hardy enough to lead them ... besides they won't be officered by anyone but those of their own choosing'.[127] Bell was making the assumption, correctly as it turned out, that 'Verner's thousands' were Orangemen. Orangeism in the yeomanry had a similar effect on traditional landlord influence, as ex-Volunteers electing their yeomanry officers. Indeed, given the Williamite tradition in the Volunteers, the distinction was a fine one in some areas. Annesley's Castlewellan Infantry, whose condition of service was that they would not permit any Catholics to join, originally

125 24 Nov. 1806, N.A. O.P.323/39(62).   126 22 Feb. 1797, P.R.O.N.I. Abercorn Papers, T2541/1B3/6/5.   127 24 Aug. 1796, N.A. R.P.620/24/153.

offered 'under the idea of the old Volunteer scheme'.[128] In 1798, John Waring Maxwell entered into an arrangement with two local Orange societies to form yeomanry corps near Strangford and Downpatrick. Maxwell's correspondence with members of the Orange societies shows he had to compromise, allowing the Orangemen to elect their own leaders as yeomanry officers. This was the consequence of having to utilise groupings who were organised before yeomanry. If the new organisation was to successfully harness the power of such pre-existing local-defence groups, it would have to adhere to the dynamics of the older structure. Maxwell had to deal with two such societies at Strangford and Raholp and, in contrast to the norm of landlord selection, he had the job done for him. In April 1798 he was trying to raise yeomanry near Castleward. Richard Anderson of the Raholp society, though elected yeoman officer by that society, turned it down on the grounds that it would be 'highly objectionable' to the Strangford Orange Society 'which will constitute, at least, two thirds of the corps'.[129] Though Maxwell was to head the corps, the jostling and negotiation between the rival Orange societies dominated the levying of the corps. Maxwell was thrust to the periphery, getting only a copy of the correspondence. Although Orangeism in the yeomanry can be seen as another of the many compromises necessary to make the force function, unlike the toleration of Volunteer practices it was not harmlessly absorbed and retained the potential to shake itself clear of landlord control. In August 1798, from Blaris military camp, Poyntz Stewart, one of the smaller landowners and captain of the Derriaghy Infantry, chaired a meeting of Orangemen who sent resolutions to 'all yeomanry captains and masters of Orange lodges in Blaris Barracks'.[130] The occasion was sectarian trouble between yeomen and militiamen. The resolutions stressed the law-abiding aspect of Orangeism and demonstrated the efforts of landlords to control it by means of the yeomanry. Yet the fact that they were necessary, and the very issuing of such resolutions from a military barracks, shows that Orangeism in the yeomanry had the potential to set itself above both traditional landlord influence and military authority. Not long afterwards the Reverend Hudson, told Charlemont about the spread of Orangeism through a corps quartered near his own, and the predicament of his yeomanry officers 'who, trying to check it, are imputed Catholic sympathisers'.[131] Not all landowners availed themselves of the Orangemen. It was precisely this sort of loss of control that prompted Alexander Knox to caution Sir George Fitzgerald Hill, 'I hear of an Orange lodge in Derry. I trust you and your connection will keep clear ... it cannot strengthen you, circumstanced as you are, you do not need it'.[132]

As we have seen, the formation of yeomanry corps could certainly be harnessed

---

128 R. Annesley to Cooke, 9 Nov. 1796, N.A. R.P.620/26/37. 129 Murphy to Maxwell, 28 May 1798, P.R.O.N.I. Perceval-Maxwell Papers, T1023/150; Anderson to Raholp Orange Society, 26 April 1798, T1023/147. 130 N.A.M. 6807–174 ff. 503–6, Nugent Papers, 6 Aug. 1798 131 Hudson to Charlemont, 6 Oct. 1798, H.M.C. *Charlemont*, ii, p. 336. 132 n.d. [Sept.] 1798, P.R.O.N.I. Hill of Brook Hall Papers, D642/A/10/19.

to strengthen a magnate's political interest, but, once afoot, did yeomanry have a major impact on the hard practicalities of electoral politics? Did having a yeomanry corps boost a man's ability to compete in elections? The traditional pattern of Irish politics was an appeal to the electorate on the basis of paternalistic factors like length of residence and quality of landlordism.[133] This was prevalent throughout much of the eighteenth century but, like many other traditional aspects of society, was now under threat. From the 1770s county election contests could include ideological elements as well as the traditional issues of personality. The electorate was changing. Catholic 40-shilling freeholders had been admitted to vote since 1793. This change meant that elections were increasingly being fought over political issues like full Catholic relief rather than the more personal style of traditional electioneering. Such changes coincided with increasing politicization amongst the 'lower orders'. Constitutional change also had an impact. The Act of Union disfranchised many Irish boroughs with the result that they too became more competitive.[134] In this rapidly changing political world, one would expect that yeomanry would be quickly enlisted as an electoral tool. The evidence does show this happening, but only patchily, and in certain very recognisable circumstances.

Comparatively little evidence survives in the source material to show yeomanry being used in electioneering. This is hardly surprising as landowners were scarcely likely to advertise the fact to government or each other. Where such references do occur, it is often in the form of a complaint against a rival, and must therefore be treated with caution. Qualifications aside, there is still sufficient evidence to illustrate three distinct ways in which yeomanry were used for electioneering, at different times in the life of a yeomanry corps. A corps was first ripe for exploitation at its actual raising. The circumstances of the first levy meant that apolitical territorial limitations were centrally imposed and had to be fitted in as best as possible with the disposition of local interests. This was not always possible, so, principally for strategic reasons, it was sometimes permissible for a landowner who could raise corps to enroll the tenants of landowners who could or would not, particularly in the case of absentees. In some areas landowners are seen vying for the tenants of their rivals. John Wolfe of Prosperous, county Kildare was trying to get the tenants of the absentee Mr. Stanmer enrolled in his own corps with Stanmer's approval. However, he warned Cooke of a bid by a rival who 'made great exertions to get the people of Prosperous, who are all Stanmer's tenants, to quit their landlord and join them'.[135] Obviously, the tenants of an absentee without an influential enough agent were considered fair game. From the tenants' viewpoint, the ability of one gentleman to offer protection and arms via a yeomanry corps was a greater incentive than the danger of not having their leases renewed. The late 1790s were an unpropitious

---

133 Malcomson, *John Foster*, p. 157.   134 R.G. Thorne (ed.), *The History of Parliament: the Commons, 1790–1820*, i, p. 100.   135 n.d.[c.10] Jan. 1797, N.A. R.P.620/28/44.

time for looking too far ahead. A similar situation is detectable in the case of John Waring Maxwell's Ballyculter yeomanry. When Robert Ward was allowed a corps at Castleward in 1798, he permitted those of his brother, Lord Bangor's tenants, who had already enrolled with Maxwell to continue, as they had joined before the Castleward corps was thought necessary. Maxwell had obviously calculated well. One of Maxwell's officers asked the 'Ballyculter Boys' if they would serve Ward should Maxwell resign in his favour. The answer was that they would lay down their arms first.[136] Perhaps the risk of compromised control over one's tenants was worth taking if another man's tenants could be attached by means of the yeomanry and their Orange sympathies. Maxwell undoubtedly tried to strengthen his interest in this way. The 1798 list shows him with three corps against Ward's one. The Wickham Papers demonstrate how the Ward family tried to recover their interest in the corps at Maxwell's death in 1803.[137]

After formation, the second period of political utility in a yeomanry corps' existence was when they were augmented by a large addition of supplementaries, especially when a combination of supplementaries was permitted in a legion. The crucial point about supplementaries is that they were often numerically much larger than regular corps, not being restricted by limitations of pay or uniform. The two main periods of this sort of supplementary augmentation were in 1798 itself, and in the large-scale augmentations which followed the resumption of war in 1803. The sources for both periods contain definite evidence of politicking. The yeomanry of Cork city were split between the rival interests of Donoughmore and Westropp. In 1798 Robert Harding, a member of Westropp's Royal Cork Volunteers made the standard accusations of disloyalty (Donoughmore was a liberal Protestant supporter of emancipation who had many Catholics in his Cork Legion) but followed with the claim that the legion was 'raised for electioneering purposes where numbers not character was the object'.[138] This connection between numbers and electoral politics was accurate, even if the slur on Donoughmore's primary motivation was not. Similar evidence is available elsewhere. 'Mr Isaac Corry is playing a fine potwalloping game at Newry' Robert Ross told Downshire in July 1798, 'Lord Castlereagh has given him powers to raise as far as 500 men, which he is doing indiscriminately, without consulting anyone; and he swears, whitewashes and arms all who offer themselves'.[139] In August 1803, in contrast to his earlier reticence, Abercorn was going all-out to secure the opportunities afforded by the vast increase in yeomen and especially supplementaries. His correspondence of the period reveals that not only did he take a personal interest this time, but also that he pandered to popular prejudices to make absolutely sure his supplementaries were formed. 'It will be all I can

---

136 R. Ward to Maxwell, 29 May 1798, P.R.O.N.I. Perceval-Maxwell Papers, T1023/151; n.d.[late] May 1798, Reid to 'Jack' [Maxwell], T1053/154.   137 E. Ward to Castlereagh, 30 April 1803, H.R.O. Wickham Papers, 38M49/5/33/4.   138 Harding to Cooke, 24 Feb. 1798, N.A. R.P.620/35/158.   139 3 July 1798, P.R.O.N.I. Downshire Papers, D607/F/297.

do to admit 10 Catholics in a legion of 1,200, without trying too much the feelings of those whom we have to depend upon'.[140] Both Corry and Abercorn were men who needed to strengthen their political influence, Corry to feed his rising social and political ambitions, and Abercorn because Union had decimated his boroughs.[141] The political orientation was unmistakable in each case, and both men tried to enlist a rivals' tenants in their yeomanry legions. John Stewart told his patron, Abercorn, that Lord Belmore's agent 'was mortified beyond measure at all Lord Belmore's respectable friends joining my supplementary corps'.[142] The components were different – Abercorn's prior courting of Catholic support was reversed while Ross claimed that Corry included 'notoriously proscribed croppies' – but the intention was the same.[143] The opportunity afforded by supplementaries was inviting to anyone with political ambition. Five hundred men in Newry and 1,200 in Tyrone were electorally substantial. No wonder there was overwhelming reluctance among Ulster landowners to allow yeomanry to be gathered in brigades of up to 500 at the restart of war.[144] Not everyone could command.

The third electorally useful period of the life of a corps was when they were established and functioning and could be used to enhance the prestige of their patron or remind the yeomen where their loyalties lay. This was the most risky of all the political harnessing of yeomanry, as involving military bodies in politics was universally frowned on and had the potential to rebound very badly. The kind of show put on in Tyrone by Lord Mountjoy on the eve of the critical 1806 general election was just about acceptable. The Knox-Abercorn feud again provides the backdrop. Grenville's party was supporting Thomas Knox against Abercorn's candidate, Sir John Stewart. Mountjoy arranged to review local Tyrone yeomen at Abercorn's residence, Baronscourt. He had them march past the house and cheer for Abercorn, for which they were rewarded with a glass of whiskey each.[145] The line distinguishing support from intimidation was a fine line one. Landowners could and did use their yeomen against each other when occasion suited. In 1810 yeomen who answered to Abercorn were involved in cutting salmon nets on the River Foyle. When General Hart ordered the brigade-major to investigate the circumstances it transpired the fishing rights were disputed between Abercorn, who owned fisheries upstream, and Sir George Hill. Government's decision was that this was a private matter and no interference was necessary.[146] In sharp contrast was the outrage shown by Wellesley at the blatant intimidation reported to him from Downpatrick in 1807, when a candidate, Hawthorne, threatened to march his yeomanry into town in response to his rival, Croker, having asked for troops to preserve order during polling.

140 Abercorn to Littlehales, 15 Aug. 1803, P.R.O.N.I. Abercorn Papers, D623/A/81/64.   141 Malcomson, 'A lost natural leader', op. cit., passim.   142 5 Oct. [1803], P.R.O.N.I. Abercorn Papers, D623/A/142/21.   143 Ross to Downshire, 31 July 1798, P.R.O.N.I. Downshire Papers, D607/F/343. 144 G. Knox to Abbot, 4 Aug. 1801, P.R.O. Colchester Papers, 30/9/123/ff. 170-3.   145 J. Hamilton to Abercorn, 4 Nov. 1806, P.R.O.N.I. Abercorn Papers, D623/A/97/46.   146 Hart to Gordon, 2 June 1810, P.R.O. H.O.100/158/f. 190.
147 Croker to Wellesley, 18 May 1807, P.R.O.N.I. Wellington Papers, T2627/3/2/113.

The singularity of this is shown in Croker's astonishment that Hawthorne would threaten to use 'the King's volunteers against the King's soldiers'.[147] This is the only evidence that has come to light of yeomanry being used in overt electoral intimidation, and it is clearly the exception which proves the rule. With the repeated attempts to improve the yeomanry militarily and the consequent omnipresent scrutiny of general officers, such intimidation would have been too risky for any gentleman to contemplate who had regard for his reputation. Government had always the ultimate sanction, to break a yeomanry captain and disband his corps, and no political influence would survive such social disgrace. The overall conclusion to be reached is that yeomanry corps were an addition of power through the linkages they built with the tenants by means of obligation and patronage, but their full electoral potential was only realised when exceptional circumstances allowed a bid to be made for another man's tenants or to get control of a block of yeomen in a legion.

Did the yeomanry shore up the position of the Anglo-Irish? Although a prominent feature in many landowners' lives, it could not reverse trends already in progress. The influence of the landed interest continued to decline, though the benefits yeomanry gave in terms of government patronage for themselves and their supporters, government indebtedness and a partial clawing back of lost influence over their tenants slowed the rate of decline. Without yeomanry the Anglo-Irish twilight of the nineteenth century might well have been a sudden eclipse in 1798. Through the yeomanry, the Anglo-Irish proved Ireland's security problems could only be tackled with their co-operation, yet at the same time, more than ever opened to scrutiny the practices of the landed interest in the control of law and order. It is to the impact of the yeomanry on Ireland's law and order problems that we must now turn.

9

The Irish Yeomanry and law and order, 1796–1834

'We'll fight for our King, and our country's just cause,
Fair Liberty, Property, Order, and Laws.'[1]

Ireland's law and order situation could be described as sometimes difficult but always controllable up to the 1790s when it was transformed utterly. Apart from open insurrection, there were three broad challenges to law and order during the yeomanry's span – political, sectarian and agrarian disorder in the Whiteboy tradition. All three had degrees of overlap and could, at times, react with each other. Disorder in the 1790s was first and foremost political in nature. Economic problems were still there, but, rather than an *a priori* motivation, were now being deliberately manipulated to harness unrest behind demands for radical political change, which were in turn used to drive the United Irish military strategy for revolution. Whiteboyism re-surfaced in the early nineteenth century but, in the polarized and embittered conditions following 1798 it is sometimes difficult to draw any meaningful demarcation between traditional agrarian protest and disaffection. The south and west of Ireland suffered periodic waves of disturbances from various rural combinations during this period. These were neither continuous nor general, but their persistence meant that government viewed them collectively as an ongoing law and order problem. The Home Office Papers show the reactions of officials to the flow of 'state of the country' reports and bespeak a weary resignation which saw autumn and winter as virtually an 'outrage season' in parts of Ireland. Speaking of Tipperary, Limerick, Westmeath and Kildare between 1806 to the 1840s, Galen Broeker considers agrarian secret societies to have had sufficient continuity to constitute a 'standing army of the disaffected'. Though these were the worst places, they were by no means the only areas disturbed or threatened with disturbance. Broeker memorably describes early nineteenth-century Ireland as 'the despair of the governing and the governed – threatening, gloomy, stubborn, too disturbed to respond effectively to civil government, not disturbed enough to justify full-scale military occupation'.[2]

The malevolent influence of the 1790s can be seen in the changing nature of

1 Loyalist Ballad: 'The New Paddy-Whack', n.d. [c. Jan. 1797], N.A. R.P.620/28/81.   2 G. Broeker, *Rural Disorder and Police Reform in Ireland, 1812–36* (hereafter Broeker, *Rural Disorder*), pp. 1, 6.

Irish disorder. The limited nature of popular protest and the relative bloodlessness of agrarian crime has already been noted. More people, around 600, died in the few days of London's Gordon Riots in 1780 than in all Irish eighteenth-century Irish disorder, apart from the last decade. However, comparing early nineteenth-century Irish disorder with its English equivalent, Stanley Palmer considers that Irish crime was both distinctive, in being usually collective as opposed to individual, and more severe in that, according to statistics from 1805, Ireland was twice as 'crime-ridden'.[3] For one thing Irish disorder was now more violent than its contemporary cross-channel equivalent. If eighteenth-century agrarian crime was typified by the maiming (houghing) of farm animals, its nineteenth-century equivalent frequently involved the disfigurement of people. The nomenclature of rural combinations bespeak violence. The Carders took their title from the wool-cards – steel combs designed to refine raw sheep wool – they used to excoriate their victims. These attacks were designed as both punishment and warning to those breaking the combination's 'rules', frequently regulation of prices, rents or tithe or an embargo on informing. Such warnings were to be taken seriously. In 1813 Lord Castlemaine, telling the under-secretary Gregory about an informer's murder, excused his erratic prose style on the grounds that he wrote 'with his bloody corpse before me a shot, stabbed and battered with stones as flat as a board'.[4] Castlemaine may not have been the Macbeth of county Longford – indeed Peel witheringly dubbed him the 'grand alarmist' – yet there are too many other examples of similar mutilation to avoid the conclusion this was typical treatment for breaking the 'rules'.[5]

In an analysis of the yeomanry's role in trying to enforce the laws and tackle disorder it makes no sense to try to categorize their duties into mutually exclusive civil and military functions. In reality they overlapped in a somewhat similar way, as did much of the Irish army's duty in this period, which was considered 'police' work in the older sense of the word, denoting domestic peacekeeping. The vast majority of yeomanry duty can be seen in the same light. However this is not to say that it was the same. At the lower end of the scale, a yeomanry corps could function like a beefed-up version of the parish constabulary, readily available to help magistrates with arrests or process-serving in their capacity as civilian volunteers without being under military law. Like the regulars, yeomanry on this type of duty were meant to be accompanied by a commissioned yeomanry officer and a civil magistrate, in the event of the officer not being one.[6] The yeomanry's role extended from these localised functions to peacekeeping in its wider sense, as represented by full national call-outs during invasion scares or apprehensions of rebellion, in which case they voluntarily put themselves under full military control. However, to attempt a full analysis of the yeomanry's impact on law and order by dividing up their

---

3 S. Palmer, *Police and Protest in Ireland and England, 1780–1850* (hereafter Palmer, *Police and Protest*), p. 45.   4 Castlemaine to Gregory, 22 Nov. 1813, P.R.O. H.O.100/174/f. 242.   5 Peel to Whitworth, 1 Dec. 1813, Parker (ed.), *Peel, Private Papers*, i, p. 125; Palmer, *Police and Protest*, pp. 46–7.   6 Circular, 25 July 1811, Lurgan Yeomanry Detail Book, P.R.O.N.I. D3696/A/4/1.

duties into neat functional categories would risk imposing order where little existed. The legislation was hazy as to their actual role, confining itself to generalities
about national defence and the preservation of life and property.[7] As they were a
quintessentially *ad hoc*, emergency force, it is therefore more realistic to examine
their response to the different types of disorder.

SMOTHERED REBELLION, 1796–8

When urging government acceptance of offers of service from loyal associations in
August 1796, Thomas Knox described county Tyrone as 'teeming with treason and,
what is worse, treason methodized'.[8] Knox bluntly described what he saw around
him. Historians, with the benefit of hindsight and abstract judgment, can distinguish motive from method. Nancy Curtin describes the United Irishmen's activities as 'propaganda by deed'. It began by demonstrations of strength in, for example, public rejoicing at French victories, but, when the United Irishmen reorganised militarily from 1795 onward, included intimidation and actual attacks on the
system of law and order. The purpose was to give confidence to their members and
attract recruits, who sought the protection of the strongest party while concurrently
either scaring weak magistrates into inactivity or physically opposing active ones to
discourage popular loyalism, the magistrates' natural local support.[9] This campaign
subjected the creaky law and order system and a magistracy of uneven quality, commitment and coverage, to intolerable strain. The ordinary civil watchmen and constables, ineffective at the best of times, were swamped. Around Aughnacloy, county
Tyrone, it was 'almost impossible to rely on the constables ... where law is to be
executed against the United Irishmen'.[10] Even the ultimate expediency of calling
for military assistance was fraught with difficulty. For one thing, protection by troop
detachments was necessarily temporary, the United Irishmen could go to ground,
creating apparent tranquillity until the soldiers were recalled, then target the magistrates responsible. This local scenario could be enacted on a large scale if the army
had to concentrate its forces to meet invasion.[11] Moreover, wartime troop shortages
meant militia were heavily used in peacekeeping, raising concerns about possible
United Irish or Defender sympathies. In effect the United Irishmen held the initiative, being able to turn disorder on and off strategically. The United Irish areas of
Ulster, at this stage most of Antrim, Down, Derry and parts of Tyrone, Armagh,
Cavan, Monaghan and Fermanagh were in what one magistrate described as a state
of 'smothered rebellion'.[12]

7 37 Geo. III c. 2.   8 Knox to Cooke, 4 July 1796, N.A. R.P.620/24/16.   9 Curtin, *The United Irishmen*,
pp. 228–53.   10 Moore to Lees, n.d. [Feb. 1797], N.A. R.P.620/28/206.   11 Stoddart, 'Counter-Insurgency and Defence in Ireland, 1750–1805', pp. 64–78.   12 Curtin, op. cit., p. 68; Griffith to Cooke,
27 Aug. 1796, N.A. R.P.620/24/177.

When the initial propaganda campaign against yeomanry enlistment failed, those becoming yeomen were added to the hate-list of Ascendancy figures such as magistrates and Anglican clergy. Thomas Knox reported attacks on yeomen in Stewartstown, 'many of whom were dangerously wounded' after taking the yeomanry oath, and noted that this was general in Tyrone.[13] United Irish military strategy gave added impetus as the yeoman was more than an Ascendancy Aunt Sally, he was a source of arms. The United Irishmen's local dominance was such that early attempts to arrest members met an arrogantly confident response in their ability to prevent the judicial system operating. Sir George Hill told Cooke, 'it is impossible to get respectable people to serve on petty juries' in county Derry and that the courts freed all United Irish prisoners, a circumstance which, according to a local cleric, led to massive increases in threatened lawlessness.[14] The government's next move was to arrest United Irish leaders. This provoked perhaps the most ominous tactic in the entire United Irish arsenal: the potato digging. Large numbers of men would appear under the pretext of digging an arrested man's potatoes, but in reality they demonstrated numbers and organisation in a way that intimidated without coming under the Riot Act. They also contemptuously cocked a snook at the magistrates by bidding them to do their worst. Physical attacks increased. Informers were murdered and assassination attempts made on two key clerical magistrates: Philip Johnston of Lisburn and John Cleland, Lord Londonderry's agent. Signs of desperation set in. At Moneymore, county Derry, Richardson's friend, the clerical magistrate Isaac Ashe, even contemplated a cut in tithe to give no pretext for 'a combination which may eventually overturn church and state'. By late 1796, some rural magistrates were abandoning their districts for the protection of the towns. James Stewart complained he would soon have nobody assisting him to execute the law in west Tyrone.[15] The situation the new yeomanry force faced was one where the normal writ of law was demonstrably not running in United Irish areas.

Notwithstanding, the government's initial expectations for the new force were high. It was hoped that, after an initial period when the army would help the formation of yeomanry by its protective presence and by providing training, the yeomen would be able to take full responsibility for law and order, thus freeing the army of peacekeeping and improving its anti-invasion capacity.[16] Viewed in the light of such shining expectations, the yeomanry seems a dull failure: the army became more rather than less involved in peacekeeping from 1796. Moreover, ordinary peacekeeping having failed, the recourse to the Insurrection Act and eventual martial law, which involved both the yeomanry and the army, made the yeomen appear as sullenly vindictive, incapable of ordinary peacekeeping and functioning either as agents of lawlessness themselves or a legitimizing stimulus for disorder.

13 Knox to Cooke, 2 Oct. 1796, N.A. R.P.620/26/9.   14 Newton to Bourne, 13 Aug. 1796, Hill to Cooke, 15 Aug. 1796, N.A. R.P.620/24/112, 120.   15 Ashe to Cooke, 10 Sept. 1796, N.A. R.P.620/25/ 84; Stewart to Cooke, 5 Nov. 1796 620/26/20.   16 Stoddart, op. cit., p. 196.

Any analysis of the yeomanry's law and order role must squarely confront their part in this coercion and its implications. However, to begin an analysis at that point would be misconceived. The luxury of retrospective judgment beckons historians towards anachronistic conclusions when the yeomanry's role should be examined first in the contemporary context, remembering that those subjectively involved in the events acted according to what they saw as their best interests. This is especially true for the 1790s, when the very real danger of political revolution and the inadequacy of traditional responses made the outcome unpredictable.

Three weeks after the first yeomanry commissions were issued, the Insurrection Act, which had been on the statute book since early 1796, was first implemented, giving magistrates a blunt coercive instrument against insurgency. Its main provisions were to make administering an illegal oath a capital offence and the taking of such oaths punishable by transportation. Local magistrates could make a request for the Act to apply in their districts whenever a quorum of seven agreed that the area was in a state of disturbance. East Down was the first district 'proclaimed' in November 1796, shortly followed by north Armagh, then the areas around Newry, Armagh and Dungannon. Large parts of Derry, Donegal and northern Tyrone followed in early 1797 while Antrim's avoidance of proclamation only proved the United Irishmen were sufficiently prepared to make disturbance unnecessary.[17] Magistrates in proclaimed districts had wide-ranging additional powers, including being able to impose curfews, search for arms at will with military assistance, and arrest anyone considered disorderly and send them to serve in the fleet.[18] The newly formed yeomanry's first activity was providing assistance to active magistrates acting under the Insurrection Act. In December 1796 Thomas Knox's yeomen had arrested two 'noted leaders' and 'righted' the Dungannon district. Knox wanted a propaganda victory as much as a strategic strike, adding ominously that 'mystery' was to surround the removal of the prisoners to distant jails, a move designed to 'terrify the disaffected'. By January 1797, his yeomen were mopping up more suspects for administering oaths and escorting them to goal.[19] In March, Newry magistrates John Goddart, William Beath and George Anderson told Downshire how local yeomanry assisted magistrates and baronial constables in escorting prisoners arrested by the Cavan militia.[20] Where magistrates were prepared to take an active part against the United Irishmen, yeomanry had the advantage over regulars, fencibles or militia, of possessing local knowledge and being immediately available. With Carhampton's precedent in mind, the presence of yeomanry and the Insurrection Act gave active magistrates the confidence that they could turn the tables on their opponents. In a stringent coda to the United Irishmen's overture to the Derry ju-

17 Curtin, op. cit., pp. 72–3.   18 36 Geo. III c. 20.   19 Knox to Pelham, n.d. December 1796, 5 Jan. 1797, N.A. R.P.620/26/151, 620/28/62.   20 2 March 1797, P.R.O.N.I. Downshire Papers, D607/E/ 145; Magistrates' memorial, 18 March 1797, B.L. Pelham Papers, add. mss. 33103f. 249; Goddart to Pelham, n.d. March 1797, N.A. R.P.620/29/269.

rors, by February 1797 Sir George Fitzgerald Hill was ranging far and wide with his Londonderry Cavalry, arresting people he felt were leaders and arranging for informers. With these measures available, Hill could seize the initiative, confident of official approval. He asked Cooke to sanction the stretching of a point of law as the men, whom he intended to send to the fleet, were taken in a parish that was not proclaimed until *after* the arrests.[21] The point about informers is important. The successful establishment of a yeomanry corps functioned locally as an alternative power network to that of the United Irishmen, thus making the procurement of informers more feasible as permanent local protection could be provided.

However men like Hill and Knox may have been predisposed to 'activity', the evidence from the yeomanry's first six months of existence, shows that their effectiveness against insurgency was generally outweighed by problems. The difficulty of raising yeomanry in various parts of Ulster has been noted. In conjunction with governmental limitations on numbers and delays in supplying arms and equipment, this meant inadequate yeomanry coverage in the worst affected areas. In late November 1796, Thomas Knox told Pelham that 'from Dungannon to the northern ocean, with the exception of Stewartstown, there is not one corps likely to be raised'.[22] Following the Bantry scare, a programme of rapid augmentation began in tandem with military protection, to help gentlemen get their corps started and maximise recruitment. In central Ulster, General Knox was personally involved in helping to establish new corps which, in addition to freeing the regulars, he intended would stimulate those magistrates, previously overwhelmed by the United Irishmen, 'to oppose violence with violence'. Camden was optimistic that 'in the worst affected parts of the north ... I shall by degrees establish the yeomanry principle, so as even there to ensure domestic security without interference or awe of the troops'.[23] By mid-February, when financial considerations stopped further augmentation, around 10,000 yeomen had been added to the establishment.

Nevertheless, the United Irishmen remained dominant. Indeed, the Bantry Bay episode, rather than discouraging by its failure, seemed to increase their confidence further by providing proof of French commitment to the cause. Attacks on magistrates continued. In Donegal, Hamilton, a clerical magistrate active in organising yeomanry, was murdered at Raphoe. Disturbing reports came from other areas that United Irish strategy had changed to infiltration of the yeomanry. They either enlisted falsely, taking the yeomanry oath or, where this was impossible, exerted their local dominance to force existing yeomen to take the United 'oath of secrecy'. John Kincaid told Hill the majority of Donegal yeomen were either 'United *in toto*' or bound by the secrecy oath 'to save their families and property from ruin'.[24] Kincaid's

21 Hill to B[eresford], 7 Feb. 1796, N.A. R.P.620/28/230; Hill to Cooke, n.d.[Feb. 1797], 620/28/241. 22 27 Nov. 1796, N.A. R.P.620/26/83.   23 J. Knox to Pelham, 2 Jan 1797, N.A. R.P.620/28/13; Camden to Portland, 10 Jan. 1797, P.R.O. H.O.100/69/f. 66.   24 Rowley to Knox, 7 Mar. 1797, N.A. R.P.620/29/49; Kincaid to Hill, 4 Mar. 1797, 620/29/61.

report was exaggerated by panic following Hamilton's murder yet similar reports were so widespread they clearly had substance. Cavan, Fermanagh and Tyrone reported infiltration.[25] Even the Armagh Orangemen were not immune from the psychological pressure. An anonymous letter from Drumcree claimed that 'whole boddys [*sic*] of Orangemen are turned over to the United men' between Markethill and Newry and around Lisburn, 'for they could not withstand so many enemies'.[26] Some saw the problem in the yeomanry. The Newry magistrates complained to Lake about 'the defect in the Yeomanry Institution itself'. They claimed the yeomen were 'liable to no coercion except honour', were difficult to assemble, and in so doing advertised their intentions, that many could not afford to serve without pay and, as part-timers, were unavailable to follow-up any good they might do. The structure of the yeomanry as a force of civilians who were vulnerable to individual attack when not gathered as a body has been described as 'the weakness in the yeomanry'.[27]

There was undoubtedly a relationship between United Irish strength and yeomanry weakness. However, in this case one cannot blame the egg for producing the chicken: in reality the United Irishmen had a head start on those trying to organize loyalism. It was impossible to expect the yeomanry to tackle insurrectionary disorder in the first months of its existence. This period should be seen as transitional. Despite setbacks, the very fact some yeomanry corps were established in the United Irish districts of Ulster and remained in existence during this critical early period was in itself a significant contribution to law and order by giving a basic structure on which to build. The United Irishmen were well aware of this, and their attacks, for instance on the Stewartstown yeomen, were all the more ferocious because they were against the first breach in their monopoly of local power. This 'weakness in the yeomanry' reflected the wider truth, that the strength of the United system in Ulster had so far proved resilient to all government's efforts. Arrests provoked potato diggings and propaganda; the militia was infiltrated; the Defender alliance went on apace; and, despite Lake's efforts to protect magistrates and loyalists in the yeomanry, even the Insurrection Act was failing. Moreover, though Ulster remained the focus of disaffection, the United Irishmen had branched out from Dublin and were establishing their system in Leinster, particularly in counties recently disturbed by Defenderism. It is reckoned that by late April 1797, 16,000 of the United Irishmen's total strength of 128,000 were in counties Dublin, Louth, Meath, Westmeath and Kildare.[28] Despite increasing coercion, Lake and Knox, the northern generals daily facing the problem, knew that the thinking behind the government's measures was flawed. Treating the problem of insurgency within the framework of the civil law, even if that law was 'stretched' (to quote Sir George Hill), fatally mis-

---

25 Johnston to Pelham, 5 Mar 1797, N.A. R.P.620/29/23; Leith to Pelham, 21 Mar. 1797, 620/29/100. 26 21 March 1797, N.A. R.P.620/29/205. 27 Stoddart, op. cit., pp. 196–206. 28 Quoted in T. Graham, 'An Union of Power? The United Irish Organisation', Dickson, Keogh and Whelan (eds), *The United Irishmen*, p. 246.

diagnosed the problem. Lake complained to Pelham, 'United Irish terror has destroyed all ideas of exertion in most magistrates and gentry throughout the country'.[29] Lake and Knox believed they faced *de facto* war, which should be tackled accordingly under martial law. The Castle's response was a typical Camden fudge, trying to get something done yet dodging the potential political implications of an extreme measure. In March, Lake was given discretion to act independently of the magistrates if he felt the conditions justified him. While some districts were under *de facto* martial law and the generals others were still nominally under the civil law and the magistrates. This ambivalent approach revealed a crucial weakness in the yeomanry: its ambiguous, indeterminate status as an organization comprising civilian volunteers inheriting an expected civil role was now thrust into the realm of military policy and strategy in what has become notorious as the 'dragooning' of Ulster.

One of the first objectives was to search disturbed districts and take up arms. Given their local knowledge, yeomen were inevitably involved. Indeed, Knox intended to use yeomen exclusively. 'Having so few troops' he told Pelham, 'I must depend on the yeomanry.' He had other reasons too. In the atmosphere of wavering yeomanry and Orange loyalty, Knox planned to exploit the early Orange-yeomanry connection in his area. Telling Lake that he intended to 'scour' a district reportedly full of unregistered arms, he admitted the purpose was 'not so much with a hope to succeed to any extent, as to increase the animosity between the Orangemen and the United Irishmen. Upon that animosity depends the safety of the central counties of the north'. Knox thought in terms both of strategy and propaganda. The Orange district of central Ulster combined with the natural features of Lough Neagh and the Lower Bann river to form a line of defence against further United Irish westward expansion. The United Irishmen had disingenuously begun calling themselves 'Liberty Men', clearly feeling this would be more acceptable to the Orangemen, having echoes of the Glorious Revolution divested of any association with the Defenders.[30] By counteracting fraternization between the Orangemen and the United Irishmen, Knox could drive a wedge between areas of old and new United Irish strength in the north and ensure that Orangeism remained as a vigorous counter-revolutionary force. The use of yeomen was critical. With their Orange connections in this district, they would ensure that the 'right' guns were lifted, thus advertising the fact that the Orangemen now had official approval. This strategy linked with Knox's other moves to strengthen the extant connection between the Orange order and the yeomanry, by purging suspect yeomanry corps while encouraging Orange enlistment in others.

The first arms searches failed. Knox said it was bad planning to apply the proclamation in areas where there was insufficient force, yeomanry or otherwise, to im-

29 21 March 1797, B.L. Pelham Papers, add. mss. 33103/ff. 276–8. **30** 19 March 1797, B.L. Pelham Papers, add. mss. 33103 f. 263, Knox to Pelham, 11 March 1797, add. mss. 33013 ff. 256–6.

plement it and that only full martial law would work.[31] The United Irishmen were probably well informed and simply hid their arms or arranged the surrender of unserviceable weapons. Unfortunately statistics for weapons seizures in Knox's district do not survive, but Nugent's returns for Down and Antrim show that while these in no way reflected United Irish strength, given their relatively small numbers, yeomanry were at least effective as the fencibles who did most of the searching. At this time yeomanry were scarce in most parts of Antrim and Down, with the exception of clusters around Lisburn and Hillsborough. Yeomen from these areas searched their own districts and provided cover elsewhere. Nugent used yeomen from Lord Hertford's estate, virtually all Orangemen, for both the Killinchy and Ards sides of Strangford Lough, where 'native' yeomen were scarce. Hertford's yeomen then searched around Antrim while Downshire's men covered the Lurgan district.[32] The total of arms seized by 25 March was 3,303 muskets and 356 pistols, of which the Hillsborough yeomen had 88 guns and 2 pistols while those from Lisburn retrieved 250 guns and 27 pistols.[33] However these very moderate returns were more than cancelled out by a range of problems. For one thing, Knox's toleration of loyalist weapons was not implemented uniformly in other districts: at Omagh, Downpatrick and parts of Charlemont's Armagh estate, although yeomanry guns were immune, the arms of non-embodied loyalists were seized indiscriminately.[34] This was especially damaging at Omagh where, due to Abercorn's hostility, no corps existed and local loyalists had associated in a peacekeeping association in lieu of proper yeomanry.[35] Moreover, there were discipline problems. Knox had early accepted the strategic benefit of 'animosity', and the need to 'oppose violence with violence', but where the local man saw strategy, his English superior saw indiscipline. Yeomanry in arms searches were not under permanent duty and therefore not under proper military discipline. Technically they should have been accompanied by a magistrate, but, with the logistics of arms searches necessitating small detachments, this was not always possible. Lake noted that 'in some instances the yeomanry may have shown a dislike to their neighbours and been rather sharp'.[36] Despite differences in detail, both men agreed that the first disarming had failed and nothing short of full martial law would work. Accordingly, in May 1797 Lake received authority to issue a new proclamation demanding the surrender of unregistered arms, and authorized the generals to 'make war upon property until the surrender can be

---

31 Knox to Pelham, 4 April 1797, N.A. R.P.620/29/177; Knox to Pelham, 12 April 1797, K.A.O. Pratt Papers, U840/0164/1.   32 Nugent to Downshire, 11 March 1797, P.R.O.N.I. Downshire Papers, D607/E/173; Lake to Pelham, 13 March 1797, B.L. Pelham Papers, add. mss. 33103 ff. 220–1.   33 Returns, 15–25 Mar. 1797, B.L. Pelham Papers, add. mss. 33103 ff. 210–11, 227.   34 Lake to Knox, 20 March 1797, N.L.I. Lake Papers, MS56/f. 35; Lindsay to Pelham 27 March 1797, N.A. R.P.620/29/115.   35 Knox to Pelham, 19 March 1797, B.L. Pelham Papers, add. mss. 33103 f. 263.   36 Lake to Pelham, 17 March 1797, B.L. Pelham Papers, add. mss. 33103 ff. 240–1.

made'. Remembering the first attempt, Knox added grimly: 'arms may be hid, ring-leaders may conceal themselves but houses and barns cannot be removed'.[37]

This further policy change delegated still more power to the generals, sanctioned more arbitrary methods and inevitably drew the yeomanry further into in the darkening scenario. Before examining the yeomanry's role in this most radical measure to restore law and order, the wider context needs to be established. The backdrop to martial law is the see-saw battle between loyalism and the United Irishmen for the local dominance necessary to either implement or baulk the operation of the laws. The struggle had been going on since the establishment of yeomanry in 1796. The United Irishmen had recovered from the set-back to effect serious infiltration both of yeomanry corps and Orange societies but Knox's pro-Orange, anti-militia policy was counteracting this at the time of Lake's second proclamation. An explosion was inevitable in this torrid atmosphere, where unrealistic hopes and atavistic fears mingled. The heavy yeomanry involvement in martial law inexorably drew the flame and powder together in such conditions. The 'dislike of their neighbours' that Lake had noted in March blazed into uncontrollable aggression in some places. Henry Joy McCracken's brother John told him of yeomen in Armagh and Tyrone hanging suspects by the heels on a twisted rope and lashing them with belts.[38] The yeomen were not alone in their violence against suspected United Irishmen. Many army officers were prepared to turn a blind eye to the indiscriminate violence of their regulars and fencible troops if it resulted in a strengthening of loyalism.[39] The Newry yeomen, who had earlier inspired so little confidence in the magistrates, now competed with the Ancient Britons, a Welsh fencible regiment, in their ruthlessness towards the inhabitants of areas of presumed United Irish support. In county Armagh, Robert Livingstone, Charlemont's agent complained that Jonathan Seaver's Orior yeomanry, some Ancient Britons and 'a mob', wrecked and beat indescriminately on the estate and seized all arms, including those of Protestants who had registered them.[40] Around Keady, Lord Blayney complained that 'several self-created magistrates have sprung up ... and march about with parties of Orange yeomen levying contribution which if they [the local inhabitants] refuse to pay, threaten the burning of houses on the supposition of having concealed arms'.[41] As a liberal, Blayney naturally opposed such tactics but the 'counter-terror' was severe enough to cause some loyalist gentry to recoil. John Giffard, later a prominent Dublin Orangeman, commanded a detachment of Dublin militia in the Newry arms searches and was disgusted by the behaviour of the Britons and yeomen, who fired randomly at anyone they saw, reportedly killing between 10 and 20, burnt houses and took prisoners, all subsequently proved innocent.[42] In spring 1798 yeo-

---

37 Knox to Pelham, 28 May 1797, B.L. Pelham Papers, add. mss. 33013 f. 140.   38 26 July 1797, T.C.D. Madden Papers MS 873.   39 Stoddart, op. cit., p. 176.   40 Livingstone to Charlemont, 8 Nov. 1797, H.M.C. *Charlemont*, ii, pp. 310–11.   41 Blayney to Pelham, 20 Nov. 1797, N.A. R.P.620/33/71.
42 Quoted in Lecky, *Ireland*, iv, p. 41.

manry were used in disarming Dublin and disturbed southern counties. It seems some lessons had been learned. The corps were now under permanent duty and military discipline and apparently co-ordinated better with the military. In Dublin yeomanry were used exclusively to search houses while the military patrolled the streets during the search.[43] Yet the southern disarming was no less violent. Martial law was an horrific instrument to deal with a dangerous problem. The extent of the danger has recently been highlighted by Nancy Curtin who notes that, notwithstanding military repression, at least 27,000 United Irishmen turned out in the Ulster rising.[44]

The sad and sanguinary end-game of 'smothered rebellion' is not the entire story of the yeomanry's law and order role in this period. Inevitably the focus has been on the more lurid aspects which have fuelled the common perception of the yeomanry's role as one of gratuitous violence against ordinary people. However, though these operations did represent a centrally co-ordinated offensive, there was equally a *defensive* aspect to their duties. The protection of property and persons was the Yeomanry Act's first objective.[45] Concurrently with the first 1797 disarming, the yeomen were ordered onto 'piquet duty' for guards and night patrols simply to 'preserve the tranquillity of the neighbourhood and give immediate protection to any person whose security may be threatened'. There were problems with yeomen on protection duty but these were the discipline problems of civilians unused to the rigours of night duty rather than the uncontrolled ferocity of disarming raids. The success of these early protection duties, and the lack of reported violence when engaged on them, contrasts sharply with the performance on arms searches, though in neither duty were the yeomanry under the Mutiny Bill.[46] The reason concerns human nature more than military theory. The same yeomen who were self-disciplined and effective when defending their own property were often licentious when attacking the property of others.

Protection duty on its own did not make immediate inroads into the problem of 'smothered rebellion' where the United Irishmen were strong. Indeed, by its very nature it confirmed United Irish strength; in some areas yeomen on protection duty still needed the wider screen of army protection. Even Richardson admitted, 'if you are weak [in regulars] the yeomen are lost'.[47] However, this was to miss the point. The highly visible guards and patrols meant that the yeomen were establishing a tangible alternative presence, thus encouraging loyalism by demonstrating that an alternative party to the United Irish-Defender alliance could operate unmolested and be a foundation for future expansion. This was extremely important in the local context but the value of the yeomanry system in being able to provide this sort of

43 Camden to Portland, 22 May 1798, P.R.O. H.O.100/76/f. 246.   44 Curtin, op. cit., p. 277.   45 37 Geo. III, c.2 , section 1.   46 Nugent to Downshire, 23 March 1797, P.R.O.N.I. Downshire Papers, D607/E/220; Circular, 5 March 1797, Lurgan Yeomanry Detail Book, D3696/A/4/1.   47 Richardson to [?Pelham], 8 April 1797, John Wright, to Pelham, 10 Apr. 1797, N.A. R.P.620/29/200.

cover nationally, in what can be termed 'peacekeeping by presence' proved a crucial factor in maintaining law and order during invasion scares.

The campaign against the United Irishmen drew inexorably out of the realm of civil law towards its full military denouement. This process left indelible changes on the character of the law and order system in that it became much more militarised. This is not to say that magistrate's powers were removed, rather that local army commanders had what could best be termed an overseeing role, which arose out of necessity in the period before the rebellion, for example in the institution of military magistrates. The new organization of yeomanry into county brigades in 1798 further propelled the militarisation process. Yeomanry brigade majors had a remit to gather information and their inspection reports were combined with the district general's observations before being submitted to government. The 1797–8 period left a lasting imprint on the character of law and order. Emergency legislation and militarisation went hand-in-hand. The Insurrection Act was not repealed until 1802, but renewed again between 1807–10, 1818–18 and 1822–3. Habeas Corpus was suspended until 1802, then again between 1803–6 and in 1822, while martial law was reintroduced after Emmet's rising and remained in force till 1805.[48]

AGRARIAN COMBINATIONS

It would be both confusing, unhelpful and probably impossible to try to make an exhaustive analysis of the various combinations and their locations, in order to assess the role of the yeomanry in opposing them. This section will examine yeomanry use against the Connacht Threshers of 1806–7 and the various secret societies in Munster, mainly in counties Tipperary, Limerick and Cork over the period 1808–23 to convey an impression of an essentially impossible task.

Threshing was a form of economic protest in the 'agrarian' tradition, directed against tithes, priest's fees, wage rates and land prices.[49] Threshers forced farmers to take oaths binding them to 'reasonable' payments or prices. These 'rules' were enforced by acts of violence, such as flogging, thus imposing a alternative system of law based on locally orientated, custom-based notions of justice. In 1806, the Sligo magistrates noted that people were more afraid of breaking the Threshers' rules 'than the stated and common laws of the land'.[50] Threshing was non-sectarian, opposing priest's fees and Anglican tithe equally. In the eyes of the government, the Irish magistracy still suffered from the same weaknesses as it had in 1796, particularly 'supineness' and the tendency to let electoral politics or personal rivalries split the county bench into factions and so militate against the co-ordinated approach

48 *Parl. Debs.*, Second Series, ix, p. 1439.   49 S.J. Connolly, in *N.H.I.*, v, p. 17.   50 9 Oct. 1806, P.R.O. H.O.100/138/f. 236.

necessary in tackling combinations. Bedford's administration encouraged the magistrates to form traditional law and order associations, to raise rewards for information and organize patrols using their yeomanry. This happened in the badly affected Mayo baronies of Tyrawley and Tyreragh. Yeomanry formed a main plank in this scheme: captains were asked to call in all yeomanry arms to safe places, government was petitioned to put the corps on permanent duty, and in the interim this duty was paid from association funds. The association worked in co-operation with the district general, who decided which corps went on duty. This achieved some success: many Threshers were arrested and the 'lower orders' now seemed 'afraid of the law'. However General Rosslyn noted that close communal links and memories of 1798 made resistance so formidable that more regular troops were necessary.[51] Reports soon claimed the Threshers were regaining the initiative. Detachments of corps were used and, despite orders, it was impossible to prevent off-duty men taking their arms home, offering the Threshers an easy target. At Crossmolina, one yeoman, 'visited' for the second time, lied that his gun was in the guard house and provoked an attack which saw him and his family beaten until he surrendered his musket and ammunition. Even those on duty were failing. The brigade major's inspection revealed how the Threshers also used their nocturnal visits forcibly to gain advance knowledge to avoid the roads the corps were to patrol.[52]

It is difficult to define culpability in such cases, to deduce where sympathy ended and fear began. There were certainly grounds for fears of sympathetic collaboration: many rural yeomen were small tenant farmers, subject to similar economic pressures as the protesters. Yeomanry structure in western counties proved as problematic as its personnel. The isolation of non-embodied yeomen, plus the relatively low numbers and scattered locations of corps, militated against effectiveness. James Body, a private in the Mohill (Leitrim) yeomanry and an illiterate cottier, described armed men forcing him to swear 'to be true to Captain Thresher's laws' which he felt unable to resist given his isolated and unprotected location.[53] There is evidence of collaboration from other areas. The earl of Granard made the entire Longford yeomanry sign a test oath swearing they had not nor would not take the Thresher oath. In Mayo Denis Browne blamed the disturbances and the yeomen's untrustworthiness on the neglect of his fellow magistrates and warned against permanent duty as 'those of them who get one shilling a day were half of them the authors of this mischief'. This seemed to have some substance. In June 1807, two Swinford yeomen were put behind bars for allowing Thresher prisoners to escape from gaol.[54]

51 Association of the baronies of Tyrawley and Tyreragh, 16 Jan. 1806, P.R.O. H.O.100/135/f. 41; Rosslyn to Floyd, 5–6 Feb. 1806, H.O.100/135/ff. 42,46.   52 Battersby to Marsden, 12 Mar. 1806, P.R.O. H.O.100/138/f. 15; Bridgeham to Elliot, 27 Mar. 1806, H.O.100/138/f. 33.   53 Statement of James Body, 5 Oct. 1806, P.R.O. H.O.100/136/f. 103.   54 Granard to Bedford, 9 Dec. 1806, P.R.O. H.O.100/136/f. 280; Browne to Trail, 19 Sept. 1806, H.O.100/138/f. 48; Floyd to Wellesley, 18 June 1807, N.L.I. Kilmainham papers, MS1022.

Aside from the possibility of collaboration, despite the plans of government there was still the danger the yeomanry's utility could be compromised by gentry divisions. For one thing associations cost money and effort. Petitioning for the Insurrection Act, as some Sligo magistrates did in September 1806, would in practice mean the old expedient of calling in more troops.[55] In such cases it was not in the magistrate's interest to make too much use of yeomanry. Indeed, the Mayo magistrates tried to misuse the association to push for their preferred option of the Insurrection Act. Apparently the 1798 proclamation of the two baronies had not been formally revoked and the association tried to have it reintroduced. The government was livid, as it had encouraged the association as a means of making the magistrates carry out their responsibilities, as well as tackling the protesters. The alternative, allowing them to call for troops at will under the Insurrection Act, would, as Charles Kendal Bushe later described it, 'relieve the gentry of responsibility, and at the same time invest them with power'.[56] The government consulted the law officers to confirm that the Mayo magistrates could not effect a back-door proclamation, and the association limped on. Unseemly squabbles broke out over pay, while there were insufficient yeomen on duty to allow commanders to use them as static replacements for regulars to move to trouble spots.[57] Moreover, their use was further hampered by the government's need to keep down the costs of permanent duty. Even the scant yeomanry resource was therefore not applied to its best effect.

The local nature and local connections of the yeomanry force combined with government's competing financial and security interests to make the force at best an equivocal tool against the Threshers in the west. Clearly there was a correlation between the density of yeomen in an area and their ability to resist, let alone tackle, combinations. Figures are not available for Longford in 1806, but in December 1803 there were only 680 yeomen in the county. Sligo, another disturbed district, was not much better with 892, while the large and mountainy county of Mayo had only 1,140.[58] In 1805 Tyrone, which proved immune to the spread of Threshing, had 24 yeomanry corps, whereas Mayo and Sligo, the seat of the disturbances, had eight and seven respectively.[59]

Eventually, in December 1806, the government used the yeomanry system to better effect by putting whole county establishments on duty in the worst areas. The entire yeomanry of Cavan, Leitrim, Longford, Mayo, Roscommon, Sligo and Westmeath were put on duty, whereas in counties bordering on the Threshing area, Limerick and Fermanagh, detachments were put on duty for the winter to stop its spread.[60] By keeping the corps embodied, and under military command and disci-

55 Soden to Afflech, 22 Sept. 1806, P.R.O. H.O.100/138/f. 63.   56 Bushe to Sexton, 10 Sept. 1808, P.R.O. H.O.100/148/f. 352.   57 Trail to Elliot, 11 Oct. 1806, P.R.O. H.O.100/138/f. 189; General Vansittart to Col. Gordon, H.O.100/136/f. 213, 18 Nov. 1806.   58 *Parl. Papers*, H.C. [10] 1803–4, A return of all the Volunteer and Yeomanry corps, xi, pp. 65–100.   59 1805 Yeomanry List , N.L.I. ref. 355942.   60 Bedford to Spencer, 8 Dec. 1806, P.R.O. H.O.100/134/f. 368.

pline, a number of the previous weaknesses were automatically obviated. Gentry division and lack of co-ordination were avoided, as were the related problems of isolated residence and non-centralized arms holding. The civil authorities considered that generalized permanent duty for the yeomanry as a whole was the first really effective measure against the Threshers in 1806.[61] In reality the maintenance of law and order in disturbed districts was a military problem. Arthur Wellesley was less optimistic. Recognizing that the yeomanry's structural and manpower weaknesses coincided with the areas most under threat of disturbance, and realizing the force's effectiveness against combinations increased or lowered in ratio to its connection with the military, he warned that if invasion was added to stir the pot further, 'let those who think the loyal inhabitants and the yeomanry could keep down the rebels ... think what would happen if the troops were withdrawn'.[62] When the yeomanry of Sligo and Connemara were stood down in 1807 they were replaced by regulars.[63] The response to Threshing is therefore an example of the equivocal and paradoxical nature of yeomanry as a law and order force. They had the potential to exacerbate disturbances, either by joining in or providing a source for the protesters to arm themselves. Permanent duty made them more effective, but only worked with the assistance of troops in areas where the yeomen were numerically 'swamped', whereas in Ulster the numerical density of corps automatically stopped the progress of Threshing.[64] In one sense, the yeomen were most numerous where they were least needed. Yet by the same token, it could be argued that if sufficient yeomen were not there, such districts would quickly become disturbed. Wellesley's optimism was no higher in January 1808, when he punctured more unrealistic expectations about Ireland's law and order situation, telling the lord chancellor, 'I long for the time when I can say that any one law is obeyed ... when I shall witness that ... I shall believe we can carry into execution in Ireland the system of the British constitution ... without the aid of general officers and bayonets'.[65] He would have a long wait.

Soon afterwards, the next cycle of cycle of agrarian crime started in Limerick, which had been disturbed previously in 1801. The magistrates were again told to hold baronial meetings and form law and order associations. As a result, yeomanry patrols were started and lists of inhabitants complied for arms searches in disturbed areas. Despite this the disturbances continued and spread. In May 1808 the Kilkenny yeomanry brigade major reported few nights free of large gatherings of Whiteboys intending to commit outrages, but 'so secret are their proceedings as to evade the vigilance of either civil or military power'.[66] However the seat of the dis-

61 Bushe to Littlehales, 7 Sept. 1807, P.R.O. H.O.100/148/f. 360.   62 Wellesley to Hawkesbury, 7 May 1807, *W.S.D.*, v, pp. 28–36.   63 Memo, 21 Apr. 1807, Wellesley to Littlehales, 29 June 1807, *W.S.D.*, v, pp. 9, 98–9; McManus to Littlehales, 22 July 1807, N.L.I. Kilmainham Papers MS1022.   64 Harcourt to Littlehales, 20 Nov. 1806, P.R.O. H.O.100/136/f. 222.   65 Wellesley to [Manners], 14 Jan. 1808, S.U.L. Wellington Papers, WP1/189/74.   66 Ormsby to Wellesley, 1 May 1808, P.R.O. H.O.100/147/f. 168.

turbances was in Limerick and northern Kerry. As in Connacht, neither county had a particularly large yeomanry establishment. The nearest yeomanry returns to this period are for 1810. They show that Kerry had 17 yeomanry corps, with an effective total of 761 infantry privates and 95 cavalry, while Limerick had 23 corps, comprising 740 and 231 effectives respectively, though no less than nine of these were based in Limerick city.[67] When the limited numbers, scattered location and static nature of the yeomanry force is compared with the ability of localized combinations to mobilize large numbers of men unexpectedly and at will, the imbalance speaks for itself. The practical results were familiar. Those members of the Askeaton yeomanry living outside the village all had their arms stolen, a pattern repeated throughout Limerick and north Kerry, according to the district general.[68] Here too these structural weaknesses were compounded by the politics of law and order, with the yeomanry caught in the firing line in the battle between magistrates and central government over how best to tackle the problems. The Kerry brigade major, Daniel Mahony, totally overstepping his authority, took it upon himself to advocate the Insurrection Act, claiming that most magistrates were 'supine'.[69] Mahony's response is less surprising when it is considered that brigade majors visited all corps on permanent duty and could assess at first hand the deleterious effect of yeomen risking everything by doing duty in which some of their commanders had no heart. This is not to say all were inactive. Harding, the Limerick brigade major, admitted some did their best, seeking information on Whiteboys and following up with patrols; none the less, the outrages 'were not subsiding but increasing'.[70] The task was daunting even for the best magistrates. In Kerry Lieutenant-Colonel Godfrey, commanding the Milltown yeomanry, combined his military experience with zealous and fearless activity as a magistrate. Godfrey was exceptional enough to merit the high sheriff's praise to government for using his yeomen to suppress the local banditti in September 1808. Even so Godfrey's valiant attempts to restore order encapsulated and typified many of the elements of the problem. By November he could not function without military reinforcements, reluctantly admitting it was 'impossible that his corps, one of the most active and loyal in Kerry, could preserve the peace in so extensive a district'.[71] Meanwhile arms raids continued relentlessly. The 'state of the country' reports convey the distinct impression that permanent duty, so positive and effective when intelligence gave the authorities the initiative during invasion scares, was a negative measure in the current context, used more to protect the yeomen and their arms rather than to restore law and order. Harding spoke of yeomen on duty being allowed out to their farms during daylight to get the harvest in,

67 Abstract of inspection reports, 24 Mar. 1810, P.R.O. H.O.100/155/ff. 176–7; War Office list, (London, 1805). 68 Mahony to Lee, 25 Aug. 1808, P.R.O. H.O.100/148/ff. 245–6, Lee to Littlehales, 29 Aug. 1808, H.O.100/148/f. 259. 69 Mahony to Littlehales, 29 Aug. 1808, P.R.O. H.O.100/148/ff. 267–72. 70 Harding to Saxton, 9 Oct. 1808, Harding to Littlehales, 29 Oct. 1808, P.R.O. H.O.100/ 149/ff. 13–15, 50–2. 71 Judge Day to Littlehales, 14 Sept. 1808, 7 Nov. 1808, P.R.O. H.O.100/148/ff. 402–11, 149/ff. 101–03.

then hurrying back to the guard house in the evening.[72] In reality, they were under siege.

With Richmond determined against the Insurrection Act, the government's next initiative tacitly symbolized the yeomanry's severe limitations in acting against secret societies. Two 'proper persons' – Richard Willcocks and Edward Wilson – were sent down as 'Castle' magistrates to liaise with General Lee, who was concurrently reinforced with regulars, about taking out parties of troops 'to put the laws into execution'.[73] Yeomanry were not mentioned. The only link with the force was tenuous: Willcocks had once commanded a corps in county Dublin. Meanwhile, yeomanry in disturbed districts continued to prove a liability. In Tipperary and Waterford arms raids featured in another round of disturbances in 1809. Richmond asked the respective brigade majors to investigate, but his practical response was to direct the commander-of-the-forces to send in more regulars.[74] Peel's secretaryship saw outbreaks of 'Carding' in Westmeath, Roscommon, Waterford, Limerick, Tipperary, Kilkenny and King's county. By now there was a worrying tendency that growing awareness of the Catholic question, albeit crudely conceived locally, meant that traditional agrarian grievances were entangling with political and sectarian jealousies. From around 1813 Protestants were being singled out for attack and yeomanry arms raids featured even more.[75]

The problem of yeomanry arms deserves consideration at this stage, as it was an ever present, widespread dilemma which well illustrates, indeed epitomizes, the yeomanry's double-edged nature as a law and order force. Guns were a problem *per se*. Many government guns issued to the Volunteers ended up in private hands and eventually were turned against the laws they were meant to defend. There was also a political dimension. Despite Catholic relief measures in 1793, in the eyes of some conservative Protestants, the right to bear arms meant membership of the polity. The frequency of requests for yeomanry to lodge their arms centrally, and the lack of any statutory obligation compelling them to do so, mutely testifies that yeomen were very reluctant to part with their guns and that the voluntary nature of their service meant they could not be forced to part with them. The reasons varied, from simple personal protection to a desire for the status afforded by possession of a gun; indeed some may well have joined for the very purpose of obtaining firearms. From a law and order perspective, this could be self-defeating. The United Irishmen had raided for yeomanry weapons. Although by the early nineteenth century yeomanry arms raids were more a southern feature, their intensity should not be underestimated. In 1807 raids in Limerick were so frequent that the brigade major saw his main monthly task as establishing how many yeomanry arms were stolen since the

72 Harding to Littlehales, 29 Oct. 1808, P.R.O. H.O.100/149/ff. 13–15.   73 Littlehales to Jenkinson, Littlehales to Morrison, 20 Nov. 1808, P.R.O. H.O.100/149/ff. 136–7, 152–60.   74 Littlehales to Wellesley, 20 Jan. 1809, S.U.L. Wellington Papers, WP1/230/26.   75 Broeker, *Rural Disorder*, pp. 26–7.

last inspection.[76] The symbolic aspect was as important as the functional. To the extent that guns were seen as a status symbol by the yeomen, they were viewed as a symbolic prize as well as an asset by arms-raiders. At local level capture of a yeomanry musket could mark a symbolic victory over government and its laws, or a defeat for 'Ascendancy'. Where lack of numbers led to isolation, instead of being active agents of control, the yeomanry goaded disorder by unintentionally setting their weapons up as an achievable prize.

Peel aptly summarized the position in 1814, telling Littlehales, 'I think we may assume that the efficiency and good discipline of yeomanry corps will be in a great measure proportionate to their numerical strength'.[77] Faced with ongoing disturbances, Peel had by now introduced a new component to Irish peacekeeping: the Peace Preservation Force. This force of 'outrage specialists' was first introduced to the Tipperary barony of Middlethird in 1814 and, after early problems in efficiency and the fact that government expected them to be paid for by the local authorities as long as they remained in disturbed districts, had spread to thirteen counties and achieved success, in cases where they were backed by sufficient troops.[78] A comparison between the 'Peelers', as they became known, and the yeomanry will be made later; suffice it to say for now that yeomanry were delegated to a third-level peacekeeping force, behind the regulars and the new Peelers. However, the supply of troops was never equal to demand. The disturbances took place against a wider backdrop of the final stages of the European war, particularly the logistical convolutions occasioned by Napoleon's return from Elba, and subsequently the severe postwar retrenchment in all military establishments, including yeomanry. In these circumstances, and despite Peel's negative opinion, yeomanry corps in disturbed southern areas were again drawn in to the struggle with the secret societies, often merely as a holding measure in default of regulars or Peelers. The old problems recurred. Where the yeomanry were weak they were vulnerable; where they were Catholic they were suspect – Peel spoke ironically of 'Captain Carder's Tipperary Yeomanry';[79] and, in the few areas where they were strong, they were dangerous. The Limerick city yeomen were accused of using yeomanry duty as a pretext for involvement in what amounted to sectarian outrages, so much so that they could not be considered for duty in disturbed areas of the outlying country except 'under the most imperious circumstances'.[80]

The next major wave of disturbances further amalgamated traditional Whiteboy grievances and crude sectarian politics. The Ribbonmen, a lower-class Catholic self-defence secret society similar to the Defenders, which started in Ulster in 1810, had

76 Harding to Littlehales, 29 Sept. 1807, P.R.O. H.O.100/142/f. 340.   77 5 July 1814, B.L. Peel Papers, add. mss. 40287 f. 66.   78 For a full discussion of the P.P.F. see Broeker, *Rural Disorder*, chaps 4–6 and Palmer, *Police and Protest*, chap. 6.   79 Peel to Littlehales, 30 April 1815, B.L. Peel Papers, add. mss. 40288 ff. 214–15.   80 General Meryick to Littlehales, 4 Nov. 1815, P.R.O. H.O.100/187/ff. 200–02; Broeker, *Rural Disorder*, p. 84.

spread south and west, along the old Defender routes, from around 1819 and en-
meshed itself with the Rockites, the latest southern combination. The Rockite disturbances of 1821–4 were widespread, affecting all three southern provinces at some
level.[81] The same weaknesses in the yeomanry, of structure and numbers, were now
compounded by post-war reductions. Troop numbers were low. Only 17,000 were
voted for Ireland in 1819 while the Peelers stood at around 1,000.[82] The following
year the yeomanry totaled 31,000 the vast majority, well over 20,000 were in Ulster.
As the southern yeomanry diminished its problems multiplied, yet the static nature
of the force as a whole meant that its full potential could not be realised. In 1821 the
Tarbert yeomanry and the three Palatine corps, put on duty in a badly disturbed
district, only involved around 300 men.[83] Another aspect of the logic of yeomanry
reductions in the south was that Protestant corps were more likely to be retained. In
October 1821 Warburton, a 'police' magistrate sent to Kerry, recommended the
arms of a corps at Ballylongford, believed to be Rockite sympathisers, be confiscated and redistributed to a 'loyal' corps at Tarbert.[84] In Limerick this policy included the encouragement of yeomanry corps formed from Palatine villages. Palatines were originally German Protestants deliberately settled by improving landlords in the early eighteenth century.[85] They maintained their ethnic and cultural
distinctiveness, which Warburton saw as a security advantage as it set them apart
from the rest of the populace. They were, he claimed 'an insulated people and equally
to be depended upon as the best troops'.[86] This policy of exclusion mirrored the
sectarianism of the southern peasantry. Recent research has highlighted the
millenarianism in the Rockite movement, particularly deriving from 'Pastorini's'
prophecies, which predicted the overthrow of Protestantism in the year 1825.[87] Protestants were targeted by the Rockites, and the Palatine yeomanry were accorded
special attention. It was a two-way process: the yeomen and protesters reacted against
each other, making the force more of a hindrance than a help in preserving law and
order. Charles Grant, the chief secretary, noted that 'it cannot be denied that the
employment of them (the yeomanry) has a tendency to excite irritation, to give the
whole business the appearance of an array of Orangemen against Catholics'.[88] The
increasing tempo of the Rockite disturbances is reflected in the ferocity of their
attacks on the Palatines. In addition to the usual yeomanry arms raids, in 1823 they
burnt an entire Palatine village, Glenasheen.[89] It is a caution against simplistic interpretations of Irish history to note that this was an almost exact parallel to the actions
of some northern yeomen and others in Lake's disarming of Ulster in 1797. Yeo-

81 J.S. Donnelly Jnr, 'Pastorini and Captain Rock' in Clark and Donnelly (eds), *Irish Peasants and
Political Unrest*, pp. 102–39.   82 Broeker, *Rural Disorder*, pp. 107, 116.   83 Talbot to Sidmouth, 22
Oct. 1821, P.R.O. H.O.100/121/f. 134.   84 Warburton to Gregory, 7 Oct. 1821, P.R.O. H.O.100/200/
ff. 7–8.   85 Lecky, *Ireland*, i, p. 351.   86 Warburton to Gregory, 15 Oct. 1821, P.R.O. H.O.100/201/ff.
11–13.   87 Donnelly, op. cit., p. 112.   88 Grant to Sidmouth, 19 Nov. 1821, P.R.O. H.O.100/202/ff.
114–17.   89 Donnelly, op. cit., p. 129.

manry, never a good instrument against the southern secret societies, increasingly became part of the problem rather than part of the answer. Only in Ulster were there sufficient numbers of yeomen to make an impact on internal disorder, yet there they were needed least. Despite efforts to make the force more mobile, weighty factors made yeomanry mobility problematic. For one thing, yeomen were civilian residents, with families and occupations; for another, there was concern, and a division of official opinion, about the political impact of using northern yeomen in the south. Sidmouth, the home secretary, was in favour, as he had long been opposed to complete reliance on the army, but Talbot, the viceroy, and particularly Grant were opposed. In the event, around 1,000 Ulster yeomen were called out, not to move themselves, but to free regulars for southern service, and moves were made to reactivate some of the Dublin corps. The replacement of Talbot with the marquis of Wellesley in December 1821 saw the abandonment of even this limited role for the yeomanry, which remained moribund till 1831, when it was briefly and bloodily revived and rearmed by Anglesey's administration for use in the 'tithe war'.[90] This short-lived renaissance signalled the beginning of the end for the force, as predictable clashes occurred between members of a self-evidently Protestant force, perceived as representing as well as defending property, and those protesting against a form of property right. The most notorious was in Newtownbarry, county Wexford when a magistrate called for yeomanry assistance against a mob trying to rescue cattle distrained for tithe. All the ingredients for trouble were present; indeed one of the magistrates involved was agent for the prominent Orangeman, Lord Farnham. Although 40 county constabulary were also involved, the mob, reportedly of 2,000, focused their attack on the yeomen. The outcome was that fourteen of the mob, one yeoman and the son of another were killed.[91]

This introduces a point about yeomanry doing police duty in general. They were not good at dealing with crowds. Nothing in their training could prepare them for the tension which could build up on such occasions. This was a perennial problem going right back their first experience of United Irish 'potato settings'. In May 1797 Alexander Ker, a magistrate of Newbliss in county Monaghan, faced around 300 diggers with his mounted yeomanry and ordered them to disperse. They refused. Ker fired his pistol over their heads, sparking a melee in which his yeomen killed six unarmed men.[92] In the nineteenth century sectarian polarization ensured the same intense feelings on both sides, and a high risk of panic reactions. Even apparently innocent occupations like sports were held to be, and sometimes were, a cover for demonstrations of political or religious strength.[93] In 1804 some Dublin yeomanry

90 Sidmouth to Grant, 28 Nov. 1818, P.R.O. H.O.100/195/ff. 272–4; Broeker, *Rural Disorder*, pp. 122, 209.   91 *Parl. Debs.*, Third Series, iv, p. 1178; Anglesey to Stanley, 23 June 1831, P.R.O.N.I. Anglesey Papers, D619/31J/38; Palmer, *Police and Protest*, p. 328.   92 Ker to [?Pelham], 22 May 1797, N.A. S.O.C.1016/40.   93 Bartlett, *Fall and Rise*, pp. 313–14.

accompanied by a magistrate 'routed' a large crowd which had gathered at Rathmines to play football and hurling, and arrested 54 men, believing it to have been a ploy by the disaffected to show their numbers. There was the ever-present danger of over-reaction through mis-interpretation. A classic example happened at Rathdowney fair, Queen's County in 1807. What Lord Norbury described as the usual 'country clans' came to 'settle scores'. Whereas in the past the magistrates might well have been content to let them fight it out, the local magistrate, Prior, intervened, panicked, called out his yeomen armed with ball cartridge, and, after unsuccessfully trying to negotiate, ordered them to fire, killing five people.[94]

It should however be noted that yeomen were not alone in having problems in dealing with crowds. Though Anglesey considered the constabulary at Newtownbarry 'exempt from blame', a similar but less well-publicised incident occurred at Castlepollard, county Westmeath where the police were attacked after arresting a man at a fair and opened fire, killing seven. In this incident the magistrates had been content to use police, and only called out the yeomanry *after* the riot.[95] There is also evidence that the presence of yeomen in numbers discouraged the formation of crowds. Surveying Tyrone in 1814, William Shaw Mason noted that 'since the institution of the yeomanry it (hurling) has been seldom practiced. Cock-fighting also is nearly out of use'.[96] There was however one law-enforcement duty when the yeomen could not be relied on to take the side of the authorities against the popular will of the people: the revenue laws.

YEOMANRY AND THE REVENUE

As 'Threshing' showed, where lawbreaking was neither political nor sectarian and the yeomen's interests overlapped with those of the lawbreakers, their support of the laws could not be assumed. As in Britain, it was common for military detachments to help enforce the revenue and excise laws. Theoretically this 'peacekeeping' role should have devolved on the yeomanry, and there is some evidence that they could do it successfully. Foster Archer, the inspector general of prisons, touring Connemara in 1806, had one of his local guides shot dead by yeomen who caught him smuggling.[97] However, there is much more evidence that yeomen were frequently involved in *contraventions* of the revenue laws, ranging from passive acquiescence in smuggling and illicit distillation to active and violent participation in both.

The problem was so bad that the government had to act. In 1801 General Barnett

94 Nepean to King, 27 Feb. 1804, P.R.O. H.O.100/124/f. 74; Norbury to Littlehales, 13, 24 July 1807, H.O.100/141/ff. 354, 394.   95 Thompson to Stanley, 24 May 1831, P.R.O. H.O.100/238/ff. 221-2.
96 Mason, *A Statistical or Parochial Survey of Ireland*, p. 124.   97 Archer to Trail, 5 Oct. 1806, P.R.O. H.O.100/138/f. 162.

complained to Littlehales that, around Mullingar, 'I have every reason to believe that it [illegal distillation] is countenanced by many of the most respectable yeomanry'. The following year Wickham recommended that regular soldiers should tackle illegal distillation, as 'it has been found from experience that yeomanry will not do for this service'.[98] Wickham's caution was well grounded. In 1806, members of the Dromahair, county Leitrim, yeomanry were berated by the local army commander, General Afflech, for operating what would today be called a 'protection racket'. Dromahair was ideal for poteen-making and marketing, being near a wild, mountainous and sparsely populated district. The experiment of attaching revenue officials to the corps as yeomanry officers was tried. However things went badly wrong, as the gamekeepers soon became poachers and began operating a 'system' whereby poteen-makers were allowed immunity from the laws in return for protection money, reportedly £2,000 – a vast amount in contemporary terms. Reading between the lines, it is likely the revenue men directed the operation and the yeomen used their arms to enforce it. 'Every kind of outrage' was allegedly committed by them but all attempts at getting information met a conspiracy of silence from the locals. Warrants issued against certain yeomen were not executed due to 'the partiality or negligence of the constable'.[99] The Dromahair case cautions against automatically assuming a sectarian or political context to all disorder. Four years later, at nearby Drumkeerin, a revenue officer complained to Palmer, the magistrate and local yeomanry captain, that he could not do his duty without military protection. Palmer ordered his yeomen to parade at Drumkeerin fair but 'without any sort of provocation' they were 'cut, beat and battered' by a mob of over 500. It would be easy to assume a yeomanry redcoat being the usual red rag to the Catholic peasantry. However, the Dromahair precedent and the fact that a revenue officer was obstructed in his duty makes it far more likely the indignation against the Drumkeerin yeomen was based on expectations that they would take the stance of the Dromahair men on distillation.[100] There is also evidence that yeomen ran stills themselves. In 1815 General Hewitt accused some Antrim yeomen of using 'the arms placed in their hands by government for the maintenance of order and the laws, for the very purpose of defending their own illegal and most mischievous practice' and for attacking revenue officers. According to Hewitt, this licentiousness was part of a wider problem, with yeomen at the cutting edge of protests on a range of economic issues. He claimed 'the yeomanry in arms naturally insulted and drove from Antrim the collected bench of magistrates, assembled for the purpose of addressing parliament on the Corn Bill' and that this was linked to protests about grain prices and demands for rent reduction. The situation was serious enough for troops to be summoned to 'protect the magistrates from the violence of our armed yeomanry'.[101]

98 2 Feb. 1801, P.R.O. H.O.100/103/f. 49; Wickham to Addington, 18 Sept. 1802, H.R.O. Wickham Papers, 38M49/1/46/21. 99 Afflech to Adjutant General, 15 June 1806, P.R.O. H.O.100/138/f. 17. 100 Stewart to Marshall, 29 June 1810, P.R.O. H.O.100/159/ff. 881–2. 101 Hewitt to Peel, 21 Mar.

Violence and contempt for authority feature in many of these incidents. Revenue officers seized a quantity of malt near Dundalk in June 1808 and were transporting it to poundage with a detachment of the Scots Greys when they were ambushed and fired on by a party of men who retrieved the malt. Of the six men arrested, five were members of a local yeomanry corps. At times such activity by yeomen was quite overt. The Wexford brigade major investigated reports that regulars detachments assisting an excise officer had been shot at by men in yeomanry jackets. This indicates considerable degrees of local connivance both within and without the corps. Being in uniform, the men were either going to or coming from parade or duty, implying both the tacit consent of their colleagues and complete confidence that local people would not betray them. Moreover, even if yeomen themselves were not personally involved, the practice of keeping arms at home meant that other members of the same community could easily utilize them illegally. In two related incidents at Portglenone, county Antrim, an 'active gauger' was shot at doing his duty and a water keeper murdered. As a principal crossing on the lower river Bann, Portglenone was an obvious transit point for contraband, and also a centre for salmon poaching. The bishop of Down was a major local landowner and strongly suspected that the muskets of an inactive supplementary yeomanry corps were used in both attacks.[102]

Such issues of local lawbreaking must be seen in context. They were certainly anti-authoritarian but not necessarily against local authority figures. In many English coastal districts it was common for gentry and their tenants to connive at smuggling. Not surprisingly, the sources are usually silent on the subject of gentry connivance. A more important feature however is that the yeomen themselves probably felt they were not breaking the law in these disputes. Indeed the dichotomy between law-breaking and law-enforcing can be anachronistic in a context in which conceptions of local 'custom' were strong. Traditional usage operating to the benefit of the majority of the local community could constitute an alternative system of local 'law' to be defended against central or outside interference and internal treachery. In north Armagh, local yeomen were central to a dispute in 1808 which, had it occurred in Munster, would have been considered Whiteboyism in its purest form.

William McNamara, an absentee landlord, had sold off large parcels of his estate in the townlands of Bleary and Ballynagarrick 'over the heads' of the current occupiers, causing wider concerns about lease renewals and turbary rights on the bog of Clare, an area with a tradition of agrarian protest going back to the Steelboys. The intrusion was seen by the entire community as an assault on long-standing local custom. Local yeomen, all of whom were also Orangemen, were joined by the few Catholic residents in a series of attacks on the new occupiers. Houses were shot up,

1815, B.L. Peel Papers, add. mss. 40244 ff. 184–9; Hewitt to Whitworth, 22 June 1815, P.R.O. W.O.30/ 79/ff. 23–30.   102 Lambert to Wellesley, 26 June 1808, P.R.O. H.O.100/147/f. 240; Brigade major's report, Nov. 1816, H.O.100/191/f. 299; Bishop of Down to Saxton, 3 Jan. 1811, H.O.100/163/f. 6.

a mill dam smashed and anonymous notices under fictitious names sent to would-be purchasers. Anyone cutting turf under the new terms was similarly threatened and effigies of two of the main hate-figures were 'hung' on the public road with Cromwellian theatricality, bearing labels marked: 'Behold the heads of the traitors Bell and McMurran'.[103] The participation of Catholics in this incident is interesting, especially as it was in a part of Armagh which had suffered from sectarian disputes, and foreshadows a similar movement in 1829–30 when, during food shortages, Protestants, including yeomen and Orangemen, and Catholics came together in west Down and north Armagh in a curiously named faction called 'Tommy Downshire's Boys' under the slogan 'half-rent and no tithe'. Here too the yeomen were prominent, in shooting up and wrecking a barge on the Bann canal which was taking away potatoes for export. An amalgamated orange and green flag was hoisted at Shane's Hill between Lurgan and Portadown, and the local magistrate, Handcock, feared sending his yeomanry against them in case they joined in.[104] This 'ecumenical' incident was perhaps the exception that proved the rule. Handcock had continual difficulties in controlling the Lurgan yeomen due to their Orange leanings; indeed his liberal Protestant views earned him the nickname 'Papist' Handcock. As the initial gentry involvement with Orangeism was intended to control loyalism as much as counteract insurgency, Handcock's experience invites the question, did the yeomanry generally facilitate this control and therefore contribute to law and order by removing some of the components of disorder?

CONTROL OF LOYALISTS

As events in county Armagh had demonstrated, loyalists could represent as big a threat to law and order as the southern agrarian combinations. Obviously control of loyalism was never spelt out as an objective of the yeomanry, yet when one examines the way the force was organised, this hidden aspect of control becomes plain. Even at the planning stage Camden thought in terms of dual control, wanting to oppose the United Irishmen yet at the same time to ensure that the threatened loyalists' natural tendency to form defence groups was harnessed and put under government control and pay. The same tacit principle applied after formation. In 1797 Richardson claimed that the law-abiding Orangemen had stopped meeting as such and joined the new yeomanry, while the more unruly elements continued their banditry as usual.[105] Richardson's claims about Orangemen not meeting were absurd – he was

---

103 Littlehales to Johnston, 16 Aug. 1808; Memorial of Richard McNamara to the Assize Judges, 18 Aug. 1808; Sexton to Beckett, 7 Sept. 1808, P.R.O. H.O.100/148/ff. 33–55, 105, 315–16.   104 Chief Constable Patton to Gregory, 6 May 1829, P.R.O. H.O.100/226/ff. 331–2; *Parl. Papers*, HC 1835 [476] Select Committee on Orange Lodges, xvii, p. 184 and appx.   105 Richardson to Abercorn, 22 Feb. 1797, P.R.O.N.I. Abercorn Papers, T2541/1B3/6/5.

trying to persuade Abercorn to support the yeomanry wholeheartedly, yet his point about control was accurate. By joining a yeomanry corps, men bound themselves by ties of honour, reputation and deference to the local gentry, and by oath, arms and pay to central government and ultimately the King. By including some who would otherwise form irregular combinations, yeomanry added significant weight to the scales against disorder. The toleration of Orange enrollment after 1797 accelerated this process. General Knox told Abercorn, 'I have found it necessary to encourage that party', but 'they are inclined to be licentious and it requires much difficulty to keep them within bounds'.[106] The scales may not have risen to the level where the law had full control but neither did they plummet to anarchy. Rebellion involved a faction; anarchy involved all factions.

It is better to see yeomanry as a brake which gave sufficient control over popular loyalism rather than stopping its impetus altogether. Inevitably the balance between latitude and licentiousness worked itself out locally. Thomas Lane told Downshire that his yeomen refused to serve under the district general and wanted their own officers: 'I do not know how the general may like it, my lord, but they are Kilwarlin Boys, and though most truly attached to your lordship and very loyal, yet somewhat ungovernable at times'.[107] Sufficient momentum was necessary for the yeomen to be effective, yet if the brake was inadequate yeomanry contributed to the problem rather than ameliorated it. Hardwicke succinctly summed up the danger to Wickham, when yeomanry disbandment was considered in 1802: 'some of the individuals who are now in their embodied state, preservers of the peace of the country, may hereafter become disturbers of the public tranquillity'.[108] It was a delicate balance for turbulent times. Too little control, and loyalists were a threat; yet to be useful, they needed to be under some degree of threat themselves. Castlereagh believed that yeomanry were best at 'police' work when they felt themselves to be under threat.[109] This balance could not be taken for granted, as unpredictable combinations of circumstances could upset it. When yeomen felt their own interests or those of their community to be threatened, and especially when this coincided with their being in no direct physical danger themselves, they could prove agents of disorder rather than control. This was a perennial problem. At Stewartstown, county Tyrone, on 12 July 1797 local yeomen wearing orange ribbons, and Scottish fencibles became involved in a riot with Catholic Kerry militiamen, in which twelve people were killed.[110] In the early nineteenth century the practice of drilling several local corps together could lead to problems. In 1810 one such inspection ended in a near-riot when men from the Ban Infantry refused to be inspected with the Scarva Infantry, since the latter included six Catholics. As both parties were armed, Brigade-Major Wallace

106 11 May 1797, P.R.O.N.I. Abercorn Papers, D623/A/156/14.   107 23 June 1799, P.R.O.N.I. Downshire Papers, D607/G/179A.   108 7 April 1802, B.L. Hardwicke Papers, add. mss. 35771.   109 Castlereagh to Wellesley, 28 Dec. 1807, *W.S.D.*, v, pp. 279-83.   110 Camden to Portland, 17 July 1797, P.R.O. H.O.100/72/f. 109.

averted a potentially explosive situation by deciding to inspect both corps on separate fields. When the Armagh yeomanry were disbanded in 1812 following a virtual mutiny over their lieutenant signing an emancipation petition, the district general noted that there had been similar misconduct among various other corps in the area.[111] In the tense atmosphere following the granting of emancipation there was trouble from the Lurgan yeomanry. One yeoman was arrested by his own captain, Handcock, for leading a riotous mob and yelling at the police: 'we have plenty of arms and ammunition and can use them as well as you'. This was true. The permanent sergeant, an Orangeman, had been giving out yeomanry arms to nominal members of the corps who had never formally enrolled.[112]

Although these examples certainly qualify the thesis that the yeomanry helped control lower-class loyalism, it should not be assumed they were typical. The very fact that they entered the official correspondence argues their exceptional nature. Given the sectarian problems of Armagh immediately before yeomanry formation, and considering the threats to established order in the 1796-8 period, it must be said that yeomanry were generally successful in controlling and harnessing loyalism in this critical early period. Moreover the scenario of the military guardians of the law occasionally presenting a challenge to public order themselves, was certainly not peculiar to Ireland. British volunteers joined food rioters on more than one occasion.[113] Considering the ease with which all types of military force, especially wartime levies, slipped into disorder, and the passions aroused in a period roughly circumscribed by the 1798 rebellion and Catholic emancipation, it can only be concluded that yeomanry contained militant loyalism fairly successfully. They helped to direct this power towards the interests of law and order, yet still left the opportunity to defend local property and sectional interests. Without it, many of the weavers and tenant farmers who filled their ranks would have defended their interests in ways which would have exceeded the normal operation of law far more than the disarming campaigns of 1797. Such actions, given the tinder-box condition of Ulster in these years would have resulted in complete anarchy, with the government and its generals helpless spectators. It would be overstating the case to say that yeomanry alone achieved this. It operated in consort with other related phenomena such as the gentry influence in Orangeism. Yet the fact remains that when Catholic emancipation passed in 1829 there were approximately 25,000 armed yeomen in Ulster, many with their arms kept at home, and, despite threats, not one of these muskets was raised in response.

Was this generally positive effect overbalanced by the negative impact the yeomanry had in changing attitudes to the laws among lower-class Catholics? Yeomanry

111 *Parl. Papers*, H.C. [474], xvii, Report of the Select Committee on Orange Lodges, p. 184; (ibid.) [475], xv, appx. p. 80.   112 Handcock to Power, 31 Dec. 1830, Lurgan Yeomanry Detail Book, P.R.O.N.I. D3696/A/4/1; *Parl. Papers*, H.C. [184], op. cit. xvi, pp. 184-5.   113 C. Emsley, 'The Military and Popular Disorder', pp. 105-6.

got off to a bad start in this respect. Their formation coincided with the wartime shelving of reform and emancipation and the concurrent introduction of waves of emergency legislation. By its largely Protestant composition and increasing Orange connections, the yeomanry was inevitably an agent of change in popular Catholic attitudes to the law. The first real contact yeomanry had with the population at large was in implementing the Insurrection Act which was first activated on 24 October 1796, just days after the Yeomanry Bill had become law and habeas corpus been suspended.[114]

The identification with emergency legislation deepened when the yeomanry went into service. One of the first things they did in central Ulster was to assist in the new proactive policy. The involvement of the yeomanry in disarming Ulster in 1797 further cemented their association with emergency legislation. The yeomanry were placed in an uncomfortable and ill-defined position. In their oath they had sworn to 'support and maintain the laws and constitution of this kingdom'.[115] This meant the ordinary criminal code of laws to protect property and public order as well emergency measures. In short, their association with coercion meant that an odour of constitutional ambiguity lingered about them and never fully cleared, though some argued they were very constitutional. Charlemont took the old line, that they were volunteer citizens arming to defend their country. His whiggish mind could separate his yeomen from men and measures which he found abhorrent. Not all were able to make the distinction. Grattan publicly branded Lake's disarming as illegal and unconstitutional.[116] The experiences of 1798 strengthened the association with coercion. The Rebellion Bill allowed rebels to be tried before martial law courts.[117] Yeomen could bring prisoners before the courts and also sit in judgment on them. After Emmet's rising a complete call-out of yeomanry was the inevitable follow-up to the re-suspension of habeas corpus and the re-introduction of martial law.[118] In many respects the association with coercion is an accident of history. The 1782 Volunteers also dealt with law and order as they found it, yet they are seen as defenders of a 'constitution' endangered by exploitative government.

To the majority of Irish people the tangible effects of the yeomanry engaged in the execution of the laws had more of an impact on their lives, thoughts and attitudes than the legal niceties. The typical countryman's first reaction to the presence of yeomanry would have been to assume that law enforcement had taken on a new dimension. This would not have been visually unfamiliar to those who remembered the Volunteers. Moreover the red coats of regulars and militia were a common sight. However, the introduction of yeomanry did mark a break with more recent practice

---

114 Camillus [pseud. Sir R. Musgrave], 'To the magistrates, military and yeomanry of Ireland', L.H.L. N8517.   115 37 Geo. III c.2, section 9.   116 Charlemont to Haliday, 12 Sept. 1796, Haliday to Charlemont, 30 Sept. 1796, H.M.C. *Charlemont*, ii, pp. 283–5; Camden to Portland, 21 March 1797, P.R.O. H.O.100/69/f. 162.   117 39 Geo. III c.11.   118 Hardwicke to Yorke, 29 July 1803, B.L. Hardwicke Papers, add. mss. 35702.

insofar as *local* men were concerned. Before yeomanry were established in his part of Down, Captain Robert Waddell, faced with Orange wrecking, spreading from Armagh, resorted to the only means available to protect his district. He embodied 'a body of decent people ... who should act as a *posse comitatus*'.[119] They consisted of about sixty men whom he made temporary constables, and who took turns at mounting nightly guards of ten until things quietened. These would have seemed very much the same as the fifty men gathered by a neighbouring magistrate, Richard Johnston, against the Steelboys in the 1770s.[120] Yet in 1797, if a magistrate wanted to mount a guard, and there were yeomanry available, they were put on piquet duty for the purpose. Though still under the local control of the magistrates, they ultimately answered to the War Office, received regular army pay, and presented a much more martial appearance with their muskets, uniforms and officers. By the early nineteenth century such piquet guards would normally occur under permanent duty and full military discipline. In these respects the yeomanry were quite different from the old Volunteers and their impact must have been to highlight the militarisation of local law enforcement. The *posse comitatus* reverted to being ordinary citizens again when the trouble was over, but the yeomen, as their weekly parades emphasised, were always the yeomen. One argument advanced for Ireland's relative stability in the earlier eighteenth century was the flexible local implementation of the laws.[121] Admittedly, the disorders of the 1790s made this impossible and necessitated stronger, less *ad hoc* law enforcement. Nevertheless, the changes in yeomanry control added momentum to the militarisation of Irish law enforcement, a point confirmed by the paramilitary nature of the Peace Preservation Force.[122] The critical point is that all disturbances were now being dealt with by some form of 'soldiers' and as these represented the state both in its central and local aspects the political context of disorder was increased.

Attitudes are difficult to correlate with written evidence, because they are often either implicit in what is written, or shared by the correspondents and consequently not made explicit. The historian trying to trace the development of separatist nationalism in the nineteenth century must assess attitudes to the laws held by that level of society whose attitudes are most hard to detect, those who did not or could not correspond in writing. The impact of the yeomanry on this level of society is difficult to adduce by standard evidential techniques. However, by contrasting yeomanry law enforcement duties with earlier attitudes towards the law amongst rural Catholics, an informed speculation about likely turning points can be made.

Mid-Ulster may not be typical of the north, and much less of the whole of Ireland, because of its peculiar denominational mix, its rural industry, burgeoning

119 Waddell to [Pelham], 8 Nov. 1796, N.A. R.P.620/26/27.   120 Beames, *Peasants and Power*, p. 154. 121 S.J. Connolly, 'Albion's Fatal Twigs: Justice and Law in the Eighteenth Century', in R. Mitchison and P. Roebuck (eds), *Economy and Society in Scotland and Ireland, 1500–1939*, passim.   122 Beames, op. cit., p. 158.

population and troubled sectarian background. However this exceptionality is useful, as it forces ordinary peoples' attitudes to the law into the correspondence of the controllers and governors. Although the Defenders swore: 'The French Defenders will support the cause; the Irish Defenders will pull down British Laws', there is clear evidence of a considerable measure of respect for the laws among lower-class Catholics.[123] When local government in the form of the Armagh magistrates failed the Catholics, they had no hesitation in seeking protection from General Dalrymple, the nearest representative of central government. Such attitudes were already under pressure before the yeomanry appeared. In August 1796 Mark Devlin, a Tyrone Catholic, admitted, 'I tremble for the fate of my country, but especially for that of loyal Catholics in this country, between the unrestrained persecution of the Orangemen, and that of the union men, where are they to find shelter'.[124] Evidently, in parts of Tyrone, at any rate, some still thought they could find it in the protection of the laws, and the local defence group which would soon be incorporated into the yeomanry. The following month W.C. Lindsay, a magistrate in Charlemont's interest, told Cooke that 'the Roman Catholics, at least in my neighbourhood, are satisfied to receive protection from a Protestant Loyal Association, provided the gentlemen of property are at their head'.[125]

Obviously, despite the sectarian disorders and the apparent inability of some magistrates and Armagh grand jurors to stop the Orangemen, this did not automatically mean an antagonistic attitude to the law. The modification of such attitudes, positive or negative, was intensely local in its generation, and would have been conditioned by the accumulated experience of events. The first time that many people in Armagh and Tyrone would have experienced a large-scale yeomanry operation directly was the 1797 disarmings. Although Knox's yeomen may have accidentally disarmed some Protestants while winking at Orange guns, they certainly left no guns in Catholic hands if they could help it. The fact that this religiously selective disarming was carried out by yeomen under the control of the local gentry and magistracy in a martial-law type activity, can only have discredited the civil law. Central as well as local government would have lost credibility, and endangered the consent which was as necessary an element in obeying the law as fear of the consequences of breaking it. Local people would have seen it in plainer terms: the local yeomanry, wearing government uniforms, carrying government guns and accompanied by local magistrates, were acting under the government's orders exactly as the Peep O'Day Boys had done: re-imposing the penal laws at parochial level. The law must have appeared as the Orangeman's law. United Irish claims that government was protecting the Orangemen, wholly and mischievously incorrect when first made in August 1796, now made sense.[126] That was plain: as plain as a pikeshaft.

123 Copy of Defender Oath, 21 June 1795, P.R.O. H.O.100/56/f. 201.   124 Dalrymple to [Pelham], 7 Aug. 1796, Devlin to Corry, 10 August 1796, N.A. R.P.620/24/88,103.   125 7 Sept. 1796, N.A. R.P.620/ 25/29, 7 Sept. 1796.   126 Camden to Portland, 6 Aug. 1796, P.R.O. H.O.100/64/f. 168.

The regional extent of such attitudes are hard to assess, but it is reasonable to speculate that the total national call-outs of yeomanry following each emergency helped spread the belief amongst lower-class Catholics that this force represented sectarian laws. The wartime change from familiar, well understood ways of applying the laws must have been more frightening because it was enacted by local men at a local level. This exacerbated the process of polarisation which had been going on since the 1780s. Indeed, as attitudes to the law became one of the major points by which the communities defined themselves against each other, the yeomanry were active agents in the dynamic of polarisation. District generals' reports provide a good source of evidence into local conditions and attitudes in the early nineteenth century, since they were outside the political, social and emotional undergrowth in which the Irish gentry became increasingly entangled in the aftermath of 1798 and Union. One of the first tasks for a general arriving in a new district was to tour his area and inspect the local yeomanry. In July 1801 General Payne toured Westmeath and Longford. His report to Dublin, shows how the law had been drawn into the vortex of polarisation, and how yeomanry, for both sides, represented the point where each met, the crucible where attitudes were formed. On his yeomanry inspection Payne noted 'great jealousy' between Protestant and Catholic, and the Protestant gentry prejudiced in their administration of justice because they believed the Catholics wanted to destroy them. Payne's predecessor had spent most of his time acting as a military magistrate. He was popular with the poor, who 'regarded him as their protection against persecution', but was detested by the magistracy, who viewed him as a stranger 'who has wrested from their hands the administration of justice'.[127] The yeomanry were one of the main features of such Protestant control of the local law and order system. Viewed in this light, the reluctance of yeomen to move from home was possibly not the only factor operating against the force's fuller integration into the military system.

Perhaps the inevitable price of delegating such a powerful instrument to the Protestant gentry, which it could recruit selectively, was a change in Catholic perceptions of the law and the likelihood of impartial justice. After frequent sectarian clashes in Tyrone, James Hamilton Junior noted how 'magistrates and indeed almost all the country gentlemen show a disposition to support those who chose to style themselves Orangemen, whether right be on their side or not'.[128] Although the midlands was probably influenced by lack of yeomen in the area while weight of numbers told in Tyrone, the impact on Catholics would have been the same: the yeoman's law was not their law.

---

127 Payne to Littlehales, 6 July 1801, P.R.O. H.O.100/103/f. 293.   128 Hamilton to Abercorn, 24 April 1802, P.R.O.N.I. Abercorn Papers, D623/A/94/15.

ASSESSMENT

By what criteria should we assess the yeomanry's role in the maintenance of law and order? The most obvious one is the government's own intention for the force, which was to free the army from domestic 'police' or peacekeeping. This never happened. However, to judge the yeomanry by this criterion would be to measure it against unrealistic expectations. Some contemporary government officials did just this, assuming English solutions to Irish problems. Arthur Wellesley was under no illusions about the unique nature of Ireland's law and order problems. A report on the Irish magistrates' position written in 1807 but covering the period from 1798 concluded:

> the ordinary duty of the office here and in England is very different; there it is little more than to announce the laws by peace officers to a quiet and compliant people, here it is partly a military office; the offender must be conquered to be taken ... also [magistrates] must deal with intimidated witnesses, obstinate prejudice and religious factions ... this representation applies to what is called a state of tranquillity.[129]

It is therefore more realistic to accept, given the variety and extent of Irish disorder, that 'police' would continue to be a military responsibility, and that the yeomanry role would always be supportive, and evaluate their role against this criterion. Once this has been done, the yeomanry's contribution emerges more clearly. Within this context there were strengths and weaknesses. Their utility against 'smothered rebellion' in 1797–8 increased in proportion to the proximity to regular soldiers and the structures of the military system, both physical and in terms of command. In ways this was facilitated by the nature of the problem: the areas of greatest United Irish strength, Ulster and Leinster, were also the areas with the greatest numbers of yeomen. The problem with numbers and distribution in Munster and Connacht would militarily have rendered any force ineffective against opponents who had local depth of numbers and the support of the local populace. The fact that yeomen were local residents was an equivocal benefit to peacekeeping. Connections with the wider Protestant community, and their Orange linkages generally helped keep popular loyalism on the side of the law, though the implications of these connections damaged the proper operation of the laws by making non-acceptance of the law virtually a sectarian shibboleth for large sections of the population. Moreover, this same localism could have detrimental effects on the yeomanry's ability to tackle crimes like smuggling and illegal distillation, and could involve yeomen in sectarian clashes. Indeed, though the yeomanry was not intended as a civil police force, the new developments in policing, the Peace Preservation Force and the County Constabulary,

129 1 Aug. 1807, *W.S.D.*, v, pp. 139–40.

defined themselves as opposites in many ways. The Peace Preservation Force was outside the direct control of local magistrates; cost the locality money rather than made disorder profitable through yeomanry permanent pay; and being territorially mobile it subverted the central yeomanry principle of local men dealing with local disorder. Unlike the permanent presence of the yeomanry, the 'Peelers' were only to remain until peace was restored. Despite Peel's intentions for a 'neutral' force, the 'Peelers' took on some of the characteristics of yeomanry insofar as Orangeism began to permeate their ranks. The County Constabulary, which began in 1822, included by design members of both denominations, a fact underlined by the disposition of northern loyalists to give the chief constables the prefix 'Papist' no matter whether they were Protestant or Catholic. It too kept its men separate from the local populace, by their origins and their permanent residence in barracks. To be fair, some of the better aspects of the yeomanry system were pragmatically used in the developing police. The yeomanry brigade major's overseeing role enabled him to grasp what was going on in a county. This experience was drawn on. One of the most effective stipendary magistrates was George Warburton, who had served as a brigade major in Kilkenny.[130]

Where they were used, mainly in the south, the 'Peelers' relegated the yeomanry to the status of a third-line defence force. They were therefore the first nail in the yeomanry's coffin as a viable peacekeeping force. It is very obvious from Peel's private correspondence that he would have been happy to abolish the yeomanry had it not been for political considerations. In his calculations concerning the yeomanry, Peel the frugal administrator and Peel the politician were at odds. In September 1812 he reviewed all civil and military resources, including the yeomanry, and considered replacing the latter with a local militia. This had taken place in Britain as a 'conversion' of the volunteer infantry, designed to improve its efficiency and get a better return for the vast amount spent on voluntary forces.[131] Anything which promised more utility attracted Peel and the conversion scheme also had the backing of the commander-of-the-forces, Sir John Hope. However, in Ireland economics and efficiency were not the only considerations. Given that since 1798 the yeomanry had been the darlings of the Protestant 'Ascendancy', there were political constraints. Peel trod warily. 'Do not hint it to a soul on earth' Peel pleaded with his confidante Lord Desart, 'that I ever alluded to the subject.'[132] In early 1814 the prospect of European peace threatened financial retrenchment and inevitable reductions in the Irish army and ushered in measures designed initially to compensate for cuts but ultimately to ameliorate the problem of disorder. The Irish Yeomanry were also to be reduced but, realising the 'bad moral effect' this would have on loyalists and the corresponding 'great encouragement to the disaffected', Peel and Whitworth, the

130 Palmer, *Police and Protest*, pp. 198–203, 212; Broeker, *Rural Disorder*, chaps 4–5, passim. 131 P.J. Haythornthwaite, *The Armies of Wellington*, p. 183 132 14 Oct. 1812, B.L. Peel Papers, add. mss. 40280 f. 60.

viceroy, agreed that reduction should be partial and the force trimmed to its active component of attending members; that cavalry corps should disappear; and that small, scattered corps be reduced or combined in 'unions'.[133] In early 1815, faced with more troop withdrawals caused by Napoleon's 'hundred days', Peel was forced to look again at the yeomanry to see if it could function to any degree as an aid to the army. He immediately faced opposition from the new commander-of-the-forces, Sir George Hewitt, who wanted the force disbanded. Peel admitted that 'they are generally speaking unfit for the performance of those very duties in ... which their main utility would consist – namely in relieving the army from the maintenance of internal order and the collection of the revenue'.[134] Although not the first to recognize the yeomanry's inbuilt weakness, of being most numerous where least needed, Peel trod where others feared, in trying to free the force from its geographical constraints, administrative and indeed parliamentary constraints. He proposed an 'experiment', to see if the surplus of yeomanry strength in Ulster could be utilised to any extent in the south. Peel's 'experiment' had its roots in earlier discussions about the viability of converting the yeomanry into a local militia force. As with their British local militia counterparts, many Irish yeomen had offered service anywhere in the kingdom. Receiving loyal gestures was quite another thing from putting them into practice however. Peel initially thought in limited terms: 'at a distance from home, two or three hundred Protestant yeomen on permanent duty might be very serviceable to us'. Like the local militia, it was intended that this 'relief' would consist of extended permanent duty of around two months.[135] Even such a limited proposal aroused the wrath of Hewitt, who had a measurably worse view of the yeomanry than his predecessor. Hewitt immediately cited one of the readily available instances of yeomanry licentiousness: the notorious Antrim corn law riot. Peel was daunted neither by this or by legislative and administrative complications. He countered: 'if we required the yeomanry of Donegal to be employed in Ennishowen to prevent the manufacture of potsheen [*sic*] there would be something in Sir George's argument', but it was nonsense to claim that because they made whiskey in Donegal they would be unfit to keep the peace in Athlone. Whitworth agreed. Peel's next obstacle was the Yeomanry Act, which limited service to the home barony or that adjoining. As far as he was concerned, 'the Gordian knot' of local sensitivities and administrative complexities was to be cut.[136] Peel, with Whitworth's backing, originally envisaged detachments of northern yeomen being sent to Limerick and Clare.[137] By June they had circularised corps in Cork, Kilkenny, Wexford, Waterford, Clare, Galway, Kerry, Limerick, Leitrim, Roscommon, Carlow, Kildare, Queen's and

133 Peel to Littlehales, 5 July 1814, B.L. Peel Papers, add. mss. 40287 ff. 66–8; Whitworth to Sidmouth, 11 July 1814, P.R.O. H.O.100/179/f. 136.　134 Peel to Hewitt, 27 March 1815, B.L. Peel Papers, add. mss. 40288 ff. 136–7.　135 Broeker, *Rural Disorder*, p. 83.　136 Peel to Littlehales, 27 Apr. 1815, B.L. Peel Papers, add. mss. 40258 ff. 204–5; Peel to Gregory, 17 June 1815, add. mss. 40289 f. 109.　137 Peel to Whitworth, 19 May 1815, B.L. Peel Papers, add. mss. 40289 ff. 46–7.

Queen's counties asking for offers of 'extended service'.[138] Peel was putting the onus on the yeomen to prove their use in the same way in which he subjected magistrates' reports to rigorous scrutiny, assuming exaggeration unless proven otherwise. He told Saurin, now attorney general:

> If we do not at such a time try the yeomanry, we ought without a moment's delay abolish the establishment for I cannot conceive a more convincing proof of our want of confidence ... and of their utter uselessness than our own refusal to employ them in preserving the peace at home when we have scarcely any other force to employ.

In reality, though, he was making the best of a bad job. By September 1815, the experiment petered out ineffectually. The circulars went largely unanswered as the 1814 reductions were still in the process of decimating the force in many of the counties involved. Hewitt ordered substantial reinforcements to Clare and Limerick, whether against the banditti or the northern yeomen is a moot point.[139] The actual total of yeomen on permanent duty between June and September was 140 men from five northern corps, excluding those from Omagh who 'quit' after a few weeks, while a similar number in Tipperary had remained on duty for five days. It is not clear how far the northern yeomen marched from home, though those from Monaghan town got as far as Kells in county Meath.[140] The conclusion cannot be avoided that the political connections of yeomanry, once so beneficial to government, were now prolonging the existence of an anachronistic force and thereby, however indirectly, functioning as an impediment to further developments in the national introduction of a police force. This went back before Peel. During the Peace of Amiens, the attorney general, Kilwarlin, envisaged police institutions as a peacetime alternative to yeomanry, suggesting the County Police Act be extended as the yeomanry was reduced.[141]

After 1815 yeomanry feature less in government's law and order policies, and only as a stop gap in lieu of sufficient regulars. In June 1817, during severe food shortages in Meath, Dublin, Kildare and Carlow, around 500 yeomen were called on duty to guard stores and escort the movement of provisions, though not before the government satisfied itself of their fitness by having brigade majors inspect each corps which was to supply detachments.[142] Attempts to break the political gridlock of the northern yeomanry were not now considered as policy, but only as expedients driven by extreme necessity. Although the use of 'Peelers' mushroomed in response

138 Circular, 26 June 1815, P.R.O. H.O.100/184/ff. 233–5.   139 Hewitt to Littlehales, 19 Sept. 1815, P.R.O. H.O.100/185/f. 235.   140 Warburton to Littlehales, 29 June 1815, P.R.O. H.O.100/184/ff. 231–2; Return of yeomanry corps on permanent duty, 16 Sept. 1815, H.O.100/185/f. 47.   141 Abstracts of all laws for maintaining public peace in Ireland, 15 Jan. 1802, P.R.O. Colchester Papers, 30/9/133/ff. 4–5.   142 E.B. Baker [Littlehales] to Cosby and Hamilton, 18 June 1817, P.R.O. H.O.100/192/ff. 415–8.

to the serious Rockite and Ribbon disorders of 1819–21, the situation eventually became so serious and troop numbers so parlous, that Talbot, viceroy since 1817, was forced to look at the yeomanry as a stop-gap. Under pressure from a Home Office bent on retrenchment, Talbot reluctantly tried to overcome the old north-south yeomanry imbalance and have 3,000 Ulster yeomen sent south. Although over 1,200 northern yeomen and some in Cork and Kerry, were put on duty at the end of the year, the measure was abruptly halted with the arrival of a new viceroy, Marquis Wellesley. Wellesley was dead against using yeomanry, and only ten corps were called on duty in 1822, while the following year's entire permanent duty consisted of four Wexford corps doing arms escorts.[143] In late 1823 Wellesley unequivocally told Peel, now home secretary, 'I should prefer any other mode of augmenting ... our military strength to the embodying of the corps of yeomanry'. From 1823 until 1828, and presumably until the force was disastrously reactivated by Anglesey and Stanley in 1831, not one corps was put on duty.[144] Largely concentrated in Ulster, the yeomanry remained, in a state of stasis, functionally redundant but politically symbolic. Although it maintained some of its negative capability, as a control on loyalism, it was a potentially dangerous anachronism which had long outlived its main usefulness because the rules of the game had changed. The law and order problem was now one of localised disturbances by agrarian combinations rather than a general insurrection. In the south there were insufficient yeomen to make an impact; in the north, the political and religious affiliations of the yeomen meant that they could add to the problems. In April 1815 the district general concluded a report for the northern district by expressing his distaste that 'magistrates should resort to yeomen for assistance as it often leads rather to increase than prevent disturbance'.[145]

The yeomanry's most important contribution to law and order is to be found in the earlier period, when permanent duty was used in response to the periodic invasion scares which bedevilled Ireland, particularly before the Battle of Trafalgar (1805) had severely damaged French seapower. The fear was that, although the leadership of disaffection was broken after 1798, support for the French remained and news of possible invasion would spark off disorder. With yeomanry considered part of the stationary force, it was normal to put the force on permanent duty on such occasions. The difference between this sort of permanent duty and that used against 'Whiteboys' is a subtle one. It was a question of initiative. The government could rely on their own intelligence on the French movements and had, in the country-wide structure of yeomanry brigades, a latent system which, though uneven in its coverage, could be activated in advance of invasion rumours. On the sailing of the Brest Fleet in April 1799, Cornwallis ordered the entire yeomanry on permanent duty to show that government was prepared and ready for any insurrectionary dis-

143 Broeker, *Rural Disorder*, pp. 121–2; *Parl Papers*, H.C. [17] 1828, xiv, pp. 283–7.   144 Wellesley to Peel, B.L. Wellesley Papers, add. mss. 37301 f. 322; *Parl. Papers*, 1828, op. cit.   145 Hart to Pole, 22 July 1810, P.R.O. H.O.100/158/ff. 539–40; Monthly Report, April 1815, H.O.100/184/f. 85.

turbances timed to coincide with the prospect of invasion. They guarded major roads and strategic passes to 'overawe the country'.[146] Moreover, given the rudimentary nature of military communications, a temporary standing force like this could minutely observe local developments and transmit news of them to the military. Yeomanry also functioned as a deterrent, simply because their very existence meant a constant local presence. The weekly exercise parades were a continual reminder of their potential. Thomas Knox's brother George, in giving Charles Abbot his opinion against amalgamating the local corps into larger brigades, astutely noted, 'they are of much more service in watching and overawing the disaffected'.[147]

Moreover yeomanry permanent duty, being a flexible instrument which could be activated as locally and for as long as the authorities wished, had the potential to be a useful tool against 'ordinary' crime, and in areas with good yeomanry coverage and no secret society network, this was often the case. In county Dublin in 1800 General Craig kept corps on permanent duty near a part of the Dublin-Drogheda road notorious for robberies, throughout all the dark nights of winter. Craig also put the Fingall Cavalry on peacekeeping permanent duty for a week, during which time the mounted yeomen maintained the 'presence' by patrolling a chain of towns, while the dismounted men did 'town duty', arresting robbers and murderers, seizing illegal spirits, and holding fair-day drunks till they sobered up.[148] Where conditions were suitable, yeomanry had many advantages over regular soldiers, militia or fencibles. Being territorially-based, they provided local cover in a more effective way than the army or militia, and could remain in an area without the need for billets, which were hard to get in some districts and frequently the cause of more disorder.[149] Their baronial, parish and town system of organisation meant they fitted the structure of local civilian society better than the military districts which were organised with defence against invasion in mind. The United Irishmen were also grouped on baronial lines. Being local men alert to the nuances of the district, their observations and intelligence was more accurate. A Hillsborough yeoman would have a better idea how to read what was going on locally than an English light dragoon, a Tay fencible, or a Monaghan militiaman. This 'peacekeeping by presence' particularly during invasion scares was of the first importance and explains why commanders like Cornwallis and Fox, though they personally detested the yeomanry, could not control the country without its assistance.

In conclusion, during the whole period of its existence, the yeomanry emerges as an equivocal aid to law and order. Local residence and depth of numbers were the critical points which defined their capability against the various types of disorder. Because the areas of greatest United Irish numerical strength, Ulster and Leinster, coincided with the heaviest concentrations of yeomanry, after a shaky start the yeo-

146 Circular from Adjutant Gen. Hewitt to District Generals, 22 April 1799, P.R.O. H.O.100/83/f. 368. 147 4 Aug. 1801, P.R.O. Colchester Papers, 30/9/123/ff. 170–3.   148 Craig to Littlehales, 3 Dec. 1800, P.R.O. H.O.100/94/f. 287.   149 Hardwicke to Pelham, 7 Aug. 1802, P.R.O. H.O.100/109/f. 173.

manry's most effective active role was against planned insurrectionary disorder. A numerous yeomanry meant significant levels of support for the force in the local community. This too helped make them effective. This situation was reversed in the nineteenth century when agrarian combinations in the south and west, by their local depth of numbers virtually overwhelmed the few scattered yeomanry corps and made their members easy targets for arms raids. The degree of threat felt by yeomen was related to their efficiency. If the danger was too great, the yeomen were useless either as a deterrent or an offensive, corrective force. In such cases, their duty structures operated to defend the yeomen rather than tackle the problem. Where the degree of threat and the ability to respond were less uneven, as in Ulster in 1797 and 1798, much more could be expected from the force. However, where weight of numbers was not cancelled out by a substantial threat, the yeomanry could endanger law and order themselves. This is seen in their involvement in sectarian disputes in Ulster in the nineteenth century. Where the local threat was not perceived in religious or political terms, but rather seen in the upsetting of tenurial customs or the unofficial economy of distillation or smuggling by encroachment of 'outsiders', whether private individuals or government agencies, the yeomen could operate in a Whiteboy-like manner. However, despite these weaknesses, as a force raised primarily against insurrection, they were most effective when they were most needed: in the late 1790s. Given their largely Protestant and Orange connections, the yeomanry and the laws they enlisted to defend, were inexorably drawn into the polarisation of the nineteenth century. We must now turn to examine the yeomanry's impact on the Irish Protestant community, perhaps the most crucial of all its influences, both in contemporary terms and for future developments.

10

The Yeomanry and Irish Protestantism

> But mark now the fun, how thousands do run,
> At sight of our brave Orange Yeos.
> Not Murphy[1] or hell, book, candle or bell,
> Could make them such striplings oppose.[2]

In 1832, Sir Hussey Vivian, the commander-of-the forces, dismissed the idea of using yeomanry any further in the tithe war, claiming that though their use might 'put down the Catholics it would not restore order as you will then have the yeomanry themselves to be put down, for they will not be satisfied (in the north at least) without the restoration of Protestant Ascendancy'.[3] Had Camden read this he would have been horrified. When forming the yeomanry he dreaded being construed as arming the 'Protestant against the Papist', or creating a force which would involve itself in politics. Yet this was precisely the essence of Vivian's letter. The Irish Yeomanry were so identified with political Protestantism they could not be trusted not to use their government guns to overturn locally what they perceived as the advantage Catholics had gained with the granting of emancipation three years earlier. Had the force Camden raised for defence and domestic peacekeeping become the standing army of militant Protestantism? To answer this we must examine the yeomanry's relationship with the Protestant community to see how representative it was, numerically, socially, denominationally or doctrinally, and how it interacted with political developments affecting Protestantism. First, it will be necessary to summarise the position of Irish Protestantism, 1790–1830.

The relations between the main Protestant denominations and between Protestants and Catholics all underwent major changes in the period. 'Protestant Ascendancy' received a series of major blows. The onslaught on Protestant privilege started with the 1793 Catholic Relief Act and continued during the Fitzwilliam episode. It rallied under Camden, only to be hit by the 1798 rebellion and the Union. Politically, and at times physically, Protestants felt insecure and defensive. Both main Protestant denominations were subjected to rigorous changes, with the growth of evangelical movements in response to 'the current climate of social convulsion and apocalyptic expectancy'. Evangelicals saw the new ideological wine from France in

1 Father John Murphy of Boolavogue.   2 'Orange Triumphant', 'Loyal Songs no.2 as sung in all the Orange Lodges in Ireland' (Dublin, c.1800), B.L. 11622d2.   3 Vivian to Anglesey, 12 Jan. 1832, P.R.O. H.O.100/241/f. 83.

the old bottles of an Irish Catholicism with implacable designs on Protestantism. Methodism injected a populist vibrancy into the moribund eighteenth-century Anglican church and cut across its class-based hierarchy through the medium of uneducated itinerant preachers, while Presbyterian evangelism bonded doctrinal divisions in a similar way. The Evangelical Society of Ulster was founded by five seceding Presbyterian ministers and, at its first meeting in October 1798, included thirteen ministers from four different Presbyterian denominations. Although the evangelical tendency had its origins in the prevailing atmosphere, the 1798 rebellion was crucial in its increase. The tendency to link the dangerous weakness in the structure of Protestantism with the threat of resurgent Catholicism had been growing in the latter part of the century. The bishop of Cloyne's interpretation of the Munster Rightboys as 'popish plots' was a theme returned to in the 1790s. Methodists openly interpreted the rebellion in this light, and indeed Methodism more than doubled its membership in the three years after 1798. However, the evangelical tendency went further than trying to change the Protestant denominations from which it arose. It quickly became involved in missionary work among Catholics actively seeking converts. This too was given added stimulus by the 1798 rebellion, and naturally drew angry responses from Catholicism. As well as linking with and contributing to anti-Catholicism, evangelicalism contributed to the development of a more cohesive and more conservative Protestantism by its advocacy of a return to basic principles, its stress on the mutual interdependence of rich and poor as part of the divine order, and by channeling energies away from political debate.[4]

A major factor in Protestant concerns was obviously the campaign for full Catholic relief. Although this had been staved off by Camden, many feared that emancipation would follow Union. Renewed Catholic agitation began in 1805. On top of this came reforms in the local magistracy, a traditional bastion of Protestant power. 'Hostile' administrations like Bedford's had removed partisan magistrates for political reasons, but even 'sympathetic' ones like Peel's seemed to undermine Protestant domination by increasing central government questioning, intervention and reform of the old law and order system. If by 1830 Irish Protestantism was a more defensive entity than in 1790, in the face of these challenges it was certainly also much more politically homogeneous.

The predominantly Protestant composition of the yeomanry was inevitable. Over a year before its birth, Fitzwilliam's linking of the yeomanry concept with emancipation ensured that denominational division would be an issue when the force was eventually raised. Although Camden envisaged a yeomanry distinguished from the mass of the people by its social and propertied connections, rather than by religious affiliation, first the background, then the circumstances of its raising, established a tendency towards Protestant membership which would continue and increase. Local delegation regarding choice of members, coupled with the involvement of many

4 Hempton and Hill, *Evangelical Protestantism*, pp. 23, 28–39.

Anglican clergy and their use of the parish for loyal associations and offers of service, all mitigated against heavy Catholic participation, as did the Catholic Committee's attempts to discourage enlistment. Moreover, the yeomanry's ethos, to defend the constitution in church and state, can only have helped point it in the same direction. Its appeal was not limited to doctrinaire churchmen, as the eager participation of both Methodists[5] and conservative Presbyterians shows. The fact of its being a property-based force also helped lock the yeomanry into the Protestant community: as the great majority of landowners were Anglican so was the local yeomanry leadership. Whatever the circumstances of local raising, whether the initiative came down from the landowner, up from his tenants, or a combination of both kinds of movements, this had the effect of replicating traditional forms of social conservatism, paralleling the similar process wrought by evangelicalism. Thus the yeomanry quickly came to reflect many current strands in Protestantism, through its wide social, clerical and denominational connections. Just how representative was it of Irish Protestantism? If we take its optimum figure of at least 80,000 (attained frequently between 1803 and the end of the Napoleonic war) and a combined Protestant population of about one million, containing some 500,000 males of *all ages*, this would mean one in every six male Protestants was a yeoman in, say 1810. Given that the young and the very old would not be able to serve, that the figures omit supplementaries and give no indication of those who *had* once served, in reality and taken over time the proportion must have been even higher. Indeed, there can have been few Protestant families not associated with the yeomanry during the years of its existence. Thus the strong links, social and religious, binding the force into the fabric of the Protestant community were reinforced by connections of kin and blood. Does this fully explain the situation described in 1832 by Sir Hussey Vivian, where it was feared that yeomanry corps were likely to function as nineteenth-century Peep O'Day boys and break the law in struggles for local dominance with Catholics? The period 1800–70 has been described as 'the dawning of democracy' in a recent work which highlights *inter alia* O'Connell's politicization of the Catholic masses.[6] This process had its counterpart on the Protestant side. The history of the Irish Yeomanry is both more and less than the history of popular Protestantism; however, in this area lies much of the explanation of the force's symbolic significance. To consider this we must again turn to the connections between the yeomanry and Orangeism.

This process has been traced from its limited beginnings in mid-Ulster in 1796, through General Knox's 1797 Orange augmentations in the same area, to the heavy cross-fertilisation and spread in 1798 by the use of Orange supplementaries during the rebellion and the indiscriminate gathering of loyalists and government forces in garrison towns. It is known that Knox's moves were a development of a process

5 Hempton and Hill, op. cit., p. 36.   6 D. McCartney, *The Dawning of Democracy: Ireland, 1800–1870.*

ongoing amongst several mid-Ulster families, all of whom, like Knox's, were to become prominent in the yeomanry, whereby they formed links with their Orange or proto-Orange tenants to keep them under control. Knox's primary intention was of course to harness popular loyalism against the United Irishmen rather than to keep the Orangemen from disorder. Indeed, he encouraged 'animosity' to ensure that he had a party in guaranteed opposition to insurrection. However, the point here is not the reasons for the liaison but the means by which it was secured. In the late 1790s traditional deference could not be assumed.

Before yeomanry was approved by government, Knox's elder brother Thomas may have promised membership and guns to the local lodges in August 1796, but, faced the following year with republican infiltration and fears about wavering Orange loyalty, the connection had to be locally promoted and made to interest government. It is known that General Knox took up the earlier gentry theme of stressing the law-abiding nature of the Orange clubs and their readiness to help the magistrates. Indeed, Knox arranged for Orange resolutions to be sent to Pelham on the back of his request for approval to add Orangemen to James Verner's yeomanry. These resolutions were designed for Castle consumption, making conciliatory gestures towards Catholics provided they remained loyal.[7] If one contrasts these resolutions with others published in Armagh on exactly the same day, 21 May 1797, a very different construction can be seen at a local level. 'The Armagh Orangemen's answer to the United Irishmen' berates the 'heterogeneous mass of Presbyterians and Papists [who] hate our church and would gladly destroy it' and concludes, 'We gave you only a taste at the *Diamond*, but the next time we come to blows, you shall have a bellyful'.[8] This curious production seems to ignore the fact that Presbyterians fought against the Defenders at the Diamond. It is clearly designed for loyalist rather than republican consumption. However, its significance becomes clear when seen in the context of United Irish infiltration of yeomanry corps and the subsequent purges and Orange augmentations. By placing the conflict in the canon of Protestant victories, in the tradition of the Boyne, Knox intended to make its appeal stretch beyond the exhortations of clergymen and gentlemen, above the cry of 'church in danger' and back to an imagined unity in the Williamite wars. This appeal to emotion and instinct could therefore be anti-Catholic without being anti-Presbyterian and was calculated to draw on the planters' fear of elimination.

Other evidence exists to suggest that while the gentry put themselves at the head of the gathering body of popular loyalism, in both its official and unofficial forms in the yeomanry and Orange clubs, notwithstanding their overall strategic objectives to maintain the peace or subdue insurrection, they deliberately reawakened and utilised martial feeling at a popular level. This was no metropolitan Boyne Society,

7 Knox to Pelham, 21 May 1797, B.L. Pelham Papers, add. mss. 33104 f. 91; Senior, *Orangeism*, pp. 68–9.   8 21 May 1797, P.R.O.N.I. T1689/21.

washing down gargantuan meals and antique politics with the best claret, but rather an ignorant rural proletariat whose folk memories of the Williamite wars were a mixture of fact and superstition not dissimilar to that of the Catholic peasantry so berated by evangelicals. In short, John Knox and others re-invented the Boyne tradition. This shows in all sorts of ways. Blacker tells of going out to inspect yeomen, riding a horse with a saddle and bridle dating from the Williamite period, and the country people crowding him to touch it as a 'relic'. Toleration of yeomen wearing orange ribbons on anniversaries was common and some corps even adopted names from the Williamite period. Those at Enniskillen called themselves 'Enniskilleners', the name of the famous regiment of northern Protestants who fought in William's campaign and the new town defences were given names like Orange Redoubt.

From the viewpoint of the gentry, the leadership of the Orange Order and their allies in the military hierarchy, the overriding intention was to defeat the rising of the United Irishmen. The offer of Orange auxiliaries in March 1798 was the culmination; the public side of all this local effort.[9] Although this offer was not fully utilised – indeed the use of Orange supplementaries was Castlereagh's compromise – the strategic, controlling animus of its instigators can be seen working at a local level in the yeomanry corps, now that Orangeism was spreading in the force and was receiving *de facto* toleration. General Knox used the lodge structure as an aid to discipline in the Crowhill yeomanry and as a means of using local knowledge to sniff out disaffected members, while its captain, Joseph Atkinson, made use of the naturally corporate structure of the corps to get each member to relinquish his full right of resignation, in that each yeoman had to swear an oath avowing such action would only be taken when the outgoing member had found, *and paid for*, a substitute.[10] During the rebellion, the yeomanry and Orange auxiliaries stationed at Blaris Camp near Lisburn were under the immediate direction of an Orange 'committee' which intervened to head off the danger of sectarian disorder between yeomen and Catholic militiamen.[11] This incident alerts us to the inherent difficulties of harnessing turbulent popular loyalism, after having first attracted it by pandering to the very turbulence the gentry leadership now tried to control. The fact that this incident happened only weeks after both parties had been engaged on the same side against the rebels serves to show how transient were the beneficial effects of the Orange liaison and how powerful was the dynamic popular loyalism that was now embedded in the yeomanry. The simultaneous process, whereby popular loyalism was attached to the yeomanry by a conscious re-invention of the traditions of 1690, and mustered against the United Irishmen, was already under way before 1798. However, the rebellion ensured that this became irrevocable, and that another Protestant victory was added to the Boyne, Aughrim and the Diamond. In the popular mind, from 1798 onwards the yeomanry epitomised the Orange traditions and were at the

9 To the loyal subjects of Ireland, March 1798, P.R.O.N.I. D215/2.   10 n.d. *c.*1800, P.R.O.N.I. Atkinson of Crowhill Papers, T2701.   11 N.A.M. 6807–174 ff. 503–6, Nugent Papers, 6 Aug. 1798.

cutting edge of Protestant defence. If evangelicalism reawakened spiritual zeal, the 'Orange yeomanry' no less jolted its military equivalent. The situation that Hussey Vivian feared had its immediate roots in the politics of the Catholic question, though, as regards the yeomanry, its origins dated from this 'harnessing' process in 1797–8. Before turning to the wider issue of the yeomanry and the Catholic question, it is necessary to examine their impact on the nature of Irish Protestantism itself.

For one thing, yeomanry contributed to the growing militancy and simplified loyalty of Protestantism by soaking up ex-radical Presbyterians or those shrewd enough to wait to see which party was strongest. Many of these yeomen demonstrated the zeal of the convert. The process was in train even before the Ulster rising broke. James McKey told Downshire that many former Belfast republicans were eager to join the yeomanry to prove their loyalty.[12] A very subtle change in what was officially encouraged in yeomanry corps is implicit in developments around the beginning of 1798, when there is less evidence of pandering to Volunteering sensibilities and more of trying to attract Presbyterians by reawakening their instinctive fear of Catholicism. The ground had been prepared by a combination of official and private action, in which the resurrection of the 1690 traditions played a critical role. General Knox told Cooke, 'depend upon it the Presbyterians will not abide a popish plot'.[13] Affidavits taken by Sir Hardinge Gifford concerning the massacre of Protestants at Scullabogue were widely circulated in the north in a bid to get radical or undecided Presbyterians to coalesce with Anglicans in a common loyalty.[14] The scheme had government backing: Castlereagh considered Steel Dickson dangerous enough not to be included in the policy of 'acting against the Catholic rather than the Presbyterian members of the union'.[15] By 1 July, McKey gleefully told Downshire that 'every man in Belfast has a red coat on'.[16] Yeomanry corps began to be formed in Presbyterian areas of Down and Antrim. Hudson noticed a 'schism' between Presbyterians and Catholics in Antrim. Telling Charlemont that 'the brotherhood of affection is over', he utilised the split to enroll Presbyterians in his yeomanry corps. Yeomanry corps were an important ingredient in the transition. In frightening times, they were able to offer Presbyterians a familiar tradition to contrast with despotism in France and civil war in Ireland, one which catered for the fact that, in the last analysis, they too were planters. Government had the commitments of oath and pay with little risk: if a corps proved disloyal, it could easily be disbanded and the members branded ever after with the mark of Cain. With the United Irishmen defeated, it mattered little if Presbyterians joined in the same spirit, as those who Hudson noticed joining the Orange Order to 'screen themselves' and take revenge on their 'quondam associates of a different persuasion'. By 1799 Castlereagh noted

12 1 June 1798, P.R.O.N.I. Downshire Papers, D607/F/192.   13 Gen. Knox to Cooke, 6 June 1798, N.A. R.P.620/38/61.   14 *Parl. Papers*, H.C. 1835 [377] Report from the select committee ... on Orange lodges, xv, p.82.   15 N.A.M. 6807–174 ff. 457–8, Nugent Papers, Castlereagh to [Nugent], 6 June 1798.   16 P.R.O.N.I. Downshire Papers, D607/F/293.

'the Protestant dissenters in Ulster have in a great measure withdrawn themselves from the union and become Orangemen'.[17] By this stage that was saying much the same thing as saying many of them had joined the yeomanry.

It would, however, be an over-simplification to claim all radical Presbyterians suddenly did ideological somersaults in 1798 and joined the yeomanry and Orange Order. There is clear evidence that Presbyterians in formerly United areas which did not see fighting in 1798 were slower to change. Nevertheless when they did change, the yeomanry were the catalyst. References in the sources to ex-radical Presbyterians joining the yeomanry cluster around two distinct periods: after the failures in 1798 and 1803. In August 1803 the Reverend Fowler noted that disaffection in counties Tyrone, Derry and Donegal was now a Catholic affair and 'the Presbyterians are indubitably [*sic*] completely disunited from the Catholic body and wish much to enter into yeomanry corps'. General Hart, speaking of the upper liberties of Derry, where the wealthy Presbyterians had been solidly United Irish, noted they were wanting to express their new loyalty by forming yeomanry corps.[18] Hart's military objectivity allowed him to see a secondary motive deriving from a fear of Catholics getting too much power. Despite this, he recommended acceptance, obviously realising that Presbyterian yeomen at this stage, for whatever combination of reasons they enlisted, were a good investment for future security. No better way existed of turning the loose change of mixed motives into a currency acceptable to central and local government, to the gentry, the army and other Protestants. Yeomanry were the very best way back for ex-radical Presbyterians, because joining a corps was a public, often corporate act; one which, with its oaths and submission to discipline, carried more weight than mere professions of loyalty. In this sense, the yeomanry oath was a rite of passage marking the end of the flirtation with revolution. Yeomanry, with their property associations, pointed to a better future than the pike rusting in the thatch.

Although Protestant liberalism was not entirely extinguished, and there were some Protestant supporters of emancipation (like the captain of the Lurgan Yeomanry, 'Papist' Handcock) such figures were decidedly in the minority.[19] The 1790s left a sad legacy of polarisation. As the eighteenth century waned, Hudson prophetically told the ageing Charlemont 'the word Protestant, which was becoming obsolete in the north, has regained its influence'.[20] This paralleled the impact of evangelicalism, which encouraged anti-Catholicism, and facilitated and justified the replacement of political radicalism with conservatism, a symbiotic relationship which gave strength and direction to the overall process and saw the yeomanry contribute

17 Hudson to Charlemont 18 July 1798, 12 Aug. 1798, 6 Oct. 1798, H.M.C. *Charlemont*, ii, pp. 326–7, 332–3, 336; Castlereagh to Portland, 3 June 1799, P.R.O. H.O.100/87/f. 5. 18 Fowler to [Marsden], 13 Aug. 1803, N.A. S.O.C.1025/73; Hart to Littlehales, 29 Aug. 1803 S.O.C.1025/35. 19 *Parl. Papers*, H.C. 1835[476], Third Report from the Select Committee ... on Orange Lodges, xvi, p. 113. 20 5 July 1799, H.M.C. *Charlemont*, ii, pp. 354–5.

significantly to the broadening of Protestant loyalty and the narrowing of loyalty to Protestants.

Because of the now overt and substantial Orange connection cemented by the reawakened 1690 tradition, yeomanry clearly had a major impact on Protestant militancy. However, it is less clear where cause and effect lay, as the general climate in Protestantism was one of increasing anti-Catholicism, something which the yeomanry both drew on and contributed to. Yeomanry did not create anti-Catholicism, but acted as a channel through which such attitudes could travel and manifest themselves in both their defensive and triumphalist forms. Moreover, with yeomanry being a main point of contact between the Protestant establishment and the bulk of the population, such manifestations inevitably produced or provoked the anticipated reaction, and achieved the mutual fear and distrust on which sectarianism thrives.

To understand the yeomanry's contribution to *defensive* anti-Catholicism it is necessary to identify the *zeitgeist* of the formation period. This can be described as one of panic and fear, produced by rapid and seemingly uncontrollable new developments in Ireland being interpreted in the light of past events. Clare put words to these feelings when he told Camden, in deadly earnest, 'if the opportunity comes we shall see the scenes of 1641 renewed'.[21] Clare's opinions were formed during a period which had just witnessed the terrifying spread of Defenderism, with its strong anti-Protestant ethos, and now saw military liaison between those same Defenders and the United Irishmen.[22] Shortly after the formation of yeomanry, General Knox spoke of the need to drive on 'the yeomanry spirit' into County Derry to 'oppose violence with violence'.[23] This aggressively defensive spirit had its roots in the Williamite tradition, but it was not the whig tradition of the bloodless Glorious Revolution of 1688 but rather, its Irish concomitant: the apocalyptic blood-sacrifices of 1641 and 1690.

The collective act of offering to form a yeomanry corps offered a local Protestant community the opportunity to publicly declare or to restate their principles. In county Down, the Ballyculter Supplementary Yeomen produced resolutions which read 'The above are Protestant men who ever made public profession of their loyalty', thus confirming that their stance had the authority of the past, as distinct from current uncertainty and confused alliances.[24] Indeed, by forming a yeomanry corps on this basis, they drew a line of demarcation between themselves and other groups as decidedly as that drawn by the apprentices who shut Derry's gates in 1689. Forming such a corps formalised the growing polarisation of Irish society.

The very way in which the yeomanry was organised locally also contributed to anti-Catholicism. Because both Catholic and Anglican churches shared similar ter-

---

21 28 Aug. 1796, K.A.O. Pratt Papers, U840/0183/6.   22 Bartlett, *Fall and Rise*, pp. 211–12.   23 Knox to Pelham, 2 Jan. 1797, N.A. R.P.620/28/13.   24 n.d. [May 1798], P.R.O.N.I. Maxwell of Finnebrogue Papers, T1023/153.

ritorial divisions, and because the lower classes of both communities informally organised themselves around these divisions, the potential for sectarian polarisation was high. Yeomanry infantry offers tended to come in aggregate from one group or the other. As time went on and more corps were embodied, these offers were inevitably from the Protestant communities, which defined the differences clearly and symbolised local superiority. In this respect, local yeomanry corps fit the tradition of the fair-day faction fight as well as the 'nation-in-arms' of the French wars. Moreover yeomanry also contributed to anti-Catholicism in their application. Professor Bartlett notes that when yeomanry came into contact with the mainly Catholic rebels in the south, they 'envenomed an already sectarianised atmosphere'.[25] Doubtless the campaign of expelling Catholics from corps, because of the United Irishmen's campaign to use them for infiltration, contributed to this.

As noted earlier, Catholics formed a small but important minority in the yeomanry of 1796. In addition there were also 'liberal' corps who supported Grattan.[26] Henry Joy McCracken contrasted the Dublin yeomen favourably with those from the north as 'quite a different sort of people, many of them professing the most liberal sentiments'.[27] However as time and events moved, and the Orange connection grew, yeomanry provided a means by which anti-Catholicism could be expressed. It provided the opportunity of being able to act on suspicion. The puritanical Calvinism of many Irish Protestants had conditioned them to fear, as had their Elizabethan and Cromwellian forebears, evil jesuitically masquerading as good. There were two occasions when this attitude was particularly manifested in the yeomanry, in 1798 and 1803. In 1798 the panic had some grounds in reality. Myles Byrne admits that the United Irishmen did indeed try to use Catholics as a point of entry into yeomanry corps in Wexford.[28] However the extent of the reaction shows the propensity to use yeomanry as a means of demonstrating Catholic disloyalty. Captain Green of the Grand Canal corps told Major Sirr that in 1798 he had discovered a plot on his life among some Catholics in his corps. He had 'determined not only, not to receive any more of that description, but also to require that those who were in the corps should quietly resign'.[29] The 'plot' may well have been an attempt to clear the corps of Catholics, as a group of Orangemen had enlisted *en bloc* in Green's corps.[30] This process whereby Protestants saw themselves as the only true loyalists was highly subjective. The mainly Catholic militia fought as hard as the yeomanry in 1798. The Monaghan militia, still smarting from the disgrace of the Defender infiltration, fought furiously at Ballynahinch, where Nugent pitched them against the best of Munro's pikemen, and took the heaviest casualties on the government side.[31] Cornwallis commented on the ease with which people substituted 'the word

25 Bartlett, *Fall and Rise*, pp. 222–3. 26 Senior, *Orangeism*, p. 76. 27 H.J. McCracken to M. A. McCracken, 15 March 1797, T.C.D. Madden Papers, MS 873. 28 S. Gwynn, (ed.), *The Memoirs of Myles Byrne*, pp. 12–13. 29 8 Sept. 1801, P.R.O. H.O.100/107/f. 29. 30 Bartlett, 'Militarisation and Politicization', p. 134. 31 Stephenson to Downshire, 13 June 1798, Lane to Downshire, 19 June 1798,

Catholicism for Jacobinism'.[32] In thus providing a channel by which anti-Catholicism could be directed, and a platform on which it could be enacted and disseminated into the wider population, yeomanry contributed greatly to the constant renewal and re-invigoration of militant Protestantism. This was not simply a matter of local squabbles. With emancipation ominously in the background there would inevitably be a political dimension.

YEOMANRY AND THE CATHOLIC QUESTION

The Catholic emancipation campaign has traditionally attracted more scholarly attention than Protestant opposition to it. Recent work by Professor Bartlett has examined other sides of the question, particularly the 'two nations' in their military manifestations, the militia and yeomanry.[33] However, more work is needed on the Protestant dimension, especially in its popular dimension. Indeed, the tendency to view Protestant Ireland through the medium of the Anglo-Irish can prove distorting. In Bartlett's recent and comprehensive work on the Catholic question, he assesses reactions to Emmet's rising in 1803 and suggests 'it is from this point that the yeomanry came to be completely identified with the Protestants of Ireland'.[34] The context of the suggestion is the readiness of the Castle, particularly Hardwicke and the chancellor, Redesdale, to identify the Emmet affair as a plot which had the tacit approval of the Catholic hierarchy, and a subsequent popular and gentry reluctance to admit Catholics into yeomanry corps. Bartlett is certainly correct in highlighting the political significance of 1803 but, as the Orange-yeomanry connection shows, the identification started in 1797 and was firmly established by 1798.

It must be re-emphasised that yeomanry were one element in this process: re-awakened religious zeal, rivalry and fear interacted with perceptions of the 1798 rebellion in a complex equation where cause and effect became confused. However the result was clear: though emancipation was submerged when Union passed, polarisation and sectarianism continued to grow. The yeomanry's involvement in the emancipation issue predated even its Orange connection: it was bespoken from 1795 when Fitzwilliam proposed a largely Catholic yeomanry once the removal of grievances made it safe to entrust them with arms. The Catholic question re-emerged to become the major political issue in early nineteenth century Ireland. But before examining the yeomanry's impact and role it will be necessary to provide a brief summary of the development of the Catholic question after 1800.

With George III's insistence that emancipation would break his coronation oath, the question of full Catholic relief was shelved with Union. Hardwicke's adminis-

P.R.O.N.I. Downshire Papers, D607/F/236, 255.   32 Cornwallis to Portland, 26 June 1798, P.R.O. H.O.100/77/f. 200.   33 Bartlett, 'Militarisation and Politicization', p. 134.   34 Bartlett, *Fall and Rise*, p. 276.

tration was, as Cooke hypocritically complained to Camden, 'obliged to act upon Protestant principles exclusively' with only 'a profession of impartiality'.[35] The political organisation of Catholics was correspondingly dampened. Although alluded to in a debate on Emmet's rising, parliamentary agitation for further relief did not start again until 1805, in the usual form of a petition which was heavily rejected. However, the incoming 'Talents' ministry in 1806 again raised hopes, as Grenville and Fox supported emancipation. The king remained implacable, however and Grenville's administration fell over the issue, to be replaced by Portland's 'No Popery' ministry in 1807, which signaled its intentions by cutting the Maynooth grant. Catholic agitation sharpened in the period 1807–12 and there was, from 1807 onwards, a strong and growing Catholic electoral interest which demanded that its candidates oppose Richmond's government. This period saw aggressive changes in the means of agitation and in the government's response. For one thing, the leadership was shifting away from the remaining Catholic peers like Fingall towards a more impatient middle-class group. The more assertive policy which resulted from this between 1810 and 1813 saw more regular meetings and proposals to elect delegates and the adroit reconstitution of the Catholic Committee as the Catholic Board to keep outside the terms of the 1793 Convention Act.

Catholic agitation, and government's policy towards it, fluctuated. In 1812 Lord Liverpool's ministry made emancipation an 'open' question, a matter for ministers' personal choice, and opinion in parliament began to move in favour of relief, but Peel, a political 'Protestant', rallied opposition to ensure the defeat of Grattan's relief bill in 1813. The Catholic campaign then went through a period of stagnation, torn apart by internal disagreements, particularly over the issue of whether a government veto on episcopal appointments should accompany emancipation as a safeguard. Daniel O'Connell had been involved in Dublin Catholic politics since 1804 and was a major influence in the aggressive Catholic Board phase. However he really came to the fore in the next main round of agitation, when, from 1822, the Catholic Association which had replaced the Catholic Board was creating a broad support base, extending beyond the Dublin politicos to encompass all levels of Irish Catholicism: the hierarchy and parish clergy, and the mass of the laity by means of parochial associations and the 'Catholic Rent'. Moreover, O'Connell saw the need to politicize all grievances, including those of the agrarian secret societies, and organise them behind the emancipation campaign. Although forced to dissolve and reform as the New Catholic Association, this powerful alliance formed the basis for the final push which made emancipation inevitable in 1829.[36]

The Catholic issue had a range of political contexts from parliamentary debate between the conflicting interests, through central government's policy on how the issue should be handled, to local electoral conflict and, ultimately, to local lower-

---

35 13 Sept. 1803, K.A.O. Pratt Papers, U840C/104/5.   36 Bartlett, *Fall and Rise*, passim; C. C. Trench, *The Great Dan*, p. 67.

class struggles for sectarian dominance. Yeomanry were active in all these contexts. Whatever their operational utility, the yeomanry remained a dynamic political symbol. Throughout their nineteenth-century existence they were a rich river brimful of political arguments for those who knew how to fish for them. Initially, this was the Irish government and the Protestant interest.

With the Dublin parliament gone, Irish Protestants well knew their political position ultimately depended on their maintaining their 'Ascendancy', both locally and at the ultimate source of power in London. The means of altering or maintaining their position was the British government and the king. Loyalty was the direct line to this power-source but it was essential that Protestants monopolised it. Robert Emmet gave them their opportunity, the heavy yeomanry augmentation following the end of the Peace of Amiens was their means. The official hysteria was well-orchestrated. One of the law officers advised against 'rummaging old books and musty councils, to prove men willing to stake their lives and property against Bonaparte cannot be good subjects'.[37] However the Castle's negligence in not detecting the plot under their very noses was conveniently lost in the resulting cloud of dust. This made the opportunity of yeomanry monopoly golden. Wickham told Castlereagh, 'the determination not to receive Catholics into many corps has increased since the last rebellion, so that we must either reject the services of loyal Catholics altogether, or create Catholic corps ... a measure which would not be *cried* but *roared* out against throughout all Ireland'.[38] Wickham read the Yeomanry Office runes correctly. Up in Tyrone Abercorn sensed the mood. Once a supporter of Catholic relief, he now proposed a legion of 1,200 supplementaries, assuring Hardwicke 'in all this force I shall admit not more than 10 or 12 papists, just to save the appearance of total exclusion'. In Wicklow Sir Edward Newenham declared that he 'would not trust them [Catholic yeomen] with even a sword, let alone making them drill serjeants for the rebels'. Passing through parts of Kildare, Queen's County and Tipperary on circuit, the prime serjeant, Arthur Browne, noted that all corps in the towns he passed, especially Monasterevin and Rosscrea, 'refuse to admit a Papist', a tendency so complete that the only debate was whether it was better to exclude Catholics collectively, signifying general distrust, or by ballot, conveying individual stigma.[39]

Clearly the members of the Protestant interest felt they could rely on the support of the government in such cases. The value of yeomanry as a political conduit and governing tool has been emphasised. However, with Addington's ministry unstable, and the possibility of new arrangements involving Pitt or Grenville, who both favoured emancipation, Hardwicke had to tread warily. Late the previous year

37 J.L. to Colclough, 21 Feb. 1804, P.R.O. H.O.100/119/f. 203.   38 14 Aug. 1803, *Castlereagh Corrs.*, iv, pp. 294–8.   39 10 Aug. 1803, P.R.O.N.I. Abercorn Papers, D623/A/81/65; Newenham to Wickham, 15 Sept. 1803, H.R.O. Wickham Papers, 38M49/5/32/11; Browne to Redesdale, 3 Aug. 1803, P.R.O.N.I. Redesdale Papers, T3030/9/10.

he had admitted confidentially to Wickham, 'though it is very desirable to have Protestant yeomanry, yet the less that is said about it the better'.[40] Hardwicke had used a Protestant yeomanry to help him govern Ireland; after Emmet, a Protestant yeomanry and a Catholic conspiracy were necessary to keep him governing Ireland. The Castle's weakness was the Protestant interest's opportunity. Any stirrings of the Catholic issue assumed a heightened significance after the Union, and, if the identity of government and Ascendancy interests of 1798 could be revived, so much the better. New offers of yeomanry service flooded in to the Castle. In an echo of 1798, Foster extravagantly praised the yeomen for saving the day against Emmet. The rejuvenated yeomanry offered physical security, a reassuring affirmation of the *status quo* before Cornwallis, and an advance argument against any future threat to Protestants' political position. By using their hold over the yeomanry – the fraternal correlation between admittance to yeomanry corps by ballot and Orange lodge membership are significant here. This monopoly of loyalty could send a blunt message to Westminster: if Catholics were not trusted as yeomen, could they be trusted in parliament?

The politics of loyalty are interesting. Since Fitzwilliam's aborted yeomanry scheme and Grattan's subsequent attempt to link the formation of the 'Ascendancy Army' with the Catholic issue, there had been no moves to utilise the state of the country as an argument for emancipation. Obviously, perceptions of 1798 and 1803 compromised Catholic agitation, ensuring that it would follow the traditional pattern. Innate conservatism was also a factor yet there is evidence of what might be best described as a trusting naiveté. In November 1804, as the new Catholic petition was preparing, one commentator attributed Catholic irritation to Protestants monopolising the yeomanry since July 1803, supposedly for financial gain.[41] The Protestant interest therefore had a head start in harnessing the yeomanry politically. This took a variety of forms and fluctuated in response to perceived 'crises', when the Catholic interest seemed most threatening.

Bedford's viceroyalty raised Catholic hopes. Grenville's 'Talents' ministry supported emancipation and measures were soon being taken to win the confidence of Irish Catholics. An obvious area was reform of the magistracy and purges of ultra Protestant magistrates soon began. A prime target was Archibald Jacob, who commanded a Wexford yeomanry corps, the Vinegar Hill Rangers. The removal was openly political: Jacob was considered 'obnoxious to Roman Catholics'.[42] His response was no less political. He resigned his yeomanry commission in a protest tacitly co-ordinated with Wexford's Protestant interest. Jacob's action was followed by the resignation of every other member and left government with no option but to disband the unit, thus incurring the embarrassment of appearing to destroy a corps

40 12 Nov. 1802, H.R.O. Wickham Papers, 38M49/5/10/90. 41 Thomas McKenna to Nepean, 18 Nov. 1804, P.R.O. H.O.100/123/f. 112. 42 Trail to [?Hawkesbury], 13 Aug. 1807, P.R.O. H.O.100/142/f. 48.

with obvious links to 1798. Given the substantial yeomanry connection with the wider Protestant community, the resignation of arms had the effect of firing a political broadside at government and at the growing Catholic electoral interest. The fall of the 'Talents' and the advent of Portland's 'No Popery' ministry marked a change of policy. The backers of Jacob's actions came out in the open. Lord Ely, himself snubbed by the Bedford government,[43] recommended to Arthur Wellesley that Jacob have his corps back. Wellesley agreed, though with electoral interests in mind, attempted 'balance' in making Jacob reapply formally rather than make the decision appear to be a political reward. However, Wellesley absolutely refused to allow Jacob to dance on the grave of Bedford's government by parading his yeomen on the anniversary of the Battle of Vinegar Hill, on the grounds that it would annoy the Catholics.[44] This was precisely what Jacob wanted, but the real prize would have been to provoke disorder because the Catholics were finally waking up to the politics of loyalty.

Around the same time, in Waterford, Michael Evelyn, first lieutenant of the town's Merchants' Infantry, wrote confidentially to Littlehales at the Yeomanry Office about Catholics in his corps. He recalled that he had lived and worked with Catholic gentlemen, and felt them to be loyal, but he had recently noticed that their 'demeanour is totally changed'. Friendliness had been replaced by a very obvious 'coldness, reserve and sullen silence'. This spoke volumes for Evelyn, who saw his captain's disobeying orders to parade the corps on the king's birthday as evidence of Catholics refusing to serve, particularly when it was seen in parallel with moves by priests in Waterford and Wexford to stop people enlisting in the militia.[45] Though the Castle dismissed Evelyn's concerns as unsubstantiated, subsequent events revealed that Catholic loyalty in the forces was emerging as a new form of leverage on an otherwise unsympathetic ministry. With war raging and manpower in short supply, this argument side-stepped 1798 and 1803, and was intended to wrong-foot the opponents of emancipation. In an 1808 pamphlet addressed to Bedford, William Parnell, a liberal Protestant, highlighted troop shortages and claimed that by withholding emancipation 'you have an army that can't recruit, a people for an enemy'. However, if the government would treat Protestants and Catholics equally, 'the yeomanry, strengthened by the accession of all the wealthy and respectable Catholics' would not only secure the country but allow the militia to be sent on foreign service.[46]

By 1810, informers' reports from Catholic meetings noted an eagerness to calculate the numbers of Catholics in the forces, and construe militia interchange as a deliberate weakening of their interest, coupled with threats to withdraw Catholics from the yeomanry, army and navy.[47] This tactic had a multiple purpose. Catholic

43 Bartlett, *Fall and Rise*, p. 286.   44 Wellesley to Beevor, 1 June 1807, *W.S.D.*, v, p. 71; Wellesley to Richmond, 26 June 1807, N.L.I. Richmond Papers, MS58/f. 5.   45 18 Aug. 1807, P.R.O. H.O.100/142/f. 120.   46 W. Parnell, 'An historical apology for the Irish Catholics', pp. 156–7.   47 Pole to Ryder, 26 July 1810, 'J.W.' to Pole, 22 Sept. 1810, Pole to Ryder, 27 May 1811, 31 Dec. 1811, P.R.O. H.O.100/158/ ff. 489–93, 159/ f. 246, 165/f. 348, 163/ff. 319–20.

loyalty was used as an argument for entitlement to emancipation.[48] Failing this, the small numbers of Catholic yeomen could be used to turn the Protestant yeomanry monopoly against the Protestant interest by establishing a counter claim to undermine the political kudos of 'loyalty'. The yeomanry were partisan, and, as every viceroy knew, it was a small move from being partisan to being dangerous.

If disturbances in the early nineteenth century was not political per se, then arguments about who was responsible for the disorder certainly became highly politicized. The centrality of the Catholic question ensured that other events were interpreted in relation to it. Since the later eighteenth century there had been the tendency for commemorations and public gatherings to become politicized. Bartlett notes the facility with which any popular gathering, festive, religious, or otherwise, in the early nineteenth century became an occasion for the demonstration of Catholic numbers, a cause of concern to the government and a source of strength to the participants.[49] Protestant commemorations had similar effects on participants and opponents. Parnell noted how Orange celebrations in July and November produced Protestant 'outrages', while Catholics felt them to be parades 'of insulting domination'.[50] If local domination could not be demonstrated in numbers, then displays of armed strength could substitute, as the Jacob incident shows. Any apparent advance by the Catholic interest meant that this dominance needed to be restated. To Catholics, it mattered little whether such displays were worked through the medium of the gentry, as in this case, or were spontaneous. The message was the same: a demonstrably Protestant yeomanry meant local 'Ascendancy'. While Jacob trailed his coat in Enniscorthy, even the token Catholics in Abercorn's legion had disappeared: the 1,400–1,500 men were now 'all Protestants'. Here too the message was unmistakable. This total exclusion and the snub it implied 'would have an effect on those who by their resolutions would abolish the Protestant and establish the Roman Catholic church'.[51]

Struggles for domination did not need an anniversary as pretext. They could be conducted at a wide range of gatherings including sports, horse races, funerals, and fairs. The politicization of funerals was one of the United Irishmen's propaganda devices and was a tactic now taken up by their opponents. It became customary for yeomen to appear in uniform at Orange funerals. Apart from the obvious motive of respect for someone who was a fellow lodge and corps member, these occasions were both public displays of Orange-yeomanry solidarity and aggressive political statements reminding Catholics of 1798. They were certainly received as such. In Belfast the body of an Orange yeoman, Quail, was reportedly disinterred and left on the public road, the fact of his being buried at Friar's Bush, a mainly Catholic burying ground, doubtless adding venom to the display.[52] Fairs were especially potent,

48 *Parl. Debs.*, First Series, xxii, p. 753.   49 Bartlett, *Fall and Rise*, p. 314.   50 Parnell, op. cit. p. 174.   51 Manners to Richmond, 7 Sept. 1807, N.L.I. Richmond Papers, MS61/f. 350.   52 Verner to Peel, 10 Jan. 1814, P.R.O. H.O.100/176/ff. 294–5.

because they involved a large influx of rural dwellers coming into the towns. In many areas this brought Catholics and Protestants eyeball to eyeball. Even where this did not happen naturally, the fact that fairs happened on different set days in the towns of a district meant that advance 'understandings' were possible, where the factions could meet, perhaps to resume the conflict of a previous meeting. In many instances yeomen were involved, officially and unofficially, in these affrays.

One important point must be made: Orange displays in the yeomanry, or yeoman participation in Orange events, had a wider frame of reference than faction fights. The tolerance by the local authorities, civil and military, of such involvement was an essential part of the Orange-yeomanry liaison in 1797–8. Although overt official toleration of such displays was increasingly eroded from the time of Bedford, they had become established as custom in many corps and were continued, often with the connivance of the local gentry. Such occasions could be marked by arranging a yeomanry parade or inspection to fall on the special day, a decision which could only have been taken at command level. Initially, these displays also served a strategic function: the men would have celebrated the occasion anyway and were easier controlled under yeomanry discipline. However, in the polarised atmosphere of the early nineteenth century, as the strategic imperative lessened, the sectarian potential increased.

An ugly incident at Bandon in county Cork shows how powerful and potent these yeomanry displays could be. On 1 July 1809, the anniversary of the Boyne on the old style calendar, the earl of Bandon tried to stop the traditional yeomanry parade, as it had produced 'party' problems in the past. The brigade major was briefed not to carry out any inspection that day but the officer in command saw an ugly situation developing as the men assembled and ordered an exercise parade, as 'all who know their temper know they would have assembled without orders and it was judged most prudent to gratify their wish in moderation'. The Bandon Legion was based on an earlier Boyne Society, which had similarly marked 1 July, and custom overcame orders and deference. The men broke from inspection and formed columns to parade the town as usual, but 'contrary to any former usage', with Orange lilies in their caps. The earl of Bandon, seeing this, intervened, but despite his using 'all his eloquence ... they refused to be commanded by any one but an Orangeman and would rather lay down their arms than their lilies'.[53] However, in this case, it was Lord Bandon who was being anachronistic. This incident represented a larger process which amounted to a deliberate rejuvenation of the Orange-yeomanry connection of 1797. From 1809 the Lurgan yeomanry, entirely illegally, used an unofficial version of the yeomanry oath, a *de facto* Orange oath, for all officers, non-commissioned officers and privates.[54] In Tyrone on 1 August 1810, 'one of the most

53 Auriol to Littlehales, 8 July 1809, Bandon to Littlehales, 9 July 1809, P.R.O. H.O.100/153/ff. 345–7, 347–8. 54 9 March 1809, Lurgan Yeomanry Detail Book, P.R.O.N.I. D3696/A/4/1.

particular days of the year for Orange meetings and displays of banners', yeomen gathered for their customary parade at Strabane, in spite of a ban by the district general, Hart. The local magnates here did not toe the line, as Lord Bandon had tried to do. The brigade major, doubtless answering to Abercorn, to whom he probably owed his position, countermanded Hart's order. A riot had occurred at the previous year's 1 August parade at Omagh between yeomanry, parading 'with some Orange badge', and privates of the Queen's County militia, in which two yeomen were killed and the remainder barely prevented from storming the barracks where the militia had taken shelter. Hart put his finger on the origin of the custom: 'every person of consideration who has been made acquainted with the merits of the armed Orangemen in times of rebellion, must respect and do give them every due merit'. However, missing the point entirely, he went on, 'when in the wisdom of the legislature, it is not thought proper to give the Roman Catholics all they have asked for', such proceedings were imprudent and would cause trouble as local Catholics took such displays as 'a pointed insult'.[55]

The point was that ordinary Protestants felt physically insecure and their leaders felt the political need to keep one step ahead. This was done by means of the Orange Order: the vigour of the yeomen on commemorative occasions was symbolically important. The medium became the message. The message was that if political agitation could be construed as rebellion, then fear was the drill sergeant for the opposition. The deliberate rejuvenation of the Orange-yeomanry connection shows that, notwithstanding a sympathetic administration, Protestants distrusted the long-term ability of any Irish government to defend their interests. To Protestants, the increasing tempo and various strands of the Catholic challenge began progressively to coalesce into the ultimate nightmare: that they would be overwhelmed through sheer weight of numbers.

The growing Catholic electoral interest was further enhanced by the formation of local clubs to elect delegates. Political agitation drew strength from the accession in 1810 of the Prince Regent, a one-time supporter of emancipation. For Protestants, the concurrent rise and spread from Ulster of the Ribbonmen, a sectarian self-defence society similar to the Defenders[56] gave the lie to arguments about Catholic loyalty and cast the whole process as potential insurrection. Riots became commonplace, particularly in west Tyrone, Derry and Donegal where new Ribbonism and resurgent Orangeism fed off each other. The crude violence of these sectarian affrays has been frequently noted[57] though this perhaps disguises a subtle change in the Protestant response. From 1811 the 1797 part of the Orange-yeomanry connection – the zeal for Williamite commemorations – having been rejuvenated, Protestant propagandists then faithfully recreated the Orange auxiliaries of 1798.

55 Stewart to Littlehales, 12 Aug.1809, Hart to Littlehales, n.d Aug. 1810, P.R.O. H.O.100/153/ff. 366–8, 159/f. 43.   56 Bartlett, *Fall and Rise*, p. 318.   57 See Bartlett, ibid., pp. 322–3; Jenkins, *Era of Emancipation*, pp. 97–8; Senior, *Orangeism*, pp. 184–7.

In December 1811 Richmond received an anonymous letter from Lisburn, warning of a 'treasonable association' in Antrim and Down, and promising that the Orange auxiliaries of 1798 'have renewed their vigilance'.[58] The yeomanry were of course the key element in this policy: their continued existence and ostentatious Orangeism proved that Irish Protestants could and would defend themselves. In the debate on Grattan's motion for Catholic relief in 1812, Patrick Duigenan blurted out, 'Why, Sir, the Protestants of Ireland are able, without any assistance from this country at any time, to keep them [the rebels] down'.[59] In 1813 'The Honourable, the Protestant Loyal Society', representing 104 lodges in county Down, published a 'declaration' which recalled the Orange yeomen and auxiliaries of 1798. Conflating Ribbonism, 'treason once more agonizing this kingdom', and Catholic political agitation, 'seditious poison daily issuing from the press', the Orangemen bound themselves in a new association against the attack 'on the state and its venerable religion ... by *self-constituted inquisitors*' including 'pardoned conspirators of the late rebellion'.[60] At around the same time, Blacker made the same point in verse. At the foundation of an Apprentice Boys' Club in 1813, he drew the siege tradition and the yeomanry and 1798 together in a song 'The Crimson Banner':

Again when treason maddened round, and rebel hordes were swarming,
Were Derry's sons the foremost found, for King and Country arming.
Forth, forth they rushed at honour's call from age to boyhood tender,
Again to man their virgin wall and sang out, No Surrender![61]

In the same city, the following year Sir George Hill noted the impact on local Protestants of Catholics drawing O'Gorman (one of the solicitors the Catholic Board engaged to fight cases where they believed partial justice operated) around the streets in triumph and, to add injury to insult, smashing through a toll gate on the bridge. Hill's response, which had Peel's approval, was to 'remove the rebels from the Derry corps', in other words purge the 32 Catholics from the thousand or so members of Hill's Londonderry Legion, and, 'instead of discouraging the spread of Orangeism as I have done heretofore, I must for public safety promote it and head it'. Convinced as he was of the complicity of the Catholic Board and the 'Ribbon system' in agitating the lower orders, Hill's actions echoed the yeomanry purges of 1797 and 1798: as Catholics were removed from the corps, its numbers were augmented by numbers of Protestant farmers. Hill thought this would shore up local Protestant confidence, which was subjected to 'threatening letters, petty offences and malicious injuries' at the same time as showing the Board in its true colours. Peel agreed

---

58 30 Dec. 1811, N.L.I. Richmond Papers, MS60/f. 284a.   59 *Parl. Debs.*, First Series, xxii, p. 753.
60 B.L. 8274bb (2) (North Shields, 1813).   61 R.M. Sibbett, *Orangeism in Ireland and throughout the Empire*, i, p. 192.

and in a rare moment of exegesis, turning one of the Ribbonmen's passwords against them, claimed: 'Thus shall the eyes of the blind be opened'.[62]

The Duigenan line had the immediate advantages of lumping all reformers as rebels and chiming in with the views of the Castle: Peel felt the Orange institution 'truly loyal', as opposed to the Ribbonmen.[63] It also hit a familiar note with ordinary Protestants, resonating with both the Williamite and the more recent past, and having the moral justification of contemporary evangelical religious practices. However, in its present strength lay its greatest future weakness. This is the crucial point about the Orange-yeomanry connection in the second and third decades of the nineteenth century. The Orange-yeomanry may have proved a retreat for a besieged Protestant interest, but when Union moved the battleground of Catholic politics from west Tyrone to Westminster, it proved a political liability. The Protestants of Derry and elsewhere were slow to see the writing on their own wall but the eyes of more astute Catholics like O'Connell were already open to the political possibilities inherent in the yeomanry's Orange connections.

The first inklings had emerged in 1812. The supporters of emancipation shifted the emphasis from the military numbers game and Catholic loyalty to use the Protestants' own yeomanry monopoly and its Orange connection as a means of attack. The radical *Dublin Evening Post* struck at Protestant interests in Fermanagh, where the earl of Enniskillen was a prominent Orangeman. A smuggling dispute was used as a pretext to produce a wide-ranging criticism not only of the yeomanry but also the local magistracy. Apparently a group of Fermanagh yeoman and Orangemen were involved in firing at revenue officers. Some were arrested but the others, despite having bills of indictment found against them, were able to attend their yeomanry parades under the inspection of the captain and brigade major, both grand jurors, without any action being taken.[64] The truth of these assertions is unclear, since they were derived from an anonymous letter. However, the point is that yeomanry were now enlisted as a source of argument on *both* sides of the Catholic question. Peel, proving himself better as an administrator than a prophet, soon felt the impact.

The opening shot had been already fired. From 1813, Orangeism came under scrutiny in parliament. The emancipationists had chosen their ground well. In a debate on Orange legality, as an oath-bound society following the suppression of the Catholic Board, a succession of incidents involving the yeomanry provided ammunition to attack the government. The Catholic spokesmen could point to riots in Carrowkeel, county Donegal, in which nine lives were lost while Peel, clearly rattled, could only counter rather tamely by alluding to the case of the Armagh yeomanry, disbanded the previous year for refusing to serve under a lieutenant who had

62 Hill to Peel, 1 Jan, 10 Jan. 1814, P.R.O. H.O.100/176/ff. 123–4, 286; Peel to Hill, 7 Jan. 1814, P.R.O.N.I. Hill of Brook Hall Papers, D642/A/14/2; Hill to Gregory, n.d. Jan. 1814, B.L. Peel Papers, add. mss. 40212 ff. 43–4. 63 Jenkins, op. cit., p. 93. 64 7 May 1812, P.R.O. H.O.100/167/f. 18.

signed an emancipation petition.[65] The attack was renewed the following year. It was believed that a new petition against Orange societies by Sir Henry Parnell would use the issue of yeomanry bands playing party tunes in the July processions as a means of proving that the Irish government supported societies which had engaged in outrages against Catholics. Peel had prepared for this in 1813, but taken no effective action, relying on the gentry to influence their corps against 'ceremonial pageantry', and instructing the captains and brigade majors, where exercise days were not set to fall on 12 July, to find alternative days rather than run the risk of damaging the Irish government's political interest by issuing a public order against it (as recommended by the military hierarchy). It is worth noting *en passant* that this resurrected the old problem of clashes between the civil and military hierarchies. Peel the administrator could work with the system where the district generals had a formal role, giving advice and assistance on civil peacekeeping to the magistrates, Peel the politician had difficulty taking advice from the same quarters, even though it was for the same reasons. 'Why not' he fumed to Gregory 'order uniformity of religion by a circular from the Royal Hospital?' In reality, as the emancipationists knew only too well, Peel was caught between the potentially conflicting demands of maintaining the connection with the Protestant interest to govern the country, and maintaining tranquillity. It was a delicate balance. Peel justified his approach on the old grounds of the lesser evil: to 'inflame' Protestants meant that 'government would lose a steady friend and the Catholics find a bitter enemy'.[66]

In the event the bands issue was not raised in 1813 but, though regular army and militia bands had been prevented playing in Orange processions, despite Peel's plea for gentry influence the previous year, the yeomanry bands continued as usual. Peel's continuing discomfort with the issue is clearly seen in a long and frank dispatch to Whitworth. Splitting all kinds of hairs, he drew a distinction between his wish to encourage loyal feeling but at the same time discourage any display which might give offence. In a further refinement, he blamed those who were predisposed to take insult. He ascribed the cause to lower-class religious divisions, but drew some comfort from the fact that the Protestant peasants were loyal while their Catholic equivalents were the reverse, and derided any attempt at 'false unanimity' which would merely make the Protestants the same as the Catholics in hating Britain. Hoping that they 'may always be disunited', Peel reckoned 'the great art is to keep them so, yet at peace, or rather not at war with each other'. All this meant that he had to allow Orangemen to parade, but saw the danger of yeomanry involvement as they would make the government a party to it. Yet his perceptive mind anticipated problems: if the government made 12 July the only day yeomen could not parade it would mark the day even more. Hence the sanction for exercise parades on the day. Similarly, Peel instructed the brigade majors to stop yeomanry bands from participating in

65 *Parl. Debs.*, First Series, xxvi p. 982.   66 Peel to Littlehales, 30 June 1813, B.L. Peel Papers, add. mss. 40284 ff. 31–6; Peel to Gregory, 1 July 1813, 40284 ff. 38–9.

processions, yet refused to ban the playing of party tunes at other times on the grounds that this would multiply their popularity on the one hand and their offensive potential on the other.[67] As well as conveying the subtleties and difficulties of governing Ireland, this letter clearly shows that the yeomanry, once a source of political strength to Irish administrations because of their connections to the Protestant community, were now becoming the weak link in the government's political armoury because that connection was symbolised by an increasingly militant Orangeism.

Alarm bells also rang about a sectarian riot at Kilkeel in county Down which involved yeomen, especially since the local magistrates appeared reluctant to prosecute the Protestant party despite the fact that all reports suggested that neither side was blameless. A number of Protestants had been beaten at the fair, but had then returned in strength, some with yeomanry muskets, and wrecked around 40 Catholic homes. Members of both groups were arrested but the judicial aftermath mirrored the affray itself. The Catholic Board sent its lawyers to defend the Catholics and the jury promptly acquitted the Protestants. Sir Henry Parnell's petition against Orange societies raised the possibility of the matter being harnessed by emancipationists, but Peel, perhaps better aware than his opponents of his political vulnerability, was relieved when no government comment was required on Parnell's petition, telling Gregory that he 'had no wish to court discussion'. Shortly afterwards Peel gave Whitworth a revised opinion of the Orange Order, admiring its loyal principles but expressing grave concern about its military, particularly its yeomanry, connections.[68] Peel's relief was short-lived. Although the July parades passed, the Orange-yeomanry issue sprang back into prominence from an unexpected quarter. At his summing up after the Wexford summer assizes, Judge Fletcher, always a loose cannon in the establishment, fired a broadside at the assembled grand jury about judicial partiality, recollecting his experiences on the North-West circuit where 'those disturbers of the peace, assuming the name of Orange yeomen, come into the fairs and markets with arms ... under the pretence of self-defence or of protecting the public peace, but with the purposed [*sic*] view of inviting attacks from the Ribbonmen'.[69] The political intention was clear to Peel and, in November he warned Sidmouth that the matter would be taken up in parliament as proved the case in July 1815 when Parnell quoted Fletcher in an attempt to petition the Prince Regent on Orange lodges.[70]

This parliamentary onslaught was ultimately intended to weaken the opposition to emancipation, by prising apart the connection between the Irish government and

67 Peel to Whitworth, 16 June 1814, B.L. Peel Papers, add. mss. 40287 ff. 35–7. 68 Peel to Sidmouth, 13 April 1814, P.R.O. H.O.100/177/f. 343; Peel to Gregory, 3 May 1814, B.L. Peel Papers, add. mss. 40286 f. 142; Bartlett, *Fall and Rise*, p. 316; Peel to Gregory, 14 June 1814, B.L. ibid., add. mss. 40287, f. 33; 23 July 1814; Parker (ed.), *Peel Correspondence*, i, p. 159. 69 n.d. July 1814, P.R.O. H.O.100/176/ff. 79–111. 70 10 Nov. 1814, P.R.O. H.O.100/176/ ff. 76–9; *Parl. Debs.*, First Series, xxxi, p. 1096.

the majority of Irish Protestants, the 'Protestant interest'. To an extent this worked. Peel was put in a position where he had to take action against Orangeism, or the Orange 'spirit' in the yeomanry, and this left him open to criticism from the 'ultras'. He complained to Gregory about being 'blamed by the one party for going too far in the vindication of Orangemen, and by the other in not going far enough.[71] He had already seen an example of this in the case of the Armagh yeomanry which he had used to fend off attacks in 1813. 'I hear', he told Richmond, 'that the rebels of Armagh are putting a misconstruction on the disbanding of the yeomanry corps'. He proposed to re-embody the Armagh yeomanry corps and give it back to Lord Charlemont, whose father had originally raised the unit. However, Peel aroused the ire of the ultra-Protestant party, particularly the Primate of Armagh and Duigenan himself, whose antennae were strained to detect any snub to the Ascendancy, by favouring a liberal, despite Charlemont's impeccable family claim to the corps.[72] The danger of course was that, in trying to hold the ring, the Castle would caught between Catholic agitation and Protestant alienation. 'The more I think about the subject [Orangeism]' he told Gregory, 'the more I am convinced that even the most loyal associations in Ireland for political purposes are dangerous engines.' Peel then warned, in a clear reference to the yeomanry, 'we may derive a useful lesson from the Volunteers'.[73] At ground level, there was the additional danger that the attacks on the Orange yeomanry would be interpreted as attacks on Protestantism rather than the Protestant interest, and every attempt by government to decrease its vulnerability in this area would be evidence that government support was waning, that Protestants would eventually have to defend themselves.

The government's stance was critical. Although Hill described a sectarian riot at Donemana fair in county Tyrone as 'a *champs de Mars*' in August 1815,[74] Peel's crackdown on the Catholic Board eventually convinced anxious Protestants of the government's continued support, and thus outweighed his limited moves against Orangeism in the yeomanry. This continued support was heavily underlined by the yeomanry's retention after the end of the war. From a Protestant perspective, however, their fate was no longer in their own hands. In contrast to the boasts after 1798, that they could defend themselves and the country by means of the yeomanry, the support of future Irish administrations was at the mercy of unpredictable governmental changes in Britain. Although the same situation of general government support continued from Whitworth's into Talbot's administration (with the partial exception of Grant, Talbot's secretary from 1818), the reality was that with emancipation an 'open' issue from 1812, nothing could be taken for granted.

Castlereagh, one of the architects of the Orange yeomanry in 1798, had told

---

71 n.d., July 1814, *Peel Corrs.*, i, p. 159.   72 Peel to Richmond, 13 Oct. 1813, B.L. Peel Papers, add. mss. 40285 f. 83; Whitworth to Sidmouth, 25 Jan. 1814, P.R.O. H.O.100/176/ f. 505.   73 Peel to Gregory, n.d. July 1814, *Peel Corrs.*, i, p. 159.   74 Hill to Peel, 23 Aug. 1814, B.L. Peel Papers, add. mss. 40212 f. 110.

parliament in June 1813 'there might have been formerly some cause for them, but they had survived the danger', and that 'such associations were ever dangerous, but especially so when extended to military bodies'.[75] The arrival of a political 'catholic', Marquis Wellesley, in late 1821 was greeted by a riot in a Dublin theatre, when Orangemen threw bottles and other missiles at the new viceroy. The Orangemen had cause to worry, as their opponents rallied on a number of fronts. Wellesley's arrival was followed shortly by a strong revival of Catholic agitation, in the form of O'Connell's Catholic Association, and the establishment of the county constabulary, which further removed any functional justification for yeomanry retention. It also sparked a renewed parliamentary assault on the Protestant interest, mediated via Orangeism in the magistracy, the Peace Preservation Force, and, more particularly, the yeomanry. Eventually, a bill against unlawful societies was passed and Peel, now home secretary, insisted it include Orange societies. In March 1825 the grand lodge dissolved itself.[76]

Yeomanry were little used in the period between 1822 and the brief reactivation under Anglesey in late 1830. This period coincided with the final push for and eventual achievement of Catholic emancipation. It has been noted how the dissolution of the grand lodge removed a vital link between those at the social apex of the Protestant interest and those at the bottom.[77] Attempts to defend the yeomanry had been ineffectual, and threw up anachronistic arguments or unrealistic claims. In 1823, George Dawson, MP for county Derry and Peel's brother-in-law, in response to Spring-Rice's critique of the force in the annual army estimates debate, made use of the entire gamut of argument: the yeomanry was constitutional; it had saved Ireland in 1798; and it was an effective law and order force.[78] In 1825, as O'Connell's Catholic Association mobilised its resources in an all-out electoral assault on a range of 'Ascendancy' candidates, the same historical justifications of the yeomanry were used in defence. On the anniversary of the shutting of Derry's gates Dawson tried to 'cheer up the Protestant spirit' in as 'warm a manner' as possible. However, rhetoric was of little consolation to ordinary Protestants, faced in the south with the Rockites, and Pastorini's 'year', and in the north with the Ribbonmen and a neglected yeomanry. There is much evidence of panic and spontaneous unofficial action. In Cavan rumours of insurrection led to members of yeomanry corps applying for their arms, which had been kept in storage. The captain, Knipe, could not act on his own authority and sent the request up the line to the brigade major, and eventually the district general, who refused it as unnecessary. However, the Protestants acted on their own initiative and, 'without the sanction of the magistrates', formed nightly armed patrols much to the alarm of local Catholics.[79] Similar reports came from around the country. At Clogher in county Tyrone, a sectarian riot caused irregular

---

75 *Parl. Debs.*, First Series, xxvi, p. 986. 76 Senior, *Orangeism*, pp. 204, 214–15. 77 Senior, ibid., p. 217. 78 *Parl. Debs.*, Second Series, viii, pp. 758–66. 79 Knipe to Semple, 24 Dec 1824, Semple to D'Arcy, 27 Dec. 1824, Egerton to Goulburn, 1 Jan. 1825, P.R.O. H.O.100/214/ ff. 26–7, 28–9, 38–9.

bodies of armed Protestants 'to pour into the town all day and part of the night' In Carlow and Wexford, the brigade major reported that Protestants were panicking, gentlemen barricading their houses and yeomanry arms deficient or completely unfit for service. At Dundalk, in an echo of 1796, Lennox Biggs, an ex-magistrate, convinced the Ribbonmen were armed and ready, and swearing it would be 'the work of a day' to exterminate the Protestants, wanted government to arm the yeomen and loyalist civilians to defend themselves. In Wexford Archibald Jacob claimed that hundreds of loyalists wanted to join his yeomanry 'to stand or fall in support of our glorious constitution in church and state'.[80]

At this stage, particularly in parts of the north, the atmosphere of panic engendered by the emancipation campaign and the official neglect of the yeomanry was in danger of making the yeomanry become what its detractors had long claimed it was, and what Peel had feared it would become: armed Orangemen who would maintain 'Ascendancy' by force. The nearest this came to happening was in 1828, when Orangemen at Ballybay, county Monaghan and at Armagh, with proletarian leadership and yeomanry muskets, stopped O'Connell's lieutenant, Jack Lawless, and thousands of supporters marching into Ulster.[81] Arguably the concurrent formation of Brunswick Clubs, which imitated the Catholic Association in structure, embracing peasants, gentry and clergy, provided a response which redirected dangerous energies away physical force to political action. The reconstitution of the grand lodge in the autumn of 1828 also helped re-establish the plebeian-gentry nexus in Orangeism.[82] The emancipation crisis passed without serious bloodshed. However, as the Lawless affair had shown, the potential for spontaneous ground-level physical resistance did exist, and yeomanry were one of its main agents. There is evidence that some yeomanry commanders had extreme difficulty in checking the tendency, encouraged by years of governmental neglect, for the yeomen to see themselves as local defenders of Protestantism.

William Handcock took over the captaincy of the Lurgan Infantry in 1829. As a liberal Protestant he was destined to have many problems with a totally Orange corps. He initiated an investigation into the practices of the corps and discovered that many men had been admitted and armed without taking the yeomanry oath, presumably taking instead the unofficial Orange oath. Worse still, arms were being transferred without consultation with any officers so that no record was kept of their whereabouts. The consequences became clear during a riot in the town, when one of the yeomen was arrested after heading a crowd which confronted the constabulary, and threatened to use yeomanry guns against them. Fearing a Ribbon attack at Cookstown in January 1829, some armed yeomen came into the town demanding orders. On their being refused, the remainder of the corps were on the

80 Chief Con. Brien to D'Arcy, 3 Jan. 1825, Beevor to Goulburn, 9 Jan. 1825, Biggs to Goulburn, 22 Nov. 1826, Jacob to Peel, 30 Dec. 1826, P.R.O. H.O.100/214/ff. 58–9, 60–1, 216/ ff. 7–8, 114–15.   81 Senior, *Orangeism*, pp. 228–9.   82 Senior, ibid., p. 236.

point of mutiny, which it required the permanent sergeant's best efforts to prevent.[83] Control was not always possible. During 1829 yeomen and Orangemen were involved in violent clashes with Ribbonmen at various places across Ulster, including Ballintra, near Coleraine, Ballyshannon, county Donegal, and Poyntzpass, county Armagh.[84] Though more serious clashes followed the 1829 July parades, in which lives were lost, the year of emancipation passed relatively quietly given the inflamed passions involved. In the following year's parades, yeomen were prohibited from assembling 'in any way or in any garb' on 12 July, either for exercise or for joining Orange parades.[85]

The anger many yeomen felt after emancipation was directed at the British government for their 'treachery', as well as at local Ribbonmen. O'Connell had long aimed at repeal of the Union to accompany emancipation, and pragmatically saw the possibilities in Protestant disenchantment. In late 1830 he made moves to attract Orangemen to repeal, to the extent of drinking a glass of Boyne water in a toast. On the face of it this seems improbable. However, when it is considered that O'Connell was astutely pulling at a submerged strand in the Orange tradition, the true whiggery of the Volunteers of 1782, which some yeomen had previously used to justify opposition to Union in 1800, the attempt assumes a different aspect. Melbourne took it seriously enough to advise Anglesey to re-activate the northern yeomanry.[86] The context of the 1831 re-armament was therefore political as well as military. The consequences have already been noted. Anglesey, under pressure following the sanguinary affair at Newtownbarry, claimed the rearmament of the force was the lesser evil, as 'the Orangemen were upon the balance. A feather would have turned the scale against us ... I had nothing to trust to but the yeomanry, and I had to save them from fraternizing with O'Connell'.[87] The incident became the subject of intense parliamentary scrutiny. Petitions flooded into parliament demanding the disbandment of the yeomanry following Newtownbarry, including some from Protestants. O'Connell featured largely in the debates. Having recently failed in his attempt to win over the Orangemen, he was unrestrained in his criticism of the 'miscreant Orange Yeomanry', though still alert to the possibility of Protestant support for repeal. The July processions, he said, were 'not Protestant but Orange. There was a wide difference between the two'. The disbandment issue brought the Irish Yeomanry to the centre of the parliamentary stage as never before, and provoked an extravagant response. Sir Robert Bateson, member for Belfast, claimed that 'it would be the destruction of the Protestants in Ireland to disarm the yeomanry'.[88] The

83 Power to Handcock, 4–5 Dec. 1830, Handcock to Power, 31 Dec. 1830, P.R.O.N.I. Lurgan Yeomanry Detail Book, D3696/A/4/1; McCormick to Richardson, 5 Jan. 1829, P.R.O.N.I. Richardson of Drum Papers, D2002/C/17/4.   84 Ross to D'Arcy, 19 Jan. 1829, State of the County Report, n.d. April 1829, Gahan to Gregory, 15 May 1829, P.R.O. H.O.100/226/ f. 124, /227/ ff. 5–7, 18.   85 Gregory to Scott, 6 July 1830, P.R.O.N.I. Richardson of Drum Papers, D2002/C/17/10.   86 Senior, *Orangeism*, p. 249.   87 Anglesey to Holland, 4 July 1831, P.R.O.N.I. Anglesey Papers, D619/27B pp. 26–7.   88 *Parl. Debs.*, Third Series, iv, p. 803, vi, pp. 1028, 1243.

consequences of such publicity were felt most strongly in the north, where the Or-ange-yeomanry connection was strongest and where the vast majority of the corps were based. At a local level, this certainly had the immediate effect of making the yeomanry appear as the last defence of 'Ascendancy', as Hussey Vivian noted in 1832, but it also arguably had a long-term impact, giving northern Protestants an additional reason to associate repeal with Catholic 'Ascendancy', and to express their reactions to this new threat by traditional means through the well-established custom of locally raised self-defence.

The carnage at Newtownbarry precipitated a gradual run-down of the yeomanry which was completed in March 1834. In April the government sent out question-naires to the inspectors of police, to assess local reactions to issues such as tithe, repeal and the recent disbanding of the yeomanry. The response to the latter was mixed. In Leinster the Protestants were strongly opposed, while their Connaught counterparts saw it as a victory for O'Connell. Munster was indifferent, but the reaction in Ulster was surprisingly muted. There Sir Frederick Stoven noted what can be best described as a sense of hurt: 'Many of the yeomen feel themselves *ne-glected* and are indifferent about their arms'.[89] This stunned reaction tells its own story. Hurt pride was one thing, but the real damage cut deeper. As the descendants of the of the original planters, the northern Protestant psyche was heavily influ-enced by factors relating to their security, such as defence and a strongly defined sense of territory. As a local defence force, Yeomanry occupied a familiar place in the collective memories of many Protestants, whether Presbyterian or Anglican. One of the lasting impacts the yeomanry had was in reuniting northern Protestants through the re-activated Williamite tradition, and, by weight of numbers, making them more confident than their co-religionists elsewhere about their capacity to defend themselves. As early as 2 June 1798 Cooke told Wickham that the force of 'Orange yeomanry' in Ulster was 'really formidable'.[90] Its territorial nature, shown so clearly by the reluctance of the yeomen to move from their homes into large military brigades, reflected the logic of the Ulster plantation. Indeed, the Derry yeoman John Shoales pointedly referred to the yeomanry as the direct descendants of the Protestant settlers.[91] The gentry commanders and even the emergency as-sembly point, often the landowner's house, echoed plantation requirements for un-dertakers to arm their tenants. The weekly parades and drills doubled as a way of marking territory in much the same way as painted kerbstones and lambeg drum-ming in the twentieth century. Moreover, the desire to band together defensively, and to sign for service had religious connotations. Charles McCarthy spoke of the Orange elements at Strangford, county Down, which were later to end up in John

89 2–18 April 1834, P.R.O. H.O.100/245/ ff. 118, 122–3, 120, 138–41, 144. 90 2 June 1798, P.R.O. H.O.100/77/f. 21. 91 Enclosure in Farnham to Wellington, 14 Aug. 1828, S.U.L. Wellington Papers, WP1/247/25.

Waring Maxwell's yeomanry as 'a remnant of the Scotch covenant of 1638 when the covenanters subscribed to defend each other against all opposition'.[92]

Though officially disbanded in 1834, given how neatly the yeomanry fitted into the Protestant experience it is not surprising that the force left an imprint on the Irish and particularly the northern Irish Protestant consciousness discernible at various times since. Stoven, recognizing that the permanent sergeants were the most influential members of corps and, also the real danger that yeomanry guns would be difficult to reclaim, wanted their pensions made contingent on the arms being collected.[93] He had cause for concern. A later parliamentary enquiry showed that many yeomanry guns were missing. All 230 of the Lurgan yeomanry's muskets were still in the hands of a private individual in 1841 and the ex-permanent sergeant had to be ordered to retrieve them, with police assistance if necessary.[94] It is very likely therefore that the local yeomanry organisation remained in unofficial existence as a latent defence network in parts of Ulster, possibly under the structure of the local Orange lodge, in a nineteenth-century equivalent of the old Boyne Societies. Certainly the template, and the idea of the force remained. In 1859, when there was an attempt to re-establish volunteering in England, William Sharman Crawford, one time captain of the Moira Infantry in county Down, advocated a renovation of the Irish yeomanry force.[95] Indeed, the Ulster Volunteers of 1912 were raised by some of the same gentry families involved in the yeomanry. They show remarkable similarity to the yeomanry right down to their reluctance to leave their homes for larger brigades.[96] The yeomanry's imprint can also be seen in modern Orangeism, both in nomenclature and ethos. Sharman Crawford's old corps gave their name to the Moira Yeomanry Orange Lodge. Furthermore, if the progenitors of present-day Orangemen are the first lodges of 1795, the ancestry of the flute bands they march to owes more to the yeomanry, with territorial collectiveness being expressed in an aggressive militarism. If a survey was taken of the most popular names for Protestant bands 'Defenders' would be in the great majority. Yeomanry, therefore occupy an important in Irish history as the first modernisers of the Williamite tradition.

---

92 McCarthy to Pelham, 20 Nov. 1797, N.A. R.P.620/33/74. 93 18 April 1834, P.R.O. H.O.100/245/ f. 140. 94 Handcock to Moore, 25 April 1841, P.R.O.N.I. Lurgan Yeomanry Detail Book, D3696/A/ 4/2. 95 Sharman-Crawford to Palmerston, n.d. 1859, P.R.O.N.I. Sharman Crawford Papers, D856/ D/146. 96 I am grateful to Dr A. Jackson of Queen's University, Belfast for this information.

Epilogue

The story of the Irish Yeomanry is a complex one which resists being neatly parcelled in an eye-catching overall conclusion. The force's military significance is undeniable and certainly belies the historical neglect under which it has languished. However, the yeomanry's influence was also tangible across a range of non-military contexts. Even within these different contexts, the yeomanry's longevity and regional diversity make generalisations difficult. Indeed, this very diversity makes it a subject eminently fit for more detailed local studies. However, some broad conclusions do emerge from the analysis of the political, social and religious contexts. When examined together these point towards some key features about the yeomanry. We can certainly say that out of its 38 years of existence, the first ten years were the period of its greatest actual and practical significance. Thereafter the yeomanry's significance was more symbolic than factual, though no less important for being so.

Historians of the Irish Yeomanry's nearest equivalent in Britain, the volunteer infantry, are divided over whether the volunteers were a useful adjunct to the regular army or an expensive and wasteful extravagance. The Irish Yeomanry casts little light on this debate as, unlike their British counterparts, they actually faced a formidable armed insurrection and invasion scares which had definite if inchoate support from the disaffected, whereas the British force faced an invasion which never happened in a country where real disaffection was a minority pastime. The Irish Yeomanry reached the peak of its military potential between the years 1797 and 1805, a period which witnessed the end of organised revolutionary disaffection and the reduction of the invasion threat following Nelson's victory at Trafalgar. In these years, the static nature of the yeomanry force made it possible for military commanders to make viable contingency plans against either invasion or domestic insurgency. After this period, starting roughly with the outbreak of 'Threshing' in 1806, the nature, and to a large extent, the location of disorder changed in a way which militated against the yeomanry being either an effective deterrent or a sufficiently powerful instrument of suppression. This said, the yeomanry was conceived mainly as a counter-insurgency force rather than an antidote to agrarian secret societies. They were therefore militarily most effective at the time and in the places of greatest need.

Their main period of political value both to the government and the gentry coincides with that of their military utility to the generals and the magistrates. From the Castle's perspective, the yeomanry gave access to a range of Irish landowners which included some of those normally in opposition like Charlemont. Sensitive implementation of the yeomanry regulations allowed a measure of individual autonomy. The 'egalitarian' practices of the old Volunteers were allowed to continue in the election of officers, and the voluntary service principle, dear to the hearts of whigs steeped in Locke, was permitted to override the dictates of martial law if necessary. Although the reaction to Cornwallis' more conciliatory policy towards the beaten rebels and opposition to legislative Union showed the limits of the yeomanry's value as a political tool, they also showed its ultimate strength as, after 1798, the yeomen needed the government even more than the government needed them. Indeed the highpoint in the yeomanry's utility as an aid to governing came just after Union when official praise of the force helped soothe Protestant feelings and its patronage helped compensate for the loss of military patronage. It is little wonder that Hardwicke's administration were keen to avail themselves of every opportunity to augment the force. This conception of the yeomanry, as a political conduit between the government and the Protestant community, remained valid throughout the rest of the force's existence. However, starting with the re-emergence of the Catholic question in 1805, and particularly when Catholic political agitation became more aggressive from around 1810–12, the yeomanry's close association with Orangeism made it an equivocal aid to government. As Peel discovered when contemplating yeomanry abolition at the end of the war, the potential political difficulties from outraged Protestant opinion outweighed any positive consideration. Moreover, as O'Connell discovered, the Orange-yeomanry connection was the Irish government's weak link at Westminster.

The main impact of the yeomanry on the position of the landowners also occurred early on. The response of the landed gentry to the invitation to raise yeomanry was found to be generally favourable, despite some initial reluctance from reformists opposed to the coercive policies of Camden's government. Politically, there was much to be gained from being involved at the initial stages of raising the force in the counties as this presented the magnates and major landowners involved in co-ordinating the response of the gentry with opportunities to strengthen their electoral interest. For the average yeomanry captain, usually a smaller landowner, there were also solid advantages in being involved in the force. In the social and political turmoil of the 1790s, having a yeomanry corps offered the landowner the opportunity to reclaim influence over his tenantry by giving him patronage, in the form of yeomanry pay, and the obligations of military discipline to reinforce traditional paternalism. Colonel Blacker claimed that no one who obeyed him in his yeomanry corps ever disobeyed him anywhere else. However, here too, the yeomanry's impact lessened after the immediate dangers of insurrection and invasion had passed. Yeomanry corps could not be used as overt instruments of electoral pressure. The main periods of their electoral utility were either when they were raised initially or when large-scale augmentations took place in 1803. As the nineteenth century went on, active gentry involvement in the yeomanry declined somewhat. For one thing, the decline in cavalry and rise in infantry altered the social mix of the force. More critically, many captains delegated much of the responsibility for their corps to their lieutenants and even the permanent sergeants. However, by this stage, the main dangers had passed and the yeomanry had helped the Anglo-Irish maintain their privileged position as landowners and magistrates, albeit after having sometimes to compromise with the 'alternative' influence of the Orange lodge.

The yeomanry's most profound impact is found in two related areas: Protestant-Catholic relations and the changes within Irish Protestantism itself. Problems in the first area were inevitable. Relationships between Protestants and Catholics, deteriorating since the Munster Rightboy disturbances in the late 1780s, were further soured by the relief acts of 1792 and 93 and by the spread of Defenderism. The Fitzwilliam viceroyalty escalated matters by its gratuitous dispensation of hope and fear to each group. The United Irish alliance with the Defenders continued the process. Given this background and the fact of the Camden government's 'rallying of the Protestants' and given that the new yeomanry linked easily, if not seamlessly, with the long-established tradition of Protestant self-defence, Protestants had much less difficulty, ideologically, politically or practically in joining the new force than their Catholic fellow-countrymen. Those Catholic yeomen who overcame these difficulties in 1796–7 were therefore in many ways a tragic anachronism, a throwback to a healthier political climate in the 1770s and early 1780s. Given these difficulties, their numbers are significant as they point to what might have been. Arguably, had a more denominationally-balanced yeomanry been raised in 1795, as Fitzwilliam proposed, the bloodshed of 1798 could have been averted. However, by making full Catholic relief the key to such a force, the opposition to emancipation in Westminster and College Green ensured that this door would be shut.

The formation of yeomanry in 1796 was a defining moment in Protestant-Catholic relations, not because it automatically engendered animosity, but because it required a response. By inviting a stance to be taken it became, not so much an agent of division, as a symptom of pre-existing divisions. However, once stances are taken or imposed, divisions are formalised, 'justified' and rendered susceptible to the influence of wider events. The yeomanry played a major role in the events of 1797–8 which re-defined relationships. The 1798 rebellion was the crucible in which the opposition to emancipation and repeal in the nineteenth century was formed. As the yeomanry oath became a shibboleth of loyalty, membership of the force came to symbolise 'Ascendancy'. This symbolic dimension was as important as any of the yeomanry's earlier practical aspects. The infamous Newtownbarry incident of 1831 illustrates this emphatically. The official reports noted that, despite significant numbers of police being present, the protesters singled out the *yeomen* for attack. Given that no Wexford yeomanry corps had been on duty for over a decade, probably some of the crowd could scarcely remember ever seeing a yeoman on duty before. This, however, was not the point. As one side demonised the yeomen the other lionised them: it was what the yeomen represented that determined reactions on both sides. In the eyes of Catholics, after O'Connell's public attacks on the yeomanry, the force was perceived as symbolising not just Protestant but Orange Ascendancy. For Protestants, if the yeomanry in 1798 represented defence, after 1829 it epitomised defiance.

The yeomanry offered Protestants a familiar re-emergence of various strands of the self-defence tradition: official and unofficial, central and local, elite and populist. It was the old militia, the Volunteers, the Boyne Societies and the loyal associations rolled into one. It was a force which attracted all social and most political elements within contemporary Irish Protestantism. The landed elite's natural leadership position in any local law and order force was reinforced by the yeomany's property-protection dimension as the ramifications of the French Revolution drew ever closer. For the middle and lower classes, the government's policy of letting the yeomanry grow on the structure of the old Volunteers and include the loyal associations, meant that the new force encompassed and tolerated the main ideological strands in eighteenth-century Protestantism, the liberal 'true whig' and the conservative Williamite. By making loyalty the lowest common denominator, the yeomanry accommodated both middle-class reformers and proletarian Orange or proto-Orange groupings. For most old Volunteers outside eastern Ulster, the yeomanry was the natural successor to the Volunteer movement. If the United Irishmen captured the vanguard of refined Volunteer radicalism, the yeomanry got the big battalions, the liberal legions of the middle ground and the growing reactionary rearguard.

These broad linkages to the Protestant defence tradition had important long-term consequences. The ideological differences within the yeomanry's component elements were flattened by the juggernaut of larger events in 1798 and 1803. Ex-radical Presbyterians joined in significant numbers in these years. The yeomanry provided more than a link between eighteenth-century Protestant nationalism and nineteenth-century Protestant loyalism, it proved an agent of and an explanation for change. Nationalism flourished when Protestants did not feel under direct threat; the hydra-like defence tradition could re-emerge with national defence against foreign invasion as the governing principle. Conversely, when threatened from within Ireland, the 'planter against native' element came to the fore. The name given to this in the late 1790s was loyalism, meaning loyalty to and support of the status quo in church and state. This 1790s loyalism certainly drew on tradition but it was also new in being socially broader-based. By providing a rallying point against the United Irishmen and Defenders, the formation of yeomanry helped create a loyalism which was popular yet still contained within traditional power structures. General Knox's scheme of using the yeomanry strategically to access and harness the power of the Orange movement is the best example of this. In this sense there were two forces within the yeomanry. The official institution of the Yeomanry Office, the brigade majors and the landed gentry co-existed with popular loyalism in its yeomanry dimension.

This popular loyalism also formed itself in the image of its opponents. The yeomanry's territorial logic was, in practice, locally conceived to counter the pre-existing structure of the United Irish clubs. Moreover, Orangemen were to the yeomanry what Defenders were to the United Irishmen: organisations that offered manpower and a background of aggression which could be harnessed militarily. Anyone disposed to a romantic view of the 1790s would do well to reflect on the ruthless pragmatism of each side. The United Irish leadership and those controlling the yeomanry played for the same stakes and ran the same risks. The Orangemens' anti-Catholicism and the Defenders' anti-establishment, anti-Protestant attitudes were used in a cynical military numbers game, played by both sides. Indeed the United Irish attempt to woo Orangemen in 1797, by disingenuously changing their name to 'Liberty Men', was matched by the Orange leadership's courting of Catholic loyalism the following year, at the same time as Catholics were being expelled from yeomanry corps, and Orangemen enlisted as supplementaries.

The yeomanry left an impression on this developing popular loyalism which long outlived the force itself. The militarism in nineteenth and twentieth century Orangeism is a direct legacy of the yeomanry connection. This is still seen in the military regalia, the pikes and swords, carried at Orange processions, while the accompanying military-style flute bands, and their aggressive party tunes, are directly descended from the yeomanry bands and their 'ceremonial pageantry' so disliked by Peel. A more immediate legacy was the tendency in the mid-nineteenth century for Orangemen to parade with firearms. This could result in major clashes, like the Dolly's Brae incident of 1846, when a party of Orangemen, on being assaulted by Ribbonmen near Castlewellan in county Down, opened fire, killing six of their opponents. The Orange-yeomanry connection of 1797-8 and the gentry sanction it implied, although conceived as an emergency expedient, a lesser evil, nevertheless left memories of arbitrary law-enforcement which could emerge as assumed sanction for Orangemen to take the law into their own hands, long after the real emergency had subsided.

However, the other side of this coin of militancy was vulnerability. Although the sanguinary affrays can mask this, the yeomanry's original raison d'être was not Ascendancy but defence. Protestants liked to think that their destiny was in their own hands, through their yeomanry monopoly; but, particularly after Union, it self-evidently was not. These changes can be charted in the yeomanry. In 1798, the Hillsborough yeomen, celebrated three battles: the Battle of the Boyne, the Battle of the Nile and the Battle of Ballynahinch. They faced the future, confident of their identity as Protestant Irishmen defending themselves and their country as part of the imperial war effort. They had the thanks of parliament, the blessing of government, the authority of the past and the victories of the present. In 1830, however, their neighbours in the Lurgan Infantry, disgusted with the reforms of the imperial government, were battling it out with the new county constabulary in the streets of the town.

The yeomanry also left a notional template for Protestant self-defence, which continued into the nineteenth century and beyond, particularly in the north. In 1912 when the Ulster Volunteers were being organised in county Tyrone, a battalion was photographed in front of Northland House in Dungannon, family seat of the Knox family. Arguably, the memory of the heavy concentrations and longevity of the Ulster yeomanry, encouraged the feeling that the north could defend itself. The very same self-sufficiency, which had been used as an argument against Union, had come to be ranked against Home Rule. Had Grattan been alive, he would not have missed the irony of the direct descendants of the 'Ascendancy Army' gathering to defend the Union in the heartland of the Volunteers of 1782.

Select Bibliography

PRIMARY SOURCES, MANUSCRIPT MATERIAL

British Library, additional manuscripts
Bexley Papers (Vansittart), 31229–30
Hardwicke Papers, 35701–4, 35706,
    35711–3, 35716, 5719–21, 35724,
    35770–6.
Pelham Papers, 33101–5
Peel Papers, 40212, 40244, 40258, 40280–4,
    40287–90
Percy Papers, 32335
Wellesley Papers, 37301, 37308

Hampshire County Record Office
Wickham Papers

Kent Archives Office
Pratt (Camden) Papers

Linenhall Library Belfast
Joy Mss.

The National Archives of Ireland
Official Papers, O.P.232 series
Rebellion Papers, R.P.620 series
State of the Country Papers,
    S.O.C.1015–7, 1025

National Army Museum, London
Cornwallis Papers 6602/45
Nugent Papers 6807/174

National Library of Ireland
Dalrymple Mss. MS809
Kilmainham Mss. MS1218
Lake Mss. MS56
Richmond Mss. MS58–9, 65–74

Public Record Office, London
Colonial Office Papers, C.O.906
    Home Office Papers, H.O.100 series
Chatham Mss. 30/8 series
    War Office Papers, W.O.8/9, W.O.30/64,
Colchester Mss. 30/9 series
    W.O.30/66, W.O.31/120

Public Record Office of Northern Ireland
Abercorn Papers, D623, T2541
Aldborough Papers, T3300
Anglesey Papers, D619
Annesley Papers, D1854
Atkinson of Crowhill Papers, T2701
Belfast Yeomanry Papers, D3221
Brownlow Papers, D1928
Caledon Papers, D2433.
Castlereagh Papers, D3030
Chesney Papers, D2260
Chilham Papers, T2519
Clare Papers, T3244
Crosslé Papers, D1927
Derry Yeomanry Muster Rolls, T1021
Donoughmore Papers, T3459
Downshire Papers, D607
Dublin Military Letters, MIC67
Foljambe Papers, T3381
Gervais Papers, T1287
Gosford Papers, D1606
Hill of Brook Hall Papers, D642
Ker Papers, D2651
Knox Papers, D115
McCance Papers, D272
McGeough-Bond Papers, D288

Morrow Papers, D3696
Perceval Maxwell papers, T1023
Pollock Papers, T3346
Richardson of Drum Papers, D2002
Rossmore Papers, T2929
Shannon Papers, D2707
Shirley Papers D3531
Stewart of Killymoon Papers, D3167
Stewart Papers, T1442
Trench Papers, T3244
Wellington Papers, T2627/3

Trinity College Dublin
Wollaghan Court Martial, T.C.D. MSS.872
    Madden Papers MS 873

Royal Irish Academy
Charlemont Mss.

Southampton University Library
Wellington Mss. WP1 series.

PRINTED MATERIAL

ABBOT: *Diary and Correspondence of Charles Abbot, Lord Colchester*, ed. Lord Colchester (3 vols, London, 1861)

BERESFORD: *The Correspondence of the Rt. Hon. John Beresford*, ed. W. Beresford (2 vols, London, 1854)

CASTLEREAGH: Memoirs and Correspondence of Viscount Castlereagh, ed. C. Vane, Marquess of Londonderry (4 vols, London, 1848–53)

CHARLEMONT: *The Manuscripts and Correspondence of James, first Earl of Charlemont* (2 vols, H.M.C., London, 1891–94)

CORNWALLIS: *The Correspondence of Charles, first Marquess Cornwallis*, ed. Sir C. Ross (3 vols, London, 1859)

DRENNAN: *The Drennan Letters*, ed. D.A. Chart (Belfast, 1931)

DROPMORE: *The Manuscripts of J.B. Fortesque, Esq.*, preserved at Dropmore (10 vols, H.M.C., London, 1892-27)

HARDWICKE: *The Viceroy's Post-Bag*, ed. M. McDonagh (Dublin, 1904)

MOORE: *The Diary of Sir John Moore*, J.F. Maurice ed. (2 vols, London, 1904)

O'CONNELL: *The Correspondence of Daniel O'Connell*, ed. M.R. O'Connell (3 vols, Shannon, 1972)

PEEL: *Sir Robert Peel from his Private Letters*, ed. C.S. Parker (2 vols, London, 1891)

PLUNKET: *The Life, Letters and Speeches of Colonel Plunket*, ed. The Rt. Hon. D. Plunkett (2 vols, London, 1867)

SCULLY: *The Catholic Question in England and Ireland: The Papers of Denys Scully, 1773–1830*, ed. B. McDermott (Dublin, 1988)

WELLINGTON: *The Supplementary Despatches, Letters and Memoranda of Arthur Wellesley, first Duke of Wellington*, ed. Duke of Wellington (5 vols, London, 1860)

NEWSPAPERS

Belfast News Letter, 1796–7
Northern Star, 1796–7

Freeman's Journal, 1796

YEOMANRY ORDERS

Standing Orders for the Yeomanry of Ireland (Derry, 1798)
Orders for the Infantry Brigades of the City of Dublin (Dublin, 1803)
Printed Directions, Belfast Merchants' Infantry (Belfast, 1803)

PARLIAMENTARY PAPERS

1. *Debates*
The Parliamentary Register, or History of the Proceedings and Debates of the House of Commons of Ireland (17 vols., Dublin, 1782–1801)
The Parliamentary History of England from the Earliest Period to the Year 1803, vxxxiii (36 vols, London, 1806–20); continued as *The Parliamentary Debates from 1803 to the present time*; both cited as *Parl. Debs.*

2. *Journals*
Journals of the House of Commons of Ireland, 1613–1800 (19 vols, Dublin, 1796–1800)
Journals of the Irish House of Lords, vols. 7–8 (Dublin, 1799–1800)
Journals of the House of Commons, vols. 56–62.
Journals of the House of Lords, vols. 43–6.

3. *Reports*
First Report of the Commissioners of Public Instruction, Ireland, with appendix, H.C. 1835 [45], [46], vol. xxxiii.
Report from the Select Committee appointed to enquire into the nature, character, extent and tendency of Orange lodges, associations or societies in Ireland, with the minutes of evidence and appendix, H.C. 1835 [377], vol.xv; 2nd. report, 1835 [475], vol.xvi; 3rd. report, 1835 [476], vol. xvi.

4. *Sessional papers*
A return presented to the House of Commons of all Volunteers and Yeomanry corps, 1803–4 [13–14] vol. xi.

5. *Statutes*
The Statutes at Large passed in the Parliaments held in Ireland, vols xviii-xx (Dublin, 1799–1800)
The Statutes of the United Kingdom of Great Britain and Ireland, vols 1–2 (London, 1804–7)

6. *Votes*
The Votes of the 8th. session of the 5th. Parliament of George III (Dublin, 1797)

PAMPHLETS AND CONTEMPORARY PRINTED MATERIAL

Anon., *Loyal songs as sung in all the Orange lodges in Ireland* (Dublin, c.1800).

Anon., *Reflections on the general principles of electing Commissioned officers in the Divisional corps of Yeomanry in the Metropolis* (Dublin, 1797)

Anon., *Debate on the Proposed Union* (Dublin, 1800)

Anon., *Loyal Songs as Sung in all the Orange Lodges in Ireland* (Dublin, 1800)

Anon., *Address of the Protestant, the Loyal Society* (North Shields, 1813)

Banim, M., *The Croppy: a tale of the Irish Rebellion of 1798* (Dublin, 1828).

Barrington, *Sir Jonah: Personal Sketches* (London, 1830)

Bullingbroke, E., *The Duty and Authority of Justices of the Peace and Parish Officers for Ireland* (Dublin, 1764)

Camillus (pseud. Sir R. Musgrave), *To the Magistrates, Military and Yeomanry of Ireland* (Dublin, 1798)

Dickson, Rev. W. Steel, *A Narrative of the Confinement and Exile of the Rev William Steel Dickson, D.D.* (Dublin, 1812)

Eunomous (pseud.), *An Argument Addressed to the Yeomanry of Ireland demonstrating the Right, the Propriety, the Utility and the Obligation of declaring their sentiments on Political Subjects in their public, distinctive character as Yeomen* (Dublin, 1800)

Gordon, Rev. J., *A history of the rebellion in Ireland in the year 1798* (Dublin, 1803)

Hay, E., *A history of the rebellion in the county of Wexford* (Dublin, 1803)

Irwin, Rev, J., *Sermon on the Nature, Use and Abuse of Oaths* (Dublin, 1798)

Mason, S., *A Statistical or Parochial Survey of Ireland* (Dublin, 1814)

Musgrave, Sir R.M., *Memoirs of the Different Rebellions in Ireland* (first edition: 1 vol., Dublin, 1801; second edition,: 2 vols, Dublin, 1802)

Observer (pseud.): *A View of the Present State of Ireland with an account of the Origin and Progress of the Disturbances in that country* (London, 1797)

An Orangeman (?John Giffard), *Orange Vindicated in a Reply to Theobold McKenna* (Dublin, 1799)

Parnell, W., *An Historical Apology for the Irish Catholics* (Dublin, 1808)

Richardson, Rev. William, *A History of the Origin of the Irish Yeomanry* (Dublin, 1801)

Teeling, C., *Personal Narrative of the Irish Rebellion of 1798* (London, 1828)

Townshend, T., *Part of a Letter ... Vindicatory of the Yeomanry and Catholics of the City of Cork* (Dublin, 1801)

Wakefield, E.G., *An Account of Ireland, Statistical and Political* (2 vols, London, 1812)

Williams, T.W., *The Whole Law relative to the Duty and Office of a Justice of the Peace* (4 vols, London, 1764)

A Yeoman (pseud. Sir William Cusack Smyth), *A letter to the Rt. Hon. William Wickham* (Dublin, 1803)

———, *The Yeoman's second letter to the Rt. Hon. William Wickham* (Dublin, 1804)

SECONDARY SOURCES

Abercromby, J. (Lord Dunfermline), *Sir Ralph Abercromby, K.B., 1793–1801: a memoir by his son* (Edinburgh, 1861)

Adams, J.R.R., *Popular Culture in Ulster, 1700–1900* (Belfast, 1987)

Babington, A., *Military Intervention in Britain* (London and New York, 1990)

Barnard, T., 'The Uses of 23 October and Irish Protestant Celebrations', *English Historical Review*, cvi (1991), pp. 889–920

Bartlett, T., 'An End to Moral Economy: the Irish Militia Disturbances of 1793', *Past and Present*, xxxcix (May, 1983), 99, pp. 41–64

——, 'Indiscipline and Disaffection in the Armed Forces in Ireland in the 1790s', P.J.Corish (ed.), *Radicals, Rebels and Establishments* (Belfast, 1985)

——, 'Indiscipline and Disaffection in the French and Irish armies during the Revolutionary Period', in H. Gough, and D. Dickson (eds), *Ireland and the French Revolution* (Dublin, 1990)

——, 'Militarisation and Politicization in Ireland, 1780–1820', in L. Cullen and L. Bergeron (eds), *Culture et Pratique Politiques en France et en Irlande* (Paris, 1988)

——, *The Fall and Rise of the Irish Nation: the Catholic Question, 1690–1830* (Dublin, 1992)

——, 'Defence, Counter-Insurgency and Rebellin: Ireland, 1793–1803 T. Bartlett and K. Jeffrey (eds), *A Military History of Ireland* (Cambridge, 1996), pp. 247–93.

——, and Hayton, D.W. (eds.), *Penal Era and Golden Age* (Belfast, 1979)

Beames, M., *Peasants and Power* [Brighton, 1983].

Beckett, I.F.W., *The Amateur Military Tradition* (Manchester, 1991)

Beckett, J.C., *The Making of Modern Ireland, 1603–1923* (London, 1966)

Beckett, J.C., *The Anglo-Irish Tradition* (new edition, Belfast, 1982)

——, *The Aristocracy in England, 1660–1914* (Oxford, 1966)

Biggar, F.J., *The Ulster Land War* (Dublin, 1910)

Blackstock, A.F., 'The Origin and Development of the Irish Yeomanry, 1796–*c*.1807' (unpublished Ph.D. thesis Q.U.B., 1993)

——, 'The Social and Political Implications of the Raising of the Yeomanry in Ulster, 1796–8', in D. Dickson, D. Keogh and K. Whelan (eds), *The United Irishmen* (Dublin, 1993), pp. 234–43

——, 'A Dangerous Species of Ally: Orangeism and the Irish Yeomanry', *I.H.S.*, xxx 119 (May, 1997) pp. 393–405

Boyle, K., 'Police in Ireland Before the Union', *Irish Jurist*, vii (1972) pp. 115–37, viii (1973) pp. 90–116, 323–48

Broeker, G., *Rural Disorder and Police reform in Ireland, 1812–36* (London and Toronto, 1970)

Boyce, D.G., *Nationalism in Ireland* (Baltimore, 1982)

Bredin, Brig. Gen. A.E.C., *A History of the Irish Soldier* (Belfast, 1987)

Brynn, E., *Crown and Castle: British Rule in Ireland, 1800–1830* (Dublin, 1978)

Christie, I.R., *Stress and Stability in late Eighteenth Century Britain* (Oxford, 1984)

Clarkson, A. and Crawford, E.M., *Ways to Wealth: the Cust Family of Eighteenth Century Armagh* (Belfast, 1985)

Cobb, R., *The People's Armies* (New Haven and London, 1987)

Colley, L., *Britons: Forging the Nation, 1707–1837* (New Haven and London, 1992)

Connolly, S.J., 'Law, order and popular protest in early eighteenth century Ireland' in Corish, P.J. (ed.), *Radicals, Rebels and Establishments* (Belfast, 1985)

——, 'Albion's Fatal Twigs: Justice and Law in the Eighteenth Century' Mitchison, R. and Roebuck, P. (eds), *Economy and Society in Scotland and Ireland, 1500–1939* (Edinburgh, 1988).

——, 'Violence and Order in the Eighteenth Century', in P. O'Flanagan, R. Ferguson and K. Whelan (eds), *Rural Ireland, 1660-1900: Modernisation and Change* (Cork, 1987)

——, *Priests and People in Pre-Famine Ireland* (Dublin, 1982)

——, *Religion, Law and Power, the Making of Protestant Ireland, 1660–1760* (Oxford, 1992)

Cookson, J.E., 'The English Volunteer Movement of the French Wars, 1793–1815: some Contexts', *Historical Journal*, vol. 32, no. 4 (1989), pp. 867–91

Corish, P.J., *The Catholic Community in the seventeenth and eighteenth centuries* (Dublin, 1981)

Craig, M.J., *The Volunteer Earl* (London, 1948)

Crawford, W.H., 'Landlord-Tenant Relations in Ulster, 1609–1820', *I.E.S.H.*, xi (1975), pp. 5–21

——, 'Change in Ulster in the Late Eighteenth Century', T. Bartlett and D. Hayton (eds), *Penal Era and Golden Age* (Belfast, 1979)

—— and Trainor, B. (eds), *Aspects of Irish Social History, 1750–1800* (Belfast, 1969)

Crossman, V., 'Preserving the Peace in Ireland: the Role of the Military Forces, 1815–45', *I.S.*, xvii (1990), no. 69, pp. 261–72.

Cullen, L.M., 'The 1798 Rebellion in its Eighteenth Century Context', in P.J. Corish (ed.), *Radicals, Rebels and Establishments* (Belfast, 1985)

——, 'The Political Structures of the Defenders', in H. Gough and D. Dickson (eds), *Ireland and the French Revolution* (Dublin, 1990)

—— and Bergeron, L. (eds), *Culture et Pratiques Politiques en France et en Irlande* (Tours, 1991)

——, *An Economic History of Ireland since 1660* (London, 1972)

——, 'Man, Landscape and Roads: the changing Eighteenth Century', in W. Nolan (ed.), *The Shaping of Ireland* (Cork, 1986)

——., *The Emergence of Modern Ireland, 1600–1900* (New York, 1981)

Curtin, N., 'The Transformation of the Society of United Irishmen into a Mass-Based Revolutionary Organisation, 1796', *I.H.S.*, xxiv, No. 96 (Nov. 1985), pp. 463–92

——, 'The Origins of Irish Republicanism: the United Irishmen in Dublin and Ulster, 1791–1988' (unpublished Ph.D. thesis, University of Wisconsin, 1988).

——, *The United Irishmen: Popular Politics in Ulster and Dublin, 1791–8* (Oxford, 1994)

D'Alton, I., *Protestant Society and Politics in Cork, 1812–1844* (Cork, 1980)

Dickson, C., *Revolt in the North* (Dublin, 1960)

Dickson, D., *New Foundations, Ireland, 1660–1800* (Dublin, 1987)

—— O'Grada, Daultrey, 'Hearth Tax, Household Size and Irish Population Change, 1672–1821', *Royal Irish Academy Proc.*, C82/6 (1982), pp. 125–81.

Donnelly, J.S. (Jnr), 'Hearts of Oak, Hearts of Steel', *Studia Hibernica*, xxi (1981), pp. 7–75.

——, 'The Whiteboy Movement of 1761–5', *I.H.S.*, xxi, 81 (1978), pp. 20–55

——, 'Pastorini and Captain Rock', S. Clarke and J.S. Donnelly Jnr (eds), *Irish Peasants: Violence and Political Unrest, 1780–1914* (Manchester, 1983), pp. 102–42

Elliott, M., *Partners in Revolution* (New Haven and London, 1982)

——, *Wolfe Tone* (New Haven and London, 1989)

Emsley, C., *British Society and the French Wars, 1793–1815* (Thetford, 1979)

——, 'The Military and Popular Disorder in England, 1790–1801', *The Journal of Army Historical Research*, lxi (Spring, 1983), 245, pp.10–21; lxi (Summer, 1983), 246, pp. 96–112

Ferguson, K.P., 'The Army in Ireland from the Restoration to the Act of Union' (unpublished Ph.D. thesis T.C.D., 1980)

——, 'The Irish Army and the Rebellion of 1798' in A.J. Guy (ed.), *The Road to Waterloo* (London, 1990), pp. 88–100.

Fitzpatrick, W.J., *The Life and Times of Lord Cloncurry* (Dublin, 1835)

Fortesque, J.W., *A History of the British Army* (13 vols., London and New York, 1899–1930)

Foster, R.F., *Modern Ireland, 1600–1972* (London, 1988)

Fox, K.O., *Making Life Possible: a Study of Military Aid to the Civil Power in Regency England, 1811–20* (Kineton, 1982)

Froude, J.A., *The English in Ireland in the Eighteenth Century* (3 vols, London, 1874)

Fuller, Maj. Gen. J.F.C., *The Conduct of War, 1789–1961* (London, 1972)

Furlong, N., *Father John Murphy of Boolavogue, 1753–98* (Dublin, 1991)

Gahan, D., *The People's Rising, Wexford, 1798* (Dublin, 1995)

Gee, A., 'The British Volunteer Movement, 1793–1807' (unpublished D.Phil. thesis, Oxford, 1989)

Gibbon, P., *The Origins of Ulster Unionism* (Manchester, 1975)

Graham, T., 'An Union of Power? United Irish Organisation', in D.Dickson, D. Keogh and K. Whelan (eds), *The United Irishmen* (Dublin, 1993) pp. 244–55

Glass, D. and Taylor, P., *Population and Emigration* (Dublin, 1976)

Gooch, J., *Armies in Europe* (London, 1980)

Gough, H, and Dickson, D. (eds), *Ireland and the French Revolution* (Dublin, 1990)

Groves-White, J., *The Yeomanry of Ireland* (Cork, 1893)

Guy, A., *Oecomomy and Discipline: Officership and Administration in the British Army, 1714–63* (Manchester, 1985)

Gwynn, S. (ed.), *The Memoirs of Myles Byrne* (Dublin, 1907)

——, *Henry Grattan and his Times* (London, 1939)

Harkness, D. and O'Dowd, M. (eds.), *The Town in Ireland* (Belfast, 1981)

Hayter, T., 'The British Army, 1713–1793: Recent Research Work', *The Journal of Army historical research*, lxiii (Spring, 1985) no. 253, pp. 11–19

Haythornethwaite, P.J., *The Armies of Wellington* (London, 1994)

Hayes-McCoy, G.A., *A History of Irish Flags* (Dublin, 1979)

——, *Irish Battles* (London and Southampton, 1979)

Hayton, D.W., 'Ireland and the English Ministers, 1707–16' (unpublished D.Phil. thesis, Oxford, 1975)

Hempton, D. and Hill, M., *Evangelical Protestantism in Ulster Society, 1740–1890* (London and New York, 1992)

Hill, J., 'National Festivals, the State and "Protestant Ascendancy" in Ireland, 1790–1829', *I.H.S.*, xxiv (May, 1984), 93, pp. 30–51

Holmes, F., *Presbyterians and Orangeism, 1795–1995* (Presbyterian Historical Society, Belfast, 1996)

Houlding, J.A., *Fit For Service: the Training of the British Army, 1715–95* (Oxford, 1981)

Hyde, H.M., *The Rise of Castlereagh* (London,1933)

Jenkins, B., *The Era of Emancipation, British Government of Ireland, 1812–30* (Kingston, Ontario, 1988)

Jupp, P.J., 'The Landed Elite and Political Authority in Britain, *c*.1760-1850', in *Journal of British Studies*, 29 (Jan.1990), pp. 53–79

——, *British and Irish Elections, 1734–1831* (Newton Abbot, 1973)

——, 'County Down Elections, 1783–1831', *I.H.S.*, xviii, 70 (Sept. 1972), pp. 177–206

Kelly, J., 'The Genesis of "Protestant Ascendancy": the Rightboy Disturbances of the 1780s and their impact upon Protestant Opinion', in G. O'Brien (ed.), *Parliament, Politics and People: Essays in Eighteenth-Century Irish History* (Dublin, 1989)

——, 'A Secret Return of the Volunteers of Ireland in 1784', *I.H.S.*, xxiv, 103 (May, 1989), pp. 268–92

——, *That Damn'd Thing Called Honour: Duelling in Ireland, 1570–1860* (Cork, 1995)

Kennedy, B.A., 'Sharman Crawford, 1780–1861: a Political Biography' (unpublished D.Litt. thesis, Q.U.B., 1953)

Keogh, D., *The French Disease: The Catholic Church and Radicalism in Ireland, 1790–1800* (Dublin, 1993)

——, and N. Furlong (eds), *The Mighty Wave: the 1798 Rebellion in Wexford* (Dublin, 1996)

Kerrigan, P.M., *Castles and Fortifications in Ireland, 1485–1945* (Cork, 1995)

Kilpatrick, C. (ed.), *The Formation of the Orange Order, 1795–98* (Belfast, 1994)

Kilpatrick, C., W. Murdie and D. Cargo (eds), *The History of the Royal Arch Purple Order* (Belfast, 1993)

Lawson, C.C., *A History of the Uniforms of the British Army* (3 vols, London, 1940)

Lecky, W.E.H., *Ireland in the Eighteenth Century* (5 vols, London, 1892)

Lyttle, W.G., *Betsy Gray or Hearts of Down* (re-published, Newcastle, 1968)

McAnally, Sir H., *The Irish Militia, 1793–1816* (Dublin, 1949)

McCartney, D., *The Dawning of Democracy, 1800–1870* (Dublin, 1987)

McCavery, T.R., 'Finance and Politics in Ireland, 1801–17' (unpublished Ph.D. thesis, Q.U.B., 1980)

McClelland, A., *A History of Saintfield and District* (Newcastle, 1971)

McComb, W., *McComb's Guide to Belfast* (Belfast, 1861)

McCracken, J.L., 'Social Structure and Social Life, 1714–60', in *N.H.I.*, v, p. 44.

——, 'The Irish Parliament in the Eighteenth Century', *Irish Historical Association* (Dundalk, 1971)

MacDermott, F., *Theobold Wolfe Tone and His Times* (new edition, Tralee, 1969)

MacDonagh M. (ed), *The Viceroys' Postbag* (London, 1904)

MacDonagh, O., *The Heriditary Bondsman: Daniel O'Connell, 1775–1829* (London, 1988)

McDowell, R.B., *Irish Public Opinion, 1750–1800* (London, 1944)

——, *The Irish Administration, 1801–1914* (London, 1964)

——, *Ireland in the Age of Imperialism and Revolution, 1760–1801* (Oxford, 1979)

McNeill, M., *The life and times of Mary Ann McCracken* (new edition, Belfast, 1988)

McSkimin, S., *The Annals of Ulster* (new edition, Belfast, 1906)

Madden, R.R., *The United Irishmen, their lives and times* (4 vols, London, 1842–45)

Maguire, W.A., 'Lord Donegal and the Hearts of Steel', *I.H.S.*, xxi, 84 (Sept., 1979), pp. 351–76

Malcomson, A.P.W., 'John Foster and the Speakership of the Irish House of Commons', *Proceedings of the Royal Irish Academy*, 72, C, No.11 (Dublin, 1972)

——, *The 2nd. Earl of Massereene, 1743–1805* (Belfast, 1972)

——, *Isaac Corry, 1753–1813, An Adventurer in the Field of Irish Politics* (Belfast, 1974)

——, *John Foster: the Politics of the Anglo-Irish Ascendancy* (Oxford, 1978)

——, 'A Lost Natural Leader: John James Hamilton, first Marquess of Abercorn', *Proceedings of the Royal Irish Academy*, 88, C, No.4, pp. 61–86 (Dublin, 1988)

——, 'The Parliamentary Traffic of this Country', T. Bartlett and D. W. Hayton (eds), *Penal Era and Golden Age* (Belfast, 1979), pp. 137–61

Maxwell, C., *Dublin under the Georges, 1714–1830* (London, 1956)

Miller, D.W., 'Armagh Troubles, 1784–1795', S. Clark and J.S. Donnelly, Jnr (eds), *Irish Peasants: Violence and Political Unrest, 1780–1914* (Manchester, 1983)

——, *Peep O'Day Boys and Defenders* (Belfast, 1990)

——, *Queen's Rebels: Ulster Loyalism in Historical Perspective* (Dublin, 1978)

——, 'Non-Professional Soldiery', in T. Bartlett and K. Jeffrey (eds), *A Military History of Ireland* (Cambridge, 1996)

Mitchell, J., *The History of Ireland* (Dublin, 1869)

Morton, R.G., 'The Rise of the Yeomanry', *The Irish Sword*, viii (1967–68), pp. 58–64.

Mullen, T.H., *Coleraine in Georgian times* (Belfast, 1977)

Murphy, M., 'The Economy and Society of Nineteenth-Century Cork', in D. Harkness and M. O'Dowd (eds), *The Town in Ireland* (Belfast, 1981), pp. 125–54.

Neuburg, V.E., 'The British Army in the Eighteenth Century', *Journal of Army Historical Research*, lxi, no. 245 (Spring,1983), pp. 39–47.

Nicholson, H., *The Desire to Please: a Story of Hamilton Rowan and the United Irishmen* (London, 1943)

O'Connell, M.R., *Irish Politics in the Age of the American Revolution* (Philadelphia, 1965)

O'Donovan, J., 'The Militia in Munster', in G. O'Brien (ed.), *Parliament, Politics and People* (Dublin, 1989)

O'Snodaigh, P., 'Notes on the Volunteers, Militia and Yeomanry of the County Wexford', *The Past*, 14 (1983).

——, 'Notes on the Volunteers, Militia, Yeomanry and Orangemen of County Donegal', *Donegal Annual*, vii (1969), pp. 49–73.

——, 'Notes on the Volunteers, Militia, Yeomanry and Orangemen of County Meath', *Riocht na Midhe*, iv (1978–9), pp. 3–32

——, 'Notes on the Volunteers, Militia, Yeomanry and Orangemen of County Monaghan', *Clogher Record*, ix (1977), pp. 142–66

——, *The Irish Volunteers: A List of the Units, 1715–93* (Dublin, 1995)

O'Sullivan, N., *Conservatism* (London, 1976)

Packenham, T., *The Year of Liberty* (London, 1969)

Palmer, S.H., *Police and Protest in Ireland and England, 1780–1850* (Cambridge, 1988)

Pares, R., *King George III and the Politicians* (Oxford, 1953)

Paterson, T.G.F., 'The County Armagh Volunteers of 1778–93', *U.J.A.*, series 3, iv (1941) pp. 101–27; v (1942) pp. 31–61; vi (1943), pp. 69–105; vii (1944), pp. 76–59

——, 'The Volunteer Companies of Ulster', *I.S.*, vii (1965–6), pp. 90–116, 204–30; viii (1967–8), pp. 92–7, 210–17

Preston, R.A., S.F. Wise and H.O. Werner, *Men in Arms* (London, 1956)

Proudfoot, L., 'Urban Patronage and Estate Management on the Duke of Devonshire's Irish Estates, 1764–1891' (unpublished Ph.D. thesis, Q.U.B., 1989)

Robertson., J., *The Scottish Enlightenment and the Militia Issue* (Edinburgh, 1985)

Robinson, P., *The Plantation of Ulster* (Dublin, 1984)

Rogers, P., *The Volunteers and Catholic Emancipation* (London, 1934)

Senior, H., *Orangeism in Ireland and Britain, 1795–1836* (London and Toronto, 1966)

Sibbett, R.M., *Orangeism in Ireland and and throughout the Empire* (2 vols, London, 1939)

Smyth, J., 'Dublin's Political Underground in the 1790s', in G. O'Brien (ed.), *Parliament, Politics and People* (Dublin, 1989)

——, 'Defenderism and the Catholic Question', in H. Gough and D. Dickson, *Ireland and the French Revolution* (Dublin, 1990)

——, *The Men of No Property: Irish Radicals and Popular Politics in the Late Eighteenth Century* (Dublin, 1992)

Smyth, P.D.H., 'The Volunteer Movement in Ulster' (unpublished Ph.D. thesis, Q.U.B., 1974)

Stewart, A.T.Q., *The Narrow Ground: patterns of Ulster History* (London, 1977).

——, *A Deeper Silence: the Hidden Roots of the United Irish Movement* (London, 1993)

——, *The Summer Soldiers: the 1798 Rebellion in Antrim and Down* (Belfast, 1995)

Stoddart, P.C., 'Counter-Insurgency and Defence in Ireland, 1790–1805' (unpublished D. Phil. thesis, Oxford, 1972)

Thompson, Glenn, F., 'The Flags and Uniforms of the Irish Volunteers and Yeomanry', *Bulletin of the Irish Georgian Society*, xxxiii (1990)

Thorne, R.G. (ed.), *The History of Parliament: the Commons, 1790–1820* (5 vols, London, 1986)

Trench, C.C., *The Great Dan* (London, 1986)

Trevelyan, G.M., *English Social History* (reprint, London, 1948)

Verner, Sir W., *A Short History of the Battle of the Diamond* (London, 1863)

Western, J.R., 'The Volunteer Movement as an Anti-Revolutionary Force, 1793-1801', *The English Historical Review*, lxxi (1956), pp. 603–14

Wheeler, H.F.M. and A.M Broadley, *The War in Wexford* (London, 1910)

Whelan, K., 'Politicisation in County Wexford and the Origins of the 1798 Rebellion', in H. Gough and D.Dickson (eds), *Ireland and the French Revolution* (Dublin, 1990)

——, 'Settlement and Society in Eighteenth-Century Ireland', in G. Dawe and J.W. Foster (eds), *The Poet's Place: Essays in Ulster Literature and Society*, pp. 45–62

——, 'Catholic Mobilisation, 1750–1850', in L. Cullen and L. Bergeron (eds), *Culture et Pratique Politiques en France et en Irelande* (Tours, 1988), pp. 235–58

——, *The Tree of Liberty* (Cork, 1996)

Index